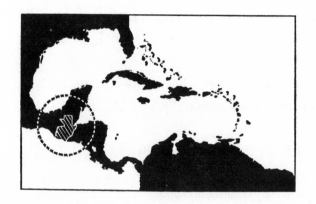

CARIBBEAN SERIES 4

Sidney W. Mintz, Editor

A descendant of the ancient Maya.

GUATEMALA

The Land and the People

by Nathan L. Whetten

NEW HAVEN AND LONDON, YALE UNIVERSITY PRESS

© 1961 by Yale University Press, Inc.

Third printing, May 1965.

printed in the United States of America by the

Carl Purington Rollins Printing-Office of the

Yale University Press, New Haven, Connecticut.

Library of Congress catalog card number: 61-7189

Dedicated to THEORA

PREFACE

This work had its inception near the end of World War II while I was in the service of the United States Department of State in Mexico. I had been asked by the State Department and the Office of Foreign Agricultural Relations to take a leave of absence from the University of Connecticut and go to Mexico in 1942 as one of three sociologists sent to Latin America to study and report on socio-economic conditions in those countries during the war. The Latin American countries had suddenly taken on tremendous importance to the United States because of the world situation, and it seemed necessary to learn more about them. Three years of studying in Mexico culminated in the publication of my book *Rural Mexico,* by the University of Chicago Press in 1948.

Opportunity to study in Guatemala came in November 1944, when I was asked by the State Department to transfer to that country for a period of five months to continue my studies. The Ubico dictatorship had just been terminated, and Guatemala was trying to set up a modern democracy. The Guatemalans welcomed me and were glad to see a North American who was interested in studying the social and economic problems of their country without any political implications.

In 1945 I returned to my post at the University but have visited Guatemala several times since then. I spent the entire summers of 1952 and 1956 there gathering additional information. I have maintained contact with Guatemala through correspondence, daily newspapers, and other publications for the past fifteen years.

This book follows an approach similar to that of my *Rural Mexico.* It is a general work designed to describe some of the major sociological aspects of Guatemalan society. Guatemala is as yet essentially a rural civilization with more than three-fourths of her total population living in small communities scattered over the mountains and valleys. An even larger proportion of the inhabitants are dependent, directly or indirectly, on agriculture for a living. Guatemala City, with an estimated population of 387,826 in 1960, is the only large city in the country, and in 1950 there were only four other towns with more than 10,000 inhabitants; the largest of these, Quezaltenango, had only 27,672. In order to understand Guatemala in its entirety, therefore, one must cut short his visit in Guatemala City and go out into the villages and country districts where life goes on undisturbed by highways, newspapers, radios, or telephones. For these reasons, major emphasis is given throughout this study to the rural population, its institutions and problems. Outside of Guatemala City, urbanization has barely begun.

The book is divided into five parts. Part 1 contains an analysis of the population in relation to the geographic environment in which the people live and carry on their various life activities. Although most Guatemalans depend on agriculture for a living, the majority live in the highlands where good farm land is scarce and landholdings are very small; yet many unused lands in the more fertile lowland areas of the coastal plains are thinly populated. These lands lie idle for various reasons, including lack of roads and fear of tropical diseases, and because land is often held in very large units (*latifundios*) by landlords who show little or no interest in developing them into productive farms.

More than half (54 per cent) of Guatemala's population consists of indigenous peoples, and therefore considerable attention is given in this section to ethnic relations. The Indian population generally is divided into numerous small isolated societies which accentuate social cohesion at the local level through perpetuation of the traditional customs, attitudes, and techniques of living that have prevailed far beyond the memory of any living man, perhaps for ages. These strong locality-centered attitudes offer stiff resistance to the development of social integration at the national level, one of the ingredients which would appear to be indispensable to the development of democracy on a national scale. Indeed it may be asserted that lack of social integration at the national level constitutes one of the most serious barriers to Guatemala's avowed aspirations of forging her people into a modern democratic nation.

Part 2 deals with the efforts of the people to make a living. Agriculture is the principal occupational pursuit of three-quarters of the employed male population; and farming consists primarily of two broad contrasting types. One involves the vast majority of the inhabitants who live in poverty trying to make a living through semi-subsistence agriculture, derived mostly from growing corn and beans on what Latin Americans call *minifundios,* or miniature landholdings, that are too small to meet their needs. The other principal type of farming, which might be called plantation agriculture, is based on large farms (*fincas*) devoted mostly to commercial agriculture, principally coffee production. Absentee management is characteristic of these plantations, which generally rely for their success on good soil and an abundant supply of cheap labor rather than on modern efficient techniques of production. Efforts by the government to carry out land reform programs are described, as are other measures supposedly designed to improve the lot of the masses.

Part 3 is concerned with the general levels of living of the people as reflected in housing, diet, and clothing. It also contains a chapter on health and mortality. Death rates, infant mortality rates, and general health conditions serve as good indices of the social and physical well-being of a society. In Guatemala, they emphasize the serious problems in existing living conditions, as manifested in the unusually high death rates.

Part 4 describes the functioning of some of the more basic social institutions including the family, education, religion, and government. Part 5 contains a single chapter devoted to the outlook.

Throughout runs the thread of Guatemala's revolutionary attempts to abolish tyranny and to carry out widespread programs of social reform. Successes and failures are noted.

Data for this work were drawn from many sources. The writer traveled widely throughout the country interviewing people from many walks of life. Statistical data were taken primarily from official sources, including the 1950 census of population, the 1950 census of agriculture, and the 1949 census of housing as well as other data collected regularly by the *Dirección General de Estadística* and other government agencies.

No census is being taken in Guatemala in 1960 because of budgetary difficulties. It is indeed fortunate, therefore, that the 1950 census was a reasonably good one, since additional data of this type may not become available for a number of years. It is my hope that data presented here will be useful in providing a mid-century bench mark from which to measure future trends. A great deal of careful planning preceded the taking of the Guatemalan census of 1950. Personnel were sent to the United States to be trained in methods used by our Bureau of Census; experimental censuses were taken in several communities in Guatemala under the guidance of experts supplied by the United Nations. The actual census was taken as carefully and thoroughly as could be expected in an underdeveloped country where geographic isolation and illiteracy constitute serious barriers to accurate enumeration. Despite all efforts, however, there are undoubtedly instances of underenumeration and misreporting in the more isolated areas which I have tried to take into consideration in reaching conclusions. The recording of vital statistics is also improving, although there are still inadequacies in the more isolated districts. In using statistical data I have avoided the more questionable materials and have tried to point out defects in the data whenever it seemed they might be sufficiently serious to influence the results.

An additional valuable source of information has been the anthropological studies made in various parts of the country in recent years. Fortunately a goodly number of investigations have been carried on by competent anthropologists which provide valuable insight into the culture of specific communities. Studies of diet and nutrition carried on by the Institute of Nutrition of Central America and Panama have also been most helpful. Many other important sources are listed in the bibliography.

It is impossible to list the hundreds of people who have contributed in one way or another to the completion of this project. I am grateful to the United States Department of State and to the Department of Agriculture for the original assignment to Guatemala. Acknowledgment and appreciation is expressed to Henry Allen Moe and the John Simon Guggenheim Memorial Foundation for granting me a fellowship in 1952, and to the Ford Foundation for assistance in publication of this book. I am indebted to A. N. Jorgensen, President of the University of Connecticut, for permitting me to arrange my time schedule so that I could carry on research in Guatemala; also to the Department of Rural Sociology at the University for assistance in many ways. Robert Burnight gave helpful suggestions on some of the demographic aspects of the study. My former graduate students, Leo Suslow and William Morrison, assisted with various parts of the work. Lillian Dotson and Thea Field each served at different times as research assistant and contributed much to the project. Richard N. Adams of Michigan State University read critically the entire manuscript and offered suggestions for improvement. A special debt of gratitude is expressed to Charlie and Lib Simmons for hospitality in Guatemala that will always be remembered.

Finally, my appreciation is expressed to the numerous Guatemalans who cooperated to make the study possible. I shall not mention them by name, since this work deals with their country, and I have no wish to involve them, even by implication, in any responsibility for the conclusions presented. The personnel of the *Dirección General de Estadística* was especially cooperative in making statistical data available to me. Many special tabulations of data were made for my use which will probably never be published elsewhere. Other government agencies also cooperated willingly.

While many individuals and agencies have left an influence on this study, they are in no way responsible for the final product. It is perhaps inevitable that in a work such as this, which deals with many important aspects of human society, some errors, whether of fact or of interpretation, may have crept in. I shall be happy if the errors are few.

N.L.W.

Storrs, Connecticut
September 1960

TABLE OF CONTENTS

Illustrations

MAPS AND CHARTS

PLATES

Following page 16:

1. Volcanic peaks stretch across the country. Courtesy of Foto Alvarez
2. Man, woman, and beast carry heavy burdens. Photo courtesy of Eichenberger.
3. Panoramic view of Guatemala City. Courtesy of *Dirección General de Cartografía.*
4. A highland village. Photo by Mitchell, courtesy of U.S.D.A.

Following page 112:

5. Poverty is widespread, but "dignified." Photo by Rickert, courtesy of Maryknoll.
6. Guatemala is highly Indian. Photo by McGuinness, courtesy of Maryknoll.
7. The Indian carries a heavy load. Courtesy of Lilly de Jongh Osborne.
8. Coffee harvest. Photo by Mitchell, courtesy of U.S.D.A.

Following page 144:

9. A sea of bananas. Photo by Mitchell, courtesy of U.S.D.A.
10. Milpa farming in the highlands. Photo courtesy of U.S.D.A.
11. Removing bark from young cinchona tree—a source of quinine. Photo by Mitchell, courtesy of U.S.D.A.
12. Clustered houses with thatched roofs in the Indian village of San Pedro Atitlán. Courtesy of Eichenberger.

Following page 192:

13. Making roof tile. Photo by Burns, courtesy of Maryknoll.
14. The stream serves as laundry and bath tub in Totonicapán. Courtesy of Eichenberger.
15. Woman and child at San Ildefonso Ixtahuacán. Photo by Burns, courtesy of Maryknoll.
16. Women in bright red skirts carrying water from Lake Atitlán. Photo by the author.
17. Man's typical dress at Sololá. Courtesy of Eichenberger.
18. At the market in Cobán. Photo by the author.
19. Mother and child in market at Chichicastenango. Photo by the author.
20. Village schoolboys of San Pedro Soloma. Photo by Burns, courtesy of Maryknoll.

Part 1 LAND AND PEOPLE

Chapter 1

THE LAND

Guatemala is about the size of the state of Ohio in land area, yet it has nearly as much geographical diversity as is found in the entire United States. It contains only 42,042 square miles but it includes high mountain ranges, low coastal plains, high plateaus, steaming tropical jungles, and even a miniature semi-desert.[1] A chain of more than 30 volcanic peaks extends across the southern part of the country at about 25 to 50 miles from the Pacific coast. Several of these are still active; and some extend to an altitude of more than 12,000 feet. In the vicinity of this volcanic chain, earthquakes occur every year and occasionally cause deep concern to the inhabitants. Guatemala has both an Atlantic and a Pacific seacoast; and such a wide range of climates and soil types that she can point to a favorable habitat for almost any agricultural product known to man.

Slightly more than one-third of the total area consists of highlands, including mountains, plateaus, and mountain valleys, most of which drain toward the Caribbean. It is in these highlands that the vast majority of the inhabitants reside. Because of the altitude they find themselves in a temperate climate even though living in the tropical zone. Thus, they live in the tropics but are not of them.

Considerably more than half of the country consists of tropical lowlands where few inhabitants are to be found. These include a broad, flat

1. Although small in size, Guatemala has more inhabitants than any other country of Central America. Thus in 1950, Guatemala had 2,790,868 inhabitants; El Salvador, 1,855,917; Honduras, 1,368,605; Nicaragua, 1,057,023; Panama, 805,285; and Costa Rica, 800,875. *Sexto censo de población,* Dirección General de Estadística, Guatemala, 1950. *United Nations Demographic Yearbook* (1953), p. 72.

Actually, Guatemala claims Belice (British Honduras) as a part of her natural territory on the grounds that Great Britain did not live up to her agreement in the treaty of 1859.

northern plain sloping gently northward toward Mexico and the Caribbean Sea; and a narrow coastal plain extending along the Pacific Ocean. Numerous rivers have their origin along the southern slopes of the volcanic chain and flow southward across the coastal plain into the

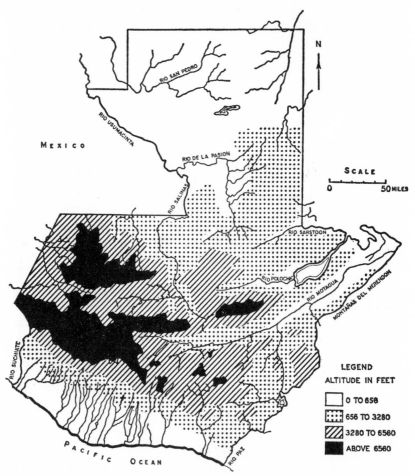

Figure 1. Altitude map of Guatemala showing river systems and variations in elevation. Adapted from *Guatemala en Cifras,* Dirección general de Estadística, 1955, p. 3.

Pacific. The Petén area of the vast northern plain which occupies nearly a third of the Republic was the center of the great Mayan civilization which flourished many centuries before the Conquest. While some of the highland sections of the country are rather densely populated, this great northern plain, so important to the ancient Mayas, is now covered with tropical vegetation and remains virtually uninhabited and unused (see Plate 1).

Climate

The climate varies greatly from one section of the country to another, reflecting differences in altitude, position of the mountains, and location with reference to prevailing winds. In the lowlands, temperatures tend to be high and rarely go below 50 degrees Fahrenheit at any time during the year. In the highlands, it is cool and invigorating, with freezing weather not uncommon during the coolest season.

Rainfall also varies greatly from one area to another. In general, there are two seasons: an alternating wet season and dry season. Each extends over a period of about six months, although the length varies in different localities. In most places, the rainy season occurs from about the latter part of May until October and is known as winter (*invierno*). The dry season extends from November until the following May and during it very little moisture falls; this long dry season is called *verano*, or summer. This, of course, is just the reverse of the nomenclature in the United States.

The average monthly rainfall over a five-year period for six different sections of the country is shown in Table 1. Examination of the yearly

TABLE 1. *Average number of inches of precipitation per month in selected localities of Guatemala over a period of five years extending from 1953 to 1957, by locality and month of the year* *

Month	Chiquimula	Quezal-tenango	Guatemala City	Quiriguá	Escuintla	Cobán
Total yearly average	19.4	35.4	51.0	72.6	96.3	101.3
January	0.1	0.0	0.0	0.5	0.0	2.3
February	0.0	0.6	0.3	2.1	0.0	2.7
March	0.0	0.2	0.1	1.9	0.1	1.9
April	0.3	1.5	0.6	1.9	3.7	3.8
May	1.6	4.3	5.1	6.0	9.4	9.1
June	4.1	6.2	11.3	11.4	21.1	16.4
July	3.7	5.8	9.8	12.1	12.2	18.8
August	3.3	3.9	6.0	9.4	10.6	16.7
September	4.0	5.4	9.8	9.9	19.1	13.3
October	2.0	6.9	6.9	6.9	16.3	8.2
November	0.3	0.3	0.7	4.8	3.1	5.6
December	0.0	0.3	0.4	5.7	0.7	2.5

* Computed from data supplied by Ing. Claudio Urrutia E., director of the National Observatory at Guatemala City.

averages for each locality indicates a variation from a scanty 19.4 inches precipitation per year in Chiquimula, in the eastern highlands, to 101.3 inches in the Cobán area of north central Guatemala. Escuintla, on the Pacific slope, received an average of 96.3 inches per year. Actually, Escuintla receives more precipitation during the month of June (21.1 inches) than Chiquimula receives during the entire year.[2] In all six areas the pattern of seasonal variation in rainfall is quite similar, with the highest precipitation occurring during the period from about June to October, followed by a definite decline which continues during the remaining months of the year.

The large range of climatic conditions, together with variations in soil type, enable Guatemala to produce a wide variety of crops extending all the way from those that are strictly tropical in character, such as bananas and rubber, to those that are characteristic of the temperate zone, such as wheat and potatoes.

TRANSPORTATION FACILITIES

The paucity of transportation facilities constitutes one reason for the lack of economic development and cultural integration of the country. Such rail and automobile facilities as do exist are usually so expensive for the average Guatemalan in relation to his level of living that he uses them very little. In most areas he continues to rely on the oxcart, the pack mule or, more commonly, the human beast of burden. Throughout western and central Guatemala it is a familiar sight to witness Indian men trudging along over the steep mountain trails from one town to another carrying huge burdens on their backs, and to see Indian women traveling barefoot to or from the markets carrying baskets full of wares delicately balanced on top of their heads (see Plate 2).

Although a relatively adequate network of narrow dirt highways has been constructed throughout most of the heavily populated highland areas of the country, the vast lowlands, including the entire Petén region of the north, are virtually without roads. One report describes the highway system in the following words:

> The system may be described as an overextended, poorly located network of low-grade, narrow roads. Maintenance is handicapped by the types and extent of roads, by climatic and geographic as

2. Some places are reported to receive more than 200 inches of rainfall per year.

well as geological conditions, and by shortages in equipment, technical personnel and funds.[3]

Obviously, highway building is expensive in the highland areas. Roads must be carved from the mountain sides and must cross deep canyons in order to connect one town with another. During the rainy season it is especially difficult to keep the highways in repair since there is constant erosion. The limited use of automobile transportation is reflected in the comparatively small number of motor vehicles per thousand inhabitants. In 1954, for example, Guatemala had only 3.6 passenger cars per thousand population as compared with 6.4 in Brazil, 7.7 in Chile, 22.6 in Venezuela, and 297.5 in the United States.[4]

The only railway service is that provided by the International Railways of Central America, which operates a narrow-gauge system. The efficiency of this railway is limited by its single track line. According to the Mission Report, railway facilities have almost reached the point of saturation and will need to be increased to meet future demands.[5]

Transportation by bus is becoming more common and in time may gradually displace the human carrier. The number of bus registrations in the nation increased from only 615 in 1945 to 2,214 in 1957. Many buses serve the dual purpose of carrying freight as well as people. It is not unusual to see pottery, baskets, chickens, or pigs loaded on top of a bus, or sometimes even tucked in among the passengers.

Mention should be made of another form of transportation that is rapidly becoming available to some of the upper and middle classes, that of travel by air. The Guatemalan government has developed an airline service, *Aviateca,* which connects most of the larger towns and cities with regularly scheduled flights for both passengers and freight. This service, however, is largely beyond the reach of the masses of the population because of the expense involved.

Fortunately, the Guatemalan government has been improving transportation facilities in recent years through the construction of three major highways. The Pan-American Highway extends across the highlands from Mexico on the west to the border of El Salvador on the east; the Atlantic Highway extends from Guatemala City to Puerto Barrios on the Caribbean coast; and the Pacific Slope Highway extends from

3. *The Economic Development of Guatemala,* Report of a Mission, (Washington, D.C., International Bank for Reconstruction and Development 1951), p. 133.

4. *United Nations Statistical Yearbook* (1955), pp. 25–28 and 323–24. Ecuador, with 1.4 passenger cars per thousand inhabitants, had a lower ratio than Guatemala. In 1953, Mexico had 9.3 cars per thousand inhabitants.

5. *The Economic Development of Guatemala,* pp. 169–70.

Guatemala City to the Mexican border along the southern slope of the volcanic chain. These three highways were nearing completion in 1960. They will provide better access to neighboring countries and connect some of the major centers of population, thus making a valuable contribution to the transportation system. The great lack of feeder roads, however, is likely to continue for a long period into the future.

Although automobilies are few in number when compared with those found in many other countries, the increase in motor vehicle registrations has been rapid. In 1945 there were only 4,711 motor vehicles of all types in the entire country, 2,695 of which were passenger cars. By 1957 the total number of vehicles had increased to 29,448 and the number of passenger cars to 17,711.

NATURAL REGIONS

The geographical environment in which the people of Guatemala live and work can perhaps be better understood through brief discussion of the major natural regions into which the country might be divided. These are plotted in Figure 2.

THE HIGHLANDS

The two highland areas indicated on the map occupy about 35 per cent of the total land area of the Republic and contain most of the inhabitants. As previously noted, volcanic peaks extend like a picket fence across the entire southern edge of the highlands from Mexico on the west to El Salvador on the east. Among the volcanic cones are a number of basins between five and eight thousand feet in elevation. One of these contains the picturesque Lake Atitlán. With a dozen Indian villages around its shores, and with volcanic peaks towering above its clear blue waters, it is generally acclaimed by visitors to be one of the scenic spots of the world.

The central highlands

The highland area may be divided into two segments consisting of the central highlands and the eastern highlands. Differences between the two areas are based on topography, altitude, and climatic conditions, as well as on demographic features. The central highlands, indicated roughly by the dark areas on the map (Figure 2), include what are often referred to as the western highlands, and are generally higher and more humid, with topography more broken than that of the eastern highlands. They are also more densely populated and contain a much higher proportion of Indian inhabitants.

Most of the central highland area is situated between 4,500 and 9,000 feet in altitude, although, as indicated, there are mountains that rise to a much higher elevation. The area enjoys a cool, invigorating climate and is often referred to by native Guatemalans as *tierra fría* or "cold

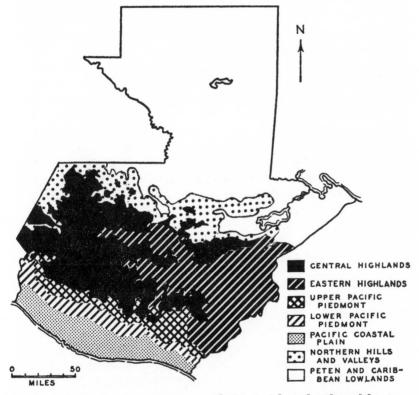

Figure 2. Natural regions. Compare with Fig. 1. Adapted with modifications from E. C. Higbee, "The Agricultural Regions of Guatemala," *Geographical Review* 37, No. 2, April, 1947, 179.

country." It is generally free from the dreaded malaria and tropical diseases that have long been a deterrent to settlement in the lowlands. It is an area of broken topography with many mountains, canyons, and ridges, and with few areas of level land. Deep *barrancas* (ravines) appear like long gashes slashed into the hillsides, and soil erosion is nearly everywhere apparent.

Farms are generally small and are usually situated on the impover-

ished soils of the crests of the ridges and on the more gentle slopes of
the hills.[6] They are mostly of the semi-subsistence variety, growing
principally corn and beans with other products added occasionally.
Many of the farms are too small to provide even a subsistence living
for their inhabitants, who must supplement their income either by
local household industries or by seeking work elsewhere. Outside employment is found largely on the coffee plantations of the Pacific slope.
This results in widespread seasonal migrations every year of thousands
of highland workers, often including whole families, to work for one or
more months picking coffee on the plantations.

The inhabitants are largely Indian in that they are direct descendants
of the pre-Conquest inhabitants and maintain their own ceremonial
organizations, traditions, and customs apart from the national life. They
have held on to their small farms over the ages, passing them on from
one generation to the next. Large landowners have tended to avoid the
area with its broken topography, and unfavorable climate, and have
been attracted instead to the more fertile lands of the southern piedmont and the level areas along the Pacific coastal plain. Rough topography, lack of roads, and the high density of Indian population have all
contributed to the preservation of the indigenous culture in this region.

The eastern highlands

This area, indicated by the striped section on the map (Figure 2),
is somewhat smaller than the central highlands, although it occupies
about 15 per cent of the total land area of the Republic. It is also an
area of broken topography with many mountains, hills, barrancas, and
valleys. It differs from the central highlands in that it has a generally
lower elevation, ranging from a low of about 1,500 feet to a height of
about 4,500 feet. There is also considerably less rainfall and the farmers
have resorted to small irrigation projects in many of the river valleys.
The climate is much warmer, especially at the lower altitudes, and
malaria is not uncommon in some sections.

In contrast to the central highlands, inhabitants of this area are
mostly *Ladino*, or non-Indian. They are descendants of former Spanish
or *mestizo* settlers and, except for a few isolated pockets of Indian
settlements, they speak Spanish. The population is less dense, with the
result that the farms are larger and there is not so much pressure for

6. E. C. Higbee, "The Agricultural Regions of Guatemala," *Geographical Review*, 37 (1947), 181. Higbee's article has been most helpful in describing the
natural regions.

farmers to seek employment off the farm. Widespread seasonal migration, therefore, is not as prevalent here as in the central highlands.

Agriculture of a semi-subsistence nature prevails as in the central highlands except that, because of irrigation and a warmer climate, a wider variety of crops is produced. In addition to corn and beans, the mild climate permits the production of tobacco, chili peppers, tropical fruits, and vegetables. Cattle and other livestock are also much more widely kept. In contrast with the central and western area, more use is made of farm animals and farm implements, such as the wooden plow. The human beast of burden is also conspicuously absent here since transportation is usually by horseback or by ox-drawn vehicles.

THE PACIFIC PIEDMONT

The most productive agricultural land in the entire Republic is found in a narrow band along the southern slopes of the chain of volcanoes which stretches across the country from east to west at the southern edge of the highlands sloping toward the Pacific coast. This area is fortunate in having a combination of favorable temperature, rainfall, and soils, making it potentially one of the most productive agricultural areas of the world. The band may be split near the middle, dividing it into two parts, the upper piedmont and the lower piedmont (see Figure 2).

The upper piedmont might well be referred to as the coffee belt since it is along this strip that most of Guatemala's coffee is grown. It is an area with fairly high relief, dissected by many streams, ridges, hills, and valleys along the slopes of the volcanic chain. Most of the coffee plantations literally extend up the mountainsides. The soils of the area are excellent, among the finest in the tropics. Their origin is volcanic and they are highly productive in spite of the erosive action of the rainfall. The coffee plants and shade trees afford protection against erosion to a much greater extent than do the tilled crops of other areas.[7]

The soils of the lower piedmont are similar to those of the upper. The temperature is warmer, however, and the land is more nearly level. It would be adaptable for future mechanization of agriculture. Coffee culture generally extends only into the northern edge of this band and there gives way to sugar cane, cotton, rice, bananas, and grazing for beef cattle. Much of the land is held in large units with considerable areas entirely undeveloped. The agricultural potential is tremendous since not only is the soil of excellent quality but in many instances the climate is such as to permit more than one crop per year.

7. Ibid., p. 194.

THE NORTHERN SLOPES

The northern slopes are somewhat like the Pacific piedmont with regard to climate, altitude, and rainfall. For the most part, the area is warm and has ample moisture. The region around Cobán is devoted to coffee production, and large plantations abound, interspersed with subsistence farming. The soil is inferior to that of the southern piedmont, however, and coffee yields are much lower. Commercial farming is further handicapped by isolation from commercial centers. There are no hard-surfaced roads or railways connecting the area with shipping centers. Much of the coffee must be transported from the farms on muleback.

It is estimated that 6 to 9 per cent of Guatemala's coffee comes from this area. It would seem that Cobán's success in coffee production is due largely to the abundant supply of cheap labor and to a favorable climate rather than to good soil. Until recently, farm workers in the area were receiving only six to ten cents per day in addition to certain perquisites, including permission to use a plot of land to grow subsistence crops for their own use.

Farther to the north and west on the map is a small area known as Zona Reina which is reputed to be an undeveloped El Dorado of Guatemala.[8] The rich soil, rainfall, and temperature conditions combine in this area to offer excellent opportunities for future development. As yet, however, the area is so isolated and inaccessible that it can be reached only by muleback or on foot.[9]

THE PACIFIC COASTAL PLAIN

This low plain extends about 150 miles along the entire southern coast of Guatemala and ranges in width from about 10 to 25 miles. The plain narrows near the eastern border, and almost disappears in the neighboring country of El Salvador. The plain rises almost imperceptibly in altitude from the seacoast on the south toward the highlands of the north. The soil is exceptionally fertile and would seem to offer tremendous opportunities for future agricultural development.

The coast line is fairly straight, without any natural harbors. There are three seaports on the Pacific—Ocos, Champerico, and San José—but in all three, ships must lie at anchor well off shore. Along the seacoast are swamps which extend intermittently almost throughout the

8. Ibid., p. 191.
9. Ibid, p. 191.

entire length. Some of these are seasonal and dry up between rainy seasons.

Near the seashore, the rainfall is inadequate for most crops, with the possible exception of corn and beans. Extending back from the seacoast, however, the rainfall increases until, in the northern half of the plain bordering the lower piedmont, the precipitation reaches about 60 to 80 inches per year which, together with the excellent quality of the soil, makes this section adaptable for tropical agriculture. Unfortunately, the rich lands in this area are sparsely settled and have produced but little. Forests of hardwoods and palms are extensive. The lands are devoted largely to the grazing of cattle.[10]

Among the reasons for the sparse settlement of the Pacific coastal area are the following: (a) tropical diseases have not been brought under control in the area; (b) much of the land is held in large units by absentee landlords who have not seen fit to open them up for agricultural settlement; and (c) roads to provide access to the area are lacking. A contributing factor in some areas of the coastal plain is lack of water. There are numerous possibilities for irrigation, however, since more than a dozen rivers flow from the mountains directly southward over the narrow plain to the Pacific Ocean. The greatest difficulty here is that the plain is narrow and the waters in the rivers coming down from the mountains flow swiftly and traverse comparatively little territory before reaching the ocean. Nevertheless, small irrigation projects could probably be developed without much difficulty.

EL PETEN AND THE CARIBBEAN LOWLANDS

This area is at once the largest section of the country, occupying about 45 per cent of the total land area and, at the same time, the most sparsely populated. It contains only 0.5 per cent of Guatemala's population and has a density of only 1.1 inhabitants per square mile.

It lies almost entirely below 1,500 feet in elevation with most of it considerably below this. The climate is tropical and the rainfall is reasonably adequate. Most of the area is covered with tropical forests, and except for the railway along the lower Montagua valley and the water transportation by small boats on Lake Izabal, the entire area is practically devoid of any means of modern transportation.[11] Produc-

---

10. An important exception to the low productivity of the area is the large banana plantation of the United Fruit Company consisting of about 22,000 acres at Tiquisate. This will be discussed in Chapter 6.

11. When completed, the Atlantic Highway will connect Guatemala City with Puerto Barrios on the Caribbean coast.

tive agriculture in the area is confined almost entirely to the banana
plantations of the United Fruit Company at Bananera.

The vast Petén area is virtually a tropical wilderness. This is a most
interesting situation in view of the fact that it was in this same Petén
area that the ancient Mayan civilization reached its highest development, from about A.D. 300 to 900. The Mayas constructed elaborate
cities and towns (Figure 3), many of whose ruins are only now being

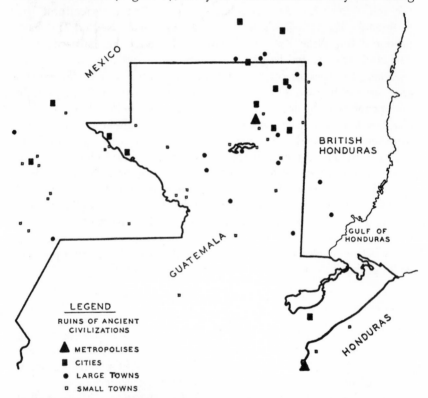

Figure 3. Ruins of ancient civilizations in Guatemala, including areas immediately adjacent. Adapted with modifications from Sylvanus G. Morley,
The Ancient Maya, Stanford University Press, 1946, Plate 19.

uncovered. They became skilled in mathematics, astronomy, and
hieroglyphic writing. They developed independently the important
mathematical principle of the zero and worked out the first accurate
calendar in the Western Hemisphere. Their art and architecture were
portrayed in the magnificence of their buildings, constructed and
carved from limestone blocks, and in the styles in which they were
designed and decorated. The ancient city of Tikal, which was being

uncovered and partly restored in 1957–60, in the tropical rain forest of this area, was perhaps one of the greatest ceremonial centers in the history of the world. It is thought by some to have contained a population approximating 100,000 inhabitants,[12] probably most of them peasants who lived on the outskirts of the city in thatched houses near their cornfields. The city proper is believed to have been largely a religious center controlled by the Mayan theocracy.

The political organization of the ancient Maya resembled that of the old Greek City States in that there appears to have been no central political and religious control, but groups of city states, each controlled by a religio-political hierarchy centered in the urban temple-palace area of each major settlement.[13]

One cannot reflect upon prehistoric Guatemala without asking why this great civilization had all but disappeared at the time of the Spanish Conquest. Why indeed did the nation apparently abandon great cities in the Petén and Usumacinta regions and trek north and eastward into Yucatán? Many reasons have been set forth and there appears to be no definite agreement among scholars. Morley has advanced the theory that perhaps their agricultural techniques, the slash and burn method, progressively lessened the productivity of the soil and destroyed the forest growth.[14] As the grasslands took over the area formerly in forest, the Mayas apparently experienced increasing difficulty in using such land again for agriculture. Their method of farming depended upon forests which could be felled and burned to make ash, in which the corn and other seeds were sown. Since they had no tools or implements to break the sod, they could not cultivate these previously burned-over lands.

Eric Thompson criticizes this theory and advances another to the effect that the decline of the Mayan civilization might have been brought about through a series of peasant revolts against the minority of priests and nobles because of the ever-growing demands for service in construction work on the urban temples and in the production of food for an ever-increasing number of nonproducers.[15]

Whatever the reason, there ultimately resulted a large-scale shift in

12. See Edwin M. Shook et al., *Tikal Reports*, Nos. 1–4, University Museum, University of Pennsylvania, Philadelphia, 1958. Also see reported interview with Edwin M. Shook in *Life* (Oct. 13, 1958), pp. 84–96.

13. Sylvanus G. Morley, *The Ancient Maya* (Stanford, Calif., 1946), p. 160. Also see Sylvanus G. Morley, *The Ancient Maya*, revised by George W. Brainerd (3d ed., Stanford, Calif., 1956), pp. 143–9.

14. *Ibid.*, p. 71.

15. J. Eric S. Thompson, *The Rise and Fall of Maya Civilization* (Norman, Oklahoma, 1954), p. 88.

population from the old Mayan areas in the Petén to the new areas located in the Yucatán peninsula of neighboring Mexico. By the time of the Spanish Conquest, five hundred or so years later, these Yucatán cities had also been abandoned, and the Spaniards found groups of inhabitants living under the rule of descendants of the old Mayan ruling houses.

Thus, when the Spaniards arrived in Guatemala, the Petén area had been virtually abandoned and the tribal nations of Guatemala were confined to the highlands. The area was ripe for conquest because the various tribes had been at war with one another for decades and, fighting among themselves, became easy prey to the organized armies of the conquistadores.[16]

STATISTICAL REGIONS

Statistical data in Guatemala are compiled largely by departments and, to some extent, by *municipios*. The municipio is the smallest unit of local government, somewhat similar to a New England town in the United States. Municipios, of which there were 315 in 1950, are grouped for administrative purposes by the Guatemalan government into larger units, or provinces, known as departments. Each of these corresponds somewhat to a state in the United States, although it does not have self-government. Each is a dependency of the executive branch of the national government. The governor is appointed by the President and serves at his pleasure. There are 22 departments in the Republic and they vary greatly in geographical size, number of inhabitants, and in the number of municipios which each contains.

For the purpose of presenting statistical data in this study, the departments are grouped by the author arbitrarily into six regions and plotted on the map in Figure 4. In this grouping an attempt is made to take into account differences in natural regions and, to some extent, demographic factors such as ethnic group composition. In some in-

16. See José Milla, *Historia de la América Central* (2 vols. Guatemala, 1879), *1*, ch. 2. The name "Guatemala" is of Indian origin and was applied to the entire captain-generalcy of Spain at the time of the Conquest. This included the five countries of Central America extending southward to the northern border of the Republic of Panama; and northward to include most of what is now the state of Chiapas in southern Mexico. After gaining independence from Spain in 1821, the entire area was attached to the Mexican Empire of Iturbide for a period of two years, after which it was broken up into separate countries. The province of Chiapas remained with Mexico, ten of the fifteen former provinces united to form the Republic of Guatemala. The remaining four separated into the independent republics of El Salvador, Honduras, Nicaragua, and Costa Rica.

1. Volcanic peaks stretch across the country to dwarf the works of man. City of Antigua at lower right; Lake Atitlán in upper center.

Above

2. Man, woman, and beast carry heavy burdens.

3. Panoramic view of Guatemala City, the largest metropolis in Central America.

4. A highland village. Note tiny farms on slopes of hills.

stances, a given department may lie mostly in one natural region but
partly in one or several others. In such cases, it has been arbitrarily
classified into one or the other. The regions, therefore, should be
thought of merely as rough approximations to more or less homogeneous units.

Figure 4. Statistical regions of Guatemala showing classification of departments into regions by the author. Compare with Figs. 1 and 2.

Comparison of Figure 4 with figures 1 and 2 shows the extent to
which the statistical regions reflect natural ones. The central region,
though small geographically, is considered as a separate unit because it
is the most highly urbanized area of the country, containing Guatemala
City, the national capital, as well as the small city of Antigua.

The departments are grouped into regions in Table 2 according to
number of inhabitants, area in square miles, and the density of popula-

TABLE 2. *Density of population, by region and department, 1950*

Region and department	Number of inhabitants	Area in square miles	Inhabitants per square mile
REPUBLIC	2,790,868	42,042.0	66.4
Central	499,037	1,000.3	498.9
Guatemala	438,913	820.8	534.7
Sacatepéquez	60,124	179.5	335.0
North	70,912	17,332.8	4.1
El Petén	15,880	13,843.2	1.1
Izabal	55,032	3,489.6	15.8
East	554,200	5,878.3	94.3
Chiquimula	112,841	917.4	123.0
El Progreso	47,872	742.1	64.5
Jalapa	75,190	796.5	94.4
Jutiapa	138,925	1,242.8	111.8
Santa Rosa	109,836	1,140.9	96.3
Zacapa	69,536	1,038.6	67.0
South	315,023	3,378.4	93.2
Escuintla	123,759	1,692.7	73.1
Retalhuleu	66,861	716.6	93.3
Suchitepéquez	124,403	969.1	128.4
West	1,095,571	9,892.3	110.7
Chimaltenango	121,480	764.1	159.0
El Quiché	174,911	3,234.7	54.1
Huehuetenango	200,101	2,857.1	70.0
Quezaltenango	184,213	753.3	244.5
San Marcos	232,591	1,463.7	158.9
Sololá	82,921	409.7	202.4
Totonicapán	99,354	409.7	242.5
North central	256,125	4,559.9	56.2
Alta Verapaz	189,812	3,353.7	56.6
Baja Varapaz	66,313	1,206.2	55.0

Source: *Sexto censo de población.*

tion per square mile. A glance shows that there is tremendous variability among regions and departments with respect to land area and number of inhabitants. This will be discussed further in the next chapter.

Chapter 2

GROWTH AND DISTRIBUTION
OF THE POPULATION

GROWTH OF POPULATION

Since reliable census statistics are a recent development in all countries, studies of population growth over long periods of time are far from accurate. Guatemala is therefore not exceptional in this respect.

The number of inhabitants in Guatemala at the time of the Conquest is unknown. Contemporaries have given estimates, but they were generally biased. The Spanish conquerors tried to demonstrate the importance of their newly won territories by exaggerating the number of inhabitants. The native chroniclers were no more accurate. However, it is quite safe to say that just before the Spaniards arrived, the population was fairly dense in the Guatemalan highlands, just as it is today. There is general agreement that the number of Indians must have been reduced upon initial contact with the Spaniards. Battle casualties, diseases, and excessive exploitation by the conquerors took their toll, but the extent of the decrease cannot be determined. Whatever the decrease, the Indian population very likely recovered over the years of peace that followed the Conquest.

Although the population before and immediately after the Conquest cannot be estimated satisfactorily, nor can its growth since then be accurately traced, we can get some conception of it by looking at the six official general censuses.[1] The population counts reported for each of these censuses are as follows:

1. Partial censuses have been conducted and estimates have been made at various times, but we shall restrict ourselves to the six official censuses which purported to cover the entire country. The 1950 figures are the latest available. The Dirección General de Estadística estimates that as of June 30, 1960, the total number of inhabitants had increased to 3,765,044. If this estimate is reliable, it would mean that the population increased 34.9 per cent during the decade 1950-60.

19

1778	396,146	
1880	1,224,602	
1893	1,364,678	
1921	2,004,900	
1940	3,283,209	(2,221,923)
1950	2,790,868	

None of the figures except that for 1950 can be taken at anywhere near face value. The 1778 count, taken by parish priests on orders from Spain, was hardly a census by modern criteria, and probably under-enumerated the Indians. The first general census for the Republic was taken in 1880. The census takers faced various difficulties in working with a population unaccustomed to such procedures. The count was especially unsatisfactory in the predominantly Indian departments of Totonicapán, El Quiché, and Huehuetenango; census officials could only estimate the number of inhabitants for those areas. The census of 1893 also left much to be desired. The 1921 census was more complete than the previous ones, but it was still of limited scope. The 1940 census might have been fairly adequate if the figures had not been deliberately tampered with. President Jorge Ubico, who wanted to show a large population for political purposes, issued orders to the local authorities to alter the count after the census was taken. Relevant papers in the central files were carefully destroyed, but enough documentary evidence has been found in the offices of local authorities to indicate that the census results were inflated by at least 900,000 inhabitants. The published result was 3,283,209.[2] An estimate of the correct total, 2,221,-923, was made by a subsequent administration on the basis of calculations from the 1950 census.[3] As indicated in the Preface, so much careful planning went into the taking of the census of 1950 that it appears to be reasonably adequate.

In spite of the unsatisfactory nature of the figures for the censuses prior to 1950, we can make the following generalizations:

1. The increases partially reflect better enumeration as the level of public administration and communication rises.
2. At least for the later republican period, there has been a fairly steady growth in population.
3. Growth has been due to natural increase, i.e., excess of births over

2. Dirección General de Estadística, *Boletín Mensual*, 26 (1950), 34–7; *Sexto censo de población*, p. 12.
   3. Dirección General de Estadística, *Guatemala en cifras* (Guatemala, 1955), p. 31.

deaths, rather than to immigration, which has been negligible since the Spanish Conquest.

4. The total population grew 25.6 per cent between 1940 and 1950. This rate was somewhat slower than that for Mexico during the same period, 31.2 per cent. Nevertheless, Guatemala, like most of the other Latin American countries, has one of the fastest growing populations in the world.[4]

FUTURE POPULATION GROWTH

The composition of Guatemala's population and her vital rates all suggest the possibility of rapid population growth. (See Chapters 3 and 11.) It seems reasonable to suppose that the death rate will decline somewhat in the near future. This is based on the assumption that health facilities now available in Guatemala City will gradually be extended to other parts of the country. In 1950 there were 420 physicians in the Republic, but almost three-fourths of them were practicing in Guatemala City, which contained only 10 per cent of the total inhabitants. Thus, there were about 900 inhabitants per physician in the capital, as compared with almost 23,000 for each doctor in all other parts of the Republic combined.[5] It seems certain, however, that physicians and health services will gradually become available in rural Guatemala. If health facilities should improve sufficiently to bring about a drastic decline in the death rate and if the birth rate continues at anywhere near its present high level, then Guatemala may suffer from overpopulation in the future.

Guatemala's population may more than double by 1980, according to projections calculated by the United Nations in 1954 for each of the Central American countries.[6] Three different estimates were made on three different assumptions. The low estimate, based on the assumption that both mortality and fertility rates would decline slowly, projected a population of 4,989,000 by 1980. The high estimate of 6,715,000 assumed that the mortality rate would decline somewhat faster than the birth rate. The medium estimate anticipated a population of 5,759,000,

---

4. For the period 1940–50, the rates of growth for the various areas of the world were as follows: Middle America, 24.4 per cent; South America, 23.3; North America, 15.1; Africa, 15.1; Asia, 12.8; Europe, 3.4; Oceania, 15.0; and U.S.S.R., 3.1 per cent. *United Nations Demographic Yearbook* (1955), p. 115 ff.

5. Data supplied by Dirección General de Estadística, 1950.

6. United Nations, *The Population of Central America* (*Including Mexico*), *1950–1980*, ST /SOA /ser. A, Population Studies, No. 16, 1954.

which would mean doubling the population by 1980. It is impossible to say how accurate these estimates of future population will prove to be. Nevertheless, Guatemala almost inevitably can expect rapid growth and may be faced with even more serious problems of education and economic development than at the present time. If the higher estimate should materialize, she may be faced with a serious population problem.

Prospects for a rapidly increasing population need not necessarily be regarded with pessimism, however, provided the economy of the nation can be developed more efficiently in the meantime. If industrialization takes place, if more efficient agricultural techniques are adopted, and if unused lands are brought into production, then the availability of human resources in the form of a young, vigorous, and rapidly growing population may prove to be one of Guatemala's greatest assets.

Density and Geographical Distribution

Guatemala has a greater density of population than most other countries of the Western Hemisphere. With 66 inhabitants per square mile, in 1950 her density was surpassed only by that of Haiti (289), El Salvador (230), Cuba (131), and the Dominican Republic (114).

The density of 66 inhabitants per square mile is, of course, only an average for the country as a whole, with much variation among the territorial units. Population density by departments and regions was given in Table 2 and varied from a low of one person per square mile for El Petén in the north to 535 per square mile for the department of Guatemala, containing the national capital. Figure 5 shows population distribution by even smaller units, the municipios, with each dot representing one hundred inhabitants.

The areas of highest density lie in the western and central highlands. The eastern highlands are fairly heavily populated, but less so than those in the west. There is a separate area of dense settlement in the southern part of Alta Verapaz in the north central region. The areas of low density are in the lowlands: the Pacific and Atlantic coastal areas and the plains of El Petén in the north.

In general, then, population is dense in the highlands, and sparse in the lowlands. Even as far back as the Conquest the population has retained essentially this distribution. The explanation appears to lie with the climate. Guatemala is in the tropical zone, but the higher altitudes are more temperate in climate and therefore more attractive for habitation than the hot lowlands where tropical diseases are prevalent.

Despite the rationale of climate, population is not distributed in keeping with the full potentialities of agricultural resources. Because of rugged terrain, good farm land is scarce in the highlands—just where population is the heaviest. The ratio of people to the land is so high that many farms are too small to provide a living for the families that

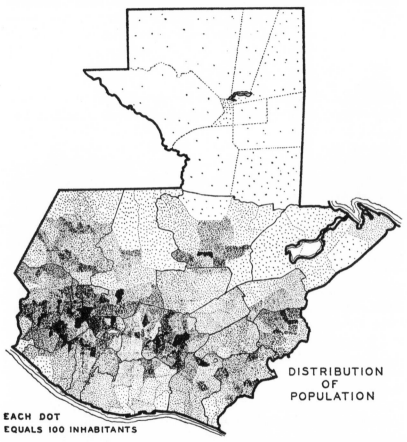

DISTRIBUTION OF POPULATION

EACH DOT EQUALS 100 INHABITANTS

Figure 5. Geographical distribution of population, 1950. Source: Sexto censo de población, Dirección General de Estadística, 1950. Compare with Figure 1.

till them. For example, in the department of Totonicapán in the western highlands, the mean average land holding is 2.8 acres and the median 1.6 acres. On the other hand, there are excellent land resources along the Pacific coast and in the north; but these regions are greatly under-populated. The department of El Petén contains nearly one-third of the total land area of Guatemala, but less than 1 per cent of its inhabitants. This region, which in 1950 had a density of one inhabitant per square mile supported a population of considerable size during the height of the Mayan empire as we have previously noted, and could probably be made to do so again. Various crops can be raised on its reasonably good soil, and its grasslands would make good grazing for livestock. At present, this northernmost department is highly inaccessible, and much road-building and malaria control will have to be undertaken before large-scale settlement can take place.

INTERNAL MIGRATION

During most of Guatemala's history, successive administrations have been aware of the imbalance between population distribution and resources. At first they sought to encourage foreigners to settle and develop vacant lands, but such immigration did not materialize. Attention was then turned to internal colonization. The government offered to sell public lands at a low price to anyone who wanted to settle on them. However, most of this land lay in remote and inaccessible areas, and the land title system was so vague that no one knew for certain just what the government did own. Some public holdings were distributed, but for the most part in districts which were already well settled.

The failure of government-sponsored colonization schemes did not mean that there was no internal migration of any sort in Guatemala. Economic and social developments abroad had their repercussions within Guatemala and led to some population movement. The people of Europe and North America in an age of growing industrialization and urbanization had become great coffee drinkers. Various tropical countries began raising coffee to meet this demand. Guatemala entered the coffee market in the latter half of the nineteenth century. Coffee plantations were established in various departments, but some of the best ones were to be found in the southern piedmont area where the population hitherto had been relatively sparse. To meet the huge demand for labor supply at harvest time, planters had to import seasonal workers from the densely populated highlands. Forcible migration was necessary at first, but in time some of the workers settled down permanently. The pressures of heavy population in the highlands helped to stimulate migration.

Banana production, the other major export industry of Guatemala, was responsible for further occupation of once relatively sparsely settled areas. The two main areas of banana production are in the southeastern lowlands of Izabal and the coastal plains of Escuintla. Historically, these hot coastal regions had appealed neither to Indians nor Spaniards.

Paradoxical as it may seem, the development of plantations which gave rise to migration into relatively unoccupied areas was also responsible, at least in part, for increased migration to Guatemala City. Plantation products came to constitute the major portion of the nation's export trade, and the administration of this trade was primarily concentrated in Guatemala City. Personnel on all levels was needed for this new function: executives, clerks, skilled and unskilled workers. The middle and upper echelons were recruited from the urban population, but many of the workers came from the countryside. In addition, it has long been a custom for plantation owners themselves to live in Guatemala City, at least for the greater part of the year. The upper classes, both commercial and agrarian, needed domestic servants. In emulation, the middle-class families also employed as many servants as they could afford. The demand for domestic servants led to further migration from rural areas. Business enterprises, large and small, multiplied to cater to the sundry needs of the ever-growing city population. This development, of course, meant more opportunities for employment and further in-migration. Moreover, the improvement of transportation and communication systems facilitated migration to the city.

The census of 1950 provides a rough measure of migration, other than seasonal,[7] among the various departments within the Republic. By recording the department of birth for all native-born inhabitants according to their department of residence in 1950, the percentage of inhabitants born elsewhere in the country may be shown for each department.

For the country as a whole in 1950, 11.8 per cent of the native-born population were living in a department other than that of birth (Table 3). This figure is only about half the comparable rate for the United States in 1950 (25.2 per cent), but it must be remembered that the United States has unusually high mobility due to superior transportation and communication facilities. The rate in Guatemala is close to that for Mexico, 12.9 per cent. However, since Guatemala is more underdeveloped than Mexico, it is to be expected that a greater proportion of her migrants move relatively short distances. The data bear out this expectation. In Guatemala, three-fifths (60.7 per cent) of the

---

7. Seasonal migration is discussed more fully in Chapter 5.

TABLE 3. *Proportion of population born in other departments by region and department of residence in 1950*

Region and department of residence	Total native-born	Born in other departments Number	Per cent
REPUBLIC	2,760,602	326,621	11.8
Central	488,561	102,976	21.1
Guatemala	428,675	96,882	22.6
Sacatepéquez	59,886	6,094	10.2
North	64,729	31,557	48.8
El Petén	14,488	3,782	26.1
Izabal	50,241	27,775	55.3
East	546,400	33,655	6.1
Chiquimula	110,273	2,705	2.5
El Progreso	47,757	5,098	10.7
Jalapa	74,918	4,134	5.5
Jutiapa	135,309	5,025	3.7
Santa Rosa	109,250	10,860	10.0
Zacapa	68,893	5,833	8.5
South	312,504	100,708	32.2
Escuintla	122,238	55,162	45.1
Retalhuleu	66,361	17,196	25.9
Suchitepéquez	123,905	28,350	22.9
West	1,092,504	51,150	4.7
Chimaltenango	121,339	8,241	6.8
El Quiché	174,849	4,264	2.4
Huehuetenango	199,635	2,694	1.3
Quezaltenango	183,473	22,004	12.0
San Marcos	231,035	9,449	4.1
Sololá	82,840	3,083	3.7
Totonicapán	99,333	1,415	1.4
North central	255,904	6,575	2.6
Alta Verapaz	189,616	3,587	1.9
Baja Verapaz	66,288	2,988	4.5

Source: Sexto censo de población.

migrants live in a department contiguous to that in which they were born, contrasting with 47.1 per cent for Mexicans.[8]

More than 30 per cent of the inhabitants of Izabal and Escuintla were born outside of their borders. These two departments include the banana plantations of the United Fruit Company. Escuintla is also one of the chief coffee-producing departments of the Republic. Generally

8. Nathan L. Whetten and Robert G. Burnight, "Internal Migration in Mexico," *Rural Sociology, 21* (1956), 145.

speaking, the departments having the greatest amount of in-migration, in terms of the proportion of their population born elsewhere, are the three departments of the southern region where plantation agriculture predominates; the two departments of the north which is sparsely settled; and the department of Guatemala which contains the capital city. These areas show the highest proportion of inhabitants born in departments other than the one in which they were living in 1950. At the other extreme, most of the departments of the northern and western highlands had the lowest amount of in-migration with less than 5 per cent of the inhabitants born outside of the confines of their respective departments. This was also true of the two eastern departments of Jutiapa and Chiquimula.

Rural-Urban Distribution

Wherever one draws the line between rural and urban communities, Guatemala is overwhelmingly rural. The Guatemalan census officials selected 2,000 as the dividing line, and by this criterion 75 per cent of the total population live in rural places.[9] In a country such as Guatemala, however, where customarily many farmers, part-time farmers, and agricultural laborers live in towns and villages and commute to their farms, this dividing line would seem to be too low. Actually, one could make a good case for classifying as rural all persons living in localities having fewer than 10,000 inhabitants. Not until a community in Guatemala reaches this size does it begin to take on very many of the characteristics of an urban society. If this dividing line were used, the proportion of the total population living in rural communities in 1950 would be 87.5 per cent.

Nevertheless, using Guatemala's criterion and classifying only places under 2,000 as rural, Table 4 shows the rural-urban distribution by region and by department. This admittedly understates the rurality of the population. The central region is unique in the high percentage of urban inhabitants. It contains the national capital, Guatemala City, and the former capital, Antigua. At the other extreme, the most rural region is the north central, with 92.7 per cent of its inhabitants living

9. According to the preface of the published results, a place with a population between 1,500 and 2,000 was also classified as urban, provided that it had "servicio de agua" (water service). The exact nature of this service is not given. There were a total of 102 urban places in the 1950 census, of which 15 had between 1,500 and 2,000 inhabitants. *Sexto censo de población, 1950.* p. xx.

in rural places. It should be noted that 14 of the 22 departments are more than 80 per cent rural; and of these, 6 are more than 90 per cent rural.

TABLE 4. *Rural-urban distribution of inhabitants by region and department, 1950*

Region and department	TOTAL INHABITANTS	RURAL INHABITANTS Number	Per cent	URBAN INHABITANTS Number	Per cent
REPUBLIC	2,790,868	2,094,410	75.0	696,458	25.0
Central	499,037	143,094	28.7	355,943	71.3
Guatemala	438,913	120,415	27.4	318,498	72.6
Sacatepéquez	60,124	22,679	37.7	37,445	62.3
North	70,912	47,968	67.6	22,944	32.4
El Petén	15,880	14,284	89.9	1,596	10.1
Izabal	55,032	33,684	61.2	21,348	38.8
East	554,200	481,154	86.8	73,046	13.2
Chiquimula	112,841	101,158	89.6	11,683	10.4
El Progreso	47,872	39,951	83.5	7,921	16.5
Jalapa	75,190	60,195	80.1	14,995	19.9
Jutiapa	138,925	125,161	90.1	13,764	9.9
Santa Rosa	109,836	96,311	87.7	13,525	12.3
Zacapa	69,536	58,378	84.0	11,158	16.0
South	315,023	251,708	79.9	63,315	20.1
Escuintla	123,759	97,425	78.7	26,334	21.3
Retalhuleu	66,861	52,113	77.9	14,748	22.1
Suchitepéquez	124,403	102,170	82.1	22,233	17.9
West	1,095,571	933,025	85.2	162,546	14.8
Chimaltenango	121,480	81,424	67.0	40,056	33.0
El Quiché	174,911	158,396	90.6	16,515	9.4
Huehuetenango	200,101	187,141	93.5	12,960	6.5
Quezaltenango	184,213	140,454	76.2	43,759	23.8
San Marcos	232,591	217,938	93.7	14,653	6.3
Sololá	82,921	65,157	78.6	17,764	21.4
Totonicapán	99,354	82,515	83.1	16,839	16.9
North central	256,125	237,461	92.7	18,664	7.3
Alta Verapaz	189,812	176,651	93.1	13,161	6.9
Baja Verapaz	66,313	60,810	91.7	5,503	8.3

Source: *Sexto censo de población.*

About half of the urban population shown in Table 4 were living in towns of less than 10,000; [10] and as mentioned before, there may be real question whether these towns can be considered truly urban. Thus,

10. Of the 696,458 urban inhabitants, 347,292 or 49.9 per cent live in places with fewer than 10,000 persons.

only 12.5 per cent of the total population lived in places with 10,000 or more inhabitants in 1950. Only five cities had as many as 10,000, and three of them hovered just over that line. The five cities may be mentioned briefly.

The smallest of these is Antigua Guatemala (usually referred to merely as Antigua), which contained only 10,996 inhabitants in 1950. For 232 years this was a flourishing little city which played a leading role in the social, economic, and political life of Central America. From 1541 to 1773 it was the capital of a large area which included all of Central America and what is now the state of Chiapas, Mexico. The entire area was ruled over from Antigua by a Captain General who was responsible to the King of Spain. In 1773 the city was almost completely destroyed by a series of violent earthquakes, and the capital was then moved to what is now Guatemala City.

During the height of its glory Antigua (which until after 1773 was called Santiago de los Caballeros) was the most important colonial capital between Mexico City and Lima, Peru. It had an estimated population of between 70,000 and 80,000 inhabitants and was the center for commercial, religious, and political affairs. It was where the Spanish aristocracy lived and where the wealth of the Church was conspicuously displayed in a large number of elaborate churches, monasteries, and convents designed and decorated by some of Spain's finest architects and artists. It was the home of the first university in Central America, founded in 1679, and of the third printing press in the New World, which was introduced in 1660, preceded only by one in Mexico City and one in Lima.[11]

Today Antigua is largely a collection of magnificent ruins which serve as a monument to the grandeur of the Spanish colonial architecture. Situated at an altitude of 5,030 feet above sea level, the city has a delightful climate; located near two towering volcanic peaks (Agua and Fuego, see Plate 1), it offers scenery that is little short of spectacular. All of these features will probably combine to increase greatly its importance as an attraction for tourists in the future.

Mazatenango, with a population of 11,067, is the regional center for the coffee-growing area of the southwest and, though small now, will probably experience considerable growth with the completion of the Pacific Slope Highway.

Puerto Barrios, on the Caribbean coast, had a population of 15,155 in 1950 and is Guatemala's principal seaport. It has remained small because of its relative isolation from the more densely settled parts of

11. Chester Lloyd Jones, *Guatemala, Past and Present* (Univ. of Minnesota Press, Minneapolis, 1940), p. 327.

the country due to the lack of adequate transportation facilities. The new highway connecting it with Guatemala City, in addition to existing railway and seaport facilities, will probably stimulate future growth.

Quezaltenango, capital of the department of the same name, is the second largest city in the Republic and had a population of 27,672 in 1950. It is situated at an altitude of 7,658 feet and is the center for a large area usually referred to as Los Altos (the mountainous region) and performs important banking and trading functions. It was formerly connected by a small railway which was washed out by floods in 1930–32 and never rebuilt. It has grown slowly and remains a small city even though it is the center of a large agricultural area. The proximity of the Pan American Highway that is now being completed may stimulate more rapid growth in the future.

Guatemala City, which is 4,872 feet above sea level, had 284,276 inhabitants in 1950, more than four times the combined population of all other cities over 10,000. Though small when compared with some of the larger cities of the Western Hemisphere, it is larger than any other city in Central America and is growing rapidly.[12] As may be noted from Plate 3, the city is virtually surrounded on three sides by deep ravines (north, east, and west), so that most of the future expansion will probably have to take place toward the south. Actually, the new location did not live up to expectations as an earthquake resisting locality. The new city was greatly damaged by a severe tremor in 1874; and was virtually destroyed by a series of violent earthquakes in 1917–18. Nevertheless, it was not abandoned but was rebuilt on the same lay-out.

The city is modern in many respects although it is evident that, like cities in many other countries, its founders in 1776 could not foresee the various roles the capital city would be expected to play in the life of the nation. The introduction of the automobile and other forms of modern transportation has exaggerated the inadequacy of the original lay-out of the city. As in many other cities of Latin America, its streets were devised for a small-town situation; they were laid out on the gridiron pattern and are extremely narrow. Even though the streets are restricted to one-way traffic, the congestion in downtown Guatemala City during the busy hours of the day has become a serious problem. Anticipated continued rapid growth may necessitate the tearing out of whole blocks in the center of town in order to make it accessible to

12. Although no census was taken in 1960, an official estimate by the Dirección General de Estadística as of June 30, 1960 places the population of Guatemala City at 387,826. If this estimate is accurate, it would mean that the city increased 26.7 per cent during the decade 1950–60.

the expanding population. Fortunately, the newer sections of the city have comparatively wide streets.

Like many other Latin American capitals, Guatemala City dominates the life of the entire country. It is where the political and economic power of the nation is concentrated. It is where the centers of learning, the hospitals, the department stores, the automobiles, and the recreational facilities are to be found; and where politicians, labor leaders, writers, and most of the nation's doctors, lawyers, engineers, and the social elite reside. Indeed, it may be said with considerable accuracy that in Guatemala all paths lead to Guatemala City.

LOCALITY GROUPINGS

The municipio

The municipio is the basic locality grouping of Guatemala. One might describe it as an administrative unit somewhat similar to the New England town. It has definite geographical boundaries which usually encompass an area ranging from an average of 30 square miles in the central region to over 1,000 in the thinly populated north. It contains one or more villages, or larger population centers, one of which is the *cabecera*, or headquarters, of the municipio. It may also contain a number of smaller population clusters as well as scattered farms. Each municipio is a political entity and tends to possess a distinct cultural individuality.

The origins of the municipio, as of many other institutions in Latin America, go back to the Conquest. Before the Spaniards came, most of the Indians lived scattered throughout the countryside. For better control of labor and souls, the Spaniards tried to concentrate the Indians into compact villages. They established territorial units which embraced these consolidated settlements and their surrounding areas. In some cases the municipio boundaries may have been based on preexisting ethnic divisions, but in many others they were quite arbitrary.

In time, each municipio came to develop a cultural homogeneity of its own. The relative lack of internal migration did much to further a distinctive character. Such matters as clothing, crafts, religious practices, vocabulary, and grammatical usages came to differ from one municipio to another, even between neighboring units. The inhabitants grew conscious of themselves as a "people," distinct from all others. The identification of the people with the municipio was buttressed by the fact that each municipio had its own church, patron saint, festival calendar, and market. The diversities persist even now to such a large extent that the anthropologist Sol Tax wrote that "studies in the ethnology of Guatemala must begin with studies of the cultures of individual municipios." [13] The cultural individuality of the municipios, especially in recent times, has become modified. In the first place, two or more contiguous municipios may be quite similar if they were originally parts of a larger unit. Administratively, divisions and combinations of municipios occur quite often. At the time Sol Tax wrote on the Guatemalan municipios in 1937, there were 355. There were only 315 when the 1950 census was taken, but 322 when the official list of territorial units was published three years later. Internal migration has also modified somewhat the homogeniety of the municipio. When Indians of one municipio move to another, they and their descendants often maintain their original customs. Thus, in the piedmont plantation areas, one sees colonies of Indians still wearing the clothing peculiar to their original highland municipios.

The municipios are by no means uniform in area or population. In the densely populated sections of the central and western highlands, the municipios are smaller in area and have more inhabitants than in the sparsely settled north. One-fourth of all the municipios have fewer than 3,000 persons and about the same proportion have more than 10,000, with the remaining half falling in between these two extremes.

The cabecera municipal

The life of each municipio revolves around the cabecera, or central village or town. In the cabecera are located the services and functions which give the municipio its cohesion as a social unit. Here are to be found the one or more churches serving all the inhabitants of the municipio, whether they live in the central village or in one of the smaller outlying communities. The festivals of the ritual calendar are all celebrated in the center. The market in the cabecera is the principal place where the inhabitants buy and sell goods. Politically, the cabecera is the seat of local government services and the channel for communications from the central government in Guatemala City via the departmental capital. The courthouse, jail, and one or more schools are also found in the cabecera.

Typically, cabeceras tend to be compact clustered settlements, inhabited by farm families who till the adjacent lands. Such a cabecera is shown in Plate 4. The men leave early in the morning, work in the

13. Sol Tax, "The Municipios of the Midwestern Highlands of Guatemala," *American Anthropologist*, 39 (1937), 425.

fields all day, and return home at night. Not all cabeceras conform to this pattern. In the larger ones most of the residents may be engaged in non-farm occupations, such as shop-keeping or manufacturing, while the farmers live outside the town, either on their lands or in smaller population clusters near their fields. In another variant type, the houses of a town are scattered over a fairly wide area, with each family living on a plot of land which it tills. The cabecera of Todos Santos, in the department of Huehuetenango, is an illustration of this type and is described by Stadelman as a "village within a maize field, as almost every house possesses its adjacent cornfield." [14]

Another type is that designated as the "vacant town" by Sol Tax, which may be inhabited by both Indians and Ladinos. Most of the Indians in this type of municipio live on farms dispersed over the countryside, but many of them also have houses in the town. Although the town dwellings stand vacant during most of the week, the Indians occupy them on market days, on fiestas, or whenever they have some special matter to attend in the center. Representative of this type is the cabecera of Chichicastenango in the midwestern highlands. Describing a Chichicastenango street where town houses of Indians are located, Sol Tax writes:

> A street in the south end of town, called Los Callejones, is lined from end to end with continuous rows of low white-washed houses, the headquarters of a thousand Indians. On Sunday it is athrob with life; but on Monday . . . not a person is to be seen nor a sound to be heard.[15]

In 1950, 31 per cent of the inhabitants of Guatemala lived in cabeceras, while 69 per cent lived either in smaller outlying communities or in the open countryside. The central region, containing Guatemala City which is also a cabecera (Plate 3), had the highest proportion of inhabitants living in cabeceras, 74.1 per cent; but this percentage is atypical of the rest of the country. By eliminating that region, one arrives at an even lower figure, 21.6 per cent, as the number of persons living in cabeceras for the Republic as a whole, exclusive of the central region. Since the cabecera is usually the largest community in the municipio, the low proportion of persons living in these places indi-

14. Raymond Stadelman, "Maize Cultivation in Northwestern Guatemala," *Contributions to American Anthropology and History*, 6 (1940), 101.
15. Sol Tax, "Town and Country in Chichicastenango," *Chichicastenango*, ser. B, Item 16, Appendix III, Microfilm Collection of Manuscripts on Middle American Cultural Anthropology, Univ. of Chicago Library, Chicago, 1935.

cates that the settlement pattern in Guatemala is predominantly one of small isolated rural communities.

The over-all pattern of small communities becomes even sharper when one turns to the size of the cabeceras themselves. From the first two columns of Table 5, it can be seen that in 1950 one cabecera out of

TABLE 5. *Cabeceras municipales by number of inhabitants and regions, 1950*

Number of inhabitants	TOTAL GUATEMALA		NUMBER OF CABECERAS MUNICIPALES					
	Number	Per cent	Central	North	East	South	West	North central
TOTAL	315	100.0	33	15	66	40	139	22
Under 500	61	19.4	2	4	7	13	28	7
500–999	81	25.7	2	5	15	8	44	7
1,000–2,499	102	32.4	14	3	31	10	40	4
2,500–4,999	47	14.9	11	2	9	6	16	3
5,000–9,999	19	6.0	2	0	4	2	10	1
10,000 and over	5	1.6	2	1	0	1	1	0

Source: *Sexto censo de población.*

five (19.4 per cent) had less than 500 inhabitants; and that nearly half (45.1 per cent) had less than 1,000. On the other hand, only 23.5 per cent of the cabeceras could be classified as urban if we were to apply the definition used in the United States census and take 2,500 as the dividing line between rural and urban.

The geographical distribution of the cabeceras is shown in Figure 6. It can be seen that the densely populated western and central regions tend to have more of the larger cabeceras as well as many smaller ones, while the sparsely settled north and north central regions have smaller and more widely scattered cabeceras, with very few larger ones.

The ciudad, villa, and pueblo

Communities within a municipio are classified by the Guatemalan government into a number of categories: *ciudad, villa, pueblo, aldea,* or *caserío.* The first three designations are reserved for cabeceras of municipios, while the others are for localities outside the center.

As a general rule, the importance of a cabecera governs its classification. The term *ciudad* (city) is usually reserved for those cabeceras of municipios which also serve as departmental capitals.[16] Thus, all

16. The ciudad of Escuintla, for example, is the cabecera not only for the municipio of Escuintla, but also is the capital for the department of Escuintla.

departmental capitals are ciudades, but there are in addition six other cabeceras of municipios which are considered worthy of this designation, bringing the total number of ciudades to 28.[17] The term *villa* is given to important cabeceras which are not departmental capitals or

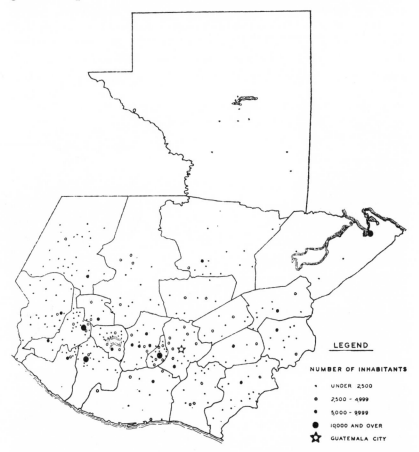

Figure 6. Municipio centers (*cabeceras*), plotted according to size and location. Data from *Sexto censo de población*, 1950.

Generally speaking, but with some exceptions, the cabecera bears the same name as the municipio. Likewise, in cases where it also serves as the departmental capital, the department usually has the same name. Thus, Guatemala City is the cabecera for the municipio of Guatemala, but is also the capital for the department of Guatemala. It also happens in this unique instance to be the capital of the Republic of Guatemala.

17. The department of San Marcos has three ciudades, while Baja Verapaz, Chimaltenango, Guatemala, and Quezaltenango have two each. All other departments have only one.

ciudades. There are 29 villas in the entire Republic. The classification *pueblo* is applied to all other municipio centers, which number 258.

Size is normally one of the important criteria for official categorization of cabeceras, but there are some exceptions. For instance, many villas and pueblos are larger than the ciudad Flores which had a population of only 1,596 in 1950 and is the capital of the sparsely settled department of El Petén. A few pueblos are larger than some villas. As a rule, however, ciudades are larger than villas and pueblos, and villas are larger than pueblos. From Table 6, one can see that 18 of the

TABLE 6. *Cabeceras municipales by size
and official categories, 1950*

| | OFFICIAL CATEGORY OF CABECERA MUNICIPAL | | |
Number of inhabitants	*Ciudad*	*Villa*	*Pueblo*
TOTAL	28	29	258
Under 2,500	3	14	227
2,500–4,999	7	11	29
5,000 and over	18	4	2
Median size	6,234	2,789	883

Source: Sexto censo de población.

28 ciudades have a population of 5,000 and over, whereas there are only four villas out of 29 which are in that category. Most of the pueblos are under 2,500. The median size of ciudades is 6,234 inhabitants; of villas 2,789, and the median for pueblos is 883.

The aldea and the caserío

We have already indicated that more than two-thirds of the total population live elsewhere than the cabeceras of municipios and that the outlying population aggregates are officially classified as aldeas and caseríos. Unfortunately, we do not know the exact proportions living in aldeas, in caseríos, or in the open countryside. However, we do know that aldeas number 2,483 whereas there are 4,441 caseríos.[18]

The aldea is larger and more important than the caserío. In most instances, a caserío is under the jurisdiction of the nearest aldea, but some caseríos are directly responsible to the municipal centers just as are the aldeas. An aldea may serve as a decentralized focus of life for the surrounding countryside, if it has, as is often the case, a church, a school, and a cemetery.

18. See Appendix Table 2 for distribution of ciudades, villas, pueblos, aldeas, and caseríos, by region and department.

In some municipios, the designations "aldea" and "caserío" are not used; instead the term *cantón* is applied to localities which elsewhere would be called aldeas or caseríos.[19] The matter is confused further by the practice, chiefly in certain parts of the west, of dividing the entire municipio into sections known as cantones. Frequently, they refer to areas containing only scattered dwellings.

Exact data on settlement patterns of aldeas and caseríos are lacking. In an effort to obtain some idea of the proportion of their inhabitants living in compact clustered communities and the proportion living scattered over the countryside, the author in 1952 with the cooperation of the *Instituto Indigenista Nacional* formulated a questionnaire which was circulated to all *alcaldes* (mayors) of municipios. Each alcalde was asked to list all of the settlements in his municipio and to indicate those where clustered settlement prevailed and those where scattered settlement was characteristic. Responses were obtained from 179 of the 315 municipios, or 57 per cent. The results are given in Table 7.

TABLE 7. *Distribution of dwellings in aldeas, caseríos, and cantones, 1952*

Type of distribution of dwellings	TOTAL		ALDEAS		CASERÍOS		CANTONES	
	Num-ber	Per cent	Num-ber	Per cent	Num-ber	Per cent	Num-ber	Per cent
TOTAL	2,501	100.0	1,153	100.0	896	100.0	452	100.0
Clustered and aligned with streets	173	6.9	124	10.8	7	0.8	42	9.3
Clustered but no alignment or streets	333	13.3	188	16.3	95	10.6	50	11.1
Scattered but mutually visible	1,407	56.3	638	55.3	525	58.6	244	54.0
Isolated and not mutually visible	588	23.5	203	17.6	269	30.0	116	25.6

Based on questionnaire formulated in 1952 by the author in cooperation with the Instituto Indigenista Nacional and circulated to all alcaldes. Responses obtained from 179 out of 315 municipios.

Caseríos tended toward scattered or isolated dwellings more than did aldeas (89 per cent and 73 per cent respectively). The intermediate

19. The category "cantón" is not used in Appendix Table 2. According to the preface of the official volume from which this table was derived, cantones which resembled aldeas were classified as aldeas and those which resembled caseríos were counted as caseríos. (Dirección General de Estadística, *Departamentos, municipios, ciudades, villas, pueblos, aldeas y caseríos de la República de Guatemala*, p. 6.)

position of the cantones is due to the varying definitions; "cantón" may correspond to an aldea, caserío, or a section of a municipio. For the sample as a whole, the prevalent settlement pattern is that in which dwellings are scattered but visible one from another. Communities of this type constitute 56.3 per cent, and by adding the category in which houses are isolated and not mutually visible, an overwhelming 79.8 per cent is shown to be of the scattered or isolated settlement pattern. Localities in which dwellings are clustered, with or without alignment or streets, were decidedly in the minority (20.2 per cent). Places having houses clustered and aligned with streets constituted the smallest category (6.9 per cent). It should be remembered that these data refer only to settlement patterns outside of the cabecera and not to those of the total rural population. Nevertheless, it would appear that even with these restrictions the settlement patterns in Guatemala differ considerably from those in Mexico where the clustered farm village is highly characteristic.

The dispersed settlement pattern is advantageous in that farmers living on their plots can take better care of their crops and are saved the time and energy they would have to spend in traveling back and forth to a clustered village miles away from their fields. Nevertheless, farm families suffer many disadvantages by being more or less isolated from their neighbors. Informal visiting among adults, play among children, and mutual aid in times of need are much easier in a clustered village. Furthermore, development of such community services as water systems, electricity, and telephone is a more formidable task when dwellings are scattered. Finally, and perhaps the most important point, families dispersed over the countryside without adequate means of communication are much more difficult to reach through such institutions as schools, farm organizations, community programs, and extension services. These institutions could serve as instruments of national integration and promote higher standards of living among the rural population. To some extent the social disadvantages of isolated settlement can be mitigated through the development of roads and communication facilities, as has happened in many parts of the United States, although in Guatemala this would appear to lie in the distant future.

The plantation community or finca

Fincas, or plantation communities, constitute a special type of locality grouping found outside the cabeceras. As defined by the Guatemalan census of 1950, a finca can mean, simply, a farm. A finca may range, however, from a single family farm to a plantation containing hundreds of inhabitants. Since the author's interest lay in these plantation communities as a distinct segment of rural Guatemala, he made special tabulations from the census data on the basis of his own definition of a plantation community as a farm or plantation containing at least 100 inhabitants. Table 8 is based on this special material.

The average plantation community having over 100 inhabitants has

TABLE 8. *Population of plantation communities having over 100 inhabitants, average number of inhabitants per community, and per cent of total population, by region and department, 1950*

Region and department	No. of plantation communities	Population of plantations	Average no. inhabitants per plantation	Per cent of plantation population to total population
REPUBLIC	1,408	431,013	306	15.4
Central	116	26,019	224	5.2
Guatemala	97	21,564	222	4.9
Sacatepéquez	19	4,455	234	7.4
North	30	9,072	302	12.8
El Petén	—	—	—	—
Izabal	30	9,072	302	16.5
East	99	27,606	279	5.0
Chiquimula	—	—	—	—
El Progreso	1	139	139	0.3
Jalapa	6	928	155	1.2
Jutiapa	4	796	199	0.6
Santa Rosa	81	23,861	294	21.7
Zacapa	7	1,882	269	2.7
South	468	152,577	326	48.4
Escuintla	165	70,155	425	56.7
Retalhuleu	106	24,617	232	36.8
Suchitepéquez	197	57,805	293	46.5
West	504	142,395	283	13.0
Chimaltenango	88	22,157	252	18.2
El Quiché	54	19,457	360	11.1
Huehuetenango	40	7,607	190	3.8
Quezaltenango	162	45,184	279	24.5
San Marcos	149	45,700	307	19.6
Sololá	11	2,290	208	2.8
Totonicapán	—	—	—	—
North central	191	73,344	384	28.6
Alta Verapaz	166	66,038	398	34.8
Baja Verapaz	25	7,306	292	11.0

Source: *Sexto censo de población.*

a population of 306. The average number of inhabitants per plantation community in the various departments having such communities ranges from 139 in El Progreso to 425 in Escuintla. There are individual plantations, however, that have over 1,000 inhabitants.

The final column in Table 8 shows the proportion of the plantation population to the total population. Inhabitants on plantations represent 15.4 per cent of the total population, making up as much as one-fifth of the total rural population, or 20.6 per cent. The importance of plantations is seen even more sharply when one turns to percentages by departments. Roughly half the population of the southern departments of Escuintla and Suchitepéquez live in plantation communities. Retalhuleu and Alta Verapaz have a third of their population in plantation communities; Quezaltenango has a fourth, and three other departments (Santa Rosa, Chimaltenango, and San Marcos) have about one-fifth.

The distribution of plantation communities having more than 100 inhabitants is plotted by municipios in Figure 7. There are two major areas where this type of settlement prevails. One lies in the southern part of Alta Verapaz. The other is a broad belt running through the southern tier of departments from the western border adjoining Mexico almost up to the eastern border. The major plantation belt lies below and to the south of the area of highest population density in the highlands. (Compare with Figure 5.) There is not a single plantation community in Totonicapán where the population density is one of the highest: 242 persons per square mile.

A plantation community is made up of a variety of persons. The owner and his family may be found there, but more often than not they live in Guatemala City. The manager and other supervisory personnel, bookkeepers, foremen, and workers charged with the maintenance of equipment are all, with their families, members of the plantation community. However, the vast majority of the inhabitants are the *colonos* (resident workers) and their families. The colono lives on the plantation throughout the year and works primarily for the owner, but he is allotted a small plot of land on which to grow a little corn for his own needs. During certain rush seasons, particularly during coffee-picking time, which extends from September to January, depending on climatical variations, the services of many more laborers are required. Migratory workers, or *cuadrilleros*, are recruited fom the highland areas, and they may or may not be accompanied by their families.[20]

20. Probably very few migratory workers were counted by the census as inhabitants of a plantation community. The census was taken in April, a month in which the services of cuadrilleros are not much needed.

Plantation workers, both colonos and cuadrilleros, will be discussed in more detail in Chapter 5.

A finca having hundreds of inhabitants must, of course, provide certain facilities that go with any other populous community. It often has

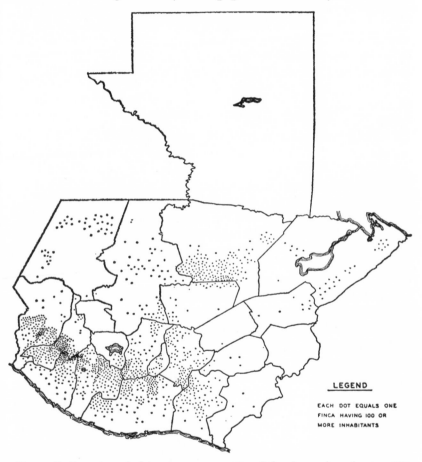

LEGEND

EACH DOT EQUALS ONE
FINCA HAVING 100 OR
MORE INHABITANTS

Figure 7. Location of plantation communities defined as a finca having 100 or more inhabitants. Special tabulation of data from *Sexto censo de población*, 1950.

a chapel, a commissary, and a jail. Theoretically at least, the plantation is integrated into the nation-wide system of local government. It may be under the jurisdiction of the nearest cabecera, aldea, or caserío, or may itself be classified as an aldea or caserío.

Although the plantation in many respects is like any other community, the inescapable fact that all the inhabitants are employees of the owner gives it a unique coloration. Life on a finca is patterned largely after the wishes of the owner. Usually he provides living quarters for the workers and their families; and since he charges no rent, he can exert whatever control he wishes over the local community. According to law he is supposed to provide educational facilities for the children; but they vary in quality, depending on the landowner in question. Participation in community activities by individuals is minimal, since the owner or his manager directs most local affairs.

Isolation of Rural Guatemala

As indicated in the first chapter, the rugged topography of Guatemala creates great obstacles to communication which have yet to be overcome by an adequate road system. The need has been recognized by successive governments at various times, but the high cost of construction and maintenance has slowed progress. Departmental capitals and the more important towns may be interconnected by roads, but some of these are narrow one-lane roads of sharp curves and steep grades, surfaced with graded sand-ash, gravel, or earth. For the most part, the smaller places are reached only by narrow foot trails, winding up and down mountain obstacles and deep canyons.[21]

The poor communication system does not exclude contact with the world outside the villages. The Indians, especially the men, do a good deal of traveling about the country. Small merchants, mostly serving as their own beasts of burden, go surprisingly long distances on foot. Moreover, thousands of Indians seasonally cross departmental lines to work on the plantations; and army service takes many to Guatemala City or other parts of the country. Physical contact in itself, however, does not bring about cultural integration. The nature of Indian society and its relations with ladino, or non-Indian, society is such that, in spite of contact, the way of life of the Indians continues pretty much unchanged.[22] The contacts the Indians have while traveling are generally limited to specific purposes, such as trade transactions, and thus are short-lived. Among themselves, the Indians live in closely knit groups in which they find psychological security. On the other hand, the Ladinos regard the Indians as inferior, and do not encourage them to emulate or identify with them.

The problem of cultural integration must be attacked through various

21. Progress in the construction of three major highways was noted in the previous chapter.
22. This will be discussed in detail in Chapter 4.

approaches, not the least of which is a reduction in rural isolation. Although the Indian sees a good deal outside his own village, he spends too much time in just getting to and from his destination. If he is carrying goods, especially on his own back, he cannot take much; and it may require several days for him to make a relatively short trip. Bus and truck transportation—the use of which is already increasing as modern highways are gradually being extended—would release more time for production. Greater productivity would result in a higher standard of living, which, in turn, might create a greater incentive toward education and eventually to acculturation.

Chapter 3

COMPOSITION OF THE POPULATION

ETHNIC GROUPS

The Indian not only survived the Spanish Conquest in Guatemala but has continued to remain the predominant element in the population. Although his numbers were greatly reduced by the conquistadores, and although a certain amount of race mixture and acculturation have taken place between Indian, white, and mestizo, nevertheless this has not been sufficient to obliterate his ethnic and cultural identity, nor even to reduce the Indians to a numerical minority.

Ethnic classification

At the present time, Guatemalans are classified into two broad ethnic groups: Indian and Ladino. In 1950 Indians constituted 54 per cent of the total population, and Ladinos accounted for 46 per cent.[1] Generally speaking, Indians are those descendants of the pre-Columbian inhabitants who have not adopted the characteristic features of modern Western culture. Ladinos are, to put it briefly, non-Indians.

Strict comparison of the ethnic situation in Guatemala with that of the United States would be misleading. In North America there are two major racial groups, White and Negro. An individual who has but a small amount of Negro ancestry and may look "White" is nevertheless classified as Negro, unless he is able to "pass" and chooses to do so. In other words, ethnic classification in the United States is quite rigid. This is not the case in Guatemala. Viewed from an historical perspective, ethnic classification in Guatemala has a dynamic nature. The

1. Although more than half of the population was reported as Indian in 1950, this represents a proportionate decline over previous census years. In 1921 the reported percentage of Indians was 64.8; and in 1940 it was 55.7. See Jorge Arias B., "Aspectos demográficos de la población Indígena de Guatemala," Dirección General de Estadística, *Boletín estadístico, 1–2* (Guatemala, 1959), 20.

44

Indian-Ladino distinction did not have the same meaning in colonial times that it does today.

Ethnic classification in the earlier colonial period was biological, based on combinations of the three racial strains: White, Indian, and Negro. The Spaniards (White), coming originally as conquerors, were at the top of the social scale. They, in turn, were divided into two groups: *Peninsulars* and *Creoles*. Peninsulars, or those born in Spain, were thought to be superior to the Creoles simply because they were born in the Old World. Indians, being the conquered aborigines, were at the bottom of the social scale, as were the Negro slaves imported to perform labor that the Spaniards could not get the Indians to do. Almost from the outset, there was miscegenation. Because Spanish women were extremely few in number, Spanish men mated with women of other races. White and Indian unions produced mestizos. Out of White and Negro alliances came *mulattoes*. Persons of Negro and Indian parentage were called *zambos*. From generation to generation other combinations developed, so that a given individual might have all three original strains in varying quantities in his genealogy. The mixed bloods during this earlier period occupied a position intermediate between Whites on the one hand and pure Indians and Negroes on the other.

In spite of the race mixture that has taken place since the Conquest, the Indian element is the predominant one today. Iberian blood did not spread extensively because, in the first place, Spaniards were never numerous in Guatemala, and secondly, they were confined almost exclusively to the capital and to the more important provincial towns. Negroes, whose ancestors were brought as slaves to Guatemala in the early colonial period, seem to have largely disappeared as a distinct group by the end of the colonial period, but physical traces of that ancestry can be recognized in individuals, patricularly along the Pacific coast. African ancestry is also evident among the so-called Black Caribs who live along the coast of Izabal, particularly in the town of Livingston, but they have a distinct history of their own. They are the descendants of fugitive West Indian Negro slaves who intermarried with the Carib Indians of St. Vincent in the Antilles. They did not come to the mainland till the close of the eighteenth century.[2]

2. The Black Caribs had cooperated with the French during the wars of the French Revolution, and so the English deported them from St. Vincent to the island of Roatan in the Gulf of Honduras in 1797. The greater portion of the Caribs soon crossed over to the mainland, and their descendants are now to be found along the coast, from British Honduras to Nicaragua. Racially they are predominantly Negroid, but they retain much of the Antillean culture, including

Genetic mixture is not all that takes place in race contact. Frequently changes in culture also result. In Guatemala, the Spanish conquerors tried to impose upon the Indians certain aspects of their culture, such as government organization and religious practices. They did not transform the colony into an image of the mother country, but a new cultural orientation which was neither old Indian nor Spanish eventually evolved. Because of the heterogeneity of the Indians themselves, there were many local variations of this new Spanish-American culture. Since some aborigines were more resistant to assimilation than others, there were also variations in the degree of emphasis given to either the Indian or the Spanish elements of the general culture. The inhabitants of the more inaccessible western highlands remained more Indian in their way of life than Spanish. The reverse appears to have held for the Indian groups who lived in eastern Guatemala, possibly because of something in their culture that made them more easily influenced.[3] Indians and mixed bloods who congregated in towns showed the highest degree of acculturation.

The acculturative process gradually became the basis of ethnic classification. The key to the shift lies with changes in the usage of the term "Ladino." The designation seems to have been first used for those Indians who worked in the towns as artisans and adopted Spanish ways, including the language. They had become "latinized," i.e., taken on the characteristics of Latinos. Mixed bloods in time also came to be called Ladinos rather than being referred to by the racial categories of mestizo, mulatto, and zambo.[4] Generally speaking, these mixed bloods were an urban group acculturated to Spanish ways, so that it is easy to see how they might have come to be called "Ladinos." The classifications for the royal census of 1778 in Guatemala consisted of only (1) Spaniards (White), (2) Ladinos, or mixed bloods, and (3) Indians and Negroes.

The category "Ladino" eventually was broadened to include any person, regardless of racial inheritance, who did not live like an Indian. This is the definition which holds today. Even a racially pure-

---

language. Douglas McRae Taylor, *The Black Carib of British Honduras*, Viking Fund, No. 17 (New York, 1951), pp. 24–7.

3. Richard N. Adams, *Cultural Surveys of Panama-Nicaragua-Guatemala-El Salvador-Honduras* (Washington, D.C., 1957), p. 271 ff. and p. 285.

4. A late eighteenth century manuscript in the Museo Naval, Madrid, reads: "they are called Ladinos, because they speak Spanish; they are mulattoes, zambos, and other castes which are not Indian. . . ." Felix Webster McBryde, *Cultural and Historical Geography of Southwest Guatemala* (Washington, D.C., 1945), p. 13.

blooded Indian could become a Ladino if he were to become un-Indian in his way of life. Persons who claim an ancestry exclusively European are likewise considered Ladino, even though they have recently immigrated from a non-Latin country like Germany.[5] Most of the foreign-born population who came from other Latin American countries are classified as Ladinos.[6] Even the few Chinese and Asiatic Indians qualify as Ladinos, although their ways of life differ somewhat from the typical ladino culture.[7]

Obviously there is a high correlation between Indian racial features and Indian culture, since persons who have retained their Indian customs have also tended to intermarry within their own ethnic group. Likewise Ladinos tend to avoid intermarriage with readily identifiable Indians.[8] Nevertheless, with ethnic classification in Guatemala based on cultural characteristics as well as upon racial background, passage from Indian to Ladino is possible, since cultural characteristics weigh more heavily in the separation of Indians and Ladinos than do racial features. Because Indians occupy a generally lower socio-economic position than Ladinos, especially where the two groups live in the same community, they have an incentive to identify with the latter. If an Indian sloughs off his indigenous ways, such as the Indian language, the Indian-type dress, and the Indian ceremonial observances, and if he learns to speak Spanish, wear shoes, and, especially, if he moves away from the Indian community into a larger town, he may in fact become a Ladino. He is then said to be "ladinoized."

Transition from Indian to Ladino may often require more than one generation. For this reason, one may consider the Indian group as consisting of two sub-groups. The first might be called the *Traditional Indian,* since its members follow the indigenous way of life in terms of religious ceremonies, dress, customs, and world view. The other group,

5. Certain upper-class Guatemalans of Spanish and other European descent may set up a three-fold classification of White, Ladino (mestizo), and Indian, but other Ladinos and Indians would consider the first two to be Ladinos.

6. Foreign-born Indians in 1950 add up to a mere 1,475 or 6 per cent of the total foreign-born from the Americas, exclusive of the United States and Canada. The largest number, 476, was found in Chiquimula, and in all likelihood came mostly from Honduras. The 294 foreign-born Indians in San Marcos, representing the next largest group, must have moved across the border from Mexico. The number in other departments was considerably lower.

7. The predominantly Negroid Black Caribs of Livingston, in the department of Izabal, were classified by the census either as Indians or Ladinos. Evidently, the more unacculturated ones who speak Carib in the home were considered to be Indians; and those who live according to ladino standards and speak Spanish were regarded as Ladinos.

8. Adams, op. cit., p. 268.

which is gradually breaking away from the indigenous customs and is acquiring the attitudes and behavior patterns more clearly represented among the Ladino, might be referred to as *Transitional Indian.* The Indian-Ladino relationship and the problems of ladinoization is the subject of the next chapter.

Although the population of Guatemala may be divided sociologically into Traditional Indians, Transitional Indians, and Ladinos, statistical information is available from the 1950 census only for the two broad groupings, Indian and Ladino. The 1921 census had also used these two categories, but the 1940 census classified the population into five racial categories: White, Mestizo, Indian, Negro, and Yellow. This resort to racial groupings was a deviation from the practice among ordinary Guatemalans of thinking in terms of Indians and Ladinos, and did not work out well in practice. With so many degrees of intermixture, it was not easy to differentiate among the groups. Besides, the numbers in some of these categories were very small. The officials who planned the 1950 census therefore decided to revert to the Indian-Ladino classification.

That this twofold categorization is common among the people of Guatemala is evident from the official instructions to enumerators. The census takers were directed to count an individual either as Indian or Ladino, according to the social position which he held in his community. "In small places," read the instructions, "there is a certain local consensus which rates the individual as Indian or as Ladino." If there were any doubts, the individual himself was to be questioned as a last resort.[9]

Ethnic distribution

As shown in Table 9, the distribution of Indians and Ladinos varies greatly from one department to another. The departmental percentages of Indians ranges from 9 to 97. Of the 22 departments, only 4 approach the national average.

Indians predominate in the western highlands and in the north central area. In eight of the nine departments in these two regions, Indians constituted at least two-thirds of the population. Alta Verapaz, Sololá, and Totonicapán were over 90 per cent Indian. Another way of emphasizing the Indian concentration in these two regions is to note that they contained nearly three-fourths (71.5 per cent) of all the Indians in the Republic, yet only 48.4 per cent of the total population. Perhaps there is some significance in the fact that the areas which are

9. Dirección General de Estadística, *Instrucciones para empadronadores; Sexto censo de población,* pp. 46–7.

the most Indian are also the most mountainous. The rugged terrain may have helped Indians to resist acculturation by making them more inaccessible, but this geographical factor should not be stressed at the expense of historical and cultural ones. There is a high degree of

TABLE 9. *Distribution of Indian and ladino inhabitants, by region and department, 1950*

Region and department	TOTAL INHABITANTS	INDIANS Number	INDIANS Per cent	LADINOS Number	LADINOS Per cent
REPUBLIC	2,790,868	1,497,261	53.6	1,293,607	46.4
Central	499,037	110,508	22.1	388,529	77.9
Guatemala	438,913	79,514	18.1	359,399	81.9
Sacatepéquez	60,124	30,994	51.6	29,130	48.4
North	70,912	13,897	19.6	57,015	80.4
El Petén	15,880	4,431	27.9	11,449	72.1
Izabal	55,032	9,466	17.2	45,566	82.8
East	554,200	163,231	29.5	390,969	70.5
Chiquimula	112,841	69,843	61.9	42,998	38.1
El Progreso	47,872	4,482	9.4	43,390	90.6
Jalapa	75,190	38,004	50.5	37,186	49.5
Jutiapa	138,925	27,249	19.6	111,676	80.4
Santa Rosa	109,836	10,294	9.4	99,542	90.6
Zacapa	69,536	13,359	19.2	56,177	80.8
South	315,023	138,608	44.0	176,415	56.0
Escuintla	123,759	19,660	15.9	104,099	84.1
Retalhuleu	66,861	34,696	51.9	32,165	48.1
Suchitepéquez	124,403	84,252	67.7	40,151	32.3
West	1,095,571	854,933	78.0	240,638	22.0
Chimaltenango	121,480	94,243	77.6	27,237	22.4
El Quiché	174,911	147,094	84.1	27,817	15.9
Huehuetenango	200,101	146,628	73.3	53,473	26.7
Quezaltenango	184,213	124,473	67.6	59,740	32.4
San Marcos	232,591	168,540	72.5	64,051	27.5
Sololá	82,921	77,817	93.8	5,104	6.2
Totonicapán	99,354	96,138	96.8	3,216	3.2
North central	256,125	216,084	84.4	40,041	15.6
Alta Verapaz	189,812	177,308	93.4	12,504	6.6
Baja Verapaz	66,313	38,776	58.5	27,537	41.5

Source: *Sexto censo de población.*

diversity among these Indians, who, for whatever reason, are little ladinoized. As indicated previously, each municipio tends to have its distinctive character in regard to such matters as clothing and religious practices, except where ladinoization has blurred the cultural individuality of the municipio.

Ladinos predominate in the central, northern, and eastern regions. The fact that Spaniards in the colonial period concentrated primarily in the central area helps to explain the high proportion of Ladinos there (78 per cent Ladino, 22 per cent Indian). Somewhere in the course of history, the east also became ladinoized, but the process was not complete. While four of the six departments in that region were more than 80 per cent Ladino in 1950, Jalapa was half Indian and Chiquimula was three-fifths Indian. The increase of Ladinos in Izabal was relatively recent, with the development of banana plantations in the lowlands and of port facilities at Puerto Barrios on the north coast at the beginning of the present century. In 1950, Ladinos constituted 83 per cent of the population of that northern department.

Although the south showed a ladino majority, 56 per cent, each of its three departments was unique in regard to ethnic composition. As stated in the previous chapter, this region was relatively unsettled until the development of plantations in the latter half of the nineteenth century. The labor supply had to come from elsewhere. Most of the colonists who went to Suchitepéquez and Retalhuleu were Indians from the densely populated western highlands. Migration did not ladinoize very many of them, as is shown by the high proportion of Indians in these two departments in 1950: 68 per cent in Suchitepéquez, and 52 per cent in Retalhuleu. Escuintla, in contrast, is predominantly Ladino. This department has drawn migrants not only from the western highlands but also from other regions which are predominantly Ladino. Plantation life amidst large numbers of Ladinos tends to break down the traditional ways of the Indians. Generally speaking, the Ladinos of Escuintla are either Ladinos from the central and eastern regions, or Indian migrants who have been recently ladinoized.

While a study of the distribution of ethnic groupings by region and department is useful for pointing out general areas of concentration, analysis by municipio must not be neglected. Since the municipio is the basic locality grouping in Guatemala, it is primarily within the confines of that unit that Indians and Ladinos interact. Thus, the respective proportions of the two groups within the municipio may have some bearing on the social and cultural basis of their relationship. For example, Indians who constitute a minority in their municipios are usually more ladinoized than Indians who are numerically dominant in their localities.

In 1950 there were 60 municipios in which the percentage of Indians was less than 10 per cent of the total population (see Table 10). At the other extreme there were 84 municipios in which 90 per cent or more of the population consisted of Indians. Generally speaking, either the Ladinos or the Indians were in substantial majority (60 per cent or over) in any given municipio. There were only 34 out of the 315 municipios in which the two ethnic groups were in roughly equal proportions, i.e., in the category of 40 to 59 per cent Indian. There were 100 municipios with less than 40 per cent Indians, and 181 with 60 per cent or more.

Figure 8 is a map showing the proportion of Indian inhabitants according to municipios. The area of Indian concentration forms a band which runs diagionally through the country. With few exceptions, the coastal areas and eastern Guatemala have relatively low percentages of Indian population, as does the large, sparsely populated department of El Petén. Guatemala City lies on the borderline between these areas.

TABLE 10. *Municipios classified according to the proportion of inhabitants consisting of Indians, 1950*

Percentage of Indians in population	No. of municipios	Per cent of municipios	INDIAN INHABITANTS Total number	Per cent
TOTAL	315	100.0	1,497,261	100.0
0–9.9	60	19.0	36,094	2.4
10–19.9	23	7.3	29,672	2.0
20–29.9	9	2.9	12,837	0.9
30–39.9	8	2.5	30,990	2.1
40–49.9	18	5.7	59,514	4.0
50–59.9	16	5.1	120,142	8.0
60–69.9	24	7.6	124,877	8.3
70–79.9	31	9.8	192,891	12.9
80–89.9	42	13.3	318,299	21.2
90–99.9	80	25.4	543,061	36.3
100	4	1.3	28,884	1.9

Source: Arias B., "Aspectos demográficos," *Boletín estadístico* (1959), Nos. 1–2, 21.

Whatever educational and social services the national government establishes for raising the standard of living in rural areas are generally found in the cabecera, or center, of the municipio. Since inhabitants of the cabeceras have greater access to these services than persons living in small isolated settlements, the distribution of ethnic groups within the municipio is significantly related to the problem of national integration.

Indians tend to live outside the cabeceras and proportionately more Ladinos live in them. According to the 1950 census, only 17.8 per cent of all Indians lived in a cabecera, as compared to 46.3 per cent of all Ladinos. About one-fifth of all Ladinos lived in the largest of all cabeceras, Guatemala City, and comprised 90.1 per cent of the total population of this municipio. If we exclude the municipio containing this overwhelmingly ladino metropolis, the proportion of Indians living in cabeceras throughout the country was 16.8 per cent, as compared with 32.7 per cent of all Ladinos.

According to Table 11, proportionately more Indians live in small communities than do Ladinos. Whereas of the total Indian population, 88.8 per cent live in places with less than 2,500 inhabitants, 63.9 per

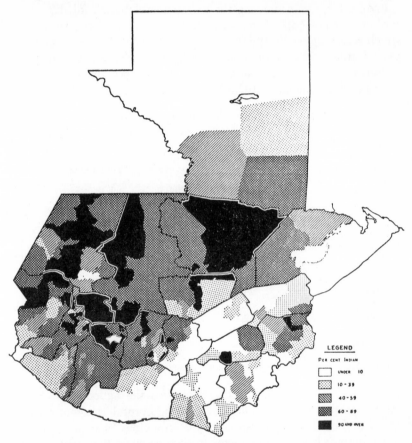

Figure 8. Per cent of total population consisting of Indians, by municipios. Data from *Sexto censo de población*, 1950.

cent of the Ladinos live in communities of that category. A slightly higher proportion of Ladinos than of Indians live in medium-sized communities. Ladinos in cities with 10,000 or more inhabitants comprise nearly one-fourth of all Ladinos, whereas only 2.2 per cent of the Indians live in cities of this size. Thus, Indians obviously predominate in the smaller communities and Ladinos in the larger ones.[10]

10. Appendix Table 3 classifies Indians and Ladinos according to rural-urban residence by departments.

In predominantly ladino areas, however, Ladinos outnumber Indians in rural places as well as in urban communities. For example, in the east where the Ladinos constituted 70 per cent of the total population, rural Ladinos constituted 69 per cent of all rural inhabitants.

LANGUAGE GROUPS

Spanish is the official language of Guatemala. It is the language of government, politics, legal contracts, schools, newspapers, and other mass media of communication. However, it is by no means spoken by all the people of the country. According to the 1950 census where information was tabulated on the language spoken in the home, 59.4 per cent of the total population three years of age or over spoke Spanish,

TABLE 11. *Distribution of Indians and Ladinos*
by size of community, 1950

Size of community	TOTAL INHABITANTS		INDIANS		LADINOS	
	Number	Per cent	Number	Per cent	Number	Per cent
TOTAL	2,790,868	100.0	1,497,261	100.0	1,293,607	100.0
Under 2,500	2,155,886	77.3	1,329,797	88.8	826,089	63.9
2,500–4,999	156,338	5.6	78,636	5.3	77,702	6.0
5,000–9,999	129,478	4.6	55,143	3.7	74,335	5.7
10,000 and over	349,166	12.5	33,685	2.2	315,481	24.4

Source: *Sexto censo de población.*

and 40.4 per cent spoke an Indian language.[11] Thus for more than one-third of the population, Spanish is not the language of their inmost thoughts or of their social relationships. They may know Spanish as a second language or they may have only the barest knowledge of it, if any. Furthermore, the Indian tongues number not just a few but at least 16. The implications for national integration of this linguistic diversity are obvious.

Since a Ladino is defined as a person who does not have the cultural traits of an Indian—and this includes a native language—all Ladinos except those speaking a foreign language are reported in the census as speaking Spanish. No Ladino was counted as speaking a native language in the home, though actually there are some, particularly in the highly Indian areas of the west, who have learned one. Of all per-

11. Only a few persons (4,128 or 0.2 per cent) spoke a foreign language. English was the one spoken by the largest single group, 3,290. Over half of the English-speaking persons lived in Izabal, and a little less than one-third lived in the department of Guatemala. German was spoken by 284, Chinese 230, French 155, Italian 64, and others 105.

sons speaking Spanish in the home, 78 per cent were Ladinos. The rest, 22 per cent, were Indians. These are probably Transitional Indians who no longer speak a native language in the home, but who have not gone far enough in the process of ladinoization to shed other cultural characteristics that mark them as Indians.

The number and percentage of persons speaking an Indian language in the home are shown in Table 12 by regions and by departments. There are more than one million persons speaking Indian languages in the home, and all of these are undoubtedly Traditional Indians. A fair

TABLE 12. *Population three years of age and over who speak an Indian language in the home, by region and department, 1950*

Region and department	Population 3 year of age and over	Persons speaking an Indian language	Per cent
REPUBLIC	2,504,922	1,011,167	40.4
Central	450,930	63,925	14.2
Guatemala	396,931	43,021	10.8
Sacatepéquez	53,999	20,904	38.7
North	63,564	10,151	16.0
El Petén	14,140	3,172	22.4
Izabal	49,424	6,979	14.1
East	496,073	17,879	3.6
Chiquimula	101,361	11,964	11.8
El Progreso	43,019	33	0.1
Jalapa	67,191	5,260	7.8
Jutiapa	123,823	10	—
Santa Rosa	98,019	585	0.6
Zacapa	62,660	27	—
South	281,984	89,235	31.5
Escuintla	111,123	8,007	7.2
Retalhuleu	59,972	20,675	34.5
Suchitepéquez	111,889	60,553	54.1
West	982,055	645,077	65.7
Chimaltenango	109,087	76,557	70.2
El Quiché	156,964	129,562	82.5
Huehuetenango	178,918	121,580	68.0
Quezaltenango	165,974	84,974	51.2
San Marcos	207,834	81,843	39.4
Sololá	73,972	68,309	92.3
Totonicapán	89,306	82,252	92.1
North central	229,316	184,900	80.6
Alta Verapaz	169,983	154,818	91.1
Baja Verapaz	59,333	30,082	50.7

Source: *Sexto censo de población.*

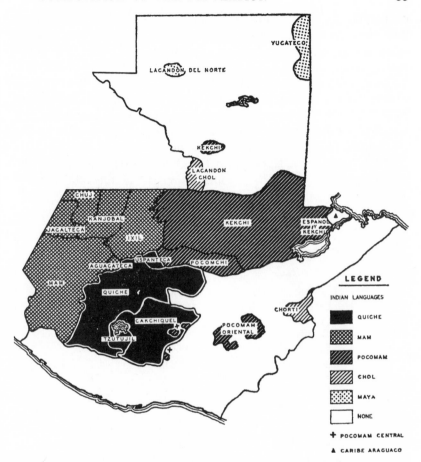

Figure 9. Map showing where each of the major Indian languages is spoken. Adapted from Lic. Antonio Goubaud Carrera, "Distribución de las lenguas indígenas actuales de Guatemala," *Boletín del Instituto Indigenista Nacional,* 1946.

degree of similarity may be noted between this distribution and that shown in Table 9. The highest proportions of Indians speaking a native tongue are to be found in the north central region and in the west, the areas of highest Indian concentration.[12] As shown in the two tables, the

12. The census takers were instructed to write only *lengua* (language) if a native language was spoken in the household enumerated. It was assumed that an Indian could not identify his language according to the classificatory scheme worked out by linguists. During the tabulation process, the name of the native language which prevailed in the municipio of birth was filled in among the data for each household.

low proportions in the central region, in the north, and in the south are quite close. In the east, fewer than 4 per cent of the Indians spoke a native language, although Indians were 30 per cent of the total population. The Indians of the east, then, appear to constitute a special case. The geographical distribution of the native languages, arranged according to the classification adopted by the *Instituto Indigenista Nacional*, is given in Figure 9. The principal groups are represented by patterned shadings, and the individual languages within the groups are identified by printed names or symbols.

Indians speaking a language in the Quiché group constituted the largest category (Table 13), a little over half of the total number

TABLE 13. *Population three years of age and over who speak an Indian language in the home, by language spoken, 1950*

Language	Number	Per cent
TOTAL	1,011,167	100.0
Quiché group	537,434	53.1
Cakchiquel	167,352	16.6
Quiché	339,232	33.6
Tsutujil	18,761	1.9
Uspanteca	12,089	1.2
Mam group	277,618	27.5
Aguateca	8,401	0.8
Chuj	10,771	1.1
Ixil	25,025	2.5
Jacalteca	13,491	1.3
Kanjobal	41,622	4.1
Mam	178,308	17.6
Pocomán group	182,951	18.1
Kekchí	133,971	13.2
Pocomchí	37,546	3.7
Central Pocomán	6,208	0.6
Eastern Pocomán	5,226	0.5
Chol group	12,048	1.2
Chortí	12,048	1.2
Carib group	1,116	0.1
Caribe	1,116	0.1

Source: *Sexto censo de población.*

speaking a native language (53.1 per cent). They are concentrated in the densely populated highlands to the west of Guatemala City. Those speaking a language in the Mam group, 27.5 per cent of the total, are to be found along a broad zone which runs from north to south in the extreme west. Languages in the Pocomán group are spoken primarily in Alta Verapaz and in small sections of adjacent departments. Pockets are also to be found in Jalapa, Guatemala, and El Petén. Persons speaking a Pocomán language constituted 18 per cent of the total Indian-speaking population. Northeastern Chiquimula is the area for Chorti, spoken by a mere 1.2 per cent of the total. The related Lacandón Chol is spoken in the southwestern corner of El Petén. The small handful of the so-called Black Caribs of Livingston who speak the Carib language (1,116 persons) are represented on the map by a printed symbol on the coast of Izabal. Adherents of the Maya language group in El Petén were not listed in the census, perhaps because they were so few in number.

One should not assume that a category of Indians speaking a particular native language is ipso facto coincidental with any ethnic grouping. The Quiché speaking Indians, for example, do not have a common culture and social organization which set them off from a group speaking another language. Moreover, there is no evidence that there was a distinct political or cultural group known as the Quiché at the time of the Conquest.[13]

As will be remembered from the previous chapter, the basic unit of cultural homogeneity is the municipio, except where modified by internal migration and ladinoization. Presumably, a single native language would predominate in an Indian municipio, but two municipios in which the same language is spoken are not necessarily similar in other respects. The individuality of the municipios combined with the diversity of languages, in a setting of rural isolation, constitute serious obstacles to the development of social integration at the national level.

AGE AND SEX COMPOSITION

The age composition of a population is one of its most important aspects, one that may greatly influence a country's social and economic life. The three dynamic factors affecting it are births, deaths, and migration, and it is in these terms that the age-sex composition of Guatemala will be analyzed.

The differences in age and sex composition of a population can be illustrated graphically by a diagram known as the population pyramid. Figure 10 represents such a diagram for the populations of Guatemala and the United States in 1950. The black bars represent the various age groups in Guatemala and the striped bars those of the United

13. Tax, "The Municipios of the Midwestern Highlands of Guatemala," *American Anthropologist*, 39 (1937), 423–5.

States. The age groups are indicated up the center of the diagram, beginning at the bottom with young children under 5 and extending by five-year groups to the top bars where persons 75 years of age and over are represented. The proportion of males in each age group is shown on the left side; the proportion of females on the right.

The chart shows that Guatemala has a much younger population

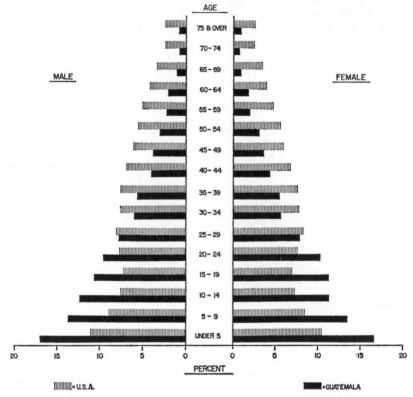

Figure 10. Population pyramid comparing age and sex profiles of population in Guatemala and the United States. Note much larger proportion of young children in Guatemala and of middle aged and older persons in the United States. Data from Appendix Table 4; and from the United States Census data for 1950.

than the United States, in that a higher proportion of its population is found in each age group under 25 and a smaller proportion in each age group beyond 25 years of age. The age-sex profile for Guatemala, as shown by the black bars in Figure 10, furnishes an almost classic example of a largely rural population of high fertility and high mortality. The broad base of the pyramid reflects the high proportion of young persons, while the narrow apex indicates that relatively few of the inhabitants are found in the older age groups. A high birth rate on the one hand and a high death rate on the other would produce such a distribution. In contrast, the age-sex profile for the United States has a narrower base and a broader apex. This indicates a smaller proportion of children as compared with Guatemala, but a much higher proportion of persons in the older age groups.

Fertility can be stated in terms of a fertility ratio which relates the number of children under 5 years of age to the number of women of child bearing age, that is, between the ages of 15 and 49. In 1950 there were 695 children per 1,000 women of these ages in Guatemala. This is a high ratio, especially as compared with a country such as the United States where the fertility ratio in 1950 was only 417. Further evidence of high fertility in Guatemala is the recorded birth rate, which was 48.8 per 1,000 inhabitants in 1955, one of the highest in the world.[14]

While many are born in Guatemala, comparatively few live very long. In 1955 the death rate per 1,000 inhabitants was 20.6, which also ranks among the highest in the world.[15] Particularly significant is the high infant mortality rate, which was 101.4 per 1,000 live births in 1955.[16] This means that approximately one out of every ten babies dies during the first year of life.

A high birth rate and a high death rate together create an age structure that has important implications for a nation's economy. When there is an extremely high proportion of children, the burden of their economic support, maintenance of adequate educational institutions, health programs, and the like falls heavily on the economically active population. This is the case in Guatemala. More than half (53 per cent) of the total inhabitants of Guatemala in 1950 were under 20 years of age, while only 42 per cent fell within the economically active ages between 20 and 59 years. In the United States, only one-third (34 per cent) of the total population were under 20 years of age, and 54 per cent were between 20 and 59 years old. In other words, proportionately fewer adults must support a much larger relative number of children in Guatemala than in the United States.[17]

14. *United Nations Demographic Yearbook* (1956), p. 613.
15. Ibid., p. 637.
16. Ibid., p. 687.
17. Perhaps these differences should be discounted somewhat, however, since dependency among children is probably less significant in a non-industrial society like Guatemala where fewer years are spent in the educational process; and where young people become partially, if not wholly, self-supporting at a much younger age than do those in more developed countries. This might reduce the actual difference in dependency somewhat, althought it would certainly not obliterate it.

A larger proportion of aged persons were found in the United States than in Guatemala. In the United States, 12 per cent of the population in 1950 were 60 years of age or over, as compared with only 4 per cent in Guatemala. The problem of support of the aged is therefore much greater in the United States than in Guatemala. Accordingly, it is not surprising to find that there are more agencies dedicated to meet the needs of older persons in the United States than there are in Guatemala.

Table 14 gives a comparison of the age composition of Guatemala

TABLE 14. *Age and sex composition of population of Guatemala and Guatemala City, 1950, in per cent*

Age group	REPUBLIC OF GUATEMALA			GUATEMALA CITY		
	Total	Males	Females	Total	Males	Females
TOTAL NUMBER	2,790,868	1,410,775	1,380,093	294,344	139,604	154,740
Under 5	16.8	17.0	16.7	14.4	15.3	13.6
5–9	13.6	13.9	13.4	10.9	11.6	10.2
10–14	11.8	12.2	11.3	9.7	10.2	9.3
15–19	11.0	10.6	11.3	11.0	10.6	11.5
20–29	17.8	17.4	18.3	20.7	20.7	20.7
30–44	15.7	15.6	15.7	18.4	18.2	18.5
45–64	10.8	10.9	10.8	12.0	11.1	12.8
65 and over	2.5	2.4	2.5	2.9	2.3	3.4

Source: Sexto censo de población.

City with that of the entire Republic. Differences are somewhat similar to those existing between the United States and Guatemala except that they are less pronounced. In comparison with the country as a whole, Guatemala City has a smaller proportion of children under 15 years of age; the same percentage of those 15–19 years of age; and a larger proportion of adults in the age groups beyond 20 years of age (compare Appendix Tables 4 and 5).

The lower rate of fertility in Guatemala City is suggested by data showing that there were only 496 children under 5 per 1,000 women between the ages of 15 and 49 in Guatemala City, as compared to 723 for the rest of the country. Here, as in cities generally throughout the world, certain social and economic factors related to urban living operate to lower the birth rate. Better medical care helps to explain the higher proportion of older persons in Guatemala City as compared to the rest of the country. Migration to the city of young adults from elsewhere probably accounts for the greater proportion in Guatemala City of persons 20–64 years of age. Guatemala City attracts numerous young adults with more job opportunities and a higher standard of living than are found in rural areas.

The lower birth rate and the heavy in-migration of young adults make the burden of supporting a dependent population much lighter for the economically active age groups in Guatemala City than for comparable groups in the rest of the country. In the capital city, persons under 20 years of age constituted only 46 per cent of the inhabitants as compared with 52.3 per cent for the country as a whole.

Indians and Ladinos in Guatemala have a somewhat similar age structure. This is not surprising when one considers the high proportion of both groups living in rural areas. Indians appear to have slightly higher proportions of persons under 20 years of age than do Ladinos (Table 15), while the latter have somewhat higher proportions in the age brackets over 20.

TABLE 15. *Distribution of Indian and ladino inhabitants by age groups and by rural-urban residence, 1950, in per cent*

Age group	TOTAL		RURAL		URBAN	
	Indians	Ladinos	Indians	Ladinos	Indians	Ladinos
TOTAL NUMBER	1,497,261	1,293,607	1,306,701	787,709	190,560	505,898
Under 5	17.0	16.6	17.3	17.7	15.5	14.8
5–9	13.9	13.4	14.2	14.5	11.7	11.7
10–19	23.2	22.3	23.3	22.8	22.1	21.5
20–44	32.8	34.1	32.5	32.3	35.2	36.9
45–64	10.7	11.0	10.4	10.4	12.6	12.0
65 and over	2.4	2.6	2.3	2.3	2.9	3.1

Source: *Sexto censo de población.*

The sex ratio

The population of Guatemala contains slightly more males than females. The sex ratio in 1950 was 102.2, meaning that there were 102.2 males for every 100 females. In the United States, the sex ratio for the same year was 98.6, showing a slightly higher proportion of females.

Ordinarily, there are proportionately more females in cities than in smaller towns and rural areas, and this is certainly true in Guatemala. There were only 90.2 males per 100 females in Guatemala City as compared with 102.2 in the country as a whole. This striking difference appears to be related to the greater proportionate migration of females to the city. Analysis of sex by age groups tends to confirm this assumption. In the capital city, the sex ratio for persons under 15 years of age was 101.4 while the ratio for persons 15 years and older drops drastically to 84.7. The heavier migration of women to the metropolis reflects the relatively greater opportunities for them than for men in such work as domestic service, commerce, and light industry.

THE FOREIGN-BORN POPULATION

Only a small proportion of the total inhabitants of Guatemala were born in a foreign country. The number of foreign-born in 1950 came to only 30,266 persons, or 1.1 per cent of the total population. Mexico, her neighbor to the north, reported only 0.7 per cent of her population as being foreign-born, while in the United States the percentage was 6.9.

Immigration has been insignificant for Guatemala since the Conquest. She was practically untouched by the influx of European immigrants which transformed the social and economic life of Argentina and Brazil. Various efforts were made throughout the nineteenth century to attract European immigration to Guatemala, but on the whole they were unsuccessful.

The 1950 census data suggest that the major sources of immigration have not changed for Guatemala since the beginning of the republican period. An overwhelming majority, or 75 per cent, of all foreign-born inhabitants came from neighboring countries: El Salvador (9,835), Honduras (6,300), Mexico (4,870), and British Honduras (1,530). Persons from the United States accounted for 5 per cent (1,558) of the total foreign-born population, and the combined remainder of the American hemisphere supplied 7 per cent. The foreign-born from Europe totaled about 10 per cent, with immigrants from Spain (970) and Germany (741) heading the list. Persons born in Italy numbered 331, France 264, Great Britain 193, and those from other European countries even fewer. China sent 567 persons, but the rest of Asia contributed hardly any.

Despite the small number of foreign-born, some of them are quite important in the life of the country. The Germans were active in business and in the production of coffee until their plantations were confiscated during the Second World War. They were particularly prominent in Alta Verapaz, where the first of them entered in 1869. The British have also played an important role in coffee-growing. North Americans own many of the larger business enterprises such as the International Railways of Central America and the American and Foreign Power Company. The United Fruit Company is also an American corporation which has exerted considerable influence on the economy of the nation. Many small Chinese businessmen are to be found in the eastern and coastal towns.

The pronounced tendency in Latin America of immigrants to congregate in the cities is modified to a certain degree in Guatemala by local circumstances—namely, that a full three-fourths of the immigrants came from adjoining countries. Most of these merely moved from rural areas in the adjoining country across the line into rural Guatemala. Of the total foreign-born population in 1950, 54 per cent lived in urban places and 46 per cent lived in rural areas. Of those persons born in adjacent countries, however, only 43 per cent lived in urban places and 57 per cent in rural areas. Among foreign-born persons from other than adjoining countries, 87 per cent lived in urban communities.

The largest single concentration of the foreign-born is in the department containing the national capital. In 1950 more than a third of the foreign-born (10,238) lived in the department of Guatemala. Most nationalities were represented here, but proportionately fewer persons from contiguous countries lived in that central department than did other foreign-born.[18]

Immigrants from adjoining countries tend to settle in departments near their borders. Six departments, in addition to Guatemala, each had more than 1,000 foreign-born. All of these except Escuintla share borders with a neighboring country.

The foreign-born in these six departments, together with that of the department of Guatemala, constituted 85 per cent of the total number in the entire Republic in 1950. Yet one must bear in mind that they formed only a negligible proportion of the total inhabitants of each of these departments. In Jutiapa, they represented only 2.6 per cent of the total population of the department; in Escuintla 1.2; and in San Marcos 0.7 per cent. The foreign-born inhabitants in El Petén and Izabal constituted about 9.0 per cent, but the comparatively high percentages are not significant because of the smallness of the total populations.

18. In 1950, 23 per cent of the nationals of El Salvador, Mexico, Honduras, and Great Britain (mostly from British Honduras and the West Indies) lived in the department of Guatemala in contrast to 65 per cent of the nationals of other countries.

Chapter 4

ETHNIC RELATIONS

THE PROBLEM OF SOCIAL INTEGRATION

A considerable part of Guatemalan social history since the Conquest can be described in terms of the integration of Indians and Ladinos. Most of the Ladinos today, as was shown briefly in the previous chapter, are descended partly from Indians who had become integrated at some time or other into ladino society through acculturation. A Ladino may have some European ancestry, but the crucial test for ethnic classification is whether or not the individual lives like a Traditional Indian. The process of ladinoization is still going on, and it will probably not be completed for many generations. Meanwhile, in the more immediate future, we may look for a certain degree of integration within the national framework. Some of the barriers to integration were taken up in the previous chapters: rugged topography, inadequate communication system, certain aspects of the rural settlement pattern, and diverse cultures and languages. In spite of these barriers, social forces are working to bring about greater integration.

In the political field, as in others, one must make a distinction between conditions before and after 1945. Between 1871 and 1944, Guatemala was politically stable under a series of strong-man dictators, from Justo Rufino Barrios to Jorge Ubico. After the overthrow of the Ubico regime in 1944, certain basic reforms were instituted which eventually should alter Indian-ladino relations.

Before 1945, laws were made on the national level by Ladinos who seemed to have little appreciation of the problems facing the Indian. In most cases, it was also the Ladino who administered locally laws emanating from Guatemala City. Indians rarely, if ever, occupied any of the higher posts in government. However, the ladino authorities usually permitted the Indians to be governed partly through their own elders, called *principales,* who rose to their position through merit and service in their own group. There was thus a dual system of local government: the formal and highly centralized ladino one focused on Guatemala City, and the informal Indian one with its roots deep in the traditional social structure. The Indians were to a large extent left alone in their daily activities, but if an Indian ran afoul of the laws, the ladino authorities were likely to mete out a more severe punishment to him than to a Ladino for a comparable offense.

Even though the government headed by Juan José Arévalo which was duly elected following Ubico's overthrow, was composed of Ladinos, it vigorously set about the task of incorporating the Indians into the national framework. One significant step toward this goal in the political field was the extension of suffrage to male illiterates.[1] This, of course, gave the vote to Indian males, most of whom cannot read.[2]

Another step was to make the municipio autonomous, at least in theory, and to allow its inhabitants to elect their own mayor (alcalde). During the Ubico administration, the principal local official was customarily appointed by the national president to whom he was held responsible, either directly or through the departmental authorities. These innovations gave the Indians a measure of political weight they did not have before. In some municipios where Indians constitute an overwhelming majority of the population, they were able to elect a mayor from their own ranks. Even though Indians did not rise to such prominence in all municipios, nevertheless many ladino politicians became somewhat more prone to respect the wishes of the Indians. For while it is possible to herd illiterate Indians to the polls and tell them how to exercise their newly won right to vote, soonor or later, as they develop political self-consciousness, they are likely to support candidates who appeal to their interests.

The beginnings of political integration have not only set the stage for modifying ethnic relations but have also introduced a disruptive wedge into the social structure of the Indians. Generally speaking, the principales have remained outside the local political groups that developed after the 1945 reforms. Meanwhile younger Indians have risen

1. Before 1945, only men over 18 years of age who could read were enfranchised. According to the constitution of 1945, all men over 18 could vote. For men who could read, voting was to be obligatory and secret. For illiterate males, the vote was to be optional and public. Literate women of the same age had the right to vote, but for them it was optional and secret. Illiterate women could not vote.

2. According to the 1950 census, 86 per cent of the Indian males over 18 years of age were illiterate, compared to an illiteracy rate of 43 per cent among ladino men. Very few Indian women gained the right to vote, since less than 4 per cent of the Indian women over 18 qualified as literate.

to positions of power through the new politics, thus by-passing the time-honored channels through which the principales had risen. If this trend continues very long, it could lead to disintegration of the traditional social system of the Indians and become an effective influence toward ladinoization (see Chapter 15).

The economic life of Guatemala shows a greater degree of integration of the Indians than do the other aspects. This was the case even before the 1945 reforms. Many Indian communities, particularly in the densely populated west, specialize in some local crop or handicraft object to be sold elsewhere for cash. Products of a particular locality frequently are sold throughout Guatemala.[3] In addition, Indians are buying more and more manufactured goods, such as imported enamel ware, metal tools, canned and dried milk, cotton goods, and ready-made clothing. Pressures of land shortage and new standards of consumption impel many Indians to migrate seasonally to work on the coffee plantations. In fact, most of the seasonal coffee workers are Indians. The economic importance of a group so necessary for the production of a crop which accounts for the major part of the nation's total export receipts should not be underestimated.

Although the Indians are incorporated in large numbers into the economic structure of Guatemala, their position within that structure is generally inferior to that of the Ladinos. If Indians own land, their holdings tend to be small and often barely adequate for subsistence. The better and larger holdings are, for the most part, owned by Ladinos, as are the enterprises of commercial agriculture. Exceptions occur, of course, for there are Ladinos who are much poorer than some Indians. The poorer Ladinos might work as manual laborers for other Ladinos, particularly in eastern Guatemala where there are few Indians, but it would be rare indeed for an Indian to employ a Ladino. Indians frequently hire themselves out, either to more well-to-do Ladinos, to Indian neighbors, or to distant plantation owners. At the present time, Indians work for others primarily from economic motives; but from the Conquest up to the 1945 reforms, there was a succession of laws designed to force them to work (see Chapter 6). The latest of these was the vagrancy law [4] which was enacted in 1934 and remained in effect until 1944, under which anyone who did not till land of specified dimensions had to work a certain number of days for someone else. Enforcement was insured by the requirement that all per-

3. For example, Sol Tax reported that the municipio of Nahualá seemed to be the source of grinding stones for the whole Republic. Tax, "The Municipios of the Midwestern Highlands of Guatemala," *American Anthropologist,* 39 (1937), 440.
4. Chester Lloyd Jones, *Guatemala, Past and Present,* p. 162.

sons carry a card on which employers would note the number of days worked. In practice, the law was interpreted as mainly applicable to Indians. Often Indians would have to work as many as 150 days a year for ladino landholders.

The inferior economic status of Indians is shown in other areas as well as in agriculture. The middle- and upper-class occupations are all filled by Ladinos. They own the shops in the towns, and if goods need to be transported, they are likely to use pack animals, and, more recently, motor trucks. Indians who have things to sell, on the other hand, operate on a much smaller scale and are likely to set up stands in the market places, rather than have shops. They often carry huge loads on their backs over the mountain trails.

Perhaps the most ambitious of the reforms following the downfall of the Ubico government lay in the economic field. The Arévalo government set up an elaborate labor code which gave workers rights unprecedented in Guatemala. They could join unions with collective bargaining powers and the right to strike. They could claim compensation for accidents and indemnity for dismissal without just cause. Minimum wages were established and working conditions were to be improved. "Vagrancy" continued to be illegal, but since no provision was made for implementing the vagrancy law after 1944, forced labor came to an end. The Arbenz government which followed that of Arévalo instituted in 1952 agrarian reforms by which unused large landholdings were to be expropriated and distributed in smaller parcels for use of the landless.[5] Most of the economic reforms suffered a temporary setback with the overthrow of the Arbenz government in 1954, brought on as a reaction to an apparently increasing communist influence in his regime. The labor code was amended and the government insisted on having the right to "approve" the officers of the labor unions, presumably to root out communists among them. The agrarian reforms were suspended, and most of the landholdings that had been distributed were returned to former owners.[6]

Some of the economic reforms, particularly of the Arbenz government, may have been used merely as tools of political action. The situation in Guatemala is comparable to that in many other underdeveloped countries where politicians have already begun to realize the potentialities of mass support. The question of these reforms may be raised again sometime in Guatemala by various political groups. The appeal of such a program might cut across ethnic lines, so that both Indians

5. See Chapter 8 for details of the law and of its operation.
6. Land reforms during the regime of Castillo Armas are described in the latter part of Chapter 8.

and Ladinos would find themselves integrated in a common movement. From the point of view of social life, the two ethnic groups in Guatemala tend to be separate entities, with the Indian occupying the inferior status. Where they live in the same community, they generally dwell in separate sections. The houses of the Ladinos are usually clustered around the central plaza, the preferred location according to traditional Latin American social ecology. The poorer dwellings of the Indians tend to be found in the peripheral zones. Members of each group rarely attend each other's social affairs as equals. Although a ladino male may occasionally have relations with an Indian woman, marriage between members of the two groups is not common.

Social distance is maintained by certain prescribed patterns of behavior. Indians generally use such formal terms as *señor* or *Don* in addressing Ladinos, while the latter use the more familiar *tu* toward the former. When they meet on a narrow sidewalk, Indians are expected to step aside to allow Ladinos to pass by. In the pueblo of San Luis Jilotepeque, Jalapa, Ladinos never doff their hats to Indians, whereas Indians usually take off their hats when encountering Ladinos.[7]

Although generalizations can be made about social distance, ethnic relations vary from one community to another. San Luis Jilotepeque appears to represent the extremes of strict stratification; Melvin Tumin, who studied it, entitled his book *Caste in a Peasant Society*. On the other hand, there is the admittedly atypical example of Chitatul, in the western highlands, where relations are on a nearly equal basis. Significantly, even there, however, intermarriage is not favored.[8] Most communities where both Indians and Ladinos are found seem to lie along a continuum between these two poles.

It should be reiterated that the inferior position of the Indians is not entirely or even necessarily based on race.[9] They may be looked down upon because they are different in the sense that they have little or no education, low standards of living, and distinctive customs and beliefs. Education and higher standards of living would diminish the cultural differences. Social separation would then decrease correspondingly.

Although complete social integration is not likely to come for a long time, a beginning was made on the problem with the 1945 reforms.

7. Melvin M. Tumin, *Caste in a Peasant Society:* A Study in the Dynamics of Caste (Princeton Univ. Press, Princeton, 1952), pp. 184–5.

8. Adams, *Cultural Surveys,* p. 334.

9. The Ladinos of San Luis Jilotepeque appear to make racial distinctions between themselves and the Indians. When Melvin Tumin asked for opinions on intermarriage, one Ladino replied: "No, I would not let my children marry Indians—you can't mix Ladino with Indian blood. The mixture comes out very bad." Another said he would disown a child marrying an Indian because of the "poorer blood of the Indian." Tumin, op. cit., pp. 287, 291.

The Arévalo government, with cooperation from the United States, organized *nucleos escolares* to serve as centers for lifting the level of the other rural schools in the region. Also, normal schools were established for in-service training of rural teachers. Cultural missions went into isolated regions to teach people agricultural techniques, sanitation, and other new ways of doing things. A National Indian Institute, organized according to a pattern recommended by the Pan American Union and established in a number of countries of the Americas, was set up under the Ministry of Education and gave considerable attention to alphabets of the Indian languages which could be used in promoting literacy campaigns and various other aspects of national policy. These social reforms were, for the most part, carried on during Arbenz's regime, but Castillo Armas, his successor, was too busy simply trying to stay in power to be very energetic in his pursuit of them.

Although efforts to incorporate the Indians seem largely to be held in abeyance at the moment of writing, they are bound to be resumed sooner or later. In addition to the political motivation of groups seeking mass support by offering Indians equal rights, the more impersonal forces of nationalism should also help to bring about greater integration. Nationalist pride is beginning to develop in Guatemala as in many other underdeveloped countries in the present century. Modern Guatemalan leaders will in all probability try to correct the backward conditions which prevail in a large segment of the population. It is not only in progressive legislation that the aspirations of nationalism will manifest themselves, but also in the form of an improved communication system and of greater industrialization and urbanization. All these changes should broaden the outlook of the Indians and thus diminish the social barriers separating them from the Ladinos.

Reforms would, of course, benefit Ladinos as well as Indians. However, it is possible that in the transitional phases, especially under the frustrations of restricted economic opportunities for all, there may be a certain amount of conflict between the two ethnic groups. The Indians, who on the whole have been outwardly content, might develop open hostility toward the Ladinos, whereas the Ladinos, accustomed to seeing the Indians in an inferior position, might begin to feel threatened. There will probably be no dearth of politicians fomenting grievances on either side.

THE TRADITIONAL INDIAN

The hostility of the Ladinos appears to be an important deterrent to the acculturation of the Indians, but it is not universal. In some sections of Guatemala, the Ladinos are quite liberal in this respect. Yet many Indians remain traditional, irrespective of hostility or the lack of it. In seeking other major factors to help explain cultural differences and social separation between the two ethnic groups, one must examine the nature of the traditional Indian society.

The Traditional Indian lives in one of numerous separate societies. These, as will be recalled from Chapter 2, are the Indian municipios, each of which has a homogeneity and self-consciousness of its own. The Indians of a particular municipio are often identifiable at a glance by their distinctive costumes (see Chapter 9). Although inhabitants of one municipio may speak the same native dialect as do those of another, there frequently are slight variations in vocabulary, pronunciation, and grammatical usages. Costume and language reinforce the self-consciousness of each society, distinct from other Indian societies and from the ladino society at large. Although physical features are perpetuated among the local Indian groups because of endogamy, they are not reliable as a badge of identification, since Ladinos may also include anyone from a "pure blooded" Indian to a peninsular-born Spaniard. One might go so far as to say, however, that most Ladinos have a lighter skin than most Indians since a certain amount of European ancestry is usually present among the former. Nevertheless, group differences tend to be primarily cultural rather than physical.

Since Ladinos live in the same municipios as do Indians, members of both groups may register births of their children in the same town hall, attend the same school (although Indians go less than Ladinos), and transact business at the same market. Nevertheless, Indians, if they are traditional, participate in a social system which functions apart from their ladino neighbors.

The society of the Traditional Indian is a closely integrated system bound together by religion. Although both Indians and Ladinos are Roman Catholics in name, their religious patterns are so different that they almost appear to be those of two separate religions. Perhaps the most important of the various factors responsible for the divergence is historical. The religion of the pre-Conquest Indians was not completely annihilated at the hands of the Spaniards, but instead merged with that of the Conquerors to form an integrated blend quite distinct from the Catholicism of the Ladinos.[10]

Life in the Indian community is organized around religious associations called *cofradías*—lay groups upon which devolve the veneration of particular saints or the preparation for certain religious fiestas. To discharge these functions, each cofradía has a series of jobs, graded

10. See Chapter 14 for a fuller discussion of religion.

in a hierarchy of age-prestige. When a boy is about fifteen, he begins at the lowest rung and works his way up as he grows older and gains in character, experience, and wisdom. The headman of the cofradía is known as the *mayordomo*. Over and above him are the principales (elders), and to become one is the greatest honor a Traditional Indian can attain. The principales are expected to personify all the traditional virtues, conduct such agricultural rites as rain-making ceremonies, and even play a role in magical curing. They appoint the mayordomos of the cofradías. The principales exercise civil functions as well as religious ones. They generally make decisions on matters affecting the community, settle disputes among its members, and sometimes call the mayordomos into consultation. The local ladino authorities tacitly recognize the influence of the principales and, until recently, hesitated to appoint any Indian to the municipal council who did not have their approval.

The values of this society prescribe that the individual feel that he lives in a world controlled by unseen supernatural forces and that, therefore, he must conform in action and attitude with the over-all scheme of things. In practice, conformity is judged to a large extent by how well he serves the cofradía system. The better he serves, the higher is the post with which he is rewarded. Not everyone can reach the top offices, which are limited in number, but the recognition attached even to the lower ones affords considerable satisfaction. Wealth per se has little prestige value among the Traditional Indians; money is something with which to fulfill the obligations of the cofradías and other ends associated with religion and the supernatural.

The Traditional Indian feels comfortable only in the group whose values he has learned. According to John Gillin, *espanto* or *susto* (magical fright), sometimes besets an individual who is out of touch with others and feels he is no longer integrated with the social group.[11] The importance of the group can be seen in numerous other ways. For example, the religious ceremonies of the Traditional Indian are held primarily to insure perpetuation to the group rather than the salvation of the individual soul.

The Traditional Indian participating in this closely knit society has a view of the universe which is limited as to time and space. Sense of time is restricted to the immediate present and the concept of change is almost non-existent. To the Indian, "Life goes on in a timeless present, it has been this way as long as anyone knows, and one will be content

11. John Gillin, "Ethos and Cultural Aspects of Personality," in *Heritage of Conquest* by Sol Tax and Members of the Viking Fund Seminar on Middle American Ethnology (The Free Press of Glencoe, Ill., 1952), p. 208.

to see the pattern continue indefinitely." [12] His social horizon does not extend far beyond the confines of the municipio in which he lives. Geographical isolation is not entirely responsible, since many Indians have visited various other localities as traveling merchants or army conscripts without much change in their outlook. Gillin has a very apt description:

> The average man in one sample could name 14 other localities with which he was familiar. Yet these other places are not part of his universe, except in a most casual sense. The nearest analogy of which I can think is that of dream scenes for normal persons among ourselves. The Indians pass through other places, remember odds and ends about them, but do not think of them as part of their structured life experience.[13]

The implications for individual mobility and national integration arising from the above analysis of the Traditional Indian society are clear. A person deriving psychological security from membership in a highly integrated group whose values militate against change would tend to stay in it. He would be more likely to leave, of course, if for some reason or other he were a marginal individual. The community as a whole, closely-knit and self-conscious to a high degree, is not prone to view itself as part of a larger group such as a nation.

The Ladino

Ladino society lacks the close integration of the Traditional Indian system. For individual Ladinos, religion may have varying degrees of meaning, but the other institutions of their society are not so deeply affected and bound together by it as among the Traditional Indians. Stratification among the Ladinos is based not on a hierarchy of politico-religious offices but on wealth and lineage. In short, Ladinos live in a secular class society.

The composition of the classes varies with the locality. Social stratification in Guatemala City, which contains over a quarter of a million Ladinos, nearly a fifth of all the Ladinos of the Republic, would differ from that in a community of ladino peasants, say, in Jutiapa. Moreover, rural communities vary among themselves. Inhabitants of some might be nearly equal in status, while in other places there may be marked differentiation.

In Guatemala City there is a wide disparity between the wealthy

12. Ibid., p. 198.
13. Ibid., p. 197.

and the poor. At the top of the social scale is a small upper class composed of wealthy businessmen, certain professionals, high government officials, and large plantation owners. The last-mentioned seem to prefer employing managers to run their fincas in the country so that they can spend most of their time in the capital. They may have business interests or exercise some profession in Guatemala City; but in some instances they live there simply because they like to and can afford to do so. In general, the members of this upper class are sophisticated and cosmopolitan, and many of them send their children abroad to be educated, either in the United States or Europe. Their style of living is generally quite luxurious: large mansions, many servants, cars, and clothes in the latest styles.

With the recent expansion of Guatemala City, there has been a concomitant growth of a middle group consisting of such persons as small businessmen, white-collar employees, teachers, and technicians. A self-consciousness distinct from the upper class has not yet fully emerged among members of this group; but in general, they tend to identify with the upper class, especially in their disdain for manual labor. Their limited incomes of course necessitate a more modest way of life, although the employment of at least one domestic servant is felt to be a primary requisite.

At the bottom of the social scale are the greater part of the workers. With increasing opportunities for education and specialized training, some of the lower class can rise a little by qualifying for better-paying jobs. Significantly, even these persons tend to validate their improved status by acquiring a servant. The structure of society in the smaller cities is similar to that of Guatemala City, though there are fewer of the very wealthy families. The size of the middle stratum also tends to be proportionately smaller.

Groupings among rural Ladinos differ with the community, depending upon the type of agriculture which prevails and upon the size of the place. In plantation communities, the top of the social scale is occupied by the owners whose power and influence are felt even though they themselves may live in Guatemala City for most of the year. Ranking below these absentee owners, in order, are the managers, bookkeepers, technicians, and lastly the workers. In keeping with the low prestige which Ladinos generally attach to manual labor, there is a sharp social division between the workers and the supervisory personnel on the fincas. Apart from the plantation communities, the local aristocracy in a fairly large rural town consists of owners of moderate landholdings, well-to-do businessmen, and professionals. The last-mentioned are likely to include very few doctors and lawyers, since they generally can earn a higher income practicing in the capital. There is a middle group of medium and small landholders, petty business-men, and artisans. At the bottom are the subsistence farmers and farm laborers. A two-class division is perhaps more general; and if a "middle" category can be said to exist, it is likely to be ill-defined and consist of persons who have risen from the bottom but have not yet been accepted into the upper group, primarily because their families have not been prominent for at least a generation. Classless ladino communities appear to be rare in number. Richard Adams reported only one, Chitatul, in his survey of some 30 towns in Guatemala.[14]

Among the Ladinos, the urban and rural social systems are linked together in several ways. We have already mentioned that many of the upper class in Guatemala City have plantations in the country. Persons in the upper and middle strata of the smaller places look to the cities, particularly the capital, for status in their own community. The me-tropolis stands at the apex of their hierarchy of values, and they make the most of any connections that they may have with the social life there. They admire the style of life of the urban aristocracy, but in view of their limited resources in a rustic setting, they cannot, of course, even approximate it. Nevertheless, many of them live in fairly substantial houses, own at least one dark suit or evening-style dress which they can wear to the parties of the local elite, and give their children as much formal education as possible. Although the lower classes cannot afford these urban amenities, they recognize the prestige of those persons who can have them. Many ladino peasants, particularly those without much land, migrate to the city in the hope of improving their lot. All this is in sharp contrast to the ways of the Traditional Indians. Very few Indians are well-to-do, but even those who are have a tendency not to display their wealth in the fashion of the Ladinos. Among the In-dians, the virtuous man who carries out his obligations to the cofradía and the community is the one who gains respect, rather than the in-dividual with the sumptuous style of life.

The fact that Ladinos find models for status symbols in the cities shows in itself that their view of the world goes beyond the local com-munity. Since they do not live in a closely integrated self-conscious society as do the Indians, they are more likely to be receptive to such a concept as nationhood which comes to them via the centralized political and educational systems. It is primarily through the educational sys-tem also that the Ladinos acquire a broader view of time and histori-cal change than do the Indians. The Ladinos tend to assume that the

14. Adams, op. cit., p. 337.

universe can be controlled or manipulated by man, and that an individual can determine his own destiny and guide that of his fellows. This manipulative view, in contrast to the submissive one of the Indians, emerges out of the ethos developed over the centuries in Western Europe.[15] It can be argued that this outlook came to the New World with the Conquest and through the process of ladinoization spread from the cities and larger provincial towns where the Spaniards tended to concentrate.

LADINOIZATION

Ladinoization is the process of acculturation from the Traditional Indian type to the ladino type. Persons undergoing this change we have grouped into the modal type, the Transitional Indian. Within this category are varying degrees of acculturation, but in each case enough of the Indian attitudes and way of life is retained so that identification with the Ladino is not complete. Physical characteristics, as we have already indicated, are not the primary basis of ethnic classification in Guatemala.

Neither of the polar types, Traditional Indian and Ladino, is constant. The culture of the Traditional Indian is not exactly like that of the pre-Columbian natives, nor is the culture of the Ladino a direct duplicate of Western European models. Both developed out of the integration of aboriginal and Iberian elements after the initial impact of the Conquest. The reintegration of the culture of many Indian groups, particularly in the west, produced the closely knit societies described in a foregoing section on the Traditional Indian. For reasons still obscure, the culture of other Indians, especially in eastern Guatemala, did not reintegrate in quite the same way, so that what eventually emerged was the loose secular society of the Ladinos. From about the middle of the nineteenth century, Guatemala began to feel the repercussions of the Industrial Revolution which had been developing in Western Europe and North America. Many of the recent changes among both Indians and Ladinos are attributable to its impact. The concomitants of the world-wide industrial culture such as improved communication systems, the growth of cities, and the diffusion of modern urban traits in rural areas, are affecting a gradually increasing segment of the Ladinos. The Indians are also subject to these forces, and those persons who have already been visibly but not completely changed we call Transitional Indians.

15. Gillin, op. cit., p. 196.

Group ladinoization

Acculturation among the Indians is a twofold problem: one aspect involves change in the culture of whole groups or communities, while the other involves change in individuals.[16] The acculturation of groups will be discussed in this section, and the problem of individual ladinoization will follow.

The earliest instances of "group ladinoization" took place in the colonial period among the Indians and mixed bloods in the Spanish towns. As will be recalled, the term "Ladino" was initially applied to Indians and mixed bloods who lived in the towns and had become "latinized." Extensive ladino areas, particularly in eastern Guatemala, also resulted from mass acculturation during the colonial period.

One of the many important factors responsible for the emergence of the Transitional Indians as we see them today was the development of the plantation economy in the latter part of the nineteenth century. This agricultural revolution was actually an outgrowth of social changes outside of Guatemala. Coffee consumption had spread widely in Europe and North America during the nineteenth century. To meet the increased demand, plantations were established in Guatemala as well as in various other tropical countries.

Since many of the plantations were located in the southern and western piedmont which had been rather sparsely settled up to that time, laborers had to be sought elsewhere. Large groups of highland Indians migrated to the plantations, or fincas, where they encountered a new environment which necessitated a modification of the old way of life. In particular, the structure of the finca society did not leave much room for the politico-religious organization which, in the native highlands, had embodied and perpetuated the traditional values. Since religion is the binding force of Traditional Indian culture, one can see quite easily that any secularizing influence would weaken its integration. Finca life has not transformed all these Indians into Ladinos, but it has shifted many of them into an intermediate status. Where nearly all inhabitants of a single plantation community are Transitional Indians, we have an example of group ladinoization. Instances of individual ladinoization on the fincas will be taken up in the next section.

The industrial age is making itself felt upon the Guatemalan Indians not only through the plantation economy but also in other ways. Native handicraft objects are giving way to machine-made products, and travel by foot over long distances is being gradually displaced by motor transportation. The adoption of new artifacts, of course, does not

16. Adams, op. cit., p. 288 ff.

necessarily alter the essence of the culture as a whole. Conceivably, an Indian can wear clothes made out of factory-woven material and still share in the traditional ethos. However, such factors as nationalism, improving communications, and a rising standard of living are all part of the world-wide industrial culture to which Guatemala is certainly not immune. To the extent that these ideas are translated into specific programs which change the ways of substantial numbers of Indians, they constitute ladinoizing influences. For example, through the spread of education Indians will gradually acquire new values which may be incompatible with their traditional ones. Adequate medical services in rural areas, to cite another example, might tend to undermine their faith in magical cures and thus have a disruptive effect on their religious orientation. The introduction of the system of political parties in local government, as will be indicated in Chapter 15, has already begun to subvert the influence of the principales and hence the very structure of the traditional politico-religious hierarchy. In short, many present-day trends are working toward group ladinoization of the entire Indian population, but any large scale results will probably not become manifest for some generations.

If one were to search in the census data for any index of the Transitional Indian, one would find very little. Statistics on the number of persons wearing shoes or able to read, for example, would not be too revealing, since barefootedness and illiteracy are found among both Ladinos and Indians. The closest thing available to an index are the figures on Indians not speaking a native language in the home. An Indian who speaks only Spanish has already lost a good deal of the traditional culture and is open to further ladinoization through education, mass media, and political activities. Moreover, he is in a better position to compete with Ladinos for economic opportunities than is an Indian who knows Spanish less intimately.

According to the 1950 census, about one-fourth of the Indian population three years of age and over (331,814 out of 1,342,981) do not speak a native language in the home. Evidently they speak only Spanish and probably most of them would qualify as Transitional Indians. In analyzing the distribution of this transitional trait by municipio, we find that generally the municipios in which the majority of the Indians use only Spanish are those in which Ladinos are numerically predominant.[17] There are exceptions, the most notable of them being certain municipios in the eastern departments of Chiquimula and Jalapa,

17. There is a Pearsonian coefficient of correlation of +.80 between the percentage of Indians speaking a native language and the percentage of Indians in the total population of the 315 municipios of the Republic.

where Indians not only are in the majority but also are likely to speak Spanish as a first language.[18] Apparently, the Indians of these municipios are not very far behind their neighbors in the acculturative process which has already made the east a predominantly ladino region. Since urbanization generally reinforces acculturation, one would expect to find proportionately fewer Indians living in cities and only a small number of those who do speaking a native language in the home. The data bear out this expectation. In localities having over 10,000 inhabitants, only 10 per cent of the population were Indians, in contrast to 60 per cent in the smaller places. Only 6,966 Indians three years of age or over spoke a native language in places over 10,000 inhabitants, and they constituted only about 21 per cent of the total number of Indians in these cities. On the other hand, the great majority, roughly 69 per cent, of the Indians living in the smaller places who were three years of age or over spoke a native language.[19]

18. The municipios of Jocotán, Chiquimula, and of San Luis Jilotepeque, Jalapa, follow the general rule that Indians living in municipios where they predominate are likely to use a native language in the home. However, they are exceptional among eastern municipios. In that region most of the Indians who live in municipios where they are in the majority speak Spanish rather than a native language. In 1950, the Indians of Jocotán constituted 94 per cent of the local population; of them, 72 per cent spoke a native language. Sixty-one per cent of the total population of San Luis Jilotepeque is Indian, and 80 per cent spoke a native language. To date, both Jocotán and San Luis Jilotepeque happen to be the only eastern municipios on which community studies have been made. See Charles Wisdom, *The Chortí Indians of Guatemala* (Chicago, 1940); John Gillin, *The Culture of Security in San Carlos: A Study of a Guatemalan Community of Indians and Ladinos* (New Orleans, 1951); and Tumin, *Caste in a Peasant Society*.

19. We have calculated the percentage of Indians three years of age and over who spoke a native language to the total Indian population because the census data do not contain age distribution by ethnic groups for these cities. If we accept the census definition of "rural" and "urban" (2,000 inhabitants as the dividing line), then we find that 77 per cent of all rural Indians three years of age and over spoke a native language, whereas of all urban Indians of the same ages, only a slightly lower proportion, 66 per cent, spoke a native language. This small difference is due primarily to the fact that there are, particularly in the west, many places whose population is over 2,000 and yet under 10,000 and which are essentially large Indian villages rather than strictly urban communities. See McBryde, *Cultural and Historical Geography of Southwest Guatemala*, pp. 85–6, for comparison of Sololá (2,600 inhabitants in 1930) with Santiago Atitlán (population of over 5,000). Sololá, with Ladinos constituting over half of its population, is a town with such features as a theatre, public library, several stores of general merchandise, and so forth; Santiago, with its predominantly Indian population can best be described as a "big agricultural village."

Individual ladinoization

In addition to entire communities of Transitional Indians which may undergo acculturation, there are also individuals who have separated themselves from a group in which the traditional way of life prevails. Ladinoization may be gradual for these individuals, and they may be quite unaware of the adjustments they are making. An Indian may leave his native village and seek work in a larger town where most of the other laborers happen to be Ladinos. He is thus cut off from continuous associations in his native village and comes under the daily influences of ladino culture. Or he may find employment on one of the large fincas where the workers are predominantly Ladinos. Such plantations are likely to be found in Escuintla, where Indians comprised only 16 per cent of the population in 1950. Either on an Escuintla plantation or in a larger town, life among large numbers of Ladinos cannot but push him into a transitional category, neither Traditional Indian nor yet fully ladino.

In some instances of ladinoization, individuals deliberately choose to become ladino because of some peculiar circumstance or personal maladjustment in the traditional society. In effect, they are ahead of their fellow Indians in responding to the ladinoizing forces which are operating in present-day Guatemala. They may move into the lowest stratum of the ladino society, but since membership in that category carries little prestige and personal satisfaction, many mobile Indians seek a middle-class position. Sometimes education provides the incentive as well as the means for upward mobility. An Indian may, for example, become a school teacher or government official. Or he may learn some modern technical skill, such as truck driving. Having acquired an occupational specialization which is associated primarily with Ladinos, the individual tends to believe he is eligible for ladino status.

If a former Indian makes the shift successfully, he then becomes a Ladino; but he would be "transitional" if his claim to being a Ladino were not completely recognized for one reason or another. His Indian origin may still be evident in certain traits like his use of dialectic Spanish, although he may have acquired some shoes (a symbol of ladino status) and may no longer participate in the cofradía system. Even if he retained no cultural trait generally associated with Indians, he might still not be accepted as a Ladino in his own community if it happens to be one where a caste-like barrier against Indian mobility prevails.

The children or grandchildren of such Transitional Indians might possibly find it easier to be recognized as Ladinos. It may take at least a couple of generations before the memory of Indian origin fades. Or an individual aspiring to ladino status may hasten the process by moving to another community where his ancestry is unknown.

PROBLEMS OF TRANSITIONAL STATUS

The Traditional Indian lives in a closely knit society in which he finds psychological security. It affords him the satisfaction of belonging to a group which recognizes his personal worth, humble as his status within it may be. He is thus shielded to a large extent from the disdain which the Ladino may feel for him. The Transitional Indian, in contrast, has no such moorings in a traditional system but he does not yet have ladino status. In the present period of rapid change, both Indians and Ladinos generally face problems of some variety or other. Those arising specifically from transitional status are the object of concern in this section.

Transitional Indians in large groups—whether workers on a plantation or inhabitants of some community undergoing ladinoization—still think of themselves as Indian and have little desire, except in certain individual cases, to be accepted as Ladino. However, their traditional goals are disappearing, and more and more they are likely to want to aspire to the apparent advantages of material well-being enjoyed by the Ladinos. The efforts of the central government to raise the standard of living among the rural masses reinforces this attitude. Since they do not have the psychological insulation of the traditional system, they tend to become increasingly sensitive to the fact that Ladinos generally regard them as inferior. Thus, in situations where large numbers of Transitional Indians are economically subordinate to Ladinos, such as on a coffee plantation, or where they are competing for limited opportunities against Ladinos who may try to put their Indian status to a disadvantage, some form of conflict in which economic and ethnic issues are merged may conceivably take place in the near future. In communities where relations with Ladinos afford no potential area of conflict, there is, of course, no particular problem related to transitional status.

The individual Transitional Indian who finds himself in an overwhelmingly ladino environment, such as a large town or an Escuintla plantation, poses a somewhat different problem. Generally, he too regards himself as an Indian and has no conscious desire to be a Ladino, although he is making personal adjustments all along toward acculturation. While he has drifted away from the traditional society, many of the Ladinos about him have also pulled up roots elsewhere. As shown during the Arbenz period, mobile persons in large aggregates tend to serve as a fertile field for political agitation.[20] Thus the Transitional Indian of this type is part of the larger problem of the rootlessness of a mobile agricultural proletariat.

The transitional individual who deliberately chooses to become a Ladino may present the greatest problem of all. He has consciously rejected Indian status and is trying to attain what he considers a superior one. He has acquired new norms, new values, and new levels of aspiration. He may have difficulty achieving his goal, since not all Ladinos everywhere are willing to concede change of status. His frustration is likely to be all the greater because his efforts toward self-improvement are more ambitious and more consciously undertaken than those of the other Transitional Indians. Dissatisfaction with his marginal position may make him prey for any political movement which professes concern for his problems. Or he may even become one of the leaders, particularly if he has some measure of education and sophistication. Thus, it would seem that government programs aimed at attaining social stability and at meeting the social and economic needs of the people might well devote special attention to those persons attempting to make the transition from Indian to Ladino.

20. Stokes Newbold, "Receptivity to Communist-Formented Agitation in Rural Guatemala," *Economic Development and Cultural Change*, 5 (1957), 338–61.

Part 2 MAKING A LIVING

Chapter 5

THE ECONOMY

Guatemala has an agricultural economy. The Industrial Revolution has made little impact there as yet outside of Guatemala City and a few of the larger towns. Production for domestic consumption as well as for export trade is predominantly of an agricultural nature. Corn is the principal crop grown throughout the country, although it is used entirely for local consumption and none of it reaches the export market. Coffee is the chief commercial crop. It alone usually accounts for about three-fourths of the total value of all Guatemala's exports. Coffee serves as a good barometer of business conditions in the nation. It is the principal source for foreign exchange; and a large share of the income for national governmental programs and services is derived from the export taxes on coffee. A fluctuation of only a few cents in the price of coffee on the world market exerts a strong impact on the whole economic system of Guatemala. When coffee prices are low, there is likely to be something bordering on an economic depression. When coffee prices rise, prosperity tends to return.

Of the total of almost 96 million dollars in exports in 1954, 94.2 per cent represented four agricultural products: coffee, bananas, cotton, and hemp. Coffee alone accounted for 77.5 per cent of the total value of all exports in 1954; and bananas 11.7 per cent. Thus, Guatemala is almost exclusively an exporter of raw materials and is dependent to a large extent upon the importation of manufactured goods. It is for this reason that any discussion of the Guatemalan economy must place major emphasis upon agriculture.

POVERTY AND WEALTH

Guatemala may be classified as one of the many countries of the world that is economically underdeveloped. The population has a low level of income derived principally from agriculture which generally fails to make use of the scientific knowledge and modern techniques of production that have brought prosperity to many other countries and could enable Guatemala to raise its level of living greatly.

This does not mean that all Guatemalans are poor or that only primitive techniques of production are used; quite the contrary. Like some other countries of Latin America, Guatemala presents striking social and economic contrasts between the few who enjoy wealth and the many who live in poverty. In terms of economic well-being, one might characterize Guatemala as having a class system shaped somewhat like a spindle with a small upper class at the top whose members enjoy most of the comforts of life. These might include a comfortable house in Guatemala City, or in one of the larger departmental capitals, as well as a home on a finca which provides much of the family income but which is managed by a hired administrator and visited by the owner and his family only occasionally during the year. Such a family might possess several automobiles, and would maintain a retinue of servants in the city and, of course, a large number of workers and servants on the country estate.

Some of these upper-class families also have business enterprises in Guatemala City or hold high positions in government or industry. Funds for travel and for educating their children are no problem for them, and many members of their families have visited European capitals and have traveled in the United States as well as in parts of Latin America.

The middle class in Guatemala would be represented by the slender middle portion of the spindle. It is small in number and composed of such occupational groups as operators of fairly large farms, school teachers and other professional groups, white-collar government workers, farm managers, shop keepers, and some of the more highly skilled industrial workers. The members of this group have modest incomes and aspire to achieve a higher standard of living, especially in the form of educational opportunities for their children, health programs to curtail the unusually high death rate in Guatemala, and improved housing facilities. Some members of this group are highly educated and well acquainted with the world's great literature, art, and music. Members of the middle class have been too few in the past to exert much influence on economic or government policy, but have been increasing in numbers and influence since the overthrow of the dictatorship in 1944. One cannot escape the feeling that much of Guatemala's hope for improved economic and social well-being in the future rests on the possibility of developing a large and more influential middle class.

The vast majority of the inhabitants, however, probably 70 to 80 per cent, are to be found in what might be called the lower class, at the bottom of the spindle. Most of them are illiterate and have very low incomes. Many are farm laborers. Others operate small farms of their own on tiny plots of land in the highlands and use antiquated techniques that result in soil erosion, poor yields, and inadequate harvests. They supplement their farming by household industries or by working as farm laborers during certain seasons of the year. Their poverty, illiteracy, and isolation exclude them from participation in the fruits of modern technology in the form of improved housing, sanitation, medical service, and education.

This lower stratum is proportionally so large that it holds down the average per capita income of the nation to a low level. Thus, a study published by the United Nations in 1957 indicated an annual per capita income in Guatemala of only 160 dollars. Guatemala ranked fifth from the bottom out of 16 countries in the Americas for which data were presented [1] (Figure 11).

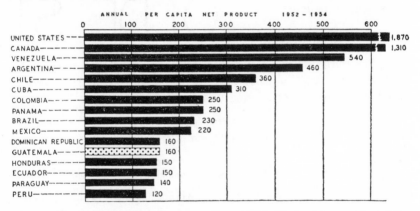

Figure 11. Annual per capita net product, 1952–54, for 16 countries of the Americas. This is equivalent to per capita net income. For source of data see footnote 1.

Perhaps it should be pointed out here, however, that although Guatemala ranks low in per capita income, it is not sunk in the depths of abject poverty to the extent found in certain other parts of the world. Most of her people live in what might be termed a "dignified poverty" (see Plate 5). As Silvert has aptly stated:

1. See *Per Capita National Product of Fifty-five Countries, 1952–1954*, Statistical Office of the United Nations (New York, 1957), Statistical Papers ser. E, No. 4, p. 8. While these data refer to "net national product," they are computed in such a manner as to be identical with "per capita income," in dollars. Ibid., p. 3.

The danger to the reader in these statistics . . . is the mental image of a land sunk deep in misery and poverty and ignorance. But ignorance is not stupidity, and poverty is in part a relative affair. Certainly, compared to Chile and Mexico in Latin America, or to such Arab countries as Egypt or French Morocco, Guatemala presents a much more agreeable face to the observer. The *roto*— the tattered city proletariat of Chile—is not to be found, nor are the street urchins of Mexico City. While the Guatemalan may be complacent about flies compared to the North American, he is a model of impatience contrasted with the Moroccan child, who learns to sleep with flies walking about his face. The general rural poverty of the Guatemalan has not allowed him to fall to the material depths of those whose livelihood depends upon impersonal and, by him, uncontrollable and complex economic phenomena. Guatemala's rural economy is based on a degree of specialization which contributes to rather higher standards in many places than might normally be expected from isolated subsistence economies.[2]

OCCUPATIONAL PURSUITS

According to the census of 1950, more than two-thirds (68.2 per cent) of all the economically active persons in the entire country were engaged in agriculture for a living (Table 16).

TABLE 16. *Economically active persons seven years of age and over, by type of economic activity and sex, 1950*

Type of economic activity	TOTAL		MALE		FEMALE	
	Number	Per cent	Number	Per cent	Number	Per cent
TOTAL	967,814	100.0	843,582	100.0	124,232	100.0
Agriculture	659,550	68.2	641,496	76.0	18,054	14.5
Manufacturing	111,538	11.5	76,851	9.1	34,687	27.9
Service industries	95,705	9.9	42,291	5.0	53,414	43.0
Non-domestic	51,950	5.4	35,446	4.2	16,504	13.3
Domestic	43,755	4.5	6,845	0.8	36,910	29.7
Commerce	52,561	5.4	35,490	4.2	17,071	13.8
Construction	26,427	2.7	26,275	3.1	152	0.1
Transportation and communication	15,352	1.6	14,986	1.8	366	0.3
All other	6,681	0.7	6,193	0.8	488	0.4

Source: Sexto censo de población, Table 50, p. 263.

2. K. H. Silvert, *A Study in Government: Guatemala* (New Orleans, 1954), pp. 20–1.

More meaningful, perhaps, are the occupational pursuits of the male population, since males constitute 87.2 per cent of all economically active persons, and are generally considered to be the principal "bread-winners" of the family. Three-fourths (76 per cent) of all male workers are engaged in agriculture for a living as compared with only 14.5 per cent of the females (Table 16).

Agriculture not only claims the attention of the vast majority of the workers of the Republic, but does so in nearly every department. There are eleven departments where more than 80 per cent are in agriculture, and only three with less than 60 per cent so employed. These three consist of the departments of Guatemala, which contains the capital city, Totonicapán where household industries such as pottery-making and woodwork are common, and Izabal in the north.

Obviously the proportion of the inhabitants employed in any industry outside of agriculture is relatively small. Next to agriculture, manufacturing is the most important economic activity, but it occupies only 11.5 per cent of the total economically active population (9.1 per cent of the males and 27.9 per cent of the females). In the department of Guatemala, 23.5 per cent are employed in manufacturing. In only five other departments are as many as 10 per cent engaged in manufacturing. One of these is Quezaltenango with 15.1 per cent. It is in this department that the second largest city in the Republic is found, which probably accounts for a somewhat higher proportion engaged in manufacturing than is found in most of the other departments.

The other departments having more than 10 per cent engaged in manufacturing are Totonicapán where 38.1 per cent are so reported, Sacatepéquez (11.4 per cent), El Progreso (12.9 per cent) and Zacapa (12.1 per cent). Although Totonicapán is highly rural in character, farm land is scarce and the landholdings are the smallest of any in the Republic, with a mean average of only 2.8 acres per farm. Many of its people make their living through small household industries, devoted to such items as pottery, woodwork and various other handicrafts. For this reason, Totonicapán has the highest proportion of inhabitants involved in "manufacturing" of any department. This in no way indicates industrialization, however, since modern industrial machines are conspicuously absent and most of the articles are made by hand in the home or in small household shops.

Manufacturing has had limited development in Guatemala for a variety of reasons. Among these are the following: (1) transportation and power deficiencies; (2) the limited availability of labor and management skills; (3) the scarcity of long-term credit and risk capital; and (4) the low purchasing power of the inhabitants and the limited size of the market.[3] Steps are being taken to remedy some of these obstacles, especially with the recent emphasis on highway construction

TABLE 17. *Economically active persons seven years of age and over, by type of economic activity, by region and department, 1950*

| Region and department | TOTAL | PER CENT ENGAGED IN | | | | |
		Agriculture	Manu- facturing	Service	Commerce	All other
REPUBLIC	967,814	68.2	11.5	9.9	5.4	5.0
Central	184,999	27.6	22.2	25.8	10.8	13.6
Guatemala	164,690	22.8	23.5	27.7	11.5	14.5
Sacatepéquez	20,309	66.7	11.4	10.8	5.0	6.1
North	26,735	58.4	6.6	13.7	13.3	8.0
El Petén	6,226	68.5	6.2	15.1	2.6	7.6
Izabal	20,509	55.3	6.7	13.3	16.6	8.1
East	182,646	81.0	7.4	6.1	2.4	3.1
Chiquimula	37,526	83.3	7.0	5.7	2.2	1.8
El Progreso	16,599	72.5	12.9	6.6	3.0	5.0
Jalapa	24,971	81.6	8.7	4.7	1.9	3.1
Jutiapa	44,475	84.9	4.6	6.0	2.1	2.4
Santa Rosa	36,136	84.8	4.8	4.9	2.1	3.4
Zacapa	22,939	68.9	12.1	10.0	4.0	5.0
South	116,363	77.3	6.5	7.5	3.7	5.0
Escuintla	48,646	76.5	5.7	7.7	4.1	6.0
Retalhuleu	23,880	76.9	6.4	7.5	3.9	5.3
Suchitepéquez	43,837	78.5	7.2	7.3	3.1	3.9
West	376,563	76.5	11.1	5.2	5.1	2.1
Chimaltenango	41,470	82.7	7.7	5.0	2.2	2.4
El Quiché	57,876	85.3	6.6	3.6	3.3	1.2
Huehuetenango	66,672	85.9	7.2	3.6	1.7	1.6
Quezaltenango	65,507	65.0	15.1	9.5	6.1	4.3
San Marcos	84,554	85.1	6.7	4.6	1.9	1.7
Sololá	27,270	84.5	6.4	4.5	2.8	1.8
Totonicapán	33,214	29.3	38.1	4.7	26.3	1.6
North central	80,508	83.0	7.4	6.0	1.6	2.0
Alta Verapaz	58,168	83.1	7.0	6.4	1.8	1.7
Baja Verapaz	22,340	82.6	8.4	5.1	1.1	2.8

Source: Sexto censo de población, Table 49.

and the organization a number of years ago of the Production Development Institute (*Instituto de Fomento de la Producción*). INFOP, as the institute is generally called, was established in 1948 for the purpose of

3. U. S. Department of Commerce, *Investment in Central America* (Washington, D.C., 1956), p. 156.

promoting the economic development of the country. It was launched with a capital of 6.5 million dollars and charged with the task of promoting activities of a productive nature that would not, or could not, be developed by private capital; and of assisting private capital in the development of new fields of promising endeavor. Its major contributions thus far have been in the provision of credit for development work and in fostering improvements in agriculture.[4]

The principal products manufactured in Guatemala arranged roughly in order of the value of the product are as follows:

1. Foodstuffs, including the processing of green coffee, milling of wheat into flour, sugar manufacturing, and candy production.
2. Beverages, including *aguardiente* and distilled alcoholic liquors as well as beer and soft drinks.
3. Tobacco products, mostly in the form of cigarettes.
4. Footwear and apparel. Shoes are made mostly by hand except for two mechanized factories, one in Guatemala City and the other in Cobán.
5. Textile manufacturing, including local weaving on household looms.
6. Chemical products, including soap and matches.
7. Other manufactured products, including cement and wood products.

The service industries which include government, professional, and personal, as well as domestic services, occupy third place in the proportion of economically active persons involved. Five per cent of the males are occupied in service industries although half of these (49.3 per cent) are concentrated in the department of Guatemala. A much higher proportion (43 per cent) of female than male workers are in service work (Table 16). This is to be attributed in part to the large number of females who are employed in domestic service. Of the male service workers, for example, only 16.2 per cent are in domestic service while of the females 69.1 per cent are so employed. Domestic workers are concentrated to a considerable extent in the department of Guatemala (44.4 per cent of all female domestics), and mostly in Guatemala City where people with middle- and upper-class standing are more numerous and where it is common to regard servants as a basic necessity for almost any family seeking to avoid identity with lower class status.

Commerce occupies fourth place in the economic activity of Guatemala. It accounts for 5.4 per cent of the gainfully employed popula-

4. Ibid., p. 167.

tion—4.2 per cent of the males and 13.8 per cent of the females. The highest percentage engaged in commerce is found in the department of Totonicapán with 26.3 per cent (Table 17). Next follows Izabal with 16.6 per cent and Guatemala with 11.5 per cent. Quezaltenango has only 6.1 per cent in commerce while no other department has more than 5.0 per cent so engaged. The department of Totonicapán, therefore, is definitely atypical in that an unusually large proportion of its economically active persons are designated as being engaged in commerce. Commerce in Totonicapán is concerned mostly with selling products from local household industries and the purchase of food products as well as raw materials.

Only 5.0 per cent of Guatemala's population was employed in other types of economic activity. These included construction work (2.7 per cent) and transportation and communication industries with 1.6 per cent. All other types of economic activity combined accounted for only 0.7 per cent.

Thus, it seems clear that male workers are concentrated to an overwhelming extent in agriculture, and to a much less extent in manufacturing, the service industries, and commerce. Female workers are engaged mostly in the service industries (particularly in domestic service), in manufacturing and in commerce.

FARM OPERATORS

According to the agricultural census of 1950, 348,687 persons in Guatemala were classified as farm operators, in that each had charge of the farm operations on the land on which he lived or worked. In some instances he was considered to be an owner. In others, he was an administrator, a renter, a colono (a combination laborer-operator), or held some other status as an operator. The farms of the various operators, however, present tremendous contrasts in size. At one extreme is plantation agriculture, with landholdings which may include both excellent farm land producing for the export market, and, in many cases, large areas of land that are not even utilized. These farms are large in size but small in number. At the other extreme are to be found the vast majority of the farm enterprises of the country, consisting of small plots of land devoted to the growing of corn. These are diminutive in size but very numerous. There are comparatively few farms that fall in between these two extreme types; or that are at all comparable to what is generally known as the "family farm" in the United States.

In Table 18, the 348, 687 farm operators listed by the census of 1950 are classified according to the size of farms they operate. At one end of the distribution are to be found what Latin Americans refer to as the *minifundios*, or tiny plots of less than 3.5 acres in size which are occupied by 47.6 per cent of the farm operators, but which involve only 3.3 per cent of the total farm land. At the other extreme are the *latifundios* or large-scale holdings possessed by only 0.3 per cent of the farm operators but which represent half (50.3 per cent) of all the farm

TABLE 18. *Farm operators by size of holding, 1950*

Size of farm (acres) °	Number of farm operators	Per cent of farm operators	Per cent of total farm land
TOTAL	348,687	100.0	100.0
Under 3.5	165,850	47.6	3.3
3.5–17.2	142,223	40.8	11.0
17.3–111.4	33,041	9.5	13.5
111.5–1,114	6,488	1.8	21.9
1,115 and over	1,085	0.3	50.3

Source: *Censo agropecuario, 1950, 1,* Dirección General de Estadística.
° This unusual grouping of acres results from converting manzanas and caballerías to acres.

land in the Republic. Only about 2 per cent of the farm operators have farms with more than 111.5 acres, but their farms comprise 72 per cent of all farm lands. Only 9.5 per cent of the farm operators have between 17.3 and 111.5 acres of land (Table 18); and only 1.8 per cent have from 111.5 to 1,115 acres.

The median farm in Guatemala contains only 3.9 acres (Table 19).

TABLE 19. *Mean and median land holdings, by region, 1950*

Region	Number of holdings	Median size (acres)	Mean size (acres)
REPUBLIC	348,687	3.9	26.3
Central	27,394	3.9	19.2
North	7,607	5.3	71.3
East	78,715	5.4	27.7
South	32,340	1.6	58.6
West	162,289	3.5	15.1
North central	40,342	5.3	39.8

Source: *Censo agropecuario, 1950, 1,* Table 1, 19.

This means that half of the farms in the entire country are no larger than 3.9 acres in size. By regions, the median is largest in the east (5.4 acres), and lowest in the south (1.6). The extremely small size of the median in the south is undoubtedly due to the fact that the plots of the colonos (resident workers) are so numerous in this area where plantation agriculture predominates.

The mean size of the farms is 26.3. The large size of the mean, as compared with the median, also shows the influence of the large plantations which have been averaged in with the small holdings. The mean size of farms is largest in the sparsely settled north, and in the south where exceedingly large farms, as well as small plots, are involved in plantation agriculture.

LAND TENURE OF FARM OPERATORS

Slightly more than half of the landholders in Guatemala (54.9 per cent) are owners of the lands they operate (Table 20). This proportion varies from one region and department to another. The highest percentage of farm ownership in any region is in the west (72.5 per cent)

TABLE 20. *Farm operators by tenure status, by region, 1950*

PERCENTAGE DISTRIBUTION

Tenure status	Total	Central	North	East	South	West	North central
TOTAL NUMBER	348,687	27,394	7,607	78,715	32,340	162,289	40,342
Owner	54.9	55.2	5.8	43.5	22.9	72.5	41.0
Renter	17.0	21.2	11.0	25.9	29.4	11.9	8.2
Colono	12.4	13.3	1.4	4.9	26.8	6.3	41.9
Squatter	10.0	4.4	64.7	19.9	4.3	6.0	4.9
Administrator	0.7	1.5	0.3	0.4	2.1	0.5	0.5
All other	5.0	4.4	16.8	5.4	14.5	2.8	3.5

Source: Censo agropecuario, 1950, 1, Table 6, 38.

which is highly Indian. Most of these Indians own small farms which are operated on a semi-subsistence basis. In this region, ownership reaches its maximum in the department of Totonicapán, which is the most Indian of all and where 98.9 per cent of the landholders own their farms.

Farm ownership is lowest in the north where it is only 5.8 per cent. Much of the land in this region belongs to the government. Individuals merely assume temporary possession of it, especially in El Petén. The second lowest rate of ownership is in the south with 22.9 per cent. As indicated previously, plantation agriculture prevails in the three departments of this region, and most of the small holdings are operated by colonos or by renters who work on the large plantations. Other regions fall in between the extremes represented by the north and the south. In the central region, 55.2 per cent are listed as owners as compared with 43.5 in the east and 41 per cent in the north central region.

Seventeen per cent of all landholders are classified as renters (Table 20). They are more prevalent in the south (29.4 per cent), the east (25.9 per cent), and the central region (21.2 per cent). They are found in proportionately fewer numbers in the north central, the west and the north. Renting of land takes various forms in Guatemala. A simple annual cash rental for a given piece of land is likely to be demanded by large landholders who do not wish to bother with a percentage of the crop. Share-cropping, however, is quite common on medium-sized and small farms. A certain percentage of the crop is paid for the use of the land. A number of variations in this practice have been reported, ranging from the sharing of expenses and dividing the crop to payment of all expenses by the renter plus sharing of the crop.[5] In some instances a subsistence farmer in the highlands may lack sufficient land of his own to meet his needs and may rent supplementary land from a plantation in the lowlands. In this sense, he could be called an absentee tenant since he goes to the lowlands only to plant and harvest the crop, with an occasional trip in between the two periods. Sometimes under this arrangement part of the harvest is paid as rent; and other times the rent is paid by means of labor.

Roughly one out of every eight farm operators in Guatemala is a colono (12.4 per cent). A colono is a laborer on a finca who is permitted by the owner to till a small plot of land for his own use while he also works on the finca. He was classified as a farm operator by the census for this particular tabulation because he tills his plot in his own way. There were 43,298 colonos listed in the agricultural census, most of them in the areas where plantation agriculture prevails. Thus in the south, colonos constitute 26.8 per cent of all operators, and in the north central region 41.9 per cent.

One out of every ten farm operators was listed in the census as a squatter (occupante). These are most numerous in the north (64.7 per cent) where there are large areas of government lands. They are also fairly common in the east.

There are 2,512 farms operated by administrators. Most of these are large, and are located in areas where plantation agriculture is most common. The highest percentage is in the south (2.1 per cent), followed by the central area and by departments in other regions where

5. A number of different practices are described by Adams, Cultural Surveys, pp. 299–300.

plantation agriculture occupies at least part of the area, such as Quezaltenango and San Marcos in the west, and Santa Rosa in eastern Guatemala.

Although the actual number of farms operated by administrators is relatively small (2,512) in comparison with those operated by owners, renters, and others; nevertheless, they have an importance far beyond anything that their relative number would indicate. Although they account for less than one per cent (0.7) of the farms, they encompass one-third of the total area of all farms in the Republic.[6]

AGRICULTURAL LABORERS

According to the population census of 1950, there were 336,024 males over seven years of age in Guatemala who were classified as farm laborers. These constituted four out of every ten economically active males in the entire Republic (39.8 per cent) (Table 21). The number of farm laborers varied as one might expect from one section of the country to another. The five departments, all located in areas where plantation agriculture prevails, in which more than half of all economically active males were farm laborers were: Santa Rosa, Escuintla, Suchitepéquez, San Marcos, and Alta Verapaz. There were six departments wherein 40 to 50 per cent of all workers were farm laborers and eight where 30 to 40 per cent were so classified. Only in the three departments of Guatemala, Izabal and Totonicapán, was the proportion of farm laborers less than 30 per cent. Naturally, the department of Guatemala had the lowest percentage of farm laborers since this department contains Guatemala City. But it is interesting to note that even in this department 15.8 per cent of all economically active males were classified as farm laborers. Attention should perhaps be drawn to the low percentage in Totonicapán. As noted earlier, although this is perhaps the most Indian department in the Republic, a relatively high proportion of the inhabitants are engaged in handicrafts and home industries. Nevertheless even here, more than one out of every eight males was a farm laborer.

When the proportion of farm laborers is related merely to the total number of economically active persons engaged in agriculture, it is found that in six departments more than 60 per cent of the males trying to make a living in agriculture in 1950 were farm laborers; and in nine departments the proportion exceeded 50 per cent (Table 21).

6. Calculated from data in *Censo Agropecuario, 1950, 1*, Dirección General de Estadística, Guatemala, 1955.

The census also listed 13,427 females as farm laborers, or 10.8 per cent of all economically active females in the nation. As was noted previously, most economically active females work in service industries, and in manufacturing. These two branches of economic activity accounted for 70.9 per cent of all female workers in 1950. Of those work-

TABLE 21. *Distribution of male farm laborers seven years of age and over, by region and department, 1950*

| Region and department | Number | FARM LABORERS | |
		Per cent of all economically active males	Per cent of all economically active males in agriculture
REPUBLIC	336,024	39.8	52.9
Central	24,980	18.2	49.5
Guatemala	18,972	15.8	51.0
Sacatepéquez	6,008	34.4	45.3
North	7,187	29.7	47.0
El Petén	1,917	33.4	45.6
Izabal	5,270	28.6	47.5
East	64,311	38.9	44.2
Chiquimula	12,514	37.0	40.7
El Progreso	4,433	31.8	37.4
Jalapa	8,567	37.7	42.6
Jutiapa	14,422	34.8	38.8
Santa Rosa	17,546	52.1	58.5
Zacapa	6,829	34.6	43.8
South	58,405	55.2	69.4
Escuintla	25,070	56.9	73.4
Retalhuleu	10,519	48.3	60.2
Suchitepéquez	22,816	57.2	70.1
West	143,363	42.2	52.1
Chimaltenango	18,171	47.8	54.5
El Quiché	22,255	40.9	46.4
Huehuetenango	23,925	38.8	42.8
Quezaltenango	24,337	43.3	61.2
San Marcos	40,331	54.0	60.8
Sololá	10,441	40.9	45.8
Totonicapán	3,903	13.5	42.4
North central	37,778	52.8	58.4
Alta Verapaz	29,574	57.4	63.4
Baja Verapaz	8,204	41.0	45.4

Source: *Sexto censo de población*, Cuadros 42 y 43. There were only 13,427 female farm laborers recorded in the census. They are not included here.

ing in agriculture, however, the vast majority (81.4 per cent) worked as farm laborers.

The coffee plantations employ a much larger proportion of the farm workers in Guatemala than any other segment of the economy. Such workers may be classified into two general types: (a) the resident worker or colono, and (b) the migratory worker or cuadrillero.

The colono

The colono or mozo colono as he is generally called on the finca, performs a dual function in that, while he is primarily a farm laborer, he is usually given a small plot of land to till for himself. On this plot he can grow a little *milpa* (corn and beans), or whatever is needed for his subsistence. In this sense he becomes a miniature farm operator and was so classified in the agricultural census. In return for this plot of ground he is expected to be available for work on the finca at specified times, usually so many days per week, weeks per month, or so many months per year. In some cases he may work regularly on the plantation during the morning period from about 6 A.M. until noon or 1 P.M., after which he is free for the rest of the day to till the plot allotted to him. The colono system assures a minimum labor supply on the finca which can be supplemented by seasonal or migratory labor during the rush seasons, particularly at harvest time.

The colono lives on the plantation with his family and is usually granted a house (*rancho*), although in some instances he builds his own. In either case it is likely to be a one-room structure, often with a lean-to in which cooking is done. The quality of housing varies considerably with the particular finca. In addition to a house he is entitled to simple medical services, mainly first aid, and has the privilege of cutting fuel from the plantation wood lots. He is entitled to send his children to the plantation school and, on the larger fincas, to purchase commodities at the plantation store. Occasionally he is permitted to pasture a few animals on the property. His wages vary from one region to another and in accordance with the amount of land he is given to till for himself. In the Cobán region of Alta Verapaz, for example, it is customary to grant fairly large plots of land for the colono's use and, as a consequence, his wages are very low. In 1950, for example, the usual wage for a day's work by a colono in that area was eight cents. In the coffee belt extending along the Pacific slope the wages paid in 1956 were in the vicinity of 50 cents per day.

Within the family of the colono, the son usually succeeds the father in the use of the plot and in the labor arrangement; or he is given a separate plot under the same conditions that prevailed with his father.

The use is generally explained in terms of custom and not prescribed by any legal document.[7]

As will be noted later, the agrarian reform program of 1952–54 attempted to destroy the colonal system because it was alleged to be a form of serfdom which kept the colono under continual obligation to the landlord, dependent on him for a place to live, a place to work, a plot of land to till, and even for the schooling of his children (see Chapter 12). Under these conditions it was argued that the colono could not very well refuse the bidding of the landlord even though it might be to his advantage to do so. The plantation system is built on the colonal system, however, and to supplant it would require drastic alterations in the present traditional arrangements. When the agrarian law was suspended in 1954, the continuation of the colono system was virtually assured.

The migratory worker (cuadrillero)

Coffee farming in Guatemala, and to a lesser extent, sugar cane production, requires a tremendous amount of hand labor especially during the harvest time, In addition to the resident labor force, large numbers of workers migrate to the plantations from the highlands to assist with the harvests. The principal migration is determined by the coffee harvest although other employment opportunities may also attract workers from the highlands. A given worker may migrate several times during the year to work for varying periods of time. Sometimes only the head of the family migrates. At others, especially during the rush season of the coffee harvest, his entire family may accompany him.

As indicated in Chapter 1, coffee is grown mostly on the slopes of the Pacific piedmont on lands that vary in elevation from about 1,000 to 5,500 feet above sea level. Because of differences in elevation, the coffee cherries do not all ripen at the same time so that the harvest may extend over a period of from one to three months. Migratory workers on a plantation live in temporary housing supplied by the landlord, either in separate family units called ranchos or in barracks or collective housing. Sanitary conditions generally are poor due to crowding and congestion during peak work seasons, when the population of the finca may be greatly increased. Although the children of the workers may attend the school provided by the *finquero* as required by law, most of them work side by side with their parents instead. In any event, they would be too numerous for the school to accommodate if they should

7. Joaquín Noval, "Algunos modalidades del trabajo indígena de Guatemala," *Publicaciones del Instituto de Antropología é Historia,* 4 (Guatemala, 1952), 47–51.

all decide to attend. The workers generally have access to some type of medical care in the form of first aid.

When they arrive at the finca, the workers are organized into small groups each responsible to the local foreman or "straw boss" known as the *caporal*. The caporales work under the supervision of a foreman called a mayordomo who has charge of one whole aspect of finca work such as coffee picking. The mayordomo in turn is responsible to the *administrador* who is operating manager of the entire finca. As one writer puts it, "the *mozos* are divided into sections under a caporal, who takes orders from the mayordomo, who receives orders from the administrador, who is responsible to the *patrón*." [8]

The migratory workers are usually paid on a contract basis for tasks performed. The task, or *tarea*, for coffee picking is usually a sackful which weighs from 125 to 150 lbs, for which the worker is paid the equivalent of a day's work. The best workers will earn slightly more than this and the poorer ones slightly less. Workers also generally receive a ration of corn, salt, and lime. Men, women and children often work together side by side. Migratory workers are paid at a somewhat higher rate than resident workers because of the urgent need for their services at harvest time and the temporary nature of the employment that can be offered them. The National Indian Institute reported that in 1948–49 migratory workers were being paid from 30 cents to one dollar per day.

In some instances, plots of land are allotted to seasonal workers for their own use without rent but with the single provision that the worker appear at the plantation during rush work periods. The land assigned may or may not be part of the main plantation. Some plantation owners have acquired land in the highlands which is assigned to seasonal workers. Rental payment to the plantation owner in such cases is in the form of an assurance that workers will be available for work at a given wage when most needed on the plantation.

As a part of the census of 1950 a special enumeration was made of all coffee farms in the Republic that produced more than 200 bags (*quintales*) of coffee per year. There were 1,744 of these farms out of a total of more than 31,000 farms producing at least some coffee (Table 22). These 1,744 farms reported a total of 80,421 colonos and 99,010 migratory workers, or 46 colonos and 57 migratory workers per farm.[9]

8. Addison Burbank, *Guatemala Profile* (New York, 1939), p. 73.

9. According to the census officials, the number of colonos reported in the census of coffee farms included all members of the families who were working on the coffee plantations during the period of maximum employment during the year. For this reason the number of colonos reported in Table 22 (80,421) is much

Thus on farms having less than one *caballería* of land (111.5 acres) there was an average of only 7 colonos and 18 migratory workers per farm. At the other extreme, on farms having more than 100 caballerías (11,150 acres) there was an average of 280 colonos and 208 migratory workers per farm, or an average of 487 workers of both types.

In addition to colonos and migratory workers, the coffee farms reported 9,551 laborers employed in coffee-processing plants and 3,351 other laborers. Along with these, there are undoubtedly many colonos, migratory workers and other laborers on coffee farms that were producing less than 200 bags of coffee per year and who were consequently not included in the coffee census; and there are many others on the sugar plantations, the cattle ranches, and the banana plantations.

TABLE 22. *Number of colonos and migratory workers on coffee farms producing more than 200 quintales of coffee per year*

| | | TOTAL WORKERS | | COLONOS | | MIGRATORY WORKERS | |
Size of farms (in caballerías)	Number of farms	Number	Number per farm	Number	Number per farm	Number	Number per farm
TOTAL	1,744	179,431	103	80,421	46	99,010	57
Under 1	533	13,514	25	3,789	7	9,725	18
1–49	1,157	143,428	124	63,829	55	79,599	69
50–99	35	13,230	378	7,488	214	5,742	164
100 and over	19	9,259	487	5,315	280	3,944	208

Source: Censo cafetalero, 1950, p. 149. One caballería of land is equivalent to 111.5 acres.

Finally, perhaps it should be pointed out that farm labor is employed on the medium sized farms, and even on the small ones, as well as on the large plantations. Workers on medium sized farms are often referred to as *jornaleros* although the term is not restricted to them. These workers may be employed, one or a few per farm, on either a seasonal or a permanent basis. Adams reports that the practice of hiring labor is not confined to the large and medium landholders, but is found throughout the ladino population in Guatemala and among all economic groups. Small landholders may act at one time as employers, at another as workers hired out to someone else. This renders the dis-

---

greater than the 43,298 reported in the regular census of agriculture, which included only the heads of families who, on the day the census was taken, were in charge of the plot of land that had been assigned to them by the finquero, and hence were classified as farm operators.

tinction difficult between employers and employees in the lower economic groups.[10]

There are also migrations of workers for purposes other than working on coffee plantations. Considerable numbers migrate to work during off seasons on the banana plantations at Tiquisate and Bananera; and as has been indicated, some of the highlanders rent lands in the Pacific piedmont areas and migrate back and forth in order to till them. In some cases the migrants work for the owners a few weeks each year in partial compensation for use of the land. As Adams says, "People from almost all the highland communities in which there are no large fincas participate in labor migrations." [11]

We have noted that according to the census of 1950, 40 per cent of the economically active males in the Republic were classified as agricultural laborers. This can be only a rough approximation to reality, however, since in many cases an individual is a farm laborer plus something else. We have already noted that the colonos usually have a small plot of land to till for their own use on the finca. Similarly, many of the migratory workers have small plots to till in their highland communities, and hence might also be called subsistence farmers.

Farm labor is a complicated problem to analyze in Guatemala because of its numerous varieties and manifestations. There is need for careful study of the whole farm labor problem to determine what economic activities are engaged in during periods of inter-seasonal unemployment on the fincas. There is also great need for more information concerning the impact of seasonal migration of the families and the communities of the migratory workers.

GOVERNMENT POLICY TOWARD LABOR

Until 1945, labor legislation in Guatemala was directed largely at the control of Indian labor, a topic which is discussed more fully in Chapter 6. In 1945, however, the government made a drastic shift in policy toward labor. This shift was based on certain provisions of the newly adopted Constitution which enunciated the obligations of the state toward its citizens. Some of the functions and obligations of the government as specified by the Constitution of 1945 were as follows: [12]

10. Adams, op. cit., p. 304. Indians also employ labor, even on small holdings. See Chapter 7.

11. Ibid., p. 305.

12. *Constitución de la República de Guatemala*, decretada por la Asamblea Constituyente en 11 de Marzo de 1945, Guatemala, 1950.

1. Responsibility of government to provide employment to those who lack it and want it. (Article 57.)
2. The right of workers to organize for socio-economic protection, including unionization, the right to enter into labor contracts, to strike and to effect a lockout, all of which are to be regulated by law. (Article 58.)
3. The fixing of minimum wages in accordance with the nature of the enterprise and the needs of the workers.
4. The responsibility to regulate the hours of work, granting, (a) one paid day of rest for each six days of work; (b) the eight-hour working day or 48-hour working week; (c) extra compensation for extra work; (d) regular pay during legally recognized holidays; and (e) annual paid vacations after one year or more of uninterrupted service.
5. Protection of female workers and minors.
6. Requiring employers to grant severance pay to employees separated from their jobs without just cause.
7. The setting up of special Labor Tribunals as a branch of the judiciary to settle disputes involving labor.

An elaborate Labor Code was drawn up and adopted by the government in 1947 spelling out in detail the rules, laws, and regulations with reference to the labor policies contained in the Constitution.[13] Labor unions began to organize and to demand their newly acquired rights under the Constitution and under the Labor Code. With special tribunals appointed to settle labor disputes, employers soon began to complain that personnel sympathetic to labor were appointed to positions on the tribunals and that decisions were almost invariably favorable to labor. Labor leaders in the cities soon began to exercise a powerful voice in government decisions involving many problems of a socio-economic nature.

At first the unions were confined mostly to nonagricultural industries located in the cities, except for employees of the United Fruit Company. This was partly because, at that time, unions were not permitted to organize in agricultural enterprises having less than 500 workers, hence few could qualify.[14] In 1948, however, Article 236 of the Labor Code was revised so that a union could be organized in any agricultural enterprise having a minimum of 50 workers. Gradually labor organizers began forming agricultural unions.

13. *Código de trabajo*, Ministerio de Economía y Trabajo, Guatemala, 1950.
14. Archer C. Bush, *Organized Labor in Guatemala 1944–1949* (Hamilton, N.Y., 1950), p. 43.

Landowners felt that their welfare was seriously jeopardized by legalizing the right of agricultural workers to strike. The finquero contemplated with considerable anxiety the possibility of a strike among his own workers at the crucial moment when his crops must be harvested quickly or lost. His uneasiness was aggravated by increased awareness that some of the labor leaders were admittedly communist-oriented and perhaps as interested in destroying the plantation economy, of which he was a symbol, as in promoting the welfare of the workers.

To add further to the finquero's apprehensions, another national organization was formed under the sympathetic sponsorship of the government. This was designed to provide additional aid and encouragement to the peasant and farm laborer. It was called the *Confederación Nacional de Campesinos,* (National Confederation of Peasants). Its membership increased rapidly throughout the country, and its leaders urged the workers and peasants to demand land for themselves as a part of the land reform program (see Chapter 8).

With the fall of the Arbenz government in 1954, this vigorous labor movement came to an abrupt halt. Many of the top labor leaders fled from the country, some of them taking refuge behind the "Iron Curtain." [15]

During the regime of Castillo Armas, a tight rein was held on labor; and most of the known labor leaders ran for cover. Labor leaders were required to receive official clearance before they could hold positions of leadership in the labor movement. This, of course, was reportedly designed to make sure that the communists did not again get control. Most of the unions were confined to Guatemala City. Exceptions to this were workers at the United Fruit Company plantations in Tiquisate and Bananera; and the dock workers in Puerto Barrios. As of 1957, no unions had as yet been permitted to reorganize on the government fincas and few existed on the private farms. Labor leaders were moving cautiously for fear of being arrested, branded as communists, and thrown into prison or exiled.

It is generally claimed that the restrictions on labor were temporary in character. The revised constitution of 1956 contains essentially the same liberal outlook for labor as did that of 1945. Only a few revisions were made of the elaborate Labor Code of 1947. One amendment prohibited farm laborers from conducting a strike during harvest time,

15. Events leading up to the fall of the Arbenz government are discussed in Chapter 16.

and stated that if a strike were in process, it would have to be called off when the crops were ready to harvest. Another amendment to the Labor Code had to do with the re-employment of persons who were discharged by the finqueros or by other employers. Under the code, a person discharged, even though he received severance pay, could appeal for reinstatement to his former position. Landowners claimed that such appeals were usually granted and that employers were often required to re-employ persons previously discharged who were definitely antagonistic to the enterprise and who could sabotage the work. The revision modified this right of reinstatement, so that discharged workers did not necessarily have to be re-employed.

As of 1959, labor had failed to recover the attention it had received during the regimes of Arévalo and Arbenz. Although progressive and humane labor legislation was retained in the revised constitution of 1956 and in the amended Labor Code, it is impossible at this time to say how vigorously this legislation will be enforced. It will probably take some time for labor leaders to live down the reputation they acquired, particularly during the Arbenz period, of being committed to promote the interests of International Communism.

It was reported in 1956 that even on commercial plantations farm labor was still paid only about 50 cents per day. Rarely was more than 75 or 80 cents per day paid except on the plantations of the United Fruit Company, which have a higher salary scale than any other plantation enterprise in Guatemala.

As of 1959, most of the farm workers were probably worse off than when the agrarian laws were instituted in 1952. For instance, the Guatemalan Minister of Labor announced in 1957 that wages had recently been reduced on about 75 per cent of the large plantations.[16] Widespread conflict developed in the rural areas between landlord and worker because of the demands of some of the workers for land. Some of the hostility engendered during the Arbenz period still lingered on, and finqueros sometimes refused employment to their former workers. In other cases they refused to give their former workers plots of land to till for their own use, as they were formerly accustomed to do, for fear that these workers might again demand permanent possession of these plots. Low coffee prices in 1958–60 resulted in a severe economic depression which affected adversely many aspects of the economy and further aggravated the position of farm workers.

16. Reported in *New York Times* (April 7, 1957), p. 11.

INDUSTRIALIZATION

As of 1960, the government is trying to promote industrialization in various ways. An aspect of this is facilitated through an Economic Integration Treaty which was signed by five countries of Central America on June 10, 1958. The treaty was designed to foster regional planning and to bring about better integration of the economies of the five countries. It specified that the country of location for certain industries of interest to these various nations would be decided on the basis of economic advantage. This would tend to avoid duplication and competition in the establishment of new industries in these countries, which are too small to support separate industries. Partly as a result of this treaty, an oil refinery and a small steel mill are now being constructed in Guatemala. The latter is being built in Guatemala City and will fabricate oil and water storage tanks, frames for low-cost houses, silos, bridge structures, and galvanized tubes and sheets. It is reported that the investment involves American, French, Colombian, and Guatemalan capital.

A Tripartite Treaty of Economic Association was also signed by Guatemala, El Salvador, and Honduras on February 6, 1960, which provides for the formation of a common market, a customs union, and a development and assistance fund. The common market feature of the treaty calls for immediate free trade among the countries for natural and manufactured products, except for certain specified items. The customs union provisions of the treaty prescribe that there shall be equal import duties among the three countries to be worked out and placed into operation not later than five years after the treaty becomes effective. The development assistance fund is designed to provide possible loans either to governments or to individuals to help finance worthy economic development projects.

Obviously, at this writing it is too early to tell just how successful these treaties will prove to be or to what extent they will accomplish the avowed objectives. In the author's opinion, however, they offer tremendous hope for economic cooperation among these countries and may greatly stimulate industrialization and international trade throughout Central America.

Chapter 6

THE ROLE OF THE INDIAN
IN THE ECONOMY

Since more than half of Guatemala's population is classified as Indian, it seems advisable to examine in some detail the role which the Indian plays in the economy of the country. At the outset it must be stated that the economic role of the Guatemalan Indian is not one of mere production for subsistence. His is a market economy, based primarily on money as a medium of exchange, and in some ways is rather highly specialized, both with respect to agriculture and in the production of other consumer goods. Many of the principal elements of an "indigenous" or underdeveloped economy are lacking. These elements, as outlined by Mosk, include:

> a high degree of self-sufficiency; limited production for the market; transactions based on custom and tradition, rather than market forces; little response to gainful incentives; insulation from fluctuations in the national . . . economy . . . including fluctuations originating in international conditions.[1]

Redfield has characterized the Guatemalan tribes as primitive merchant societies. He writes:

> The commercial spirit is strong not only within the group of communities constituting a market organization, but also within the village and even within the family. Maine, and later Weber, conceived of an original primitive society as one involving "exclusion of the unrestricted quest of gain within the circle of those bound together by religious ties." (Max Weber, *General Economic History*, p. 356.) In such a society the village was one big family, united by piety and holding property communally. These

1. Sanford Mosk, "Indigenous Economy in Latin America," *Inter-American Economic Affairs*, 8 (1954), 3–4.

particular Guatemalan societies are about as far from such a condition as is our own. The Rule of the Market has entered even within the most intimate group. Neighbors buy and sell from one another. The price of goods within the village is the same as the price in the market center, allowance being made for savings in labor or transportation or the like.[2]

The Guatemalan Indian, primitive agriculturalist though he may be, is not in most cases merely a subsistence farmer, largely because the mountainous terrain in which he lives is not capable of producing enough to make him self-sufficient. Arable land is so scarce in the highland regions of Guatemala that not all municipios are able to produce enough of the basic milpa (maize) to support the population. This factor, coupled with tradition, has led to a high degree of specialization among the Indians, not only in handicrafts and labor, but also in crops. The Indians of those areas which do not produce enough milpa have developed trade objects (which will be discussed later) or hire out as laborers in order to purchase goods to satisfy their basic needs.

These conditions have led to the development among the Indians of an exchange economy based on money rather than barter. Regional and locally organized markets in this country are not a recent innovation; they have a history which extends to pre-Columbian times. Because of the place of trade in the economy, the accumulation of wealth, whether in the form of land, goods, or money, is a socially acceptable objective, even though the differences between poverty and wealth are not as great as they tend to be in more highly industrialized societies. Market forces operate in the Guatemalan Indian economy, which is affected by national and international as well as by local conditions.

The Indian who cannot raise enough food for his family and who has no other source of income will hire out as a laborer, either to his neighbors or to the coffee plantations. Occasionally he will become a peddler selling from house to house, though this is more likely among Ladinos, and a few Indians are paid for performing ritualistic services. In the main, however, the Guatemalan Indian tends to be a farmer, a manufacturer of handmade goods, a merchant, and a laborer (see Plate 6).

THE INDIAN AS FARMER

Farming in the Guatemalan highlands takes place on small parcels of land at altitudes usually between 4,500 and 9,000 feet. One rarely finds

2. Robert Redfield, "Primitive Merchants of Guatemala," *Quarterly Journal of Inter-American Relations*, 1 (1939), 50.

level, arable plots larger than a few acres and even the slopes have become deforested as a result of tillage.

The staple food of most Guatemalan Indians is maize (corn), supplemented by beans and squash, all of which may be grown in the same plots. Wagley describes the methods of tillage in Santiago Chimaltenango where these staples are grown as a specialty of the village, over and above what is needed for subsistence, and where the surplus is used for purposes of trade.[3] Other villages specialize in other agricultural crops, although almost everywhere a little maize is grown. In Panajachel, for example, onions, garlic, and fruit are produced for sale, and maize has to be purchased.[4] Sololá supplies to its market, besides the staples of maize and beans, vegetables, fruits, poultry and eggs, pork and lard, and certain prepared foods.[5]

As indicated in the previous chapter, agricultural techniques are primitive. Cultivation is usually done by hand tools: the digging stick, the hoe and the machete. The plow is rarely found in the Guatemalan highlands except in the department of Huehuetenango where it is somewhat more common. In Santiago Chimaltenango, which has more land per capita than most villages, a plot is usually allowed to lie fallow after two years. As in many areas, no animal manure is used, and this land rest is therefore highly desirable and is practiced whenever a farmer has enough land to make it possible.

The agricultural cycle involves first, burning and clearing the land that has lain fallow; second, planting; third, weeding and cultivating; and fourth, harvesting. All of these activities must be accompanied by appropriate rituals (costumbre) which require the presence of both the husband and wife and include, as well as prayers, the burning of candles and the blood sacrifice of chickens.

Of the costumbres Wagley writes that they

> cannot be separated from the mechanical processes of cultivation. To the Chimalteco, maize will no more grow without the prayers and ceremonies than without the careful planting. The one group of activities is as important as the other, and the two spheres are closely interwoven.[6]

3. See Charles Wagley, Economics of a Guatemalan Village, Memoirs of the American Anthropological Association, No. 58 (Lancaster, Pa., 1941), pp. 31–44. Also Stadelman, "Maize Cultivation," in Contributions to American Anthropology and History, 6, 1940.

4. Sol Tax, Penny Capitalism: A Guatemalan Indian Economy (Washington, D.C., 1953), p. 12.

5. Felix Webster McBryde, Sololá: A Guatemalan Town and Cakchiquel Market Center (New Orleans, 1933), p. 114.

6. Wagley, op. cit., p. 31.

At each stage of the agricultural process appropriate rituals must be observed. For these rituals the farmer must be "clean" for the occasion. He must be continent throughout the period of making costumbre and must go alone or with his wife to perform the rituals.

For clearing the fields, the farmer prays that no snake may bite him, that he may not step on a sharp stick, and that the job may be done easily and quickly. If it is necessary to hire labor, the mozos are included in these prayers.

A *chimán* is consulted to designate a propitious day for planting. Husband and wife rise early to observe the required rituals, such as praying, sacrificing a chicken, and burning incense mixed with chicken blood.[7]

After these prayers, the father of the family goes alone to the fields, plants a makeshift cross in the plot and burns two candles before it, swinging a censer containing the incense mixed with chicken blood. The wife may help with these rituals but she must not touch the seeds. Every effort is made to complete the planting on the chosen day. After the planting, the farmer remains behind alone to burn another candle before the cross and offer prayers. After returning home, he and his wife go to the church to offer further prayers.

Each weeding of the plot requires similar rituals: prayers, incense, and the sacrifice of a chicken. Sometimes chicken eggs are used in place of chicken blood. Wives are expected to accompany their husbands to the fields for these rituals. In addition to performing these five or six separate rituals before each cultivation of the field, many farmers hire chimanes to pray for their fields. Prayers are addressed to God, to saints, and to native deities.

Even relatively unimportant aspects of the agricultural cycle, such as the gathering of corn leaves, are accompanied by a special ritual, part of the purpose of which is to notify the supernaturals of the approaching harvest.

For the harvest ritual, in which the wife participates, the husband clears a space in the field with his machete leaving two corn stalks before which a candle is burned, a chicken is sacrificed, and incense is again burned.[8]

Similar rituals are carried out after the harvest, when husband and wife take two new ears of corn to the church as an offering to the saint. It should be pointed out that the particular content and sequence of the agricultural costumbre may vary from one municipio to another, and hence may differ somewhat from that observed by Wagley, although the general pattern is roughly similar.

7. Ibid., pp. 34–5.
8. Ibid., pp. 41–2.

The Indian as Manufacturer

Even where milpa is grown in some abundance, the Indian usually supplements his work in agriculture by manufacturing home products or by hiring out as labor. Like agriculture, these handicrafts are specialized according to region, village, or even family, depending on tradition and on the availability of raw materials.

According to Sol Tax,[9] midwestern Guatemala is an extreme case of an area where communities are as dependent on trade for basic needs as cities usually are. The main factors which have brought about this condition are geography, tradition, and economic specialization, the latter being in large part an outgrowth of the first two.

Although geography provides a natural limitation upon what can be grown or upon raw materials, this factor alone does not account for variations between neighboring communities.

> Contiguous Chichicastenango and Totonicapán both have pine forests; the *Maxeños* cut their pine for timber, while the *Totonicapeños* do not only that, but fashion the lumber into furniture. Likewise, clay is not lacking in either of the two communities; but *Totonicapeños* are leading potters, while I have never heard of a pot being made by a Chichicastenango Indian.[10]

Tradition plays an important role in the Indian economy and changes come about slowly. New means of making a living are not likely to be adopted unless they are deemed to be profitable. Handicraft arts are handed down from parents to children, thus perpetuating the traditions of a village.

The supplementary productive specialties of a community may include special crops, industries (furniture, pottery, textiles), trades (chiefly building, such as masonry, carpentry, and the like), merchandising, and labor. However, there is

> an order of preference of means of making a living: Indians will not do day-labor if they have another means of making a living; they will not be traveling merchants if they can make a living at home; they will not be artisans or grow special crops at the expense of their milpas.[11]

Even so, slack seasons in milpa allow time for other occupations, and some of the industries, such as pottery, basketry and hat-making are

9. Tax, "Economy and Technology," in *Heritage of Conquest,* pp. 43–75.
10. Ibid., p. 46.
11. Ibid., p. 48.

largely women's work and do not interfere with agriculture, which is men's work.

Agricultural specialties include sugar cane and fruits from the lake town of Santa Cruz la Laguna; oranges, limes, and guisquils from Tzununa; tomatoes from Atitlán; potatoes from Totonicapán; anise from San Antonio Palopó; live pigs from Chichicastenango, to name only a few.[12] Beans grow in the highlands, especially in the Lake Atitlán area, and are sold in neighboring markets, as well as in the lowlands. Raw bean coffee, *panela* (unrefined brown sugar), salt, dried chile, and fruits are brought from the lowlands to the highlands.

Indian industry is largely of the household or cottage type. It includes pottery, basketry, rope-making, lime-burning, the making of *metates* (grinding stones), and textiles. McBryde has made an intensive study of the crafts and industries of southwest Guatemala, from which the following information may be summarized.[13] Only a few examples of the many cases of village specializations are given.

Pottery is almost always made by hand; only Ladinos use the potter's wheel. Virtually all the pottery used in southwest Guatemala is produced in fifteen villages, with Totonicapán the chief producing center. Some of this pottery is marketed in the lowlands and in Guatemala City. Pottery is made chiefly by women and the simplest techniques are used both for molding and firing.

Most of the baskets used in southwest Guatemala are made in eight municipios. There are two basic types: a deep, handled basket and an open, flat kind. The former are used by Ladinos, the latter by Indian women for displaying goods or for carrying loads on the head. Open baskets are also used as measures.

Lime-burning is found largely in San Francisco el Alto where it is a specialty of the canton Paxixil. Lime, used as a leach for corn, is a common household necessity.

Metates, which are used in every Guatemalan Indian household for grinding corn, come mainly from Nahualá. In the Huehuetenango region, they are made chiefly by Ladinos.

Textiles for home consumption are made by women on stick (or back-strap) looms. However, in some areas commercial weaving is extensive. Chichicastenango women weave shawls, belts, and blouses for sale elsewhere. Spinning is still common in the Lake Atitlán villages. Wool is woven in Chiapas and San Sebastián Huehuetenango. Treadle-loom weaving, mostly in skirt lengths, is done chiefly by men, often Ladinos. Blankets and suit cloth of wool are woven on foot-

12. McBryde, op. cit., p. 114 ff.
13. McBryde, *Cultural and Historical Geography of Southwest Guatemala.*

5. Poverty is widespread but "dignified."

6. Guatemala is highly Indian.

5. Poverty is widespread but "dignified."

6. Guatemala is highly Indian.

7. The Indian carries a heavy load.

8. Coffee harvest: the pickers select the ripe red cherries, leaving
   the green, immature ones on the tree for later harvest.

looms in Momostenango, where the soil is too poor to support agriculture and where hot springs can be used in the felting process. An example of extreme specialization is the manufacture of shaggy wool rugs in the Aldea Obotón by three brothers and their families. Palm leaf rain capes come from the municipio of San Sebastián Retalhuleu, which produces almost nothing else. Palm hats, often made on sewing machines by Indian men, come from Santa Cruz Quiché, San Sebastián Lemoa, and from some parts of Chichicastenango. Palm mats are made in three municipios. Santa Catarina Palopó is the chief rush-mat producing center among the Lake Atitlán villages; in the Antigua area, San Antonio Aguascalientes is an important producing center. Bunch-grass mats are woven by shepherds in the Totonicapán-San Francisco region.

Dance regalia, which is rented for ceremonial occasions, is a specialty of a single Indian dealer in Totonicapán, although there are two other small-scale costume makers, one in San Cristóbal Totanicapán and one in Chichicastenango.

Furniture is made in Totonicapán. Ropes come from the Cobán area, the western shores of Lake Atitlán, Comitancillo and Colotenango. Brooms are made in Quezaltenango of bunch grass, in Rabinal of palm leaves and in the lowlands of *corozo* leaf veins. Candles are made of tallow (San Andrés Xecúl), paraffin (San Cristóbal Totonicapán), and beeswax (Pueblo Nuevo). Charcoal is burned in the municipios of San José Chacaya and Cajolá. Incense comes mainly from Cuilco, Santa María Chiquimula, and Sacapulas.

THE INDIAN AS MERCHANT

Trade is an important feature of Central American Indian life today, as it has been since pre-Columbian times. There are three methods of trading: [14] 1) house-to-house peddling, which is carried on almost entirely by Ladinos or by Transitional Indians; 2) stores, which are nearly always run by Ladinos but are also patronized by Indians; and 3) local and regional markets, where the venders tend to be entirely Indians, but where Ladinos may also be customers.

The market is the center of the Indian's economic life and of much of his social life. Most of the principal towns have regular markets at least one day a week, but larger towns may have more than one a week and some towns even support daily markets. The scheduling of weekly market days permits the inhabitants of a region to attend several different area markets each week. No one knows when the present

14. Tax, op. cit., *Heritage of Conquest*, pp. 52 ff.

schedules were first worked out. Certainly the existing pattern has been in effect as long as anyone can remember. In the highlands, Sunday is often the market day, but in parts of the Cuchumatanes Mountains, markets are held every fifth day in accordance with the ancient Mayan calendar.[15] The factors which lead to the establishment of markets include 1) high population density, 2) situation on major trade routes, and 3) location between different types of production areas. All three are found in an important market.[16]

Selling at the markets is usually done by women, except for the more important commodities, such as livestock, or for goods sold in large quantities. The arrangement of the market remains very nearly the same, not only from week to week, but even from year to year. Mc-Bryde found little change in the lay-out of the market four years after his first survey of the Sololá plaza. The grouping is likely to be, first, by type of goods and, secondly, by their place of origin. Markets tend to specialize in certain commodities.

> Everybody . . . knows that Tecpán is the place to buy lime, that bananas are cheaper in Atitlán, that pitch pine and pigs are cheaper in Chichicastenango. If one wants a few ounces of lime for the weekly cooking of corn, he will not go to Tecpán for it. But if he wants a hundred pounds for building a house, it may pay him to take the journey.[17]

Commodities are brought to market almost entirely on the backs of Indians (see Plate 7). Even the heavy stone metates made in the volcanic highlands are transported either from house to house or to markets in this manner. McBryde reports that Nahualá men take a load of about a hundred pounds (two metates and six handstones) at a time.[18] According to Wagley,[19] some of the wealthier villagers of Santiago Chimaltenango have recently become muleteers, but this form of transportation is evidently confined to moving coffee from the fincas in the Cuchumatanes Mountains, not to bringing goods to local markets. Livestock is driven to market.

Considering the illiteracy of the population, the pricing of goods reflects the cost of production with considerable accuracy. There is very little barter, although maize or other products may sometimes be used as media of exchange. Basically, however, the Guatemalan In-

15. McBryde, *Cultural and Historical Geography of Southwest Guatemala*, p. 83.
16. Ibid., p. 82.
17. Tax, *Penny Capitalism*, p. 14.
18. McBryde, op. cit., p. 73.
19. Wagley, op. cit., p. 45 ff.

dian operates in a money economy. Prices depend on the scarcity of commodities, their perishability, or, occasionally, on the personal circumstances of the merchant, as well as on cost of production. Sol Tax has analyzed the Indian market as being competitive and thus capitalistic in the following respects:

a) It is atomistic, in that small merchants of identical products compete for the trade of small, independent buyers.
b) It is open, in that there are no barriers to new competitors entering the market or old ones leaving it.
c) It is free, in that prices are set by the interplay of supply and demand.
d) It is based on "rational" behavior which implies: "(1) consistent behavior in terms of cultural values, prices and quality, (2) indifference on the part of buyers and sellers as to their trading partners, and (3) information on the part of buyers and sellers concerning prevailing prices." [20]

According to Tax, the only authoritarian intervention in the free play of the market stems from the government (taxes, fees, and interference with the price mechanism), custom and tradition (such as harvesting practices), and the influence of the world economy.

Sanford Mosk, an economist who reviewed the basic studies which have been made of the highland Indian economy, concludes that the following factors are characteristic:

Production is directed toward the market, rather than towards individual and family consumption, productive effort is specialized . . . ; a vigorous and complex trade is carried on throughout the region; transactions are based on market forces, rather than custom and tradition; there is an active response to gainful incentives; the regional economy is significantly tied to the national economy . . . and to international economic conditions as well.[21]

Redfield aptly summed up the apparent contradiction between he primitive technology of the Indian and his highly developed commercialism when he wrote:

The Guatemalan case indicates that a stable society may exist which exhibits to some degree the commercial spirit and pecuniary economy of our own society, as well as some of its secular attitude, but which has a simple technology.[22]

20. Tax, op. cit., pp. 15–16.
21. Mosk, op. cit., p. 24.
22. Redfield, op. cit., p. 55.

The Indian as Laborer

The Indian has played such a prominent role as a laborer in the Guatemalan economy that it seems advisable to turn back into history and review briefly his changing position in this respect.

Since the very beginning of the Spanish Conquest there has existed in Guatemala a type of economy that has required the services of gangs of relatively unskilled labor, either continuously or seasonally. This has led at various times to the use of legal and extralegal measures to assure an adequate supply of labor through some form of coercion.[23]

The exploitative nature of the Conquest coupled with the unwillingness of the Spaniards to perform tasks of manual labor led to the subjection of the Indian population as well as to control of the land. Even while Alvarado's expedition from Mexico was completing its work of the Conquest of Guatemala there arose the problem of an adequate supply of labor with which to implement the desired economic system and assure the social dominance of the Conquerors. The transportation of goods and equipment, the opening and operation of mines in the search for precious stones and metals, the building of a seat of government, the cultivation of the fields beyond the Indian level of subsistence, and the provision of necessities and comforts which the Spaniards expected were deemed essential to the life of the colony. Added to these projects was the task of constructing elaborate cathedrals throughout the land to replace the pagan temples of the natives. The use of Indian labor to undertake these activities was considered essential, and coercion of the Indians developed as a natural result.

The pattern of coercion throughout the years of Spanish rule was a continuously varying compromise between the colonial landholders, who claimed that without coercion of native labor the colony could not exist, and the King, who, on the basis of Christian principles, was reluctant to condone coercion. The position of the Church on this matter varied with the viewpoints of particular church officials both in the colony and in Spain.

The encomienda system

The labor arrangements made at the time of the Conquest by the Spaniards were not new; they had been used before in Spain and

---

23. See Jones, *Guatemala, Past and Present,* chs. 10–12; Jorge Skinner-Klée, *Recopilación de legislación indigenista de Guatemala,* Ediciones especiales del Instituto Indigenista Inter-americano (México, D. F., 1954); José Milla, *Historia de la América Central.*

adapted to American conditions through use in Mexico and the West Indies, and were known as the *encomienda* system. As villages were conquered, it was common for the inhabitants to be given "in trust" to Conquerors or other worthy individuals. In many cases the grants included whole villages or even groups of villages. Indians living within encomiendas were allotted to the conquistadores to be converted, for the Church and the King, to Catholicism. In return for conversion of the natives, the *encomendero* was allowed to exact tribute from the natives in the form of precious metals, work, or kind. The amount of annual tribute which could be expected was limited and labor performed by Indians beyond the limit was to be paid for by the landholder.

From the beginning, the rules set by the King regarding compensation for labor tended to be overlooked and unenforced, and the system of colonial administration contained the machinery through which outright enslavement of the Indian was readily possible. In addition to Spanish administrators, some members of the ruling Indian class were kept in power and were expected to provide labor from the villages when called upon to do so. The pre-Conquest social structure of the natives had contained a system of forced labor by the lower class in the interests of the rulers; and the imposition of Spanish rule merely extended the hierarchy of authority. To facilitate the availability of labor gangs, pressure was used on the Indians to live in pueblos (villages) rather than in smaller scattered clusters.

Complaints to the King from two New World groups with widely variant motives brought about a succession of rulings from the Crown which were intended to abolish forced labor and assure payment for labor performed. Certain church officials, such as Bartolomé de las Casas, petitioned the King to put an end to what they claimed were shocking barbarities existing in the relations between the Indians and the encomenderos; [24] and the late-comers to the colony complained that the economic advantages accruing to the encomendero through his relatively free use of labor were detrimental to the long-range success of the Guatemalan venture. Principally as a result of the efforts of las Casas at Court, the King issued the New Laws in 1543 which were to apply to conditions in Guatemala as well as other American colonies of Spain.

Regarding Indian labor, the New Laws distinguished between free Indians, defined as those not living within an encomienda, and Indians legally held by encomenderos. Indians on encomiendas held by colonial officials were declared free, as were those held by any person with-

24. Lewis Hanke, *Bartolomé de las Casas* (The Hague, 1954), p. 31.

out legal title to them, those ill-treated by encomenderos; and all those held in encomienda at the death of the encomendero. Free Indians could no longer be given in encomienda, and no free Indians were to be employed against their will under penalty of death.[25] Legally held Indians were to pay a tribute to the encomendero no greater than that paid by free Indians to the Crown. They were never to be reduced to slavery, and were to be paid when used as burden bearers. All Indians, free or legally held, were to be instructed in the Catholic faith, were to be protected by local courts according to their own usages and customs, where such were considered just, and were, in general, to be treated as "vassals of the Crown of Castile."

Enforcement of the New Laws was attempted through sporadic issuance of royal decrees condemning specific violations. Las Casas continued his generally successful appeals to the King in behalf of the Indians, but his arguments were increasingly contested by the colonists, who defended their labor policy by the claim that the very existence of the colony depended upon the use of forced labor. The Crown, presumably weighing realism against humanitarianism, was swayed first by one group and then the other throughout the remainder of the period of Spanish rule in Guatemala.

The increasing need for revenue to support domestic defenses and colonial expansion, however, finally led the Crown to put an end to the encomienda system, because, through its abolition, Indian tribute became payable directly to the King. The last of the encomiendas probably continued until 1700, by which time new techniques of coercion had developed into legally recognized labor practices.

The mandamiento system

Local authorities worked out what was known as the *mandamiento* system. This was a regulation whereby orders could be issued through the magistrates commanding certain proportions of the able-bodied Indians of designated villages or municipios to work for stated periods of time on the plantations, or elsewhere, as needed. Early royal decrees against this were ignored, and in 1616 the Crown confirmed its legality through a *cédula* granting certain officials the privilege of assigning the Indians to specific places of work.

The payments to the Indians as compensation for the labor performed soon led to a refinement of the mandamiento system whereby an Indian would agree to work out an advance payment that he had requested or that had been pressed upon him by an employer. Such reciprocal agreements were declared enforceable by local authorities

25. Jones, op. cit., p. 122.

and large numbers of the Indians accumulated debts which kept them busy working off the incurred obligations for most of the year.

In 1824 the Federal Assembly proclaimed that all men in Guatemala were free and no one could ever be enslaved there. It did not occur to some of the early Liberals, however, that the Indians were anything but inferior beings who could naturally be expected to do the hardest work. Although forced labor was prohibited by a decree in 1837, except for those who did not fulfill their labor contracts or who had received advance payments for anticipated labor on the plantations, the system persisted. President Barrios reaffirmed the old standards in 1876 when he stated in a circular to the *jefes políticos* that the farmers must be given "strong and energetic aid"; otherwise all their efforts would be doomed to failure because of the negligence and "deceit of the Indians." [26] He therefore directed that Indians should be supplied to the farmers in such quantities as were needed; that payment should be made ahead of time to avoid delay; and that any Indian who tried to evade his duty should be punished to the full extent of the law. The mandamiento was theoretically supervised by the public authorities though in fact the plantation owners or their agents engaged most of the workers. If a laborer refused to work, he might be thrown into jail; if he ran away, the expense of bringing him back was charged to his account. Actually, the mandamiento continued to be utilized until 1894 when it was again abolished.

Debt peonage

In the meantime, farm labor legislation was enacted which emphasized labor contracts and debt peonage as a way to solve the farm labor problem.[27] A law enacted in 1877 called *Reglamento de Jornaleros* set forth the general regulations concerning contract labor. These were revised in 1894 and prevailed with minor variations until about 1934.

According to the decree of 1877, agricultural laborers were divided into three broad groupings, as follows: [28]

1. *Colonos.* These were persons who contracted to live and work on the plantations. They could contract for four years at a time and could not leave or accept work elsewhere until the specified time expired. Moreover, even after the four-year contract had expired, they could not leave until all debts were paid to the employer.

26. Ibid., p. 150.
27. Although this and subsequent legislation related to all workers, it was, in fact, applied more stringently to the Indian than the Ladino and is, therefore, discussed in this chapter.
28. Skinner-Klée, op. cit., pp. 37–9.

2. *Jornaleros habilitados.* These were workers not bound by a time contract but who had accepted money or goods from an employer with the promise to work for him until all indebtedness was paid off by means of personal labor. They could not leave until they had worked off the debt.

3. *Jornaleros no habilitados.* These were neither under time contracts nor in debt but must fulfill any wage contract agreed upon, usually for one or more weeks.

All classes of workers were required to carry *libretos,* or booklets, in which the employer noted the debits and the credits. Since farm workers could neither read nor write there was plenty of opportunity for the employer to manipulate the accounts so that workers might be kept almost perpetually in debt, and thus required by law to work continuously on the plantation. This process was facilitated by the extension of credit at the plantation store, the furnishing of alcoholic beverages at fiesta time, and the supplying of trinkets and sometimes a little cash on birthdays and holidays.

Fugitives fleeing from the plantation before the labor contract had expired or before all debts were paid could be pursued by the employer or his agents and brought back forcibly. The cost of the pursuit and the return of the fugitive to the plantation could be added to his account. He would then be required to work until his entire account was settled and proper notations made to this effect by the employer in the work book which the worker was required to carry on his person. Government authorities were required by law to cooperate in every way in helping employers track down fugitives and return them to the plantation. Often the recorded debts became so large that the Indian could never hope to repay them and hence was in bondage for life. Sometimes even death did not free him, because the debt was merely transferred to the heads of his sons.[29]

Subsequent legislation was enacted in 1894 through the *Ley de Trabajadores* and later revisions of the labor laws were made in 1909, but these served only to modify details with reference to the administration of the laws and to change certain aspects of the legislation. In essence these regulations continued in effect until 1934.

The vagrancy law

The system of debt peonage was abolished in 1934 and replaced by a national vagrancy law which continued in effect until 1945. To facilitate the transition to the new law, a period of two years was

29. For examples of this see Tax, *Penny Capitalism,* pp. 106–7.

granted during which time the plantation owners could try to collect whatever debts they had recorded in their books. At the end of this period all debts outstanding were to be cancelled, and it would henceforth be illegal to advance a laborer more money than that required to make the journey to the plantation to begin employment.

As justification for the law against vagrancy, it was argued that the citizen's liberty is not absolute; work is an obligation; and freedom consists only in choosing the kind of work which one prefers. As noted, the new law put an end to the debt slavery which had formerly been the basis of labor control. Jones has expressed the opinion that perhaps the real object of the law was to compel the laborer to work whether he was in debt or not.[30] The Indian's new freedom was not the freedom to be idle or to produce only what he might need for himself. The state prescribed the minimum amount of work which must be done during the course of a year in order not to be classified as a vagrant, and could punish for vagrancy those who did not comply. As Jones says, under the old law the laborer could be idle, legally, if he could manage to stay out of debt. Under the new law he must work or be punished as a vagrant.[31]

The vagrancy law required any person not having a trade or profession or not cultivating specified amounts of land to seek employment from others for 100 or 150 days per year, depending on the amount of land he farmed. A presidential decree was issued in 1935 giving more specific regulations to the above law. This decree specified that in order to be exempt from the applications of the vagrancy law, a worker would have to own and cultivate at least 4 *manzanas* (6.9 acres) of land devoted to corn, wheat, potatoes, or vegetables; or 3 manzanas (5.2 acres) of coffee, sugar cane, or tobacco. Most Indians did not have this much land to till. If the worker tilled less than these amounts he would have to seek work on the plantations for specified periods of time during the year. If he tilled less than 2.8 acres (10 *cuerdas*), he would have to work for others at least 150 days per year. If he tilled more than 2.8 acres but less than the amount specified above, he would have to work 100 days each year for others.

Each worker from 18 to 60 years of age was required to carry on his person at all times a work book containing his identification and, if exempt from the vagrancy law, a notation to this effect by the local authorities. Otherwise, the booklet must contain notations by plantation owners indicating the days worked on each plantation.[32] The booklets

30. Jones, op. cit., p. 162.
31. Ibid., pp. 163–4.
32. Skinner-Klée, op. cit., pp. 118–19.

could be checked periodically or whenever the occasion arose. Those persons whose booklets did not carry the proper notations by the plantation owners or by the local authorities could be arrested and imprisoned or forced to work on the roads without compensation. Any person suspecting another of being a vagrant could denounce him to the local authorities, who were obliged to investigate and take appropriate action against him.[33]

In addition to the vagrancy law there were other regulations requiring forced labor. For example, in 1933 a decree was issued by President Ubico to the effect that all able-bodied men would be required to work for at least two weeks per year on the public highways. Exceptions could be made for those wishing to contribute instead one dollar for each week. Since wages were very low, the Indian usually found it to his advantage to work on the roads rather than to try to pay the cash.

After the overthrow of the Ubico dictatorship in 1944, a new constitution was prepared and adopted on March 11, 1945. There had been a great deal of discussion about the necessity, in contrast with the injustice, of the vagrancy law. Representatives of the landowners repeated the argument that without coercion the Indians would not work on the plantations and that this would seriously undermine the economy of the country. On the other hand, in a supposedly liberal and democratic constitution, a provision for forced labor would look inconsistent. The following statement was finally adopted as part of Article 55: "Labor is an individual right and a social obligation. Vagrancy is punishable." Nevertheless, no provision was made for implementing punishment for vagrancy; and one might say that with the adoption of the Constitution of 1945, forced labor in Guatemala virtually came to an end.

Shift in government policy toward labor

As indicated in the previous chapter, the Constitution of 1945 marked a drastic shift in the attitude of the government toward the role of labor by recognizing government responsibility for the protection of the rights of the working man and for his general welfare. While legally there was no distinction between the benefits to be enjoyed by Indians and Ladinos under the new labor laws, actually most of the advantages went to urban workers who are primarily Ladinos. There was much more resistance to unionization on the plantations and in the rural areas where most of the Indians work. Except for some of the larger fincas, such as the plantations of the United Fruit Company, labor

33. By interpretation, the vagrancy law was applied almost exclusively to the Indian although the law did not so specify.

organizations were just beginning to penetrate rural areas when the Arbenz regime was overthrown.

During the period 1945 to 1960, Indians continued to work as colonos on the plantations and as migratory workers following the crop harvests in order to supplement the meager incomes derived from tilling their milpas in the highlands. The dismal predictions of the finqueros that the Indians would not work unless coercion continued to be used appear not to have been substantiated. Evidently the Indian is more sensitive to the economic forces that operate around him than was generally supposed.

Chapter 7

SYSTEMS OF AGRICULTURE

Since three-fourths of the employed male population of Guatemala are engaged in agriculture, it seems important to examine briefly the agricultural systems in which they spend the greater part of their lives. Guatemalan agriculture is carried on largely within two major agricultural systems. One may be called "plantation agriculture"; and the other "milpa (subsistence) agriculture." [1] In addition to these two major systems, two other types of agriculture are described in this chapter. One might be referred to as "specialized domestic crops" for trade on a regional basis. These crops are produced on small farms, and none of the products reach the export market. The other is the utilization of forestry products such as *chicle* and timber which do not require cultivation.

PLANTATION AGRICULTURE

While there is considerable variation in the organization of the plantations and in the efficiency with which they are operated in Guatemala, plantation agriculture generally displays the following characteristics:

1. It is concerned largely with the production of four major agricultural products—coffee, bananas, sugar cane and beef cattle.
2. It occupies the best lands in the country in terms of quality of the soils and favorable situation with respect to altitude, temperature, and rainfall.
3. It is oriented directly toward producing cash crops. The two major crops, coffee and bananas, are produced for the export market. The other two, sugar and beef cattle, are produced for

1. The term "milpa" is literally translated as "maize field" or "corn field." It is used here to refer to a type of farming devoted largely to raising corn on small plots of land hardly large enough to provide a living for the family.

the domestic market. More than 90 per cent of the total value of Guatemala's export trade is derived from plantation agriculture.
4. Absentee management prevails. Many owners live in the cities and visit their plantations only occasionally during the year for short periods of time. They entrust the daily operations of the farm to a hired administrator. Some owners visit their plantation about once a week; while a few may commute almost daily. Seldom, however, does the owner actually live on the plantation.
5. The plantation is wasteful of land in that it usually encompasses much more land than is used for productive purposes.
6. Plantation agriculture is dependent on a large supply of resident workers who live with their families permanently on the plantation in housing supplied by the finquero. This resident labor is supplemented by migratory workers during the rush seasons.
7. Finally, the plantation owners have an organization to represent their interests known as the *Asociación General de Agricultores* (General Association of Agriculturists). Through this organization they can make their needs known to government agencies and exert pressure for legislation favorable to their interests. This is obviously a tremendous advantage over the milpa farmer who has no such organization to influence government action in his behalf.

Coffee plantations

Coffee is the outstanding plantation crop and means more to Guatemala in terms of national prosperity and government finance than any other crop or industry. It is grown primarily in two major areas. Most of it comes from the narrow band extending along the southern slopes known as the Pacific piedmont. The coffee lands in this area extend from Mexico on the west to the department of Santa Rosa near the frontier of El Salvador on the east. Nearly all of it is grown at elevations ranging between 1,000 and 5,000 feet above sea level.

A second, but smaller and less important coffee-producing area, is the Cobán region of Alta Verapaz in the north central region. While the vast majority of the coffee is produced in these two areas, at least some coffee is produced in all of the departments of the Republic except El Petén and Totonicapán. The former has a low elevation and is essentially uninhabited, while the latter lies for the most part at elevations above 5,000 feet.

Several important factors have contributed to the success of coffee as a leading commercial crop in Guatemala. The first is the excellent quality of the soil along the Pacific piedmont; second, the favorable climate, with suitable variations in altitudes, temperature and rainfall; and third, the abundant supply of cheap labor. The combination of climate, soil and labor all converge to make this area ideally suited for the growing of coffee.

An abundance of cheap labor has made it possible to produce coffee without much attention to improved techniques and scientific develop-

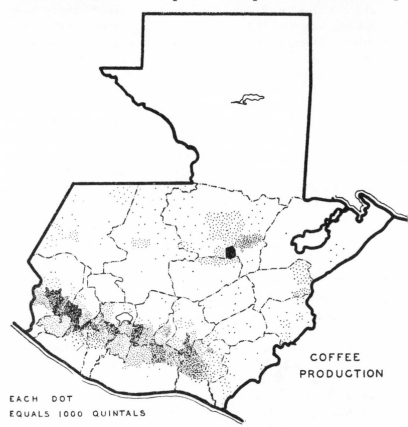

COFFEE
PRODUCTION

EACH DOT
EQUALS 1000 QUINTALS

Figure 12. Geographical distribution of coffee production. Source: *Boletín* 33–34, octubre–diciembre 1951, Dirección General de Estadística.

ments. As indicated in the preceding chapter, labor for the most part consists of two general types. First is the colono system, which assures a continuous labor supply on the plantation. The colono is expected to be available for work on a yearly basis, with some time off to till his plot. The number of colonos on each plantation may vary from a few to more than a thousand, depending on its size and organization.

During rush seasons of the year, however, the number of colonos on any plantation is insufficient to satisfy the needs for labor, especially during harvest time. Not only does coffee picking require large numbers of workers, but the larger plantations have coffee processing plants known as *beneficios* where the coffee is dried, processed, and made ready for shipping. These also demand additional workers during the harvest season (see Plate 8). Large numbers of seasonal or migratory workers are therefore employed. These usually migrate from the highlands and are available on a contract basis for the time necessary to pick the coffee or to perform other urgent assignments. After the picking season is over they move on to another plantation or return to their highland communities.

Although the agricultural census of 1950 reported more than 31,000 farms on which coffee was grown, it was noted that 87 per cent of the coffee was produced on 1,744 farms, each of which produced more than 200 bags (quintales) per year.[2] Most of the large coffee plantations are under the direct supervision of administrators who represent absentee owners. Some larger farms are operated by corporations.

Although coffee occupies a crucial position in the Guatemalan economy, little attention has been given to introducing improved techniques of production. The same practices that existed over a generation ago are still largely prevalent today. Production each year during the eleven year period 1944–55 continued to be at roughly the same level of about one million bags per year. A number of factors have encouraged inefficiency rather than progressive methods on the plantation. Some of these are as follows:

(a) Absentee management. It is estimated that only about 10 to 20 per cent of the large coffee plantation owners actually live on the plantations and direct the operations of the farm. The remaining 80 to 90 per cent are absentee owners who entrust the daily operations to hired managers. These managers seldom have adequate training for their jobs. In most cases they have risen from the labor ranks and their knowledge about coffee or about agriculture in general has been gained entirely throughly work experience.[3]

(b) Insufficient capital investment. There is general reluctance to plow profits back into the enterprise to make the plantation more productive. Little machinery is used and no thought is given to the achievement of maximum production per acre.

2. *Censo cafetalero, 1950, Boletín* de la Dirección General de Estadística, 44–45 (1953), 5.
3. Francis J. LeBeau, "Agricultura de Guatemala," *Integración social en Guatemala*, Seminario de Integración Social Guatemalteca, Jorge Luis Arriola, ed. (Guatemala, 1956), pp. 290–1.

(c) Exploitation of land and man. Land and labor are exploited because they are plentiful. Nearly all of the important tasks are performed by hand without adequate tools or equipment. Little or no effort is exerted to attain maximum productivity per man.

(c) Government ownership and management. The national government controls about 120 plantations in Guatemala. These properties include state farms, farms of certain enemy nationals, and farms expropriated from political exiles. Most of these plantations were expropriated from German nationals during World War II. Some of the national farms are reputed to be among the best in the entire Republic and include at least four of the ten largest coffee farms in Guatemala. Coffee is produced on 85 or 90 of the government plantations. It is estimated that these national farms produce about 25 per cent of all coffee grown in Guatemala.

The national farms have been severely criticized over the years for inefficient management and operation. They are alleged to be "handicapped by poor management, inadequate methods and labor discipline, and ineffective administrative and accounting procedure." [4] It is charged that many of the administrators have been political appointees, who know little about farming but are interested mostly in quick personal gain. It is widely believed in Guatemala that some administrators of government fincas have carried on "black market" operations involving the sale of coffee that was never recorded in the official records.

Many of these national farms were distributed in small parcels to the workers during the agrarian reform program of former President Arbenz. After July 1954, however, these were taken back by the government and against operated as national farms. Open criticism of inefficiency and corruption in the management of the national fincas has led at various times to proposals to dispose of them. In 1958, for example, officials were considering the advisability of auctioning some of them off to the highest bidders and thus returning them to the status of private property.

(e) Backward methods of production. As long as excellent soil, cheap labor, plenty of land, and favorable prices are available there is little incentive to experiment with new methods of production. According to LeBeau,

> There is perhaps no other crop with equivalent value that has received so little attention in the field of research. Thus, the coffee

4. *The Economic Development of Guatemala*, p. 37.

producer has had little or no information to draw on as a basis for changing his system of production.[5]

Recent agricultural experiments in Guatemala, however, have indicated a number of possibilities for increasing yields on the coffee plantations. For example, coffee is grown in the shade in Guatemala. The plantations contain shade trees scattered among the coffee trees, or banana stalks planted specifically to provide shade for the coffee. Experiments seem to indicate that coffee would probably grow just as well without shade. This would make it possible to plant coffee trees much closer together without diminishing the yield per tree. It would also cut down on the work of pruning trees used merely for shade. It is quite possible, however, that a shift to sun-grown coffee might also involve a series of problems not clearly foreseen at the present time, such as shorter life of the tree and greater need for fertilization. More research is needed to test the efficiency of various alternatives. Considerable work might be done in selecting better yielding trees through seed selection. Undoubtedly, research programs could point the way to increasing the efficiency of coffee production. There are indications that some of the suggested improvements are now gradually being adopted.

In this connection it is interesting to note that in August 1957, Guatemala signed an agreement with the United States to initiate a cooperative program for increasing and improving coffee production in Guatemala. The program called for the expenditure of $275,000 during the first year, of which $75,000 was to be contributed by the United States. In subsequent years the program would total $225,000 per year. The program was to be operated under the jurisdiction of a joint Guatemalan and United States committee and would depend for technical guidance on United States experts working through the *Servicio Cooperativo Interamericano de Agricultura*, a cooperative agency between the two governments which has been in existence for a number of years for the purpose of carrying on agricultural research and extension services. The proposed program is divided into four parts, as follows:

1. Training of technicians and production supervisors to introduce better techniques for cultivation.
2. Research to discover better-yielding varieties and strains that would grow best in the sun without the traditional tree shade. Also, research on disease control, on utilization of fertilizers, and on improved methods of processing the bean.
3. Extension services to teach growers in the field better ways of

5. LeBeau, op. cit., p. 28.

cultivation; and the promotion of increased output through several means, including new legislation.

4. Expansion of production by finding new areas fit for cultivation.[6]

In 1960, Guatemala, like some other Latin American countries, was suffering from a severe economic depression due to the declining prices of coffee. It was reported that African production was increasing and undercutting the prices on the world market of coffee grown in the Americas. If this competition should continue, Guatemala may have to consider seriously the disadvantages of having her international trade dependent largely on one crop, and explore the possibilities of developing other important products for which her excellent soil and varied climate might be eminently suitable.

Banana plantations

Bananas constitute the second most important export crop in Guatemala and usually account for about 10 per cent of the value of all exports. Commercial production is controlled largely by two fruit companies: the United Fruit Company and the Standard Fruit Company. The Standard Fruit does not operate any plantations in Guatemala, but merely purchases its total supply for export from independent growers.

The United Fruit Company has most of the export business in bananas and operates two major plantation areas. One is located at Bananera in the department of Izabal near the Caribbean coast on the north. The other is located at Tiquisate in the department of Escuintla near the Pacific coast.

The locations of these two plantation areas are shown in Figure 13, which gives a generalized map of the major farming regions in Guatemala.

The United Fruit plantations make use of efficient and modern techniques of production. On the Pacific coast, for example, there is an elaborate system of overhead irrigation through a permanent pipe network; and the plantations are also equipped with central pumping units for spraying against the *sigatoka*, or Panama disease, and for fertilization. Mechanization has been developed to a high degree. Each plantation area has its own network of private local roads and its system of private railway facilities. The company controls the seaport facilities at Puerto Barrios on the north coast as well as its fleet of ships for moving the bananas from Guatemala to North America. The company has controlling interest in the railway system running from the plantations to

6. Reported in the *New York Times* (Aug. 13, 1957), p. 35.

the seaport. It maintains a research program to provide the latest information about control of banana diseases and other related problems.

In 1955 the company reported that it was employing 8,654 persons in Guatemala, the vast majority of whom were native Guatemalans. It is generally recognized that higher wages are paid on United Fruit Company plantations than on other plantations in Guatemala, and a good

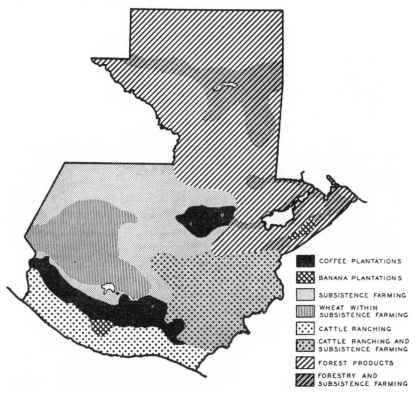

COFFEE PLANTATIONS

BANANA PLANTATIONS

SUBSISTENCE FARMING

WHEAT WITHIN
SUBSISTENCE FARMING

CATTLE RANCHING

CATTLE RANCHING AND
SUBSISTENCE FARMING

FOREST PRODUCTS

FORESTRY AND
SUBSISTENCE FARMING

Figure 13. Major agricultural regions. A generalized map showing roughly where major crops are grown. In nearly all cases there is overlapping among crops.

many perquisites are also included. The company maintains commissaries on its plantations and sells at reduced rates to its employees. The company maintains two hospitals, one in each plantation area for use of employees and their families. These contain some of the best medical facilities in Guatemala. The hospital at Quiriguá serving the Bananera area, has 160 beds while the one at Tiquisate has 320. The company maintains on its payroll 19 doctors and has 18 dispensaries at different locations on the plantations. In 1955 the company treated 14,984 patients in its hospitals and 196,190 in the dispensaries. These treatments included 1,028 major operations and 22,135 minor ones. Housing and schools for workers' families are provided of a quality that far surpasses those available on the coffee plantations (see Plate 9).

Commercial banana production requires a great deal of capital and resources with which to confront emergencies. The threats of banana disease, principally the Panama disease, and damage by windstorms are always lurking within the realm of possibility. At any time either or both of these could cause crop failure. When Panama disease strikes hard it may ruin the land for future banana production. The company claims that in 1955 it lost 2,901,232 stems of bananas. Of this number 1,900,000 were lost through heavy winds causing "blowdown" on the farms. Most of the wind damage was caused by unexpected, freakish storms during the month of May. As presently operated, the banana industry in Guatemala is big business, and also risky business, requiring immense capital with which to operate and to prepare for the various contingencies that may arise.

In addition to its own activities, the United Fruit Company purchases bananas from private growers who are under contract and supervision by the company. About 30 per cent of the total banana crop is purchased from the private growers each year. Many of the bananas purchased from private growers are from plants used as shade for the coffee trees.

The size of the commercial operations of the United Fruit Company in Guatemala may be judged from the fact that during the year 1955 the company spent a total of $14,758,512 in Guatemala. Of this amount $1,764,128 was paid to government agencies, and included, among other things, import and export duties, fiscal stamps, social security, and taxes.

Despite the recognized contribution which the United Fruit Company has made to the development of the Guatemalan economy, it has also been criticized for a number of reasons, including the following:

1. It is a foreign-controlled corporation with its top officials consisting of North Americans. This has created local jealousy on the grounds that Guatemalans have little or no voice in the policies of the banana industry in their own country.

2. Vast concessions have been made in the past by the Guatemalan government to the company in the form of low taxes and low import duties on equipment, supplies, and materials imported from the United States, thus making it difficult for Guatemalans to compete.

3. The company succeeded in acquiring a virtual monopoly over the commercial production and exportation of bananas by obtaining control over the International Railways of Central America, and the docks and shipping facilities at Puerto Barrios which is Guatemala's only adequate seaport. Since in the past virtually no other forms of transportation for commercial shipping have been available in Guatemala, and since bananas constitute a perishable crop which requires immediate attention upon harvesting, it is alleged that the United Fruit Company could strangle all competitors by merely manipulating the transportation schedules so that facilities would be fully occupied when needed by others.[7]

Following the overthrow of the Arbenz government in 1954, the Guatemalan contract with the United Fruit Company was renegotiated with more favorable terms to Guatemala. Among these was a tax of 30 per cent on the profits of the company.[8]

Cattle ranches

The production of beef cattle may also be considered as a form of plantation agriculture in Guatemala. In general, beef cattle are found on the Pacific coastal plain and along the eastern border of the neighboring republics of El Salvador and Honduras (Figure 13). Whereas many farms scattered throughout the Republic maintain a few head of

7. Evidently the United States government also became convinced that the United Fruit Company was exercising a monopoly over the production, transportation, and sale of bananas from Central America. It filed an anti-trust suit against the company in 1954, charging it with monopolistic practices. A consent decree was filed on February 5, 1958, which gave the company until June 30, 1966, "to form a suitable plan for setting up a competitor capable of importing 9,000,000 stems of bananas a year into the United States." (Reported in the *New York Times*, Feb. 5, 1958.) Other provisions of the decree prohibit the company from carrying on any of the following activities:

Acting as sales or purchasing agent for any other importer of bananas destined for the United States.

Requiring a person to accept bananas either in greater quantity or lower in quality or at above market prices, with the threat of not selling to him in the future.

Requiring a banana jobber to use specified truckmen for carrying bananas from United's terminals.

Depriving customers of the option of taking delivery by either rail or truck.

Agreeing to restrict the production, purchase, transport, distribution or sale of bananas in or to the United States market. *New York Times* (Feb. 5, 1958), p. 1.

8. *Investment in Central America*, p. 175.

cattle for domestic use, commercial production is concentrated on relatively few farms. In 1950, for example, it was reported that about 60 per cent of all cattle were found on 7.0 per cent of the farms raising cattle, and these farms had, on the average, 800 head per farm.[9] The greatest number of cattle are found in the department of Escuintla, followed by the departments of Santa Rosa and Jutiapa. About one-third of all the cattle in the country are found in these three departments.

Many of the beef cattle raised in Guatemala are imported from the neighboring republic of Honduras, and to a lesser extent from Nicaragua, and brought to Guatemala for fattening on the guinea grasses of the Pacific coastal plain. Practically all of the beef cattle sold in Guatemala are grass fed. Concentrated feeds are not used except for dairy herds, mostly in the vicinity of Guatemala City.

Like the coffee plantations, most of the large cattle ranches are operated under absentee management with the daily operations supervised by administrators and foremen. Because most of the ranches are located in tropical areas where it is hot and unpleasant to live, their owners prefer to reside in Guatemala City and visit the ranches only occasionally.

Cattle production appears to be at a low level of technical development. Little or no attention is given to good breeding practices or to the problems of parasites and disease control. It is reported that cattle ticks cause severe weight losses, and there is considerable damage from other parasites. Pastures consist mostly of bunch grass which is frequently invaded by brush. Burning is the principal method of controlling brush and ticks.[10]

Land taxes are low and labor is cheap. Employees are usually given some housing facilities, permitted to use tracts of land for the growing of subsistence crops, and may, when working, receive small daily rations of corn, beans, and salt.

Guatemala does not produce enough cattle for export; hence, the industry is devoted to supplying local needs. Trading in beef cattle often takes place out in the pastures where the cattle are grazing on the ranches. Actual weights are not always taken. It is reported that animals are sometimes judged and actually sold on the basis of height alone without any reference to weight. For this reason, it is said that some producers prefer tall rangy animals to the short, stocky type. In recent years, however, there has been some tendency to improve the breeds of beef cattle. Breeding stock have been imported from the

9. LeBeau, op. cit., p. 293.
10. Ibid., p. 294.

United States and elsewhere, including breeds of Durham, Brown Swiss, and Brahmas. The more efficient production of beef cattle has also been stimulated recently by the development of a meat-packing industry geared to the export of boneless, chilled, and frozen beef. This may prove to be an important incentive to the whole cattle industry. A cattlemen's association has also been formed to promote the welfare of the industry.

About one-fourth of all the cattle slaughtered in Guatemala pass through one slaughter house located at Escuintla. Butchering begins at about ten o'clock in the evening and is usually terminated by two or three o'clock in the morning. The fresh slaughtered beef is then loaded on railway cars or trucks and taken immediately to retail markets in the larger towns. Butcher shops in the villages fly a red flag to indicate the arrival of fresh meat. Guatemalans are not heavy meat eaters, however, and it is estimated that nearly one-third of all the beef slaughtered in the entire Republic is consumed in Guatemala City.

Cattle production in Guatemala could probably be greatly increased through the use of more efficient techniques. Some observers are of the opinion that the use of supplementary feeds for fattening would permit the development of beef animals at a much younger age than is possible under the present methods. The slaughtering of younger animals would obviously liberate a great deal of land that is now customarily used for the keeping of steers up to five or six years of age. Some have suggested the cultivation of forage crops, particularly those high in protein. It has also been suggested that agricultural by-products now going to waste, such as coffee pulp, rice hulls, and cane strippings, could be used as supplementary feeds. Veterinarians believe that production could be greatly increased through control of the various diseases, parasites, and insect pests which abound in the hot climate of the Pacific coastal plain. Others claim that some of the weight loss suffered by cattle during the dry season, could be eliminated by the use of refrigerated storage in the slaughter plants which would make it possible to slaughter the animals during a season when moisture is plentiful. Some observers express the opinion that most of the guinea grass pastures along the Pacific coast are very much undergrazed. According to Arthur T. Temple, even the present pastures could carry twice as many cattle as they are now carrying.[11]

Sugar plantations

There are two general types of sugar produced in Guatemala. One is the refined sugar which requires utilization of heavy machinery for

11. *The Economic Development of Guatemala*, p. 62.

grinding and refining. The other is panela, a crude unrefined brown sugar which retains all of the molasses and requires little machinery. The refined sugar comes from sugar cane grown on plantations situated mostly along the lower Pacific piedmont area just below the coffee belt. Panela might be called home-made cane sugar, produced on small, individual plots in valleys and semi-tropical areas, wherever sugar cane will grow.

The large refineries usually have their own plantations and mills; and like other plantations have a resident labor force living with their families in compact housing clusters located near the sugar mill. The colono arrangement is quite typical. There is also some demand for seasonal work at cane-cutting time and at other rush periods. Most of the refined sugar is processed through ten fairly large sugar mills. The owners of these mills secure about 40 per cent of the sugar cane from their own farms. The remaining 60 per cent is obtained from neighboring farms which do not have mills.[12]

The amount of sugar cane processed into sugar has been increasing slightly in recent years. There were 368,000 tons of cane processed in the year 1949–50, and this increased to 567,000 tons of cane processed during the year 1953–54.[13] Modern techniques are found more frequently on the sugar plantations than on the coffee farms. Although cutting cane is still a hand operation, the planting, cultivation, and many aspects of the handling have been mechanized to a considerable degree. New varieties of plants have also been introduced.[14]

The making of panela has been described as follows:

> In typical panela production, the cane is ground in a small wooden or metal mill, sometimes powered by oxen or a water wheel. Only a fraction of the syrup is obtained. This is filtered and limed, then evaporated in simple kettles. When ready to crystallize, the mass is poured into block molds.[15]

Besides its use as sugar, panela is widely used, especially among the Indians, for making the popular alcoholic beverage known as aguardiente, a crude distilled liquor made from the fermentation of unrefined sugar.

The Mission Report claims that there is tremendous waste of molasses in the process of sugar manufacture because of a Guatemalan law which

12. LeBeau, op. cit., p. 294.
13. Ibid., p. 295.
14. Ibid., p. 33.
15. *The Economic Development of Guatemala*, pp. 102–3.

prevents it from being made into aguardiente, or rum, as in Cuba, El Salvador and other countries. According to the Report,

> Aguardiente is therefore made from *panela,* while the molasses by-product from the plantation mills must be discarded. The Mission has no explanation for this unless it is intended to protect the market for the even less efficient *panela* producers. . . .[16]

An estimated three million gallons of molasses are wasted annually because of this prohibition. This amount might be sufficient to make all of Guatemala's aguardiente and liquor and leave an excess for cattle feed.

Speculative agriculture

Another variety of plantation farming is carried on in the excellent farm land of the Pacific coastal area of Guatemala and might be called speculative agriculture.[17] It is of recent origin, making its appearance largely since the beginning of World War II to meet the shortages in certain agricultural products. As the name implies, speculative agriculture is exploitative in nature rather than developmental. These farmers are not dependent on agriculture for a living. They usually have interests in other businesses or industrial enterprises; and regard farming as a gamble for a quick profit on the side.

Speculative agriculture differs in several ways from the usual type of plantation agriculture. It is a large-scale enterprise, highly capitalistic in nature, which utilizes modern machinery and other techniques requiring large inputs of capital. When prices decline the operations are shifted to some other crop that appears to be in demand in the world markets.

Usually there are no plantation communities of permanent resident laborers on these farms. Since the future of most of the enterprises is rather uncertain, the owners prefer to rely on temporary or seasonal labor which can be used as occasion requires but can readily be discharged when not needed, or whenever the enterprise becomes unprofitable. These workers may be housed temporarily on the property but not permanently. Ordinarily large enough wages can be paid to attract the seasonal or specialized labor when wanted.

According to LeBeau, at one time or another during the past few years the following crops would qualify as speculative agriculture: citronella, lemon grass, rice, kenaf, cotton, and to some extent, cattle.[18]

16. Ibid., p. 102.

17. This is a term used by LeBeau, op. cit., pp. 296–301.

18. Ibid., p. 297. In 1960 the production of kenaf was greatly stimulated by the introduction of a kenaf fiber bag factory at Escuintla.

During World War II the production of lemon grass and citronella became highly profitable and was greatly stimulated. In 1951 prices began to decline and by 1956 there had been a shift away from them and a concentration on other crops, such as cotton. The production of cotton is increasing rather rapidly in both quantity and quality, and much of it is being exported to Japan.

These speculative agricultural enterprises generally use modern techniques, including machinery, insecticides, fertilizers, and improved seed. The crops planted and the techniques of production change in accordance with changing prices in order to realize quick profits while market prices are favorable. Like any other form of speculation, however, this type of enterprise can prove to be disastrous when an unanticipated drop in prices suddenly takes place.[19]

Milpa Agriculture

Corn or maize is to the Guatemalan what wheat is to the Western European or rice to the Oriental—the staple food crop. Although coffee is the most important commercial crop and is grown largely in two areas, maize is grown throughout Guatemala on small family plots called milpas. It is the most widely cultivated of all crops and is basic in the diet of the Guatemalan people. In most municipios, nearly every rural family cultivates its own small milpa. Except for the fact that even where corn is grown it is not always sufficient to supply the grower's own needs, milpa agriculture might be considered synonymous with subsistence agriculture.

In contrast to plantation agriculture with its large landholdings, large numbers of resident workers, and the best lands in the country, milpa agriculture is carried on by individual families on small plots wherever they happen to live. Since most of the population lives in the highland areas, this is where most of the milpa farming is done. As noted earlier, nearly half of the farms in the entire Republic consist of plots containing less than 3.5 acres of land and nearly nine out of every ten farms have less than 17.3 acres. The vast majority of these farms are devoted to some variation of milpa agriculture (see Plate 10).

Some authorities believe that corn originated in Guatemala. It appears to have been the principal food of the ancient Mayas just as it is today of the rural inhabitants of Mexico and Central America. The closest relative to corn in Guatemala is a plant known as *teosinte,* which grows wild and abundantly in several parts of the country. Although some botanists believe that teosinte is the progenitor of corn,

19. Ibid., p. 300.

Mangelsdorf, an outstanding authority, has stated that "This ancient Bat Cave [New Mexico] corn proves beyond a reasonable doubt that the ancestor of corn was corn and not, as some 19th century botanists have supposed, the wild grass teosinte." [20] Guatemala appears to have been one of the great centers of corn cultivation. There are more different varieties here than in almost any other part of the world. One of the interesting features about corn in Guatemala is the highly localized adaptation of its varieties. Corn which grows well in the United States, for example, is not wholly successful in Guatemala; and varieties that are suited to the highlands are not adapted to coastal regions only 10 to 50 miles away.

The yield of corn in Guatemala, however, is generally low. This is probably related to a number of factors, among which are the following:

(a) Many of the types of corn planted are low-yielding varieties. There has been little emphasis on systematic seed selection or seed improvement. Some agricultural specialists believe that through seed development and improvement the yields of corn in Guatemala could be more than doubled. Corn breeding programs aimed at producing hybrids especially adapted to local conditions are in progress in a number of the Latin American countries, including Guatemala.[21]

(b) Much of the land on which corn is grown in the highlands is not particularly well suited to this crop. Some of the best areas are near the coastal regions where the climate is such that more than one crop per year could be grown on the same land and where yields would probably be several times as great as they are in the highlands. But since the Indians fear that if they do not grow their own corn they may go hungry, corn is grown where it is needed rather than where it will grow best. It is found planted on all types of land including steep mountain slopes and outworn soils, a fact which contributes to low yields.

(c) There is lack of rotation of crops. One of the common practices when soil becomes depleted is to let the land "rest" for several years. It is permitted to grow up to brush or trees and in this way restore at least some of its fertility. After a period of years it is cleared and again planted to corn. Rotation of crops for soil building purposes, however, is not a common practice.

(d) Primitive techniques of production are used. Most of the farming in Guatemala is carried on by hand labor without the use of mod-

20. Paul C. Mangelsdorf, "Corn Origins Clarified," *Science News Letter* (March 6, 1954), p. 150.
21. Paul C. Mangelsdorf, "Hybrid Corn," *Scientific American* (Aug. 1951), p. 46.

ern machinery and without either animal or motor power. According to the agricultural census of 1950, only 7.2 per cent of all farms used animal power in the form of oxen, horses, or mules. Only 0.2 per cent had anything that could be called farm machinery. Plows were reported on only 7.3 per cent of the farms in 1950 (Appendix Table 6). The departments with the highest proportion having plows were Zacapa with 26.3 per cent, Huehuetenango with 22.3, and Jutiapa with 18.0 per cent. In no other department did more than 10.5 per cent of the farms have plows. The departments having the lowest percentage of plows were Totonicapán (0.1 per cent), Alta Verapaz (0.5 per cent), and Sololá (0.6 per cent). The proportion of farms having plows exceeded 3.4 per cent in only two of the six regions. These were the east with 11.9 per cent, and the west with 8.0 per cent. The vast majority of the plows in the Republic are of the homemade wooden variety (85.5 per cent). In eight departments the proportion of wooden plows exceeds 90 per cent; and in four departments, more than 95 per cent.[22]

Agricultural implements are generally hand tools of simple construction designed to be powered by human muscle. Those most widely used in the cultivation of corn are the *machete* and the planting stick. The machete is used for cutting brush, weeds, or grass and is a long, wide-bladed knife designed for chopping single-handed. It is widely distributed and finds many and varied uses. There are variations in style; some are straight while others are slightly curved at the end. Most machetes are of foreign manufacture, many of them being made in Collinsville, Connecticut. One variation which can be made out of an old machete contains a hook on the end for cutting roots.

The planting stick is made from various types of wood depending upon the particular locality. The point of the stick is hardened through burning and sometimes contains a metal point. It is widely used in the planting of corn and beans. The hoe is also quite widely used; the metal part is of foreign manufacture with the handle hewn from wood found locally.

The ax is used in areas where trees are abundant. It is also of foreign make with the handle usually supplied by the user. There is still a great deal of forest land in Guatemala. Every year trees are cut down and burned to clear the land for crops. The underbrush is first cleared with the machete and the larger trees then are cut down with the ax. The branches are trimmed off the trees and the entire vegetation is allowed to lie on the ground for a period of time in order to dry. The peasant then sets fire to the hewn materials, having cleared a place with the hoe around the outside of the entire area to keep the fire from

22. *Censo agropecuario, 1950, 3, 76.*

spreading. After the fire has burned itself out and the ashes have cooled, the land is ready for planting. Land that has been allowed to lie fallow for a number of years so that vegetation will grow and re-fertilize may be cleared again with the machete and burned in a manner similar to that which takes place on the forest land.

Arguments have been advanced for and against the burning technique as practiced in Guatemala. On the positive side it is said to be the easiest method of clearing the land. It supposedly loosens the soil and enables planting without tillage. It is said to destroy larvae and adult insects and to clear the fields of vermin. The ashes provide fertilization through potash and mineral salts.[23]

The system has been criticized for destroying the organic matter in the soil, for the destruction of forests, and for causing excessive erosion on steep slopes through the removal of vegetation. This seems especially serious in an area so mountainous as western Guatemala.

Irving E. Melhus made extensive studies of Guatemalan corn while stationed at the Guatemala Tropical Research Center maintained at Antigua for several years by Iowa State College. He describes two corn diseases that are quite widespread, corn starvation and ear rot.[24] Corn starvation, which has been known to destroy over 50 per cent of the crop, is caused by impoverished soil and by tillage methods which facilitate soil erosion. Some practices, such as the removal of plant refuse from the fields, further both causes of corn starvation.

Ear rot, which destroys or affects the quality of 2 to 12 per cent of the annual crop, is found especially in highland areas of heavy rainfall. Much of this damaged grain never reaches the market, but is fed to livestock or consumed by the family.

There is need for a great deal of research on corn culture in Guatemala since it plays such a prominent role in the economy of the country. Seed selection, methods of preparing the soil, tilling practices, harvesting methods, storage and marketing problems, and corn diseases all need careful study.

While milpa agriculture is concerned mostly with the growing of corn, it also includes products of a supplementary nature such as beans and squash, which are often planted between the rows of corn. It may also include a few chickens, possibly one or more pigs and occasionally

23. Perhaps the most thorough description of the techniques used in corn production in Guatemala is that by Stadelman for northwestern Guatemala. This has been very helpful. See Stadelman, "Maize Cultivation," in *Contributions to American Anthropology and History*, 6 (1940), 107–15.

24. Irving E. Melhus, "A Preliminary Study of the Diseases of Corn and Some Related Hosts in Guatemala," *Iowa State College Journal of Science*, 27 (1953), 530–2.

even a cow or a steer. What few cows are kept by the Indians are largely for sale as beef rather than for production of milk.

The growing of beans, like corn, is concentrated in the highlands, although they too are grown throughout the country. They form a basic part of the diet and supply vegetable proteins necessary to supplement the carbohydrates of corn. Production of beans also appears to be inefficient. According to the Mission Report,[25] the yields are only a fraction of what the land should yield with proper management. In many instances, low-yielding varieties are used and the soil does not receive proper care. As is the case with corn, beans are often grown on land that might be much better adapted for other uses, but partly because of transportation difficulties and because beans are an important part of the national diet, they are grown where they are needed or used along with corn rather than where they can be grown best.

According to the agricultural census, there were 415,295 hogs in Guatemala in 1950. They are scattered throughout the country but generally not produced in large numbers on a commercial basis. Individual farm families may keep a few and permit them to forage around the yard. Corn is considered too precious as human food to be used for hogs, and no other feed is systematically used for this purpose. The hogs are usually scrawny and poor with no attention given to selection of breeds. Pig markets are a common feature at nearly all of the larger regional markets; and there is a considerable amount of local buying and selling. In most cases pigs are walked to market. A characteristic sight at the market is an Indian woman or man restraining three to five young pigs with a rope or string attached to each, waiting for a purchaser.

Hog production seems to offer considerable promise for the future, since about one million dollars worth of lard is imported into Guatemala each year. Agricultural experiments have been made recently with various types of feed that might be produced locally. One of these is *ramie,* a high protein forage crop which seems promising for tropical areas.[26]

The production of poultry and eggs is confined mostly to small individual farms with few large commercial flocks in the country except those now appearing in the vicinity of Guatemala City. The heaviest

25. *The Economic Development of Guatemala,* p. 45.
26. See Robert L. Squibb, et al., "Ramie—A High Protein Forage Crop for Tropical Areas," *Journal of British Grassland Society,* 9 (1954), 313–22. Other possibilities are also described by Robert L. Squibb in "Native Feedstuffs Developed by Guatemalan Research," *Foreign Agriculture,* 14 (1950), 37.

concentration of poultry is in the eastern section along the Salvadorian border and extending through the highlands. Little has been done to establish efficient breeds and build up production for commercial purposes. Also, little is known about feeds that would increase production. Generally it may be said that the breeds are poor, the feeding is not systematic, and the production is very limited. Possibilities for development along this line appear to be tremendous.

REGIONAL DOMESTIC AGRICULTURE

A number of specialized crops produced in Guatemala for regional trade do not exactly fit into the two major agricultural systems previously described. Most of these are produced on small or medium sized farms; and none are produced for the export market. They constitute small islands of regional agriculture scattered for the most part among the areas devoted largely to milpa agriculture. Wheat production is concentrated on small farms in the highlands of southwestern Guatemala as indicated in Figure 13. Considerably more than half the wheat is grown in the highlands of the two departments of San Marcos and Quezaltenango. Most of it consists of the soft varieties, since hard wheat does not grow there. The wheat is planted and harvested by hand without the aid of farm machinery. Threshing is done by driving horses over the grain and winnowing is aided by the strong winds of the region. Production is inadequate to meet national needs even though only 38 per cent of the population uses wheat bread. More than half the amount required for wheat bread must be imported almost every year, either in the form of wheat or flour. The use of wheat bread is steadily increasing.

Tobacco is grown for local and regional markets mostly by Ladinos in eastern Guatemala and in the department of Guatemala, although minor quantities are produced in all but three departments of the Republic. One-fourth of the total production comes from the department of Jutiapa. Most of the tobacco is manufactured into cigarettes to supply regional and national demands.

In addition to the commercial banana crop, numerous varieties of tropical fruits are grown for local and regional consumption. Among the most common are pineapples, oranges, mangos, papayas, cacao, aguacates, and grapes. For the most part they are grown on small farms or as supplementary crops on larger farms. Since these fruits are tropical in nature they are raised mostly in those departments which extend into the lowlands. Four-fifths (80.8 per cent) of the pineapple crop, for example, is produced in the department of Escuintla while no other department produces more than 4 per cent, although production is found in all departments except Totonicapán.

Oranges are grown in all departments but are found mostly in the departments of Guatemala, Escuintla, San Marcos, Alta Verapaz, and Sacatepéquez. Aguacate also is grown in all departments although about one-third of the total production comes from the department of Guatemala.

Commercially grown vegetables are raised on fairly small individual farms in the vicinity of Lake Atitlán, from which they are transported, often by human carrier, to local and regional markets. Extensive use is made of commercial motor boats in crossing Lake Atitlán. Human carriers and their cargos are loaded into these small boats and taken across the lake, continuing on their routes by foot to the towns, villages, and plantations located on the Pacific slope. Shipments by truck or bus are sent to Guatemala City and other large towns.

Production of rice is concentrated mostly in two major areas. The first of these is along the southeastern border near the Republic of El Salvador. Roughly two-thirds is produced in the two departments of Jutiapa and Santa Rosa. The second major area of rice production is in the west in the three adjacent departments of San Marcos, Quezaltenango, and Retalhuleu. In addition to these three major areas, there is scattered production of rice throughout all of the departments of the Republic, most of which, however, produce very little.

Owners of rice mills usually purchase the product at harvest time and then, after hulling it, sell it out as needed at much higher prices. This results in virtual monopoly of the product by the large mill owners.

Sheep are raised principally in the western highlands. There are practically none in other sections of the country (Figure 14). One-third of the sheep in the entire country are concentrated in the department of San Marcos on the border of Mexico. Another third are found in the departments of Huehuetenango and El Quiché. Goats have about the same geographical distribution, although they are much fewer in number. In 1950 there were more than 711,000 sheep as compared with only about 78,000 goats.

Few large flocks of sheep are seen in Guatemala. The industry is largely a family affair with flocks ranging in size from 3 to 25 head. The animals are grazed on whatever vegetation is available and are usually tended by one or more children of the family. There appears to be no systematic breeding for stock improvement; and usually the best appearing animals are the first ones to be sold off.

Most of the wool shorn in Guatemala is consumed at the local level.

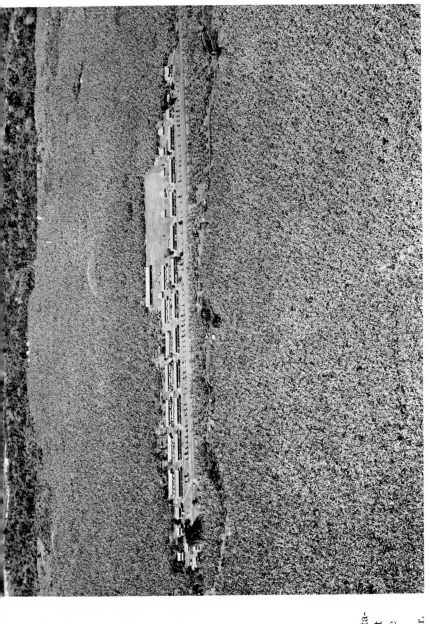

9. A sea of bananas: plantation of the United Fruit Company on the Pacific coast. Houses for the workers in upper center.

10. Milpa farming in the highlands.
Note small patches of corn.

11. Removing bark from young cinchona
tree—a source of quinine.

12. Clustered houses with thatched roofs in the Indian village of San Pedro Atitlán.

The Indians weave blankets, rugs, and other rough homespun materials, many of which are attractive in design and color. There are a few large buyers of wool in the departments of Guatemala and Quezaltenango who usually purchase the fiber through a representative sent to tour the producing areas. Quantities purchased from individual families are

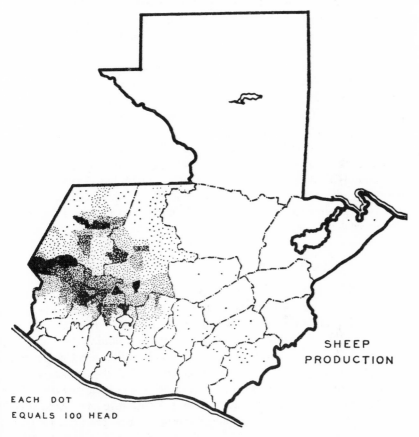

Figure 14. Geographical distribution of sheep production. Source: *Boletín* 33–34, octubre–diciembre, 1951, Dirección General de Estadística.

very small, consisting of only a few pounds. More of the local wool appears in black or gray shades than in white. In certain areas only black sheep are raised.

Guatemalan production of wool is insufficient to meet local demands and there is evidence that the sheep industry could be expanded considerably with careful management and breeding practices. The sheep generally are grazed on open pastures but flocks are confined at night to small enclosures. It is reported that parasitic infections are quite common. No use is made of dips to rid the animals of parasites and insects. It is also reported that flocks are grazed during most of the year on limited areas, with consequent damage to the land. Overgrazing on the mountainsides also results in soil erosion in some areas.

Finally, mention should be made of a few excellent dairy herds and poultry flocks that are being developed in the vicinity of Guatemala City and to a lesser extent near some of the smaller cities. While the dairy herds are few, some of them include "pure blooded" stock that demonstrate the importance of improved breeding practices if Guatemala's domestic needs for dairy products are to be satisfied. Customarily, dairy products have been imported in large amounts. In 1953, for example, the value of imported dairy products amounted to $1,333,000. Dairy cattle have been increasing in numbers and in quality, however, and the recent incorporation of a large United States dairy manufacturing concern in Guatemala will probably stimulate further development along this line. Likewise, the poultry industry has developed considerably with emphasis on broilers and on egg production. Choice breeds of poultry as well as dairy cattle have been imported from the United States.

FOREST PRODUCTS

In addition to the various types of agriculture described in this chapter, mention should be made of the closely related economic activities concerned with utilizing the extensive forest resources that abound in Guatemala. What might be called forestry exploitation is found in various parts of the country, including the Pacific coastal slope and plain; but principally in the vast, sparsely settled department of El Petén. Very little agriculture is carried on in this large area except for isolated instances of subsistence farming. The entire area is covered with forests and jungles containing important forest products (Figure 13).

One of these is chicle. This is the sap from a tree (*acharas zapota*) and is used for the manufacture of chewing gum. The importance of this product may be illustrated by the fact that in 1937 the total value of exports of chicle amounted to $306,362. This gradually increased until in 1945 the value amounted to $2,552,961. By 1956, however, the value of the product exported had declined again to $398,000.

There are no chicle plantations as such. Chicle-bearing trees are found scattered in a natural state throughout the forest and jungle areas of El Petén. Usually the chicle-producing industry is sponsored by

large buyers in the United States, such as the Wrigley Import Company
and the Chicle Development Corporation, to whom the gum is sold.
These companies deal with local contractors in Guatemala who employ
workers and then establish camps in the jungle. The camps are moved
about from one area to another depending on the supply of untapped
trees. The contractors supply provisions and furnish the collectors with
all but the most rudimentary equipment. From these camps the collectors go out into the surrounding area, locate and tap trees, collect
the sap, and boil it down into gum. The gum is delivered by the con-
tractor to the foreign purchaser who has financed in advance the entire
operation, and is transported to Puerto Barrios for shipment abroad.

Because there are no roads in these areas, transportation to and from
the chicle areas of El Petén is almost entirely by air. The gum is collected and taken to one of more than a dozen small air fields in the
forest and flown in small planes to Puerto Barrios. On the return trip
these planes bring supplies and equipment to the *chicleros* (chicle
gatherers). Tapping of the trees begins about the first of June and
continues until the end of March each year. It sometimes takes a
month or two of additional time, however, to finish collecting the gum
from the forest camps and deliver it to the airports so that it can be
sent to Puerto Barrios. Thus, work connected with chicle shipments
continues throughout most of the year.

Hundreds of chicleros are employed during the tapping season.
They are said to be well paid in comparison with other workers. This
is partly in compensation for the migratory nature of the work, which
requires long periods of absence of workers from their families, and
for the risks from exposure to tropical diseases, including fevers,
dysentery, and complications from insect bites and parasitic infections.

In recent years the production of chicle has declined and prospects
look rather dim for the future. Several factors account for this. In the
first place, the forests have been allowed to deteriorate. During years
when prices were high the trees were tapped so frequently that many
of them were either killed or their sap-producing powers destroyed.
Another and perhaps more important factor has been the development of synthetics used as substitutes for chicle at a lower cost to the
manufacturers of chewing gum.

In addition to the supply of chicle, the forests of Guatemala are also
rich in timber, principally mahogany, which is used for cabinet woods.
Such trees are found largely in the department of El Petén, although
they also exist on the Pacific slope. The absence of roads or railways
in El Petén makes it difficult to remove timber or lumber. One common
device is to float the saw logs down the rivers during flood seasons.

Many are floated down the Río de la Pasión northward to the Grijalva River and then through Mexico to the Gulf. Removal of timber for export is mostly under the sponsorship of large lumber companies in the United States.

It has been suggested in a recent study by Holdridge [27] that the Petén alone could produce about 20 million board feet of cabinet wood annually on a sustained basis, provided that adequate forestry and control practices were established and maintained, and provided that transportation facilities could be developed so that the timber could be removed. It is pointed out, however, that a great many of the practices followed up to the present time have been wasteful of the forestry resources.

Among other forest products are rubber trees upon which experiments are being made by the Guatemalan government in cooperation with the United States Department of Agriculture. It is estimated that some 2,000 acres of rubber trees could be brought into production in Guatemala in the near future. [28]

Bamboo is another forest product that may prove to be increasingly important. Certain varieties of bamboo are now used commercially for making paper, and they have long been used for structural needs in tropical areas. Their rapid growth makes them useful for quick reforestation of denuded hillsides.

Guatemalan forests contain many trees from which drug products and dyes can be extracted. During World War II considerable attention was given to the growing of *cinchona,* a quinine-producing tree in Guatemala (see Plate 11). Quinine was extracted from existing stands of trees during the war and a great many more were planted.

Although Guatemalan forests contain many plants which could yield valuable oils, drugs, dyes, extracts, and the like, for the most part their use is purely local. Except for chicle and some timber, there has been no commercial exploitation of the vast resources of the Guatemalan forests. [29] A great deal of exploration and research is needed to develop these potentially important products; but they appear to be available in sufficient quantities to justify attention by appropriate government agencies.

27. L. R. Holdridge et al., *The Forests of Guatemala* (Turrialba, Costa Rica, 1950). Cited in *The Economic Development of Guatemala,* p. 67.

28. *The Economic Development of Guatemala,* p. 71.

29. Ibid.

ETHNIC DIFFERENCES IN AGRICULTURAL PRACTICES

As previously noted, most of the plantation agriculture is under the ownership and management of the Ladinos, with Indians serving mostly as colonos and seasonal laborers. Because the ladino plantations are included in the figures, the mean average size of the ladino farms is much larger than that of the Indian. According to the 1950 census of agriculture, the average ladino farm contained 60.4 acres as compared with 7.6 acres for the average Indian farm (Appendix Table 7). The ladino farm has a larger average size in every region and department. As would be expected, the differences in size for the two groups is greatest in the areas where plantation agriculture prevails. In the south, the average ladino farm has 114.2 acres as compared with an average of 4.7 acres on Indian farms; and in the north central region, ladino farms have an average of 205.5 acres compared with 9.9 acres on Indian farms.

The ownership of large plantations by the Ladinos, however, should not obscure the fact that the farms of the majority of the Ladinos are also small. This is apparent from Table 23, which indicates that 42.0

TABLE 23. *Farm operators by size of farm and ethnic group, 1958*

Size of farm (acres)	TOTAL		INDIAN		LADINO	
	Number	Per cent	Number	Per cent	Number	Per cent
TOTAL	348,687	100.0	224,840	100.0	123,847	100.0
Under 3.5	165,850	47.5	113,844	50.6	54,006	42.0
3.5–17.2	142,223	40.8	93,870	41.8	48,353	39.0
17.3–111.4	33,041	9.5	16,391	7.3	16,650	13.5
111.5 and over	7,573	2.2	735	0.3	6,838	5.5

Source: *Censo agropecuario, 1950, 3* (1955), 117.

per cent of all ladino farms have less than 3.5 acres and 81.0 per cent less than 17.3 acres compared with 50.6 per cent and 92.4 per cent respectively for the Indians. The small size of the Indian farms in general is illustrated by the fact that the median Indian farm contains only 3.45 acres. The median ladino farm is also small (10.5 acres), but it is about three times as large as the median Indian farm.

Outside of plantation agriculture, the ladino farmers are concentrated heavily in the eastern highlands of Guatemala, while the Indian farmers predominate in the central and western highlands. A brief comparison of differences in farming in these two areas will serve to illustrate further differences in Indian and ladino agriculture.

Although the agriculture of the Ladinos in the eastern highlands is similar to that of the Indians in the western highlands, there are a number of important differences. These may be briefly summarized as follows:

1. Due to the lower density of population there is more land per person in eastern Guatemala than in the western highlands. The farms, therefore, tend to be somewhat larger. Thus, the size of the median farm in the east is 5.4 acres as compared with 3.5 acres in the west; and the farms in the east have a mean size of 27.7 acres as compared with 15.1 in the west.

2. The lower elevation and milder climate of the eastern area permit a wider variety of products to be grown than in the western highlands. For example, such products as tobacco, chile, sugar cane, and rice are grown in considerable quantities in this area. More than half of Guatemala's tobacco (56.4 per cent) is grown in the three eastern departments of Jutiapa, Chiquimula, and Jalapa.

3. There is less specialization among communities in the east than in the west. An eastern community is likely to produce a large part of the crops it needs for local consumption as well as some for sale and, hence, is not so dependent on importations. In the western highlands there is greater specialization among municipios and interchange among them.

4. Livestock plays a more important role in the economy of the eastern area than in the western highlands. Cattle and swine are more prevalent, as are horses and mules. The latter are used as beasts of burden and for riding. The human beast of burden is not so common in the east as in the western highlands. Seldom is the tumpline (a carrying strap worn across the forehead) seen here.

5. The plow is more common in the eastern area. It is found on 11.9 per cent of the farms as compared with 8 per cent in the west. Furthermore, the plows are more widely distributed in the east than in the west. Most of those in the west, 54.9 per cent, are found in the department of Huehuetenango (Appendix Table 6).

6. Fewer workers from eastern Guatemala migrate regularly to work on the plantations of the Pacific coast than from the western highlands. With more land available in their own communities they seem to find employment without such extensive migrations.

7. There is much less specialization in handicrafts in eastern Guatemala than in the western highlands.

8. One gets the impression that somewhat more modern techniques

are used in the east than in the western highlands and that there is a wider variety of crops. The climate is considerably drier and irrigation is fairly common. Some of the crops are exported to other areas. These include beans, rice, tobacco, corn, swine, and cattle.

9. There is less of a tendency for the various aspects of the agricultural cycle to be initiated through religious rites and ceremonies in the east than in the western highlands.

Chapter 8

AGRARIAN REFORM

One of the serious problems confronting Latin American countries is the inequitable distribution of available farm land. Two major contrasting types of landholding exist in Guatemala: the latifundio, or exceedingly large holding, and the minifundio, a tiny plot too small to provide a living for the owner and his family. Comparatively little land is found in holdings falling between these two extreme types.

It is not surprising, therefore, that reform governments often try to introduce programs of land reform, hoping thereby to improve the general welfare of the rural population as well as to improve the economy of the country. Such has been the situation in Guatemala since 1944.

The Guatemalan Constitution of 1945 set the stage for the land reform program which followed later during the administration of President Arbenz. This Constitution specifically prohibited latifundios and the extension of those already in existence. It provided for the expropriation of private property in the public interest, given prior indemnification, but declared that otherwise private property was guaranteed. It further stated that it was the primary function of the state to develop agricultural and industrial activities in such a manner that they would benefit the greatest number of inhabitants of the Republic.[1]

After adopting the Constitution of 1945, the government initiated various attempts to weaken the power and control of the large landowner in his relations with the renter and the farm worker.

In the first place, as we have already noted in Chapter 5, labor unions were encouraged to organize on the large plantations. With government sympathy and support they could demand benefits and privileges not previously enjoyed. The right to strike became a powerful weapon

1. *Constitución de la República de Guatemala* (1950), Arts. 88–92.

152

in the hands of the worker with which he could back up his demands for concessions from the finquero.[2]

Legislation was also adopted which was designed to force landlords to rent to others lands that were not being used. For the rental of idle lands, the owner could not charge more than 5 per cent of the annual value of the crop produced on them. This legislation became known as the Law of Forced Rental (*Ley de Arrendamiento Forzoso*). While it was intended that this law would bring into production previously unused lands lying idle on the large fincas, it would also protect the renter from undue exploitation by keeping his payments at a low level.

Evidently the law did not work out as intended, however, since it was not vigorously applied to vacant land, but largely to rentals already in existence.[3] These were found mostly among medium-sized landholders especially among the rural Ladinos of eastern Guatemala where land-leasing was rather common practice. Most of the large landowners tended to operate under the finquero-colono system and hence did not customarily rent land to others. But among the smaller farmers, where land-leasing was common, a whole cluster of customs had grown up between landowners and renters involving land tenure relationships of various types ranging from share-cropping to cash rentals; and the Law of Forced Rentals tended to destroy these relationships.[4]

Arévalo evidently was convinced of the need for an agrarian reform program, but he became involved so deeply in carrying out other reform measures that he did not get around to doing anything about the land problem. Jacobo Arbenz had repeatedly made reference to the need for land reform in his campaign speeches, however, and had committed himself to carrying out a program of this type when he took office as president in 1951.

The Agrarian Reform Law was rushed through Congress on June 17, 1952, and immediately signed by President Arbenz. The avowed purpose as stated in the preamble of the law was to bring about a substantial change in land tenure rights and in the methods of farming as a means of overcoming Guatemala's economic backwardness. It was further asserted that the purpose was also to abolish the feudal land

2. Adams, *Cultural Surveys*, p. 297.

3. One of the considerations cited in the preamble of the *Ley de reforma agraria* (Law of Agrarian Reform) adopted in 1952 was that "the laws enacted to assure the forced rental of idle lands have not satisfied fundamentally the most urgent needs of the great majority of the Guatemalan people." *Ley de reforma agraria*, Decreto número 900 (Guatemala, 1952), p. 4.

4. Adams, op. cit., p. 297. This law was abolished after the fall of the Arbenz government.

system with its "inefficient and wasteful methods of production" and to prepare the way for industrialization.[5]

THE AGRARIAN PROGRAM, 1952–54

An examination of the Agrarian Law indicates that some of its provisions appeared to be quite reasonable and appropriate to the Guatemalan situation. Others, however, gave the appearance of being politically inspired and directed toward concentrating control over land in the hands of the government.

The law provided for the expropriation of privately owned land that was not being cultivated directly by, or on behalf of, the owner. It specified, however, that no private land was to be taken that was actually being farmed by the owner or under his immediate supervision. Furthermore, no land was to be taken at all if the owner possessed less than two caballerías (223 acres) of land whether farmed or not. Thus the law, insofar as private property was concerned, appeared to be aimed mostly at large semi-feudalistic estates where much of the land was held out of production. As we have already noted, the large holdings encompassed some of the best lands in the country and it was the avowed purpose of the law to take the unused parts of these large holdings and allot them to recipients having little or no land of their own.

Government plantations, even though under cultivation, were to be broken up and allotted as plots to the workers except where the workers might be granted permission to organize cooperatives and work the land as a unit. Many Guatemalans argued that it was unwise to break up the government plantations that were producing commercial crops such as coffee, on the grounds that the plantation could be much more efficiently operated with the entire area planned as a unit than broken up into numerous smaller farms. Since the workers knew nothing about coffee culture except performance of routine tasks, it was feared that coffee production would decline, and that there would be a reversion to mere subsistence crops of corn and beans.

Nevertheless, the first lands redistributed were taken from the national fincas. In cases where the land was under cultivation, the size of the plot could vary from five manzanas (8.65 acres) to seven manzanas (12.11 acres);[6] if the land were not cultivated but tillable, the size of the plot could vary from 15 manzanas (25.95 acres) to 25 manzanas (43.25 acres). Land from the government plantations must remain the

5. *Ley de reforma agraria,* Decreto número 900, Art. 1.
6. One manzana is equal to 1.73 acres.

property of the state and the recipient would merely acquire lifetime use (*usufructo vitalicio*) of it, for which he would pay to the government as rental an amount equal to 3 per cent of the annual value of the crops raised on it.[7]

The law also provided that if there were sufficient land remaining after the needs of the workers and peasants were satisfied, nationalized lands could, on request, be leased to private individuals having capital with which to operate them, whether they were farmers or not. No person could rent more than 400 manzanas (692 acres) and would not be required to pay as rent more than 5 per cent of the value of the harvest each year.[8] The land could be leased for not less than 5 and not more than 25 years, though the lease would be extendible at the end of any period.[9] Such land could not be sublet by the renter.

Private land could be expropriated either in favor of the state or in favor of the workers. In the former case, the land would be allotted to the recipients for life-time use with the condition that the recipient pay 3 per cent of the value of the harvest each year to the government. If the land were expropriated in favor of the workers, it would be transferred to them as permanent property for which they would pay 5 per cent of the annual value of the harvest.[10]

Land allotted outright could not be sold or alienated in any way for a period of 25 years, although it could be rented to others. After 25 years, recipients would be free to dispose of the land as desired. Land distributed for life-time use of applicants could not be alienated or transferred by the recipient to any other person, although it could be rented to others by the recipient with the approval of the Agrarian Department. Upon the death of the recipient the land was to revert to the state, although the wife, children, or others economically dependent on the recipient would be given first consideration in its reassignment.

Land expropriated from private property was to be paid for by means of long term agrarian bonds; the amount of indemnity to be paid was the declared value of the property for tax purposes as recorded in the official assessment lists on May 9, 1952.[11] The assessed value of the property thus declared was to be the amount of the value of the bonds issued to the owner. In cases where no declaration had been made at any time, the value was to be determined by the average assessment of similar properties in the same general area. Payment was to

7. Ibid., Art. 27.
8. Ibid., Art. 36.
9. Ibid., Art. 37.
10. Ibid., Art. 32.
11. Ibid., Art. 6.

consist of 3 per cent interest-bearing bonds guaranteed by the govern-ment. Of different maturity dates, the maximum maturity period was to be 25 years.

One of the many problems that confront the minifundista, or very small landholder, in Guatemala is that of obtaining credit to finance his operations, small as these might be. Operating at near subsistence levels, many highland farmers find it difficult to make ends meet each year until the new crop is harvested. Some are forced to seek small loans pending the maturing of their crops. Scarcity of rural credit facilities has made loans difficult to get and resulted in exorbitant rates of interest. A study of rural credit facilities in 37 municipios made in 1950–51 by the *Instituto Indigenista Nacional* of Guatemala estimated that 10 per cent of the Indian farmers of these municipios had obtained loans of some kind during the previous year. Usually these loans were small, ranging from 5 to 100 dollars per recipient and extended over short periods of time, ordinarily not more than a few months. The rates of interest, however, were generally extremely high and computed on a monthly basis. In the 37 municipios studied the average rate of interest varied from 3.2 per cent per month to 12.6 per cent per month. The average for the 37 municipios combined was 7.9 per cent per month. This is equivalent to a yearly rate of interest amounting to 94.8 per cent.[12] Obviously, such exorbitant charges resulted in widespread hard-ship on those forced to seek loans.

As a part of the agrarian program, therefore, the government estab-lished a National Agrarian Bank to supply credit at reasonable rates to recipients of land under the agrarian program. This bank was authorized by Congress on July 11, 1953, and began functioning during that year. The initial capital of the bank was $5,200,000 which was derived from a 20 million dollar public works bond issue authorized by Congress in March of 1953.

The entire agrarian program was declared to be the immediate re-sponsibility of the President of the Republic. The President's decision was to be final.[13] In other words, there could be no recourse to the courts in the settlement of disputes concerning the applicabity of the law. This, as we shall see later, created a great deal of severe criticism and vigorous protest. Under the President, and directly responsible to him, there was organized a National Agrarian Department charged with the responsibility of putting the law into effect.

In addition to the President of the Republic and the Agrarian De-

12. Information supplied by Juan de Dios Rosales, Director, Instituto Indi-genista Nacional.
13. Ibid., Art. 59.

partment there were three committees which carried out the functions of the agrarian program. On the national level was the National Agrarian Council, consisting of nine members appointed by the President. The head of the Agrarian Department served as chairman of this Council. At the departmental level there was an agrarian commission functioning in each of the departments with the exception of El Petén. Finally, local committees functioned within the municipios and within their subdivisions. Initiation of expropriation proceedings would ordinarily begin at the local level.

Any person believing himself to be eligible to receive land under the terms of the Law could denounce land that he considered eligible for expropriation. This could be denounced to the local agrarian committee and could be done orally or in writing. On receipt of this denunciation, the local agrarian committee was supposed to verify its validity by a visual inspection within a period of three days and prepare a formal document testifying thereto. If ruled eligible for expropriation, the committee would then report to the departmental agrarian commission, proposing the expropriation or nationalization of the property denounced, and its award either permanently, or for lifetime use, to the petitioners. Such requests were then passed along for final action at the national level. Field representatives of the National Agrarian Department could also initiate expropriation proceedings by denouncing lands to the departmental agrarian commissions for processing.

Although as applied to private land owners, the law appeared to be aimed mostly at their vacant and unproductive lands, there were several important exceptions. One provision permitted plots assigned by the landlord for use by the colonos to be expropriated and allotted to the colonos permanently.[14] This created tremendous protest among the plantation owners who felt that it was unjust and unnecessary. It appeared to penalize most those landlords who had allotted large plots and better lands to their workers. The colono plots were not always concentrated in one part of the plantation, but were often dispersed in different locations. To confiscate them would mean that the landlord's property would be fragmented and interspersed with holdings belonging to others.

A second provision of the law, also protested vigorously by the landlords, granted to the colonos the housing in which they lived. The law required that any settlement of workers on the plantation inhabited by more than fifteen families would be designated as an urban center.

14. Article 9c lists as affectible those lands not cultivated by, or for, the owner directly.

Both the land and the dwellings would be expropriated and detached from the property of the finquero.[15] It was pointed out by the finquero that many of these workers' settlements were in the heart of the finca. Sometimes the finquero had to pass through them in order to reach his own dwelling.

One finquero claiming to represent the views of many others told the writer that he would not object to making plantation settlements public provided they were removed from the property of the finquero either through purchase of an appropriate tract of land from the finquero or by acquiring an adjacent site where such a community could be constructed. He asserted that workers for a whole region could then be grouped into a larger town with the necessary facilities, such as streets, schools, water supplies, electricity, and recreational facilities.

Finqueros generally claimed that the colonos did not want possession of these settlements or of the plots they were allowed to till. The finquero points with pride to his own paternalistic role in assuming responsibility for his permanent workers. He provides them with medicines, with repairs to their living quarters, with a source of water and fuel, with a school for their children, and with a ration of corn when needed. He claims that whenever in trouble the colono turns to him for assistance, and that the loss of this security would outweigh anything the colono could possibly gain in the form of additional freedom.

In defense of the nationalization of the plantation communities, government spokesmen contended that individual freedom could never be enjoyed by the colonos and their families so long as they were living on property of the landlord and dependent on him for housing, water, and services of various types. Nationalizing these communities would free the residents from complete domination by the landlord.

This part of the law aroused such bitter resentment on the part of landlords that in a number of instances the plantation owner burned the shacks of the workers and drove them off the plantation so that there would be no "community" to expropriate.

Many denounced the Agrarian Law as unconstitutional because it gave to the President both executive and judicial authority. This made the executive the final judge of his own decisions and denied the separation of powers prescribed by the Constitution. They were eager to see a test case taken to the courts in hopes that the entire law would be declared unconstitutional by the Supreme Court. They did

15. Article 13. Excluded from expropriation were any buildings for general use of the finca, such as warehouses, processing plants, and workshops. Also excluded were multiple structures designed as habitations for seasonal workers.

not have long to wait for just such a test. One of the first private individuals to be affected by the law appealed to the courts for an injunction against it. The Guatemalan Supreme Court through a split decision issued an injunction against the application of the Agrarian
Law to his property until the law could be studied more thoroughly.
The worst fears of the landowners were confirmed, however, when the
four Supreme Court justices who had voted for an injunction were
suddenly dismissed on the grounds of incompetence; and others appointed in their places who immediately reversed the decision. This
was convincing evidence that the executive would not tolerate interference with the functioning of the Agrarian Law by the judicial branch
of the government.

Article 91 of the law was also extremely frightening to the large landowners. As previously noted, this declared that any landowner who
opposed the application of the Agrarian Reform Law by violent or
subversive means could have his entire property expropriated and receive no indemnity whatsoever. This provision of the Act appeared to
place the landowners in a position where they could not even protest
in case they felt they were being unjustly and illegally treated. They
branded this as a totalitarian measure designed to give unlimited power
to the Chief Executive.

There was consternation among the landlords over the price to be
paid them for land expropriated for agrarian purposes. As noted earlier,
according to the law, the government would pay the equivalent of the
value of the property as declared by the owners for tax purposes at the
time of the latest assessment, prior to May 9, 1952. This date was presumably chosen so that land owners fearing expropriation could not
have their assessments changed after the law went into effect, merely
for the purpose of getting more for any land that might be taken. In
Guatemala, as elsewhere, it has been customary to get one's property
assessed at as low a rate as possible, and the large landowners have
been particularly skillful in keeping taxes low. The tax on rural properties, for example, is only three mills. This is based on the last general
declaration by the owner which, in many cases, was about three decades ago. There has been no general re-evaluation of agricultural
properties since 1931. Even at that time values of land were declared at
a very low rate. It is reported that lands taken from the United Fruit
Company had been declared by the Company to have a value for tax
purposes of $609,572; and this is what they were supposedly offered as
compensation during the expropriation proceedings. The Company,
however, claimed that the expropriated property had an actual value

of $15,854,849, which amount they demanded as compensation. In other words, the actual value of the property was supposedly 26 times as great as listed for tax purposes.

The composition of the local agrarian committees which were to initiate land reform was the subject of much criticism. The agrarian committees were set up in such a way that labor organizations would have a strong voice in the decisions. Each local agrarian committee was to consist of five members. These members would be nominated as follows: one by the departmental governor, one by the mayor of the municipio, and three by the local peasant organization or the local labor union. This meant that the committee would be made up of two representatives of the government and three representatives of persons eligible to receive land. The landowners felt that since the membership of the committees would consist largely of persons sympathetic to those wanting land, and, since there was no recourse to the courts, it would be almost impossible to get justice.

Finally, the program was severely criticized as an attempt by the government to gain control of the peasant rather than to help him. Most of the land recipients merely gained the right of lifetime use of the land distributed to them and for this they were required to pay to the government an annual rental. As will be noted in Table 24, 86 per cent of all recipients of land under the Arbenz program received only lifetime use of it rather than actual transfer of property rights. Much of the land taken from private individuals was expropriated in favor of the government, thus greatly expanding the role of the government as a landlord. Peasants receiving land became state tenants. The implications of this situation for possible political control appeared to be tremendous.

To the land hungry peasant in Guatemala the agrarian program probably looked like manna from heaven. As has been noted previously, policies of forced labor and debt peonage had been commonplace throughout most of Guatemala's history. Good farm land is scarce in the highland areas where most of the population resides and most of the Indian landholdings are pitifully small. Suddenly, the agrarian law promised land for the landless, more land for those having too little to provide a living for their families, and an end to land monopoly and exploitation by wealthy landlords. Advocates of agrarian reform spent a great deal of time traveling throughout the country, especially in the early stages of the program, explaining the "rights" of the peasants and workers under the law. The latter were made to feel that the government had suddenly acquired a genuine interest in their welfare.

In 1952, for example, the writer spent an evening at the headquarters of the National Confederation of Peasants [16] and noted the patience displayed by some of the leaders of this organization in listening to the problems of the peasants. The illiterate, bare-footed peasants sat on the floor around the walls of the rooms. Some of them had spent several days walking from their homes to reach the national capital. Their problems were many and varied. One wanted to know how he could acquire a plot of land under the agrarian law; another wanted to know how he could prevent the landlord from ejecting him; and a third wanted to know how to get a school in his community. They were listened to attentively, one by one, and in each case suggestions were made as to what might be done about it.[17] Sometimes a promise was made to send a memorandum to the Agrarian Department or to the Ministry of Education; sometimes a personal visit to the area was promised. In all cases, the peasant seemed grateful for the attention given to his problems and acted as if he had really found someone genuinely interested in his welfare. At 11:30 P.M. the national leader of the organization drove the writer to his hotel in a jeep and took several peasants along to converse with on the way back. The leader remarked that he expected to be listening to their problems until far beyond midnight.[18]

After the program gathered momentum, however, it became difficult to control. Left-wing labor organizers throughout the country urged peasants and workers to take advantage of the law and demand land. In some instances squatters (occupantes) swarmed onto private fincas and claimed parcels of land for themselves, without any legal authorization. Many such instances were reported from the department of Escuintla. It was also claimed that government agents could not, or would not, prevent infractions of the law by the agrarians.

It appeared that the land reform program was thus being converted into a tool for political agitation. Communists acquired some of the key advisory positions in the Agrarian Department and a barrage of typical communist propaganda began to occupy important space in the government controlled newspaper denouncing all critics, large landholders, and foreign imperialists. To many it began to appear that the program would probably destroy the existing economy rather than improve it. It was common knowledge that the secretary of the Com-

16. This was not an official government agency, but one toward which the Arbenz government was most sympathetic.

17. Nathan L. Whetten, "Land Reform in a Modern World," *Rural Sociology,* 19 (1954), 335.

18. This same leader was reported by the Guatemalan press to have fled to Czechoslovakia after the fall of the Arbenz government.

munist Party in Guatemala had become one of the chief advisors to President Arbenz and that his influence was primarily directed at advancing the long-run interests of International Communism.[19]

It should also be pointed out, however, that many of the personnel holding high government positions in the Arbenz regime had no connections whatsoever with communism. They were sincerely trying to serve their country by supporting a program which they believed would break up land monopoly, distribute land to the landless, promote the economic well-being of the masses, and provide a stronger foundation for the establishment of a true democracy in Guatemala.

Nevertheless, the extremists in various advisory capacities and in positions of leadership in some of the labor organizations succeeded in making their influence felt far beyond what would be expected from their relative numbers. The latter phases of the agrarian program appeared to consist largely of a widespread political appeal to the masses rather than a soundly conceived program for the benefit of the country. Instead of proceeding slowly and cautiously, the program was carried out so rapidly that there was not time to do adequate planning. Many of the lands distributed to peasants were not even measured. In many cases the recipient did not know what he was getting, and the landlord did not always know what had been taken, resulting in widespread unrest, confusion, and disorder.

In 1954, an invasion was launched from the neighboring republic of Honduras by Guatemalan exiles under the leadership of Colonel Carlos Castillo Armas. The Guatemalan army offered only token resistance and the Arbenz government was quickly overthrown. Castillo Armas assumed leadership of the new government. The Agrarian Law was immediately suspended, ostensibly as a means of helping to restore order pending reconsideration of the entire agrarian problem.[20]

The Arbenz government left official records indicating that by the end of June 1954, a total of 917,659 acres of land had been distributed to 87,569 persons under the agrarian reform program. This would be equivalent to 10.5 acres per person. It was further reported that 555,-098 acres, or 60.5 per cent of the total area distributed, were taken from private property and the rest from national, state, and municipal

19. A copy of the annual report of the secretary of the Communist Party in Guatemala to its members (February 1952) which fell into the author's possession makes this evident. The report was filled with denunciations of the "Western imperialists" and with praise for the Soviet Union and its satellites. It traced through the various programs which the communists had supposedly instigated in Guatemala and urged appeals to the masses as the way to achieve success. See Whetten, op. cit., p. 335.

20. These events will be discussed more fully in Chapter 16.

holdings (Table 24). Of those receiving land, 86.2 per cent received the land for lifetime use while only 13.8 per cent were granted actual property rights (bottom of Table 24).

TABLE 24. *Amount of land redistributed under the agrarian program from 1952 through June 1954 and number of recipients, by source of lands and type of grant*

Source of lands	NUMBER OF ACRES DISTRIBUTED, BY TYPE OF GRANT			NUMBER OF RECIPIENTS, BY TYPE OF GRANT		
	Total	For lifetime use	As property	Total	For lifetime use	As property
TOTAL	917,659	780,851	136,808	87,569	75,522	12,047
Private fincas	555,098	418,290	136,808	47,832	35,785	12,047
National fincas	235,647	235,647	—	23,222	23,222	—
State or municipal fincas	126,914	126,914	—	16,515	16,515	—
	Percentage distribution					
TOTAL		85.1	14.9		86.2	13.8
Private fincas		75.4	24.6		74.8	25.2
National fincas		100.0	—		100.0	—
State or municipal fincas		100.0	—		100.0	—

Source: Dirección General de Asuntos Agrarios in May 1958.

The accuracy of these data was seriously questioned by government officials of the Castillo Armas regime as well as by prominent laymen in Guatemala. It is claimed that most of the lands were never surveyed or identified; that such distribution may have been decreed but that in many cases actual possession did not take place; and that the official figures exaggerate the amount of land actually placed at the disposal of the *campesinos* (peasants).

At this time the writer finds it impossible to verify the accuracy of the above data or the claims regarding their exaggeration. The program was certainly in a state of confusion near the end of the Arbenz regime.

COMPARISON OF AGRARIAN REFORM IN GUATEMALA AND MEXICO

Why, one may logically ask, did the agrarian reform program of the Arbenz government fail in Guatemala, while a somewhat similar one had previously been carried out in the neighboring country of Mexico in reasonably successful fashion? What were the major similarities and differences between the two programs? Only few of these may be noted here. In some ways the Guatemalan program was actually more mild than the Mexican one, while in other ways it was more extreme. It was similar to the Mexican program in the following respects: [21]

1. Both programs were organized under the jurisdiction of the executive branch of the government and declared to be exempt from litigation in the courts.

2. Both programs operated through an agrarian department in the government responsible only to the president of the republic.

3. Both programs allowed for compensation to the landowners from whom land was taken by means of agrarian bonds to be paid to the former owners over a period of years. The price to be paid was to consist of the declared value of the property for tax purposes.

4. Both programs were to be financed through a national agrarian bank organized to supply farm credit to recipients of land.

The Guatemalan program differed from the Mexican program in the following respects:

1. The Guatemalan law specified that from private holdings only land in excess of 223 acres (2 caballerías) could be expropriated, and even then only those parts of the holdings that were not being farmed by, or on behalf of, the owner. Thus, insofar as private holdings were concerned, the Guatemalan law was aimed primarily at unused or rented land.

The Mexican program, on the other hand, called for the expropriation of all land, whether farmed or not, if needed, except for certain specified exemptions such as 100 hectares of irrigated land or 200 hectares of nonirrigated crop land; and larger amounts of pasture land or land with certain types of extensive crops. In this respect, the Mexican program was more radical than the Guatemalan one.

2. In Guatemala, the actual title to the land in 86 per cent of the cases (see Table 24) was vested in the government; the individual was merely assigned a lifetime use of it. For this use, he was required to pay to the government a certain percentage of the crop as a sort of rental, to help pay for the program. As we have seen, this was interpreted by many Guatemalans as a scheme to convert the recipients of land into tenants of the government and bring them under its control.

In the Mexican program the land became the property of the local community and there was no rental fee. The land received by the individual could be passed along to his heirs.

21. For a description of Mexico's entire agrarian reform program see Nathan L. Whetten, Rural Mexico (University of Chicago Press, 1948), chapters 7, 9–11.

3. Theoretically, in Guatemala the land could be received by a farmer either in the form of lifetime use or as an outright grant. In all cases a rental had to be paid to the government to defray costs. In the latter case, which actually involved only 13.8 per cent of the recipients (see Table 24), the land could be rented to others but could not be sold or alienated until 25 years had elapsed. After 25 years the land could be disposed of as desired.

In Mexico the land could never be rented, sold, or alienated. To do so would mean forfeiting all rights to it by the recipient so that it would revert to the community to be granted to someone else. Also, if the recipient failed to farm the land for two years in succession, it would revert to the community. The land, if not forfeited for these reasons, could be passed along to one's heirs for their lifetime use.

Thus, although there were some important differences, the two programs were roughly similar. The differences do not seem to have been great enough to guarantee success on the one hand and failure on the other. Perhaps we should look elsewhere for the explanation. To the author, it appears that the difference in the relative success of the two programs might be attributed, at least in part, to the matter of orientation.

The Mexicans were seeking a reversion to some of the indigenous landholding practices that had prevailed in Mexico prior to the Conquest and had persisted in attenuated form in isolated regions since that time. The scheme for agrarian reform was considered to be *native* to Mexico. It was initiated in 1915, before Soviet communism had even come into existence. The original purpose was declared to be one of restoring land to villages in those cases where it had subsequently been alienated illegally. From this beginning, the agrarian reform program later gathered momentum to include the redistribution of all large landholdings, with certain exceptions, to villagers who were essentially landless. Although criticized and resisted vigorously by the large Mexican and foreign landowners, the agrarian program was not generally attributed to the communists or to the influence of any foreign power. It was strictly a Mexican solution.

In Guatemala, the situation was quite the reverse. Large landowners and many other members of the middle and upper classes feared that the land reform program was actually a major step toward communization of the entire country, which might bring the people and their institutions under the control of the Soviet Union. Their fears were intensified by visits of Guatemalans to countries behind the Iron Curtain. Many of these visitors returned singing publicly the praises of international communism and denouncing Western imperialism. They quickly obtained for themselves key positions high up in the advisory councils of the Arbenz regime. Such persons were permitted to exercise decisive influence on the agrarian program as well as on other government programs. This contributed greatly to the intensification of fear and unrest at home as well as to the growing apprehension abroad, especially in the United States and adjoining Central American countries, lest international communism be establishing a permanent beachhead for its operations in the Americas. All of these fears tended to create a climate favorable to resistance which finally culminated in the invasion by the liberation army and the overthrow of the Arbenz government.

AGRARIAN REFORM UNDER CASTILLO ARMAS

The Castillo Armas government subscribed to the theory that, although land reform was an urgent need in the country, there was no necessity of expropriating lands that were in any way productive. It was pointed out that the government had large areas of unused and undeveloped land, especially along the southern coastal areas and in the north, particularly in the Petén region. It was readily acknowledged, however, that something should be done to bring into production those parts of large, privately owned, landed estates that were lying idle. The greatest need was viewed as a vigorous program of land colonization, reclamation, and resettlement. It was argued that families needing land should be colonized on land not in use instead of disrupting the productive enterprises that were already in operation.

Following the suspension of the Agrarian Law the government gave all landlords who had lost property through expropriation the right to have their cases reviewed as to legality. In most instances, decisions were favorable to the landlords. The agrarian recipients were gradually removed and the land returned to the original owners. In some cases, agrarians who felt that they had received the land in good faith from the previous government resisted evacuation and were removed by force. Some observers declare that during the Arbenz regime the government was invariably on the side of the peasants and workers in any dispute involving the landlords; and that in the post-Arbenz period just the reverse was true.

Not only were the expropriated private properties taken away from the agrarians and returned to the landlords, but the lands in production that were distributed to them from the national fincas were also taken back. It was alleged that since the agrarians knew nothing about farm management, production was seriously threatened.

Nevertheless, the government pledged itself to carry on an agrarian program; and in February 1956, Congress enacted into law Decree No. 559, called *Estatuto agrario* (Agrarian Statute). This replaced all other previous agrarian legislation. A new agency of the government was created known as *Dirección General de Asuntos Agrarios* (General Division of Agrarian Affairs) to develop and administer an agrarian resettlement program, which would replace the defunct agrarian department. The new law committed the government to continue to distribute both public and private lands to persons wanting them, needing them, and able to make efficient use of them. It was pointed out, however, that any lands distributed would have their titles legally transferred to the recipients and not merely rented to them for lifetime use as was characteristic under the Arbenz program.

Private lands were to be taken only if vacant and unused; and, even then, only upon payment to the owner of the actual market value of the property.[22] After establishing the price, payment would be made by the government, either immediately or in equal annual installments extending over a period not to exceed ten years in duration. In the latter case, the owner would receive 4 per cent interest annually on the unpaid balance. This was obviously a much more liberal policy toward the landowners than was specified in the previous agrarian law, where the price to be paid for expropriated land was the amount for which it was assessed on the books for tax purposes.

While the law provided for the possible expropriation of unused, private lands, the government showed reluctance to put this clause into effect. Instead it leaned toward a tax on unused private lands that was written into the law for those holding more than two caballerías (223 acres) of land. Allowing for certain specified exceptions, the tax was to be assessed as follows: For the first year it would vary from $0.25 per hectare (2.47 acres) to $1.25 per hectare depending on the classification of the land which was to be divided according to quality into five categories. If the land were to remain idle after the first year, the tax would increase each year by 25 per cent for five years.[23] Thus if the land continued to remain idle the tax would be doubled in five years. Landlords holding more than two caballerías would be required to file a sworn statement with the proper authorities indicating the uses made of their lands and designating which ones, if any, were vacant. These sworn statements would be examined and studied by the Department of Agrarian Affairs and if found accurate would be accepted and placed on file. If the accuracy were doubted, the statement would be returned to the owner for correction. Cases of deliberate

22. *Estatuto agrario*, Decreto número 559, Art. 46, Guatemala, 1956.
23. Ibid., Art. 61.

falsification would be referred to the proper judicial authorities for appropriate action against the owner.[24] It was assumed by the government that enforcement of this tax against unused lands would induce landlords either to start using their idle lands or dispose of them.

Land colonization and resettlement

The heart of the government's new agrarian policy was referred to as the Rural Development Program. Instead of a nationwide program, it was decided to select a few areas where intensive work would be undertaken in colonization and resettlement, such as land clearance, road construction, and the organization of new rural communities with provisions for water supply, sanitation, housing, schools, health services, agricultural credit, and supervised technical assistance. The three types of lands designated for resettlement were: (a) unused lands belonging to the government, (b) national fincas that were supposedly being farmed inefficiently, and (c) private lands which the state might subsequently acquire.

In carrying out this program, the Guatemalan government is relying heavily on assistance from the United States through the International Cooperation Administration and the International Development Service. United States advisors and technicians have played prominent roles in planning the colonization program and in supervising the various technical phases of the undertaking. It was decided to aim at developing farms large enough to support middle-class farm families rather than to allot plots so small that only a subsistence living could be obtained; hence, each farm was to include 20 acres or more of land.

Lands to be used in beginning the project included a tract of 110,000 acres transferred to the government by the United Fruit Company as a part of a general settlement growing out of the claims and counterclaims that had been pending from the activities of the Arbenz government. It is understood that extensive tracts of the Company's lands were in the process of expropriation when the Arbenz government was overthrown, and that the Company entered into an arrangement with the Castillo Armas government whereby new, unused, and uncleared land in the department of Escuintla on the west coast, at Nueva Concepción near Tiquisate, would be made available for resettlement provided that the other lands, which had been designated for expropriation, were left intact to the Company. Additional smaller tracts were taken from government-owned farms which were generally not productive.

Great care was to be taken in selecting the families to be settled, so that there would be reasonable chance of success, and so that loans

24. Gerardo Guinea, *Evolución agraria en Guatemala* (Guatemala, 1958), p. 86.

made through the Agrarian National Bank for developing the farms could be repaid. Agricultural extension workers were employed to work with the families and to teach them some of the modern techniques of farming, seed selection, and improved farm practices. In each zone of agrarian development, land was reserved for agricultural research and extension programs, schools, sanitary units, churches, markets, forestry reserves, playgrounds, recreation centers and other necessary services for the community.

The colonization program appears to be soundly conceived as an attempt to bring into production some of Guatemala's excellent lands that have remained idle for generations because of inaccessibility and lack of development. It should unquestionably result in improved farm techniques for those fortunate enough to be chosen to participate in the program.

By the end of December 1957, thirteen projects on rural development had been undertaken and five additional ones had been blocked out. All of these were situated in the undeveloped lowlands of the country. A total of 2,902 families had been settled on 55,688 hectares of land for an average of 19.2 hectares per family. The largest of these projects was that of La Concepción where 1,194 families had been settled on 23,905 hectares.

Numerous dwellings had been constructed, sanitary water supply had been provided in the form of 603 wells, 270 pumps, and numerous pipe lines. Agricultural extension agents had been employed to assist in promoting efficient and democratic community organization and to give instruction in gardening, poultry raising, and in improved techniques of farming. From all appearances, a great deal of careful planning had gone into the projects and the program had got off to a good start. The government may encounter difficulty in meeting the expense of the colonization program, which may turn out considerably higher than the present estimates. Much will probably depend on how long the United States continues to lend a helping hand and also on how long the policy of the government can remain stable.[25]

25. According to the *New York Times*, the record of development assistance to Guatemala during the regime of Carlos Castillo Armas, 1954–57, was briefly this:

1. A loan of $18,200,000 by the International Bank for Reconstruction and Development.
2. United States grants-in-aid totaling $35,865,000.
3. A United States gift of corn valued at $3,238,000.
4. United States technical assistance totaling $6,210,000.
5. Contributions of $25,950,000 toward the cost of constructing the Inter-American Highway in Guatemala.

"What this sudden influx of new money has done is startling. There is scarcely a block in downtown Guatemala City in which a new building is not rising. For

Some will criticize the program because it can accommodate such a small number of families when the need for land is apparently so widespread. This may be a crucial factor. Since the policy does not call for widespread redistribution of land, the big question for the government appears to be whether or not the present program can make the rural people feel that the government is working out a sound program for their benefit. Much may depend on what happens to farm wages and other factors which affect the welfare of rural people. Unless a large number of rural workers experience some improvement in their levels of living there probably will be frequent and continued agitation for a land program that will reach large numbers of rural people.

Other agrarian programs

In addition to land colonization and resettlement, the government distributed land to peasants in two other types of programs during the period 1955 to 1957. In one of these, small farms were distributed to the workers, each to be operated on a collective basis with ownership in common. The land involved in this program amounted to 45,834 hectares which were distributed to 8,590 recipients, an average of about 5 hectares (12.4 acres) per person. It was deemed inadvisable to divide the land into separate plots to individuals because it was considered uneconomical to operate in this fashion. The program has not been in operation long enough to evaluate its results.

In a second agrarian program, small individual plots of land were distributed in an attempt to liquidate the agrarian program of the Arbenz government. As noted previously, after the fall of the Arbenz government, many of the expropriated properties were returned to the original owners; but some were left in possession of the peasants, for which the latter would pay to the government annually an amount equal to 5 per cent of the harvest. This second program was largely a matter of granting land titles to persons permitted to keep land allotted to them by the Arbenz regime. Titles of individual ownership were distributed to 3,984 of these recipients during the period from July 2, 1955, to December 27, 1957, and involved 10,189 hectares of land, or an average of 2.6 hectares (6.4 acres) per recipient. Thus, in the total land distribution program through the Office of Agrarian Affairs during the period July 2, 1955 to December 27, 1957, a total of 15,476 people received a total of 11,691 hectares, or 7.2 hectares (17.8 acres) per recipient.

---

the first five months of this year, city permits for private building amounted to more than $6,000,000." *New York Times* (July 16, 1957), p. 53.

The Servicio Cooperativo

In addition to these various programs, other important work has been going on in Guatemala to improve the agriculture of the country. Some of this has been carried on through an organization known as the *Servicio Coopervativo Interamericano de Agricultura,* commonly known in Latin America by its initials in Spanish SCIDA. It is a cooperative program between the United States government and various Latin American countries and is organized through the Institute of Interamerican Affairs.

In Guatemala the program had its beginnings in 1942 when personnel from the United States was sent there in an effort to stimulate

TABLE 25. *Land delivered to peasants by the General Office of Agrarian Affairs from July 2, 1955, to December 27, 1957* *

Type of holding	Number of families benefited	Area of land (hectares)	Area of land per family (hectares)
TOTAL	15,475	111,691	7.2
Community holdings	8,590	45,834	5.3
Small individual plots	3,984	10,189	2.5
Agrarian development projects	2,902	55,668	19.3

Source: Dirección General de Asuntos Agrarios, *Boletín No. 2.* (Guatemala, 1958), p. 7.
* Does not include urban lots.

the production of rubber because of the shortage growing out of World War II. In 1944, other American specialists were also sent to assist in the production of quinine, the supply of which was cut off from the Orient and was found to be available in Guatemala in the small cinchona tree. The work was expanded in 1945 to include joint research by the two governments in other aspects of agriculture and was organized into a research institute known as the *Instituto Agropecuario Nacional.* This functioned reasonably well until 1949 when the Guatemalan government failed to appropriate its share of the funds for its continued support.[26] Little work was done after 1949 until 1955 when the institute was reorganized into the SCIDA. By the end of 1956 the personnel for SCIDA had been expanded to include 20 specialists from the United States and 215 Guatemalans. The institute was or-

26. Ministerio de Agricultura, *SCIDA, Informe anual 1956* (Guatemala, 1957), p. 1.

ganized into four divisions: administration, research, extension, and agricultural development. All of these functions were apart from, and in addition to, the functions of colonization carried on in cooperation with special missions of the International Cooperative Administration described previously as a part of the agrarian reform program.

Among the more important research studies conducted by SCIDA are those connected with improving coffee production. As indicated elsewhere, coffee trees are traditionally provided with shade in Guatemala. Shade trees greatly reduce the available space for the coffee trees and increase the additional labor costs of pruning and care of the shade trees. As noted earlier, experiments have shown that coffee grows well without shade; and some are of the opinion that if planted in the sun the yield could probably be increased several times.

Important work has also been done in nutrition for diary cattle, poultry, and hogs. Experiments have been conducted to improve seed selection for corn, beans, wheat, and other products; and to adapt the varieties of seed to variations in climate. Variations in soil types have been mapped, and diseases of both plants and animals have been studied.

An agricultural extension service was organized in 1955, and the first regional extension office was opened that year in Quezaltenango. Fifty-three persons were sent to the United States and other countries to acquire additional training. By the end of 1956 there were 22 regional offices operating in various parts of the country.[27] The work of the extension service, if adequately supported and continued free from politics, could play an important role in bringing about greater efficiency and increased productivity in Guatemalan agriculture.

At this writing, however, it is impossible to tell how effective the program will prove to be. In late 1959, the Guatemalan Minister of Agriculture became very critical of the SCIDA program and made repeated assertions to the effect that the United States was dominating the program and ignoring the wishes of the Guatemalans in some of the projects. As a result of the criticism, the United States announced withdrawal from the program. Nevertheless, some of the cooperative projects were still being continued under the jurisdiction of other agencies in Guatemala.

The Ydígoras government has recently transferred the Office of Agrarian Affairs from a dependency of the presidency to an office in the Ministry of Agriculture. This would seem to attach less importance to agrarian reform as a symbol of national policy. As of 1960, some land was still being distributed to peasants, although on a very small scale.

27. Ibid., p. 3.

It involved mostly unused lands taken from some of the national fincas.

In conclusion, it may be stated that much attention has been given to agrarian problems since 1945; that some progress has been made particularly in regard to land settlement on the Pacific coastal plain, and in programs of agricultural research and extension. It must also be admitted, however, that attempts at widespread agrarian reform have resulted in costly failures because of inadequate planning and inefficient administration due largely to the impact of political considerations. Thus, the agrarian problems have by no means been resolved. They will continue to demand attention as long as the vast majority of the inhabitants try to make a living on farms that are too small, using antiquated and inefficient techniques of production.

Part 3 THE LEVEL OF LIVING

Chapter 9

HOUSING AND CLOTHING

Housing

While there is tremendous contrast in the adequacy of housing facilities possessed by the various income groups in Guatemala, it may be said that the vast majority of the population has housing that is grossly inadequate in terms of modern standards of either health or convenience. This statement obviously does not apply to the small minority of middle- and upper-class families in Guatemala City and in the larger towns; or to the homes of the large landowners either in the cities or on the fincas. These have housing and furnishings comparable in quality to what would be found among similar groups almost anywhere in the Western world.

According to the 1950 Guatemalan census, over half the population

TABLE 26. *Population seven years of age and older living in ranchos, by ethnic group and rural-urban residence*

Residence and ethnic group	POPULATION SEVEN YEARS AND OVER		
	Total	Living in ranchos	
		Number	Per cent
TOTAL	2,151,869	1,129,286	52.5
Indian	1,149,026	811,610	70.6
Ladino	1,002,843	317,676	31.7
Rural	1,595,714	1,024,229	64.2
Indian	998,041	743,690	74.5
Ladino	597,673	280,539	46.9
Urban	556,155	105,057	18.9
Indian	150,985	67,920	45.0
Ladino	405,170	37,137	9.2

Source: *Sexto censo de población,* Table 31, pp. 179–80.

seven years of age and over live in ranchos, which may be roughly defined as "huts" or "shacks" and certainly represent minimal housing facilities. A rancho would ordinarily consist of one room with possibly a lean-to made of crude construction. Housing of this type is found largely among Indians, but is not unknown to Ladinos.

Thus, of the total population, 52.5 per cent live in ranchos. Of the Indians, 70.6 per cent live in this type of house, as compared with 31.7 per cent of the Ladinos. As might be expected, ranchos are found more commonly in the rural areas than in the urban where the multiple-family structure is much more prevalent. Nearly two-thirds (64.2 per cent) of the rural inhabitants live in ranchos as compared with 18.9 per cent of the urban.

Solow describes housing conditions in Guatemala as follows:

> The typical rural family—and Guatemala still has a predominantly rural economy . . . —lives in a hut built by the family out of local materials and lacking even the most primitive sanitary facilities. In urban centers, especially in Guatemala City, large areas of overcrowded and unsanitary houses can be found.[1]

Solow further points out that almost all rural houses need improvements and that many should be rebuilt. Most of them are of inferior construction, have dirt floors, and lack sanitary facilities. They usually consist of one room in which the family eats, cooks, and sleeps. They seldom have windows; and animals are often kept in the house.[2]

House construction depends to some extent upon the regional availability of materials. Wall construction consists of three main types: adobe, *bajareque* or wattle-and-daub construction, and cane stalks or poles. Adobe walls are made of sun-dried clap bricks and their manufacture is usually a local specialty. In the better houses the adobe walls are covered with a lime and gypsum plaster. Bajareque consists of a wooden frame plastered with clay and some rubble. According to Adams, bajareque was formerly used only by poor people but is becoming more common because of its earthquake-resistant qualities.[3] Where walls are made of poles or cane stalks, these are set up vertically and lashed together.

In 1949, the government made a housing survey[4] in all of the cabeceras in the Republic. These are commonly referred to as the

1. Anatole Solow, *Housing in Guatemala* (Washington, D.C., 1950), p. 3.
2. Ibid., pp. 13–14.
3. Adams, *Cultural Surveys*, p. 323.
4. Dirección General de Estadística, *Censo de la vivienda urbana, 1,* Guatemala, 1949.

urban areas although a number of them have less than 2,000 inhabitants (see Chapter 2). From this survey, some of the major characteristics of housing can be described.

The chief types of materials founds in the walls of the houses are evident from Table 27. Adobe is the principal material used in the

TABLE 27. *Materials of which dwellings are constructed in urban homes, 1949, in per cent*

Principal materials	All municipio centers (cabeceras)	Guatemala City	All other municipio centers (cabeceras)
A. Walls			
adobe	54.0	69.5	47.0
wood	13.5	9.8	15.1
bajareque	14.4	7.3	17.6
cane stalks	7.4	.5	10.5
sticks	3.0	.1	4.3
stones	.9	.2	1.2
brick	1.5	2.6	1.0
all other	5.2	9.9	3.2
unknown	.1	.1	.1
Total	100.0	100.0	100.0
B. Floors			
dirt	55.1	33.0	65.0
clay bricks	19.8	17.5	21.0
lumber	4.1	1.5	5.3
cement bricks	14.5	40.7	2.7
all other	6.3	7.1	5.8
unknown	.2	.2	.2
Total	100.0	100.0	100.0
C. Roofs			
tile	43.5	25.5	51.6
tin	31.2	65.9	15.6
straw	16.8	.4	24.1
palm leaves	4.6	.0	6.6
all other	3.7	8.1	1.9
unknown	.2	.1	.2
Total	100.0	100.0	100.0

Source: *Censo de la vivienda urbana, 1.*

walls of 54 per cent of the homes. It is used in 69.5 per cent of the dwellings of Guatemala City but in only 47 per cent of those in other cabeceras. Bajareque, wood (usually poles), and cornstalks follow in this order as being next most common. In the cabeceras outside of Guatemala City, bajareque and cornstalks are much more important than in the city, and would probably prove to be even more important in the rural districts if data were available for them.

Differences between ethnic groups are emphasized by Tumin in his study of *Caste in a Peasant Society* in the pueblo of San Luis Jilotepeque. He found that, of a total of 297 Indian homes, 64.3 per cent had bajareque wall construction, 27.3 per cent had cornstalk walls, 7.4 per cent had adobe and only 1.0 per cent had adobe and plaster. Among 114 ladino homes, on the other hand, 36.9 per cent were of adobe and plaster, 34.2 per cent of bajareque, 28.0 per cent of adobe and less than 1 per cent of cornstalk.[5]

The survey also gives information regarding the types of floors found in the dwellings of the cabeceras (Table 27). Over half of all the houses have dirt floors. In the cabeceras outside Guatemala City, about two-thirds of the dwellings have dirt floors (65 per cent). The percentage having dirt floors in the rural areas would undoubtedly be much greater.

Materials used for roofing include tile, tin and thatch (made of grass or palm leaves). According to McBryde, roofs in the highlands are made of grass or tile, the latter being much more expensive and requiring skilled labor to install. Grass is usually preferred to palm for thatching because it is more durable (see Plate 12).

Tile, tin, and straw were the most common roofing materials in the cabeceras, in that order (see Table 27). Tin was used most frequently in Guatemala City, being found on two-thirds of the roofs and tile on one-quarter. In the cabeceras outside of Guatemala City, however, half the roofs were of tile, 24.1 per cent of straw, and 15.6 per cent of tin (see Plate 13). Thatched roofs are probably much more prevalent in the rural areas than in the urban.

Because of large families and small houses, the homes tend to be crowded. Many have only one room in which the family eats, cooks, sleeps, stores its corn, and shelters its animals (Table 28). The most common type of dwelling has only one room (42.6 per cent); while more than two-thirds of all dwellings (68.5 per cent) have either one or two rooms. In the cabeceras outside of Guatemala City 71.4 per cent have not more than two rooms. Furthermore, it is quite likely that in most cases the second room merely consists of a lean-to where cooking is done.

In as many as 42.8 per cent of the dwellings, there were three or more persons per room (Table 28, Section B). In only 8.5 per cent was there one person or less per room. This is certainly a much more congested

5. Tumin, *Caste in a Peasant Society*, p. 105.

living arrangement than would be tolerated by any modern housing authority.

According to the housing survey, only about one-third of the urban dwellings had access to a public supply of water. In Guatemala City the percentage was 69, but only 15.6 per cent in other cabeceras. Dug wells supplied the water for 15.5 per cent of the dwellings; and 52.3

TABLE 28. *Number of rooms and number of persons per room in homes of urban residents, 1949*

Number of rooms and persons per room A. No. of rooms	All municipio centers (cabeceras)	Guatemala City	All other municipio centers (cabeceras)
		Per cent of dwellings	
1	42.6 ⎫ 68.5	43.3 ⎫ 61.8	42.2 ⎫ 71.4
2	25.9 ⎭	18.5 ⎭	29.2 ⎭
3	19.3	10.0	13.4
4 or more	12.2	27.4	14.1
unknown	.0	.8	1.1
Total	100.0	100.0	100.0
B. No. of persons per room			
1 or less	8.5	10.4	7.6
1–1.99	25.9	28.8	24.5
2–2.99	22.1	20.7	22.7
3–3.99	15.8 ⎫	14.9 ⎫	16.2 ⎫
4–4.99	10.6 ⎬ 42.8	10.4 ⎬ 39.4	10.7 ⎬ 44.6
5 and over	16.4 ⎭	14.1 ⎭	17.7 ⎭
unknown	.7	.7	.6
Total	100.0	100.0	100.0

Source: *Censo de la vivienda urbana, 1.*

per cent depended on other sources. All too frequently these other sources include open ponds, stagnant pools, and streams unprotected from contamination. Two-thirds of the homes are without running water. Only 30.7 per cent were without it in Guatemala City, but 84 per cent in the other municipio centers.

Scarcity of water outside of the larger towns virtually excludes any such conveniences as flush toilets, or bathing or laundry facilities. The women usually wash the clothes in streams or lakes with stones as washboards. In the larger villages a *pila* (stone or cement trough) is often available into which water flows from a pipe or stream to provide a place for the women of the neighborhood to do their washing.

Bathing is also common in the lakes and streams (see Plate 14). In some areas the steam bath is used. This is a small enclosure where stones are heated and water is poured over them. The bather strips off his clothes and crawls into the structure to absorb the steam.

Outside of the larger cities most homes lack any facilities whatsoever for sewage disposal. They also lack any means of refrigeration. Animals are kept about the yard; and opportunities for contamination of both food and drinking water are unlimited.

Household furnishings in the rural districts usually include only the barest essentials, especially in Indian homes. The fireplace often consists of three stones set on the floor in a corner of the house, or sometimes in the center of the room, with no chimney or opening for smoke to escape. Cooking is done almost entirely with wood. In many areas the constant cutting of wood for fuel has practically destroyed the forests and left the soil on the slopes exposed to severe erosion during the rainy season.

Near the hearth is a stack of pottery and other utensils: jars, colanders, griddle, dishes, and cups. Gasoline tins and imported enamel ware are often used. There is always at least one metate, on which to grind corn for *tortillas*. Wooden and gourd spoons, chocolate beaters, fire fans, gourds, baskets and nets are other forms of equipment. Furniture consists of wooden chests, gasoline packing boxes, platform beds with mats and blankets. Screens of matting are sometimes used to separate the sleeping quarters. There is generally a small altar. Ladino furniture tends to be somewhat more elaborate.[6]

The differences between Indian and ladino homes in the village of Santa Eulalia are brought out in the following description given by La Farge.

> The Ladino building par excellence is of adobe—the bricks being about 45 by 12 cm. in size—with a thatch or shingle roof . . . These houses are divided into various rooms and frequently have wooden floors, . . . well-made wooden walls, and ceilings in a few cases. Windows are large, barred, and closed with wooden shutters. There is no provision in any such house for a fire, and cooking is carried on in a purely Indian-style hut outside, over a typical Indian fire in the middle of the floor. It is so often chilly, if not downright cold, in this section that as a result everyone congregates in the kitchen and gets in the way of the cook.
>
> More than half of the Ladinos live in houses of Indian construction; but, where they have built these houses for themselves, they

6. McBryde, *Cultural and Historical Geography of Southwest Guatemala*, p. 45.

reverse the front-door—patio relationship in Spanish style. They divide their houses into rooms in one way or another, while the Indian sticks to a single room, building a separate house or shed for special uses in most cases . . . The Indians seem to have been in no way affected by Spanish or Ladino architecture, whereas the Ladinos have lost the Spanish kitchen entirely, taking over the Indian form, and in most cases, . . . have accepted Indian architecture with but slight changes.

The material culture of the poorest class of Ladinos is close to the Indian in every way, and those who are better off employ Indian servants almost entirely, which largely explains the importation of Indian cooking arrangements. Indians and Ladinos alike are now accepting utensils from the machine culture as fast as they can get them.

The Ladinos *on the whole* furnish their houses with full-sized chairs, tables and desks—and congregate in the warm kitchen to eat, where the widespreading smoke of the fire forces them down onto the floor, Indian fashion, and the low chairs and squatting stools become the only comfortable seats.[7]

According to Gillin, the following articles were found in ladino houses but not in those of the Indian: store or factory-made furniture, table service, chamber pots, piped water, pillows and pillowcases, and hand-cranked phonographs.[8]

Since most dwellings are constructed of local materials and are simply made, they are not very expensive. Sol Tax estimated the cost of building Indian houses in the following table: [9]

| | MATERIALS | LABOR | | TOTAL |
Kind of house		Materials	Building	
Bare cane, thatch	$ 2.74	$1.49	$ 1.73	$ 5.96
Mud and cane, thatch	2.74	1.49	2.23	6.46
Mass adobe, thatch	4.00	2.42	2.66	9.08
Adobe brick, thatch	9.50	.70	7.00	17.20
Adobe brick, tile	16.00	—	11.00	27.00
Adobe brick, "zinc"	60.50	—	8.00	68.50

For the country as a whole, the dwellings of Ladinos are more often located in villages and towns, whereas Indians are more likely to live in the rural areas. Where Ladinos and Indians live in the same village

7. Oliver La Farge, *Santa Eulalia: The Religion of a Chuchumatán Indian Town* (Univ. of Chicago Press, Chicago, 1947), pp. 32–3.

8. Gillin, *The Culture of Security*, p. 25.

9. Tax, *Penny Capitalism*, p. 146.

or town, the Ladinos live in the center around the plaza and the Indians on the outskirts. According to Tumin, as one moves from the center of the village there is a change to mixed ladino-Indian neighborhoods and then to almost purely Indian neighborhoods. The houses become poorer in quality as one leaves the center. Part of this is due to differences in wealth, but there is also a sociological factor in that it permits the Indian to maintain his separateness socially and culturally from the Ladino. Indians prefer privacy, whereas the Ladinos prize a more conspicuous position. Isolation also protects the Indian from being drafted for "voluntary labor" and allows him a freer use of the Indian dialect. The central position of the Ladino's house, on the other hand, strengthens his feelings of dominance. Thus, "the separation of the Indian places of residence from those of the Ladino helps to reinforce the general social separation which is institutionalized in the value systems of the two groups." [10]

Even in the larger urban centers, such as Guatemala City, the tendency remains for the better houses to be located in the center of the city. Suburbanization, as it is found in the United States, is virtually unknown in Guatemala. This may be attributed in part to the prevalence of the patio-centered house, the inhabitants of which can, in a manner of speaking, turn their backs to the street and remain indifferent to the neighborhood. These houses have persisted from colonial times and today even apartment houses preserve the patio form. Caplow describes housing in Guatemala City as being predominantly patio-centered. Another type of housing is

> the *barraca*, a one or two room dwelling with a doorway directly on the street, and no interior corridors, stairwells or open air spaces . . . [The] Census of 1921 . . . classified 43 per cent of the dwelling units in the municipio as *barracas*.[11]

Residential suburbs, so common in the United States, are just beginning to show signs of appearing in certain areas around Guatemala City, such as Tivoli.

Mention should also be made of housing conditions on the coffee fincas. Temporary workers are usually housed in unpainted wooden barracks, which are sometimes separated into rooms for each family, sometimes not. Permanent workers occasionally live in barracks, but are more likely to live in small houses (ranchos).

Of the 8,000 houses on fincas which were studied by Hoyt, over half

10. Tumin, op. cit., pp. 101–2.
11. Theodore Caplow, "The Social Ecology of Guatemala City," *Social Forces,* 28 (1949), 126.

had two rooms. Ninety per cent of the houses were occupied by one family only, but in 200 there were three or more families.[12] On some of the fincas the houses were clustered together to form a little village, called a *ranchería*, with streets and alleys; on other fincas, the houses were scattered. Forty per cent of the houses were made of wood, 90 per cent had earth floors, and 45 per cent had no windows. Construction varied with locality. In the highlands it tended to be less expensive and thatched roofs were most common, as compared with metal in other areas. Toilets were provided on 20 fincas, but were used on only 13.

The appearance of the houses and the grounds varied with the policy of the finquero. Some demanded neatness and regular garbage disposal, provided grass around the houses and were concerned about the external appearance of the workers' housing. Of the interiors, Hoyt writes:

> The inside of the houses was usually smoke-blackened, and there is little point in painting or whitewashing because of the smoke. The most common article of furniture was a chest, approximately three feet long by two and one-half feet wide, with a depth of about two feet. The best clothes are kept in these chests and any other articles which are highly prized. The workers for the most part slept on mats or petates made of vegetable fibres, and covered themselves with blankets, without pillows or sheets. A few rude chairs or tables were to be seen. In one corner of the house there was likely to be a shrine with a picture of some sacred person. Candles might be burned before this. Other pictures were rarely seen. The lighting of the houses on the fincas visited was a combination of candles and kerosene. Only one finca had electric light for all houses, though five had electricity for some. All cooking was done over an open fire.[13]

As in Mexico, inadequate housing in Guatemala is not entirely a matter of economics, although the lack of economic resources is certainly a major factor.[14] The persistence of culture patterns is exemplified in housing, where even in the better homes, the colonial style of architecture is still followed. This basic style has proved suitable for the climate, and there has been little attempt to introduce improvements in it. With regard to Indian houses, Wauchope's researches indicate

12. Elizabeth E. Hoyt, "The Indian Laborer on Guatemalan Coffee Fincas," *Inter-American Economic Affairs*, 9 (1955), 33–46.

13. Ibid., p. 36–7.

14. Nathan L. Whetten, *Rural Mexico* (Chicago, 1948), p. 302.

that in many respects they have retained pre-Columbian features and construction.[15]

Clothing

Clothing is one of the most conspicuous features of cultural differentiation in Guatemala. The Indian and the ladino groups are defined in part by the clothing they wear. Ladinos tend to wear Western dress except that, for the country as a whole, only about half of them wear shoes (49.1 per cent), while 43.1 per cent go barefoot.

According to the census of 1950, only about one-fourth of the total population of Guatemala seven years of age and over wear shoes, while 63.3 per cent go barefoot (Table 29). Sandals are worn by the remaining 12.4 per cent.

TABLE 29. *Population seven years of age and over who wear shoes, sandals, or go barefoot, 1950*

Ethnic group by residence	Total population 7 years and over	PER CENT OF POPULATION		
		Wearing shoes	Wearing sandals	Going barefoot
TOTAL	2,151,869	24.3	12.4	63.3
Indian	1,149,026	2.6	16.4	81.0
Ladino	1,002,843	49.1	7.8	43.1
Rural	1,595,714	11.6	15.2	73.2
Indian	998,041	1.5	17.3	81.2
Ladino	597,671	28.6	11.6	59.8
Urban	556,155	60.6	4.5	34.9
Indian	150,985	10.2	10.7	79.1
Ladino	405,170	79.4	2.2	18.4

Source: *Sexto censo de población,* Table 32.

As might be expected, the custom of going barefoot is much more prevalent among the rural population (73.2 per cent) than among the urban (34.9 per cent). It is also much more prevalent among the Indians (81 per cent) than among the Ladinos (43.1 per cent). Only 2.6 per cent of the Indians wear shoes.

The proportion of the total population going barefoot is shown according to municipios for the entire country in Figure 15. Comparison of this map with Figure 9 indicates rather close similarity between municipios having a large proportion of Indians and those having a

15. Robert Wauchope, *Modern Maya Houses* (Washington, D.C., 1938), pp. 159 ff.

large proportion going barefoot. Likewise, the map shows a rather close resemblance to Figure 20 where the percentage of illiteracy is shown.

Aside from its significance as an indication of the level of living, the wearing of shoes and going barefoot poses a health problem. As in

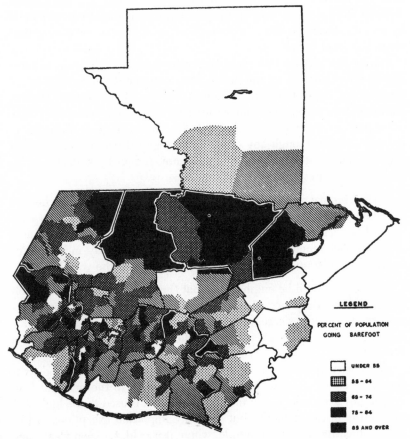

LEGEND

PER CENT OF POPULATION
GOING BAREFOOT

UNDER 55
55 - 64
65 - 74
75 - 84
85 AND OVER

Figure 15. Per cent of population seven years of age and over going barefoot, by municipios. Data from *Sexto censo de población,* 1950.

Mexico, "parasites known as *niguas* often bore into the toes under the toe nails and unless immediately removed may cause considerable damage to the toes." [16] When people go barefoot there is also danger of snake-bite in some areas, and of injuries resulting from accidents of various types.

Aside from the general lack of footwear in the rural districts, ladino

16. Whetten, op. cit., p. 324.

clothing conforms quite largely to patterns of dress elsewhere in the Western world. The middle- and upper-class males wear "white-collar" clothing including factory-made suits. They scrupulously avoid work clothing since this is generally regarded as a symbol of lower-class status. Persons struggling upward to become members of the middle class by virtue of employment in clerical or similar positions avoid wearing work clothes, even off the job. Farm people and laborers dress in overalls, khaki, or some other type of machine-made clothing purchased at local stores.

Among the Indians one finds elaborate costumes reflecting extraordinary differentiation as one moves from one municipio to another. In the western, central, and north central regions of the country, Indian clothing is so distinctive, and varies so greatly from one area to another that anyone who is familiar with the various regions of the country can wander through any of the large regional markets and readily identify the home municipio of almost any Indian by glancing at his costume. As Jones writes:

> The century-old divisions into small tribal groups and the heights which separate the lands of neighboring communities from each other seem to have perpetuated and often to have accentuated local differences and to have developed a diversity in costuming such as is found in few if any other regions of the world.[17]

Perhaps it should be emphasized that these costumes are not merely designed for special occasions, such as fiesta celebrations, visiting the market, or attending ceremonial events. They are the everyday working clothes of the Indian and often the only ones he possesses (see Plate 15).

Styles vary considerably as to length of trousers or skirt, and as to the basic colors used in the weaving, as well as to the material from which they are made. Generally speaking, wool is used in the highlands and cotton in the lowlands, but there are important exceptions to this. In Chichicastenango, for example, where it is cold, the men wear knee-length woolen trousers, while in San Marcos La Laguna, where it is much warmer, they wear woolen trousers which extend to the ankles. The women in relatively cold Chichicastenango wear knee-length cotton dresses while in much warmer Santiago Atitlán, they wear skirts of ankle length (see Plate 16).[18]

Variations in the use of clothing and textiles remain among the more persistent culture traits of the Guatemalan Indian. Undoubtedly they

17. Jones, *Guatemala, Past and Present*, p. 315.
18. Ibid., p. 315.

reflect both pre-Columbian and early Spanish influences.[19] For instance, a black wool coat found widely among the Indians in the highlands was apparently adapted from the cape-and-skirt worn by the priests. Much of the Indian ceremonial dress is copied from clothing worn by the conquistadores.

Weaving is carried on today very much as it was at the time of the Conquest. The simple stick loom is used for cotton fabrics, the foot loom usually for woolens. As described by Jones,

> Weaving is done by foot looms and hand looms, the details of their construction, like the textile products, varying from district to district. The designs characteristic of the local groups persist, though no two textile pieces are exactly alike. The weaver does not work with a pattern but carries the picture of even highly intricate designs in his head. All but a negligible fraction of the textiles are produced by weaving the design into the cloth as the work progresses. The result in the finest work carries the effect of intricate embroidery.[20]

Both men and women do weaving and embroidery. Cotton is the native fiber; wool was not used before the Conquest. Not all Indians engage in weaving. As was pointed out in Chapter 7, weaving is a specialty of some towns. For this reason, many Indians purchase their clothing or the materials for making it, either in the market or from traveling merchants.

Native dye-stuffs, though still used in many areas, are gradually giving way to imported analine dyes. The most significant aspect of dyeing is the persistence of *jaspe*, a form of tie-dyeing, usually done in blue and white. This consists of tying knots in the threads at regular intervals, after which the entire thread is dipped in the dye and then removed before the dye has had time to completely saturate the knots. This gives a most interesting shaded effect to the cloth.

Indians have only a limited quantity of clothing. Of this O'Neale writes:

> A wardrobe for ordinary wear, as we conceive of one, is unknown to an Indian man or woman. They may have complete new outfits in addition to those actually in use, but changes in costume for the mere pleasure of change is not possible for most highland people.[21]

19. McBryde, *Cultural and Historical Geography of Southwest Guatemala*, p. 48.
20. Jones, op. cit., p. 316.
21. Lila M. O'Neale, *Textiles of Highland Guatemala* (Washington, D.C., 1945), p. 105.

Very often, according to O'Neale, a woman may have only one blouse and another on the loom. Men, women, and children like to have complete new outfits for Holy Week which, as a result, becomes a very colorful occasion.

The basic items of Indian clothing are blouses, skirts, and shawls for the women; and trousers, shirts and coats for the men. Both men and women also wear elaborate sashes or woven belts. These items are subject to regional and local variations, but all are of the utmost simplicity in cut. Basically, they are all forms of rectangles. Even the men's trousers are usually made by seaming together four straight lengths of material.

> If a people change from draping woven lengths over shoulders and around hips to putting on garments, they can hardly begin with more elemental forms than the highland *huipils* [blouses] and some of the other parts of the costume.[22]

Because of its importance as a culture trait, clothing must be considered in more detail, beyond its place in the question of the level of living. Ladino dress, as has been indicated, is fairly standardized, with variation merely a matter of degree. Indian dress, however, is a part of the Indian cultural complex and the variations in it are such that they are often an index to the very village from which the Indian comes. Gillin says of the Indian dress that it

> tends to satisfy certain . . . anxieties associated with status and the attraction of the opposite sex. Indian swains regard with favor marriageable girls possessing *vestidos* [Indian costumes], but do not like that a girl should have only cotton dresses. Married women without *vestidos* suffer from social discouragements or punishments meted out by other Indian women and their husbands. Thus it is that the cotton dress is a mere utility garment adopted as an alternative on account of its lower cost.[23]

According to Gillin, the Indians also attach a magical significance to clothing and, for this reason, sometimes bury it when it is discarded.[24]

The most distinctive variations in Indian dress are found in the west and southwest highlands, although the basic items of clothing remain the same throughout these regions. The huipil, or blouse, varies in design from one area to another. Usually it is made by sewing several rectangular strips of cloth together along the sides and then making a

22. Ibid., p. 311.
23. Gillin, op. cit., pp. 35–6.
24. Ibid., p. 39.

hole in the middle for the head. If the huipil is wide, the sides extend over the arm to make rather airy sleeves. Some huipils extend only to the waist and leave a band of skin between the waist and the skirt. Others extend below the belt and may either be tucked in under the skirt or may hang loosely on the outside extending in extreme cases nearly to the knees.

> The charm of the huipil and of Guatemalan costuming in general lies in the colors and the designs woven into the fabric as well as in its cut. These show a range of stripes, diagonals, lightning patterns, and conventional figures seldom equaled in aboriginal art.[25]

The skirt is of two main types. The most common is the wrap-around skirt consisting of five or more yards of cloth wrapped rather tightly around the body and extending to the ankles. Pleated skirts are also used in some areas and these require about eight yards of cloth. While most Indian skirts extend to the ankles, there are numerous exceptions. In Zunil and Chichicastenango, for example, they extend only to the knee, while in Palín they extend half way below the knee. While variation may occur from one municipio to another, there is general uniformity within any given municipio. This is also true of other articles of Indian clothing.

The *tzute* is a decorated cloth carried by both men and women. It may serve as an article of clothing to be worn as a part of the headdress, sometimes as a shawl for women; and may be used as a hat decoration for men or as a kerchief.

In some areas the clothing of Indian men is only slightly less decorative than that of the women. They wear shirts made in much the same fashion as the women's blouses, and trousers of simple pattern, usually tied around the waist. The length varies considerably from one area to another. Some are ankle length and others extend only to the knees. Some are split up the sides with elaborate embroidery on the side flaps.[26]

Coats of European type, but more crudely made, are often worn nowadays by Indian men, but there is also a black wool coat called the *capixaij* which is something like a poncho, a large rectangle with a hole in the center for the head. When it is long it is fastened at the waist with a sash. According to Osborne, this garment was adapted from the Spanish cape-and-skirt worn by the priests.[27] In many parts of the highlands the men also wear the *rodillero,* a black and white

25. Jones, op. cit., p. 317.
26. Jones, op., cit., pp. 318–19.
27. Lilly de Jongh Osborne, *Guatemala Textiles* (New Orleans, 1935), pp. 34–5.

checked wool knee-length skirt. This is worn over trousers, and is draped around the body and tucked in at the waist. When it is not being worn it is used as a blanket or as a covering to protect loads. Men almost invariably carry knit or woven bags to hold their personal effects (see Plate 17).

Children tend to be dressed like their parents. Babies wear tight caps pulled over part of their faces. These are intended to ward off the "evil eye" and also to serve the more practical purpose of preventing the ears from sticking out (see Plate 15).

In addition to these basic articles of clothing, there are many features of dress which might be called accessories. These include the *servilleta*, or utility cloth, which is used almost universally by the Indians to cover or wrap food. It is usually lighter in color than the shawls but is otherwise hard to distinguish from them.

Sandals are generally simple leather soles, not always conforming to the shape of the foot, with single heel and toe thongs. Some models have guards over the instep. Sandals made from discarded automobile tires are becoming common in the vicinity of the larger towns. Indian women seldom wear sandals; they are usually barefooted.

Hats are never worn by Indian women and seldom by Ladinos. Indian women do, however, dress their hair in elaborate ways. The most usual consists of braiding in lengths of ribbon and wrapping the braid around the head. The most striking headdress is the "halo" of Santiago Atitlán, consisting of an inch-wide woven cotton band, over 25 feet long, usually red in color. It is wound around the head and interwoven with the hair, forming a stiff ring or halo. As a rule, men wear native straw hats, under which they often wear the tzute (kerchief).

Belts and sashes, woven or embroidered in elaborate designs, are worn by both men and women. According to Osborne, "Belts and sashes are often the only self-expression remaining in the Indian's costume." [28] Occasionally leather belts are worn and small leather bands are used to decorate hats.

Bags of an endless variety are an essential part of men's dress. Tumplines are commonly carried by Indian men, who, in contrast to women, never use baskets for carrying loads. A rain cape made of palm leaves is used during the rainy season.

Women wear elaborate necklaces of coins, figurines of silver, beads, coral and beans. Many are so heavy that they are worn only on ceremonial occasions. Some rings in the form of silver bands set with cheap stones are worn. When earrings are worn they are usually long, sometimes shoulder length. Both men's and women's clothing is ornamented

28. Ibid., p. 31.

13. Making roof tile for adobe houses (see Plate 2).

14. The stream serves as laundry and bath tub in Totonicapán.

15. Woman and child at San Ildefonso Ixtahuacán.

16. Women in bright red skirts
    carrying water from Lake Atitlán.

17. Man's typical dress at Sololá.

18. At the market in Cobán, showing typical dress of the region.

19. Mother and child in the market at Chichicastenango.

20. Village schoolboys of San Pedro Soloma.

with embroidery, and in addition men often use buttons as a form of ornamentation (see Plates 18 and 19).

Among Ladinos, the quantity of clothing owned varies to some extent with the individual but, on the whole, Ladinos own more changes of clothing than do Indians. Tumin [29] lists the clothing of ladino women as consisting of European-type housedresses, shoes, stockings, and underclothing. Unlike Indian women, they always use black, never white or colored, shawls. They wear their hair bobbed, rather than braided, and wear less jewelry than Indian women. The type of jewelry differs too. Ladino men regard a black or dark blue suit as a mark of distinction, though in the rural districts few Ladinos own one. No Indian man would wear one even if he could afford it. Neither would he wear neckties, socks, and shoes. According to Tumin,

> Aside from whatever economic circumstances enter here, Indians insist that no self-respecting Indian would ever wear shoes, even though at least some of them could afford to buy them, and many have pairs left over as souvenirs of their years of military service.[30]

Gillin [31] writes that ladino women wear only European clothing and try to keep up with the styles. For church or formal occasions they wear a black lace head covering. Only ladino women, but not all of them, wear coats. Shoes, underclothing and cosmetics are used only by ladino women. Shawls are worn by ladino women only as a wrap around the shoulders, never for carrying cloths, and are always factory-made. "The Ladino men follow European patterns on the whole although in a somewhat rustic and countrified style." [32] When ladino men go barefoot it is a sign of "demoralization and low status within the caste." [33] They may wear sandals for ordinary tasks but not for ceremonial occasions.

There is undoubtedly growing ladinoization in dress, though less perhaps than might be expected. When Indians go to work in ladino households, they may gradually adopt ladino dress. A factor here is that ladino clothing is less expensive than the Indian costume. The development of transportation and communication will continue to bring Western dress into the highlands, just as machine-made textiles are replacing hand-loomed materials.

Viewed as indices of the level of living, it appears that housing is a

29. Tumin, op. cit., p. 86.
30. Ibid., p. 89.
31. Gillin, op. cit., pp. 37–8.
32. Ibid., p. 38.
33. Ibid.

much more serious problem in Guatemala than clothing. In the urban areas, there is tremendous variability in housing ranging from the luxurious homes of some of the modern businessmen and upper income groups to the overcrowded tenements and shacks of the lower classes. In the rural areas, where most of the inhabitants live, housing is especially deficient as measured in terms of any modern standards. Large families are often crowded along with their animals into ill-equipped one-room structures. Windows are usually lacking, and sleeping facilities often consist of mats spread on the dirt floor. Cooking is commonly done over an open fire in one corner of this same room. Undoubtedly many health problems result from inadequate housing, especially in the highland areas where the climate is cool and where frosts at night are not uncommon. Clothing, on the other hand, seems to be somewhat better adapted to the needs except for the widespread practice of going barefoot.

Chapter 10

DIET AND NUTRITION

Maize as the Basic Food

As in many other countries of Latin America, maize is the basic food in Guatemala. It is grown extensively wherever people live, since they are inclined to fear that if they do not grow some of their own they may go hungry. As previously indicated, even a worker on a large commercial plantation cultivates a small patch allotted to him by the finquero. It may not yield enough corn to meet the food requirements of his family, but he derives a degree of psychological security from growing even a little.

The cultivation of maize preceded the Conquest in the New World; wheat, on the other hand, was introduced from Europe. Corn became part of the diet of the Spaniards and their mixed descendants; and a few of the Indians adopted wheat. The less urban and the less acculturated elements of the population, however, still rely much more heavily on corn than on wheat.

As shown in Table 30, only about one-fourth (24.7 per cent) of the rural inhabitants were reported in 1950 to be eating wheat bread, in contrast to more than three-fourths (77.1 per cent) of the urban population. Only one-fifth of the Indians were reported as using wheat bread in contrast to three-fifths of the Ladinos. The proportion among rural Indians is less than half of that among rural Ladinos (16.0 per cent and 39.3 per cent, respectively).

Among the regions, the largest consumption of wheat bread is in the central region, as might be expected. The lowest is in the north central region and in the west. Thus, although undoubtedly there are other factors involved, it seems obvious that the consumption of wheat bread tends to increase with degree of ladinoization or acculturation.

Wheat bread probably has not entirely supplanted corn, even among persons reported in the census to be eating wheat bread. If a person ate bread only three or four times a week, the census takers classified him as eating it, although he may actually consume more corn than wheat.[1] According to one survey, corn comprised 98 per cent of all cereals in the diets of the Indians and 95 per cent of those of the Ladinos.[2]

TABLE 30. *Consumption of wheat bread by population seven years of age and over, by ethnic group, rural-urban residence, and region, 1950, in per cent*

Region	TOTAL			INDIAN			LADINO		
	Republic	Rural	Urban	Total	Rural	Urban	Total	Rural	Urban
REPUBLIC	38.2	24.7	77.1	19.4	16.0	41.4	59.9	39.3	90.4
Central	74.1	39.9	87.1	32.6	23.1	42.4	85.7	51.1	94.9
North	51.9	37.8	80.3	21.7	12.2	79.1	59.4	46.6	80.4
East	30.9	25.6	63.8	12.6	10.9	30.0	38.5	32.3	71.9
South	45.6	36.9	79.0	30.5	26.3	59.2	57.6	47.0	86.5
West	28.4	22.4	61.5	20.4	18.1	38.7	56.6	41.7	92.6
North central	11.0	7.2	57.6	5.9	4.3	38.1	38.3	26.2	80.0

Source: *Sexto censo de población.*

The principal form in which corn is eaten is the tortilla. To prepare tortillas, a woman shells the kernels from the cob, boils them in lime water, and leaves the mixture soaking overnight to soften the hulls. Early the next morning, she rinses off the lime water and grinds the corn to a mealy paste on her grinding stone, or metate. The grinding may take from four to six hours. The paste is patted into a thin flat cake and baked on an earthen griddle (*comal*). Generally, a woman makes enough at one time to last through the day, and then warms them up as needed. In many instances, tortillas constitute a large portion of every meal.

Atole, another common form, is a thin corn gruel. It is frequently drunk at breakfast. For festive and ritual occasions, it is flavored with spices or cocoa butter.

A man may consume *posol* at work or on short trips. To prepare it, he stirs a handful of corn meal into a cup of water and drinks the concoction.

1. The census enumerated persons to be eating wheat bread if they ate it for at least one meal on the majority of the days of the week.
2. The study was made by the Carnegie Institution of Washington under the direction of Sol Tax. The field work was done by Antonio Goubaud Carrera and Juan de Dios Rosales and covered twelve rural communities of Guatemala in 1943 and 1944. It was worked up and summarized by Emma Reh of the FAO of the United Nations about 1948.

On very long journeys, he may eat *totopostes,* a thin crisp variant of tortillas. Since they contain much salt, they keep for several weeks. According to Wisdom, Indian travelers seem content to have eaten nothing but totopostes for a week or more on the road.[3]

Tamales are prepared by wrapping corn meal in corn husks or leaves and cooking them in water. For fiestas, various condiments, chicken or other meat may be wrapped inside.

Corn on the cob is eaten mostly when the young ears just become edible, during July and August. The ears may be boiled or they may be roasted on hot coals.

OTHER FOODS

Beans are the second most important food in the Guatemalan diet. A black variety is the favorite. Beans are generally boiled and are often consumed in the form of a thick black soup. Particularly among the Ladinos, the boiled beans may be mashed and cooked again in lard (*frijoles refritos*).

Coffee is drunk by both Indians and Ladinos.[4] It is toasted on the griddle with an equal amount of corn, and after the mixture is almost burned, it is boiled in water and sweetened with crude cane sugar (panela). Quantities of the beverage are consumed, particularly during breakfast and the main meal.

Meat is considered the ideal main dish, but few Guatemalan families can afford it very often. The beef cattle tend to be thin, and any visible fat is trimmed off the meat for soap and candle making. Indian families commonly keep a pig or two and a few chickens, not so much for their own consumption but to sell for cash. Some dried and salted fish is eaten, especially during Lent.

Milk is seldom consumed in liquid form except in the larger urban centers. Much of the small amount of milk that is produced is made into cheese, which can be easily preserved and transported without refrigeration.

Among the vegetables, squash, chile peppers, tomatoes, and onions are perhaps the most common. The Indians frequently eat wild plants, especially greens. There is a fairly large variety of fruits—oranges,

3. Wisdom, *The Chorti Indians of Guatemala,* p. 90.
4. Gillin points out that the Indians have taken over coffee enthusiastically from the European menu, despite its high cost. He asks if it is pure coincidence that coffee is a mild narcotic: "Here is something which gives an immediate satisfaction for which there is no substitute in the aboriginal diet." Gillin, *The Culture of Security,* p. 30.

bananas, plantains, avocados, mangos, pineapples, and so forth—but on the whole their consumption is not great.

QUANTITIES CONSUMED

Although studies of diet and nutrition are very scarce in Guatemala, a number have been conducted in rural communities recently by the Institute of Nutrition of Central America and Panama (INCAP). Several were made in the department of Sacatepéquez located near Guatemala City.

A uniform procedure was followed in each of the communities. A sample was selected from among the families of children attending school. A field worker visited each family once a day for a week. The housewife was asked what foods in what amounts were served in the preceding 24 hours. Wherever possible, the investigator weighed the food being cooked for subsequent meals and observed the actual preparation and distribution of the fare. In some instances, comparable items were prepared and weighed by the field workers away from the homes being studied.

One of the communities included in the studies was Magdalena Milpas Altas, Sacatepéquez,[5] where data were collected showing the average consumption per person during the week of various foods. The sample consisted of one ladino family and 21 Indian families. The Indian families were divided into three groups: well-to-do (*acomodado*) (6 families), moderately poor, (10 families) and poor (5 families). The single ladino family in the sample was well-to-do. The amounts were given in pounds.

It was found that with such foods as milk, meats, fruits, bananas, tubers, rice, wheat bread, and fats, the average consumption was higher for the ladino family than for the Indians. Among the Indians, the intake of these foods generally, though not consistently, descended from the well-to-do to the poor. The consumption of eggs appeared to be somewhat higher for Indians (approximately one per week) than for Ladinos in Milpas Altas; but in another community, Santo Domingo Xenocoj, the Ladinos ate much more than did the Indians.[6] Indians

5. The pueblo of Magdalena Milpas Altas had 1,092 inhabitants in 1950. Indians constituted 92 per cent of the population. The survey is reported in Marina Flores and Emma Reh, "Estudios de hábitos dietéticos en poblaciones de Guatemala: I. Magdalena Milpas Altas." *Suplemento* No. 2, *Boletín de la Oficina Sanitaria Panamericana, Publicaciones Científicas del Instituto de Nutrición de Centro América y Panamá*, pp. 90–128.

6. Marina Flores and Emma Reh, "Estudios de hábitos dietéticos en poblaciones de Guatemala: II. Santo Domingo Xenocoj," ibid., p. 138.

commonly raise chickens but sell the eggs rather than eat them, since the price of one egg is worth more than that of a pound of maize. The well-to-do Indians ate more beans and vegetables than did Ladinos and the poorer Indians. The consumption of maize tended to follow ethnic rather than economic lines. Ladinos ate an average of 5.16 pounds of maize per person per week, while the average among Indians was 8.10 pounds. The amounts consumed by the poor Indians were not markedly lower than those eaten by the others of their ethnic group. The importance of maize can be appreciated if one considers that the average Indian ate over one pound daily. The average ladino daily intake was about three-fourths of a pound per person.[7]

Nutritive Value of the Diet

Women's magazines in North America exhort housewives to serve plenty of milk, eggs, meat, fruit, and vegetables in order to safeguard the health of their families. The diet outlined above of the rural Guatemalan families would certainly seem to fall far short of such advice. However, food resources and habits vary throughout the world, and diets can differ from those recommended in the United States and yet provide adequate nutrition. Only a careful analysis of the nutritive value of the components would show whether or not the diets were really adequate.

The diet studies conducted in Guatemala by INCAP contained an analysis of the nutrients in the food known to have been eaten by the sample families over a period of a week. The values on which the computations were based were obtained through chemical analysis of native foods.[8] Standards of adequacy against which the diet findings were judged were derived from those recommended by the Food and Nutrition Board of the National Research Council (U.S.A.). In cal-

7. Quantities of the various foods consumed in Magdalena Milpas Altas showed similar patterns to those reported for other communities surveyed by INCAP. See bibliography for the references.

8. Most of the analyses were made in the laboratories of the Massachusetts Institute of Technology. See Hazel E. Munsell, et al., "Composition of Food Plants of Central America: II. Guatemala," Food Research, 15 (1950), 16–33; H. E. Munsell, et al., "Composition of Food Plants of Central America: III. Guatemala," Ibid., pp. 34–52; H. E. Munsell, et al., "Composition of Food Plants of Central America: VIII. Guatemala," ibid., pp. 439–53. Maize was the only food for which the INCAP investigators took into account loss of nutrients in cooking. Laboratory tests showed considerable loss of thiamin and riboflavin in the process of converting maize into tortillas. Hence, tortillas, not maize in raw form, were analyzed for nutritive content.

culating caloric requirements, allowances were made for age, sex, weight, and climate.

Data were computed for the 22 sample families of Magdalena Milpas Altas, according to adequacy of caloric intake and of the various nutrients consumed. Adequacy was expressed as the percentage that the amount consumed was to the recommended level. In general, the diets appeared to be more than adequate for calories, protein, calcium, iron, thiamin, and niacin. Vitamin C appeared to be adequate in only about one-third of the families. Vitamin A and riboflavin were markedly deficient, since all the families (except one in regard to vitamin A) had less than the recommended amounts. About one-third of the families had less than half of the recommended levels of these two nutrients. The amount of vitamin C consumed by the moderately poor families was adequate, but the intake among the well-to-do and the poor families was below the recommended level. In general, the adequacy of the nutrients was related to economic category.[9]

A few comments may be made concerning calories and nutrients in the diets of the Guatemalan families surveyed by INCAP.

Calories. Although the number of calories was shown to be in excess of the recommended level, there was little tendency toward obesity. The number of calories required by rural Guatemalans may be higher than the level used as the standard of adequacy. The principal source of calories is cereal foods, which provided an average of about three-fourths (74.4 per cent) of the total intake in Magdalena Milpas Altas. Sugar and beans provided about 9 per cent each of the total.

Proteins. The chief source of protein is cereal foods. They provided an average of 62 per cent of the protein consumption in Milpas Altas. Beans provided 17.8 per cent; and meats, 15.8 per cent. Proteins of vegetable sources constituted more than four-fifths (83.4 per cent) of the total protein consumption. According to nutritionists, at least one-third of the total should be animal protein. Deficiency of animal protein can lead to a serious malnutritional disease among young children known as *kwashiorkor* in Africa and Asia.[10] Vegetable proteins are low in amino acids which are essential for the growth and maintenance of the human organism. Since an increased consumption of meat is not economically feasible for most Guatemalans, investigators

9. The indices of adequacy in the other communities studied by INCAP showed the same general trend as did those in Magdalena Milpas Altas. Santo Domingo Xenocoj, however, was somewhat exceptional. In that community, riboflavin was the only nutrient deficient among all groups; and the diet of the Ladinos there was inadequate in vitamins A and C as well.

10. Described later under the heading of malnutrition.

are seeking substances which are high in amino acid content but low in cost and which can easily be added to the present diet. For example, it has been proposed that the kernels of teosinte (*Euchleana mexicana*), a close relative of corn, be ground and mixed in with wheat or corn flour.[11] Another suggestion is the addition of sesame in the preparation of tortillas.[12]

Calcium. Cereals provided an average of 87 per cent of the calcium consumed by families in Magdalena Milpas Altas. The use of lime water in the preparation of tortillas from maize appears to be responsible for the high level of calcium in the diet. It is possible for a calcium deficiency to develop among urbanized families who substitute wheat bread for tortillas without an increased consumption of milk and other calcium-rich foods. In a study made in Costa Rica, where tortillas are prepared with ashes rather than with lime water, the average percentage of adequacy of calcium in the diet was shown to be only 43 per cent.[13]

Iron. The intake of iron appears to be adequate, since it is represented by the highest percentage of adequacy among all other nutrients. Maize, beans, some greens, and crude sugar are the principal sources of iron.

Vitamin A. Nearly all the surveys in Guatemala have shown a marked deficiency of vitamin A in the diet. This nutrient is essential for growth and resistance to disease, and its deficiency can lead to a variety of symptoms. Among workers of a sugar plantation in Escuintla, a high percentage of the adults had conjunctivitis, or inflammation of the eye, *follicular hyperkeratosis,* and dry skin, symptoms indicative of a vitamin A deficiency.[14] The addition of dried ramie leaves to

11. Irving E. Melhus, Francisco Aguirre, and Nevin S. Scrimshaw, "Observations on the Nutritive Value of Teosinte," *Science,* 117, (Jan. 9, 1953), 34–5.

12. Guillermo Arroyave, *Estudios sobre el mejoramiento de la tortilla de maíz en Centro América* (Guatemala, 1955), a mimeographed publication of the Instituto de Nutrición de Centro América y Panamá.

13. Ibid., p. 11. According to Arroyave's study (p. 10), tortillas made with lime water have a higher calcium content than those made with ashes.

Tortillas made of yellow maize:	Calcium content in mg.
With lime water	107
With ashes	66
Tortillas made of white maize:	Calcium content in mg.
With lime water	83
With ashes	16

14. Emma Reh with the collaboration of Aurora Castellanos and Yolanda Bravo de Rueda, "Estudio de la dieta y de las condiciones de vida existentes entre los

tortillas has been suggested as a simple way of increasing the vitamin A content of the Guatemalan diet.[15]

Thiamin (vitamin B_1). The nutritive value computed for thiamin probably approaches the amount actually consumed, since tortillas rather than raw maize were analyzed.[16] The level of consumption of this vitamin seems adequate. The principal sources of thiamin in Magdalena Milpas Altas are cereals (70.3 per cent) and beans (15.8 per cent).

Riboflavin (vitamin B_2). Riboflavin was found to be deficient in nearly all groups studied in Guatemala. It is considered to be essential for growth, good digestion, sound nerves, defense against disease, and muscle tone. However, clinical observations in Magdalena Milpas Altas did not reveal any high incidence of symptoms traceable to a deficiency of this vitamin.

Niacin. The adequacy of niacin (a vitamin belonging to the B-complex) may be responsible for the low incidence of pellagra among the population studied. The niacin content of tortillas is quite high.[17] Cereal foods provided an average of 62.2 per cent of the total niacin intake in Magdalena Milpas Altas.

Vitamin C. Vitamin C was found to be less than adequate in a number of families studied in the diet surveys. Moreover, a certain amount of this nutrient in fresh vegetables (the chief source) is lost in cooking. Nevertheless, clinical studies of the children in Magdalena Milpas Altas did not reveal symptoms commonly associated with a vitamin C deficiency.

COST OF FOODS

The average cost per person per week of the various foods consumed by the sample families in Magdalena Milpas Altas was computed and classified according to ethnic and economic status. The values were calculated on the basis of the field workers' observations during the diet studies. In instances where the families purchased the food, the price

---

trabajadores de una plantación azucarera de Guatemala," *Boletín de la Oficina Sanitaria Panamericana,* 37 (1954), 32–52.

15. Arroyave, op. cit., pp. 17–18.

16. See footnote 8.

17. The niacin content of tortillas is higher than that of raw maize. The treatment of maize with lime water in the preparation of tortillas liberates a source of niacin which would otherwise not be available in the same amount. Flores and Reh, "Estudios de hábitos dietéticos en poblaciones de Guatemala: I. Magdalena Milpas Altas," p. 125.

paid was noted. Foods produced by the families themselves were assigned current market values. The higher the economic status of the families, the greater was the total average cost of the food. The cost for the ladino family was almost twice that among the poor Indian families, but the spread between the ladino and the well-to-do Indian families was not large. The greatest single expenditure in all categories was for cereals. It was highest in the ladino family and lowest among the poor Indians. In terms of percentages, however, the relationship was just the reverse. Cereals comprised 36 per cent of the total food cost among the ladino and well-to-do Indian families, and 40 per cent among the poor Indian families. Among the low economic groups in the other communities surveyed by INCAP in Sacatepéquez, the cost of cereals was nearly half of the total average food cost. Thus, among "very poor" Indians of Santo Domingo Xenocoj, the average cost of cereals was 46.9 per cent of the total food cost. In the aldea of San Andrés, it was 48.4 per cent. Among the "poor" families of Santa María Cauqué, the percentage was 47.9.[18]

Cereals constitute a cheap basic food which poorer families can consume in greater quantity than the relatively expensive items. According to the Institute studies, the expenditure for animal products, vegetables, fruits, and fats tended to descend with economic status. The percentage spent for beans rose as economic status went down, because beans, like corn, are another cheap basic food. The miscellaneous category did not show significant differences among the groups, perhaps because it included such items as salt, coffee, and lime (for preparing tortillas), which are essential in all Guatemalan households.

Many rural families can raise some of their own food, but they must still buy a substantial portion of what they eat. This is illustrated in Table 31, which shows the source of the various foods consumed in Magdalena Milpas Altas. The data should not be interpreted as necessarily typical of the entire year, but they give a fairly good idea of the situation in the month of May when the INCAP study was conducted. According to the table, 59 per cent of the cereals were purchased. This relatively high proportion was due to the fact that several households had exhausted their supply from the previous year's crop and therefore had to buy corn in the markets until the next harvest in December. The same explanation holds for the high percentage of beans purchased (89 per cent).[19] Milk products, eggs, and fruit were the only foods of which the inhabitants of Magdalena Milpas Altas produced a substantial proportion. Meats, bananas, tubers, sugars, fats, and miscellaneous items (including coffee) were nearly all purchased. The sole item gathered wild was vegetables, but only to the extent of 11 per cent of all vegetables consumed by the sample families.

TABLE 31. *Foods consumed by 21 sample Indian families in Magdalena Milpas Altas in May 1950, by types of food and how obtained, in per cent*

Items of food	Produced by household	Purchased
Dairy products	76	24
Meats *	2	97
Eggs	79	21
Beans	11	89
Vegetables *	36	53
Fruits	70	30
Bananas	—	100
Tubers	—	100
Cereals	41	59
Sugar	—	100
Fats	—	100
Miscellaneous	6	94

Source: Flores and Reh, "Estudios de hábitos dietéticos en poblaciones de Guatemala: I. Magdalena Milpas Altas," Table 13.

* Eleven per cent of the vegetables were "gathered" and 1 per cent of the meat was received as gifts.

Food expenditures in Guatemalan cities and towns

The proportion of family income spent on food to total family expenditures is a good index to the standard of living. Food has first claim on family incomes. Whatever income is left after the food requirements have been met can be distributed among other items, such as clothing and housing. The lower the income, the greater is the proportion of the total budget devoted to food.

We do not as yet have data on the relation of food costs to the total family budget in the rural communities of Guatemala. However, the Dirección General de Estadística conducted a study of family budgets in ten urban places in May 1953.[20] These places were, in order of their

---

ticularly high, as in the Western Highlands, the proportion of purchased maize and beans over the entire year may possibly be even higher than the seasonally influenced percentages shown in Table 31.

20. Jorge Arias B., "Estudio sobre las condiciones de vida de 776 familias en

1950 urban population, Guatemala City (284,276), Quezaltenango (27,672), Puerto Barrios (15,155), Escuintla (9,760), Chiquimula

TABLE 32. *Average annual distribution of household expenditures per family for 776 families in ten urban places in Guatemala, by income level*

Annual income level (in quetzales)	Average total per family	Food	Housing	Household furnishings	Clothing	Other
	AVERAGE EXPENDITURES PER FAMILY IN QUETZALES					
ALL LEVELS	1,462	581	285	111	223	261
Under 500	499	272	90	26	60	51
500–749	784 °	387	139	49	122	87
750–999	1,002 °	478	190	75	138	122
1,000–1,499	1,464	589	278	125	238	234
1,500–1,999	1,928	707	395	155	330	340
2,000–2,999	2,429	886	463	194	360	526
3,000–3,999	3,349	1,133	666	275	503	772
4,000–4,999	3,633	1,222	896	234	503	778
5,000 and over	5,833	1,397	1,337	340	820	1,940
	PERCENTAGE DISTRIBUTION					
ALL LEVELS		39.7	19.5	7.6	15.3	17.9
Under 500		54.6	17.9	5.2	12.1	10.2
500–749		49.4	17.7	6.2	15.6	11.1
750–999		47.6	18.9	7.5	13.8	12.2
1,000–1,499		40.2	19.0	8.6	16.3	16.0
1,500–1,999		36.7	20.5	8.0	17.1	17.7
2,000–2,999		36.5	19.1	8.0	14.8	21.6
3,000–3,999		33.8	19.9	8.2	15.0	23.1
4,000–4,999		33.6	24.7	6.4	13.8	21.4
5,000 and over		23.9	22.9	5.8	14.1	33.3

Source: Arias B., "Estudio sobre las condiciones de vida de 776 familias en 10 ciudades, 1952–53," *Boletín mensual de la Dirección General de Estadística, 3–4* (1957), Table 19. One quetzal is equal to one United States dollar.

° In these two classes the average expenditure evidently exceeded the average income.

(8,840), Cobán (7,911), Coatepeque (6,281), Huehuetenango (6,187), Jutiapa (5,162), and Flores (1,596).[21] A total of 776 families were included in the survey.

Table 32 shows the average annual expenditures for the 776 families

10 ciudades, 1952–53," *Boletín mensual de la Dirección General de Estadística,* 3–4, 1957.

21. *Sexto censo de población,* Cuadro 2, p. 5 ff.

according to the family income level. Figure 16 provides a graphic representation of the percentages given in the table.

As might be expected, the proportion of expenditures for food declined as the income level went up. Families that had less than Q500 annually [22] spent on the average somewhat more than half of their total income on food (54.6 per cent), while families who had at least Q5,000 annually spent less than one-fourth of their total income on food (23.9 per cent). The proportion of expenditures for housing

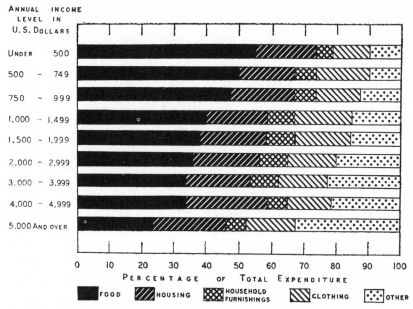

Figure 16. Per cent of annual income spent for housing, food, clothing, and other items, by size of income. Data from Table 32.

tended to rise with the income level. The proportions for clothing and household furnishings rose to a peak somewhere in the middle income levels and then declined in the higher brackets. The expenditures in the "other" category showed a definite proportionate increase as total income climbed. These would include a variety of amenities like entertainment, education, reading matter, medical services, and transportation.

The budget study conducted by the Dirección General de Estadística also showed the distribution of average weekly expenditures over the various food items, by family income level in the ten urban places. The

22. The *quetzal*, or Q, is the Guatemalan unit of exchange and is on a par with the United States dollar; i.e., one Q = one U.S. dollar.

proportion spent on cereals declined as the income level went up, as was the case in the pueblo of Magdalena Milpas Altas. The proportion spent on bread and pastries tended to rise, although it dipped sharply downward in the two of the three income categories above Q3,000. In absolute terms, the expenditure for cereals was higher than that for bread and pastries in the lowest three categories, but among families with incomes of Q1,000 or more, proportionately less was spent on cereals.

The general trend of the proportions spent on expensive items like meat, fats, dairy products, and fruits was upward as income level rose, although there were some dips in the highest income groups. In Magdalena Milpas Altas, the proportion for these items also rose, but without the dips in the highest income families, who, of course, are not likely to be found in rural communities.

The proportion spent on prepared foods did not show much difference by income level. Neither did the proportion spent on meals outside the home, except among the highest income group. The proportion spent for sugar declined as income went up, except among families with the highest incomes. The proportion spent on beverages decreased as income increased up to Q3,000, and among families above that level the trend reversed itself and went upward. The proportion expended on "other foods" showed some rise with income.

MALNUTRITION

The adequacy of the diet in Guatemala undoubtedly varies widely from one group to another in terms of economic income, education, and cultural isolation. The upper income groups in Guatemala City and elsewhere probably have a diet that is just as adequate and nutritious as that found among similar groups anywhere in the Americas. Among some of the lower income groups, however, malnutrition is certainly a serious problem and although it does not often constitute a direct cause of death, it takes a costly toll in terms of low energy output and poor resistance to disease.

According to studies made by INCAP, the principal nutritional deficiencies in Guatemala are protein of good quality, vitamin A, riboflavin, and iodine.[23] Protein builds and repairs the body tissues, so that it is particularly important for a growing child. Vitamin A and riboflavin, (vitamin B_2) are also essential to growth. Moreover, deficiency of

23. Nevin S. Scrimshaw, Moisés Behar, Carlos Pérez, and Fernando Viteri, "Nutritional Problems of Children in Central America and Panama," *Pediatrics*, *16* (1955), 378–97.

these vitamins lowers the resistance of the body to various diseases. Iodine is necessary for the prevention of goiter, which as noted in the next chapter is rather widespread in Guatemala.

The ages between one and five appear to be the most critical in terms of nutrition in Guatemala and other parts of Central America. The diets given children of these ages are often more deficient than for infants, older children, and adults of the same family. Feeding practices after weaning are poorly adapted to the child's needs. In fact, certain foods which would be beneficial are often considered improper for young children. When a child gets diarrhea, likely to be a frequent occurrence, he may be put on an even more deficient diet of thin rice-water, barley-water, or sugar-water. The diet of an older child appears to be somewhat better, for he has, in the words of the experts studying the problem, "improved his competitive position in the family and is able to obtain some food for himself." [24]

Extreme malnutrition, particularly among children between one and five, may result in bloating, muscular wasting, skin lesions, apathy, lack of appetite, and growth retardation. The part of the hair which grew during the period of severe malnutrition may be depigmented so that it appears as a light band in relation to the rest of the hair. Unless such a child is given proper treatment, he may die of a multiple deficiency disease sometimes referred to in Latin America by the name of *infantile pluricarencial syndrome*. It is identical with the disease known as *kwashiorkor* in parts of Africa, Asia, and in certain other areas of the world.[25] According to Dr. Scrimshaw and his associates, a high percentage of children in Central America are probably so poorly nourished that any further dietary deficiency or additional stress (such as a bout of infectious diarrhea) could lead to this condition.

Hopes for a weapon with which to combat malnutrition among young children in Guatemala were increased greatly late in 1959 by an announcement that an important food product of high protein quality had been developed by INCAP and placed on sale at very low cost. The new product is a powdered substance called *incaparina* after the initials of the Institute. Officials of INCAP are

> hopeful that this new product may make an important contribution to the prevention of protein malnutrition in Central America, and especially to reducing the very high rate of mortality among pre-school children.[26]

24. Ibid., p. 383.
25. Ibid., p. 386.
26. Letter to the author from Dr. Nevin S. Scrimshaw dated April 7, 1960.

The major ingredients of incaparina are cottonseed meal, corn and sorghum; all of which are found in abundance in Central America. Added to these are calcium carbonate, readily available everywhere; tortula yeast, derived from brewers yeast or molasses; and vitamin A.[27] Since incaparina is produced mostly out of local materials, it can be manufactured and sold at very low cost and does not require any change in the dietary habits of the people. The ingredients are ground to the consistency of flour and packaged into small bags, each of which may be sold for about three cents. It is soluble in water and may be used to make atole. According to Shaw, the atole made from incaparina

contains essentially the same quality and amount of protein and as much vitamin A as fresh milk. Three cents worth will provide a person with the three glasses per day needed to supplement the low protein diet on which many of the world's people are now trying to live.[28]

The problem of providing adequate nutrition for people whose incomes are at near subsistence levels is indeed a frustrating one. For this reason, the results of the important experiment in Guatemala with incaparina are eagerly awaited.

27. Richard L. Shaw, "The Flour of San Vicente: Central America Fights Malnutrition," *Americas*, 12, 1960.
28. Ibid.

Chapter 11

HEALTH AND MORTALITY

Standards of health and rates of mortality are perhaps the most adequate measures available of the general level of living in a country. If diet, clothing, housing, health practices, and medical facilities are adequate, then the incidence of disease and the rates of mortality tend to be low. From the previous chapters, we have already shown that in Guatemala the standards of nutrition and housing leave much to be desired. It remains to be seen in this chapter how these and other factors are reflected in health and mortality. The analysis of the age composition of the population in Chapter 3 gave some inkling of the conditions of mortality. The reader may recall that only a small proportion of the inhabitants were to be found in the older age groups, a fact that suggests a high death rate.

The matter of health and mortality, of course, cannot be viewed apart from Guatemala's other problems. Inadequate communication and a pattern of isolated settlements pose serious obstacles to any effort to raise the standards of health. The prevalence of illiteracy is another obstacle. If more Guatemalans could read, then knowledge of the fundamental rules of modern medicine and sanitation could be more widely disseminated. The government has to consider the fact that any program to raise the level of health—either through the improvement of communication or through the establishment of schools and rural health centers—must be realistic in terms of the financial resources of the country. So much depends on the attitude of the leaders toward the functions of government, that almost any administration in Guatemala today is likely to adhere, with varying degrees of earnestness, to the spirit expressed in one of the reform laws enacted after the overthrow of the Ubico regime:

Due to the traditional neglect of the government prior to the Revolution of October 20, 1944, there existed in Guatemala conditions of backwardness and social misery so pronounced that they make urgent and immediate the adoption of measures conducive to lifting in a systematic and gradual form the level of living of our people.[1]

DEATH RATES

The mortality rates in Guatemala indicate that the country still has a gigantic task to accomplish if the population is eventually to share in the fruits of modern technology and science. According to the *United Nations Demographic Yearbook,* only a few places had a higher crude death rate (number of deaths per 1,000 inhabitants) than did Guatemala during the period from 1940 through 1955.[2] For some of the years during that period, Guatemala's rate was either the highest or second highest. Although one may question the completeness and accuracy of the comparative data, they give some idea of the magnitude of Guatemala's health problem.

In 1955, Guatemala had a crude death rate of 20.6 per 1,000 inhabitants. This was more than twice the rate for the United States (9.3) and for Argentina (8.6) in the same year. The crude death rate for Mexico was 13.3 and for Ecuador 14.8. India had a rate of 13.1 in 1954.[3] In spite of occasional peaks, the mortality rates showed a general downward trend in Guatemala from 24.8 in 1940 to 20.6 in 1955, which would suggest that health conditions in Guatemala have improved slightly in recent years.

Since there are more adequate medical facilities in Guatemala City than in the rest of the country, one would expect a somewhat lower death rate for the capital, an assumption borne out by the data. In the three years 1949–51, the average annual rate was 17.1 for the municipio containing the capital, and it was 21.6 elsewhere in the Republic.

The crude death rate in each of the departments during 1955 is shown in Table 33. The highest rate was 27.2 in Sololá while the lowest was 15.5 in Santa Rosa. Comparison of departments shows that the higher death rates generally appear in departments having the highest

1. From the legislative decree No. 295 (1946) which created the Guatemalan Institute of Social Security, *Ley orgánica del instituto guatemalteco de seguridad social* (5th ed., Guatemala, 1957), p. 3.
2. *United Nations Demographic Yearbook* (1953), Table 9; (1956), Table 23.
3. *United Nations Demographic Yearbook* (1956), pp. 637, 639.

proportion of Indians and in those where the highest proportion of the total population live on large plantations. The relationship between high death rates and Indianism is further emphasized in a recent study by Jorge Arias B., who computed death rates for three broad groupings of municipios according to their relative proportion of Indian inhabitants. In municipios with less than 30 per cent Indians

TABLE 33. *Number of deaths per thousand inhabitants during 1955, by department*

Region and department	Deaths	Region and department	Deaths
REPUBLIC	20.6	South	
		Escuintla	26.8
Central		Retalhuleu	20.1
Guatemala	16.8	Suchitepéquez	25.7
Sacatepéquez	21.8	West	
North		Chimaltenango	24.1
El Petén	15.7	El Quiché	22.3
Izabal	23.3	Huehuetenango	20.7
East		Quezaltenango	23.2
Chiquimula	17.5	San Marcos	20.2
El Progreso	17.1	Sololá	27.2
Jalapa	16.4	Totonicapán	26.8
Jutiapa	16.1	North central	
Santa Rosa	15.5	Alta Verapaz	23.4
Zacapa	16.3	Baja Verapaz	17.3

Source: Dirección General de Estadística. *Boletín estadístico*, Nos. 7, 8, 9, 10; 1959, p. 8.

the death rate was only 17.8. This increased to 22.7 in municipios with 30–69.9 per cent Indians; and to 24.5 in municipios where 70 per cent, or more, of the population consisted of Indians.[4]

INFANT MORTALITY

The accuracy of infant mortality rates may be questioned where one suspects the vital statistics to be incomplete. The rates are generally calculated as the number of deaths of infants under one year of age per 1,000 live births. Thus, there are two possible sources of under-reporting: the registering of births and of deaths.

With these reservations in mind, one may compare Guatemala's infant mortality rates with those of other countries. A look at the *United Nations Demographic Yearbook* shows that Guatemala's are high, though some countries have even higher rates. In 1955, Guatemala had

4. Arias B., "Aspectos demográficos," *Boletín estadístico*, 1–2 (1959), 30.

101.4 deaths among infants under a year old per 1,000 live births. The infant mortality rate for Burma was 177.6; for Chile, 120.8; and Colombia, 104.2. These rates may be compared with that for the United States which was 26.5.[5]

By comparing the number of infant deaths with the total number of deaths, one possible source of error (i.e., registry of births) can be eliminated. Table 34 shows the number of deaths from 1940 to 1955

TABLE 34. *Proportion of deaths of infants under one year of age to all deaths, Guatemala and the United States, 1940 to 1955*

Year	GUATEMALA			UNITED STATES		
	All deaths	Infant deaths	Per cent	All deaths	Infant deaths	Per cent
1940	55,083	11,647	21.1	1,417,269	110,984	7.8
1945	60,332	12,310	20.4	1,401,719	104,684	.7.5
1950	61,234	15,243	24.9	1,452,454	103,825	7.1
1951	56,550	13,933	24.6	1,482,099	106,702	7.2
1952	71,994	17,036	23.7	1,496,838	109,413	7.3
1953	70,792	16,108	22.8	1,517,541	108,405	7.1
1954	58,132	14,302	24.6	1,481,091	106,791	7.2
1955	67,115	16,008	23.9	1,527,000	107,000	7.0 ·

Source: Dirección General de Estadística, *Mensaje quincenal de estadística,* No. 122 (Guatemala, April 15, 1956). *Statistical Abstract of the United States,* 1956.

for both Guatemala and the United States. The seriousness of infant mortality can be vividly appreciated if one considers that between one-fifth to one-fourth of all Guatemalans who die are infants under one year old. In the United States, only 7 per cent of the deaths were of such infants in 1955.

Seasonal variations in infant mortality show a significant pattern. The Dirección General de Estadística calculated indices based on average monthly rates during the period from 1950 to 1954 (Table 35).

TABLE 35. *Average infant mortality rate, by month, 1950–54*

	Average rate		Average rate
January	97.5	July	97.1
February	98.4	August	95.1
March	100.0	September	94.7
April	112.5	October	94.8
May	108.8	November	99.3
June	104.3	December	97.4

Source: Dirección General de Estadística, *Mensaje quincenal de estadística,* No. 122 (April 15, 1956).

5. *United Nations Demographic Yearbook* (1956), Table 26.

The indices begin to climb in January and reach their peak in April, from which month they start to decline and are lowest from July to October. The indices are ascendant during the hottest and driest months of the year, and are lowest when the rainy season is under way.

Several conditions prevalent in the dry season decrease the chances of infant survival. For one thing, excessive heat often weakens a child's resistance to illness. Moreover, food spoils quickly since most Guatemalans do not have the luxury of refrigerators. Flies are in great abundance and help to spread dysentery and other diseases which take a heavy toll among infants. Finally, drinking water, which is scarce in the dry season, is more likely to be polluted than during the rainy season.

As with the general death rates, the infant mortality rates are lower in Guatemala City than in the rest of the country. During the years 1948 through 1955, the average rate of infant mortality for the municipio of Guatemala was 89.9, while that for the rest of the country was 102.5.

As might be expected, the Indians tend to have a higher infant mortality rate than the Ladinos. In 1950, Jorge Arias B. found that for those municipios in which less than 30 per cent of the population customarily spoke an Indian language in the home, the infant mortality rate was 98.6. The rate increased to 111.3 in municipios where 30 to 69.9 per cent spoke an Indian language; and further increased to 113.4 in municipios where 70 per cent or more of the inhabitants spoke an Indian language in the home.[6]

LIFE EXPECTANCY

The figures on life expectancy can be stated from any reference point of age. We can say life expectancy at birth is x number of years in a particular country, meaning that the average native of that country can at the time of his birth be expected to live x number of years. We can also state life expectancy at any other age. For example, we can say life expectancy in that same country at the age of five is y number of years. The difference between expectancy at birth and at the age of five is not simply the passage of five calendar years but involves, among other things, probabilities of death in the intervening period. Thus, in countries where rates of mortality are high among very young children, life expectancy may even increase at the age of five. If a child has survived the hazards of his first few years, he may have a longer life expectancy at the age of five than he did at birth.

Guatemala is just such a country where the life expectancy is greater

6. Arias B., op. cit., p. 34.

at the age of five than at birth. According to Table 36, the average Guatemalan at birth could be expected to live 43.6 years, while the average native of the United States could be expected to live 68.1 years. At the age of five, the Guatemalan's life expectancy increased to 50.8, while that of the North American decreased by about two and a half years.

TABLE 36. *Life expectancy at birth and at five years of age in Guatemala and in the United States, 1949–51*

		Average future lifetime in years		
		GUATEMALA		UNITED STATES
Sex		At birth	At five	At birth	At five
TOTAL		43.64	50.81	68.07	65.54
Male		43.82	51.33	65.47	63.12
Female		43.52	50.36	70.96	68.21

Source: Dirección General de Estadística, *Boletín mensual,* No. 54, 1955. *Vital Statistics—Special Reports: United States Life Tables 1949–51, 41,* no. 1.

A longer life expectancy at age five than at birth reflects, as we have already indicated, a high mortality among younger children. The figures on mortality among children under five dramatize the critical need for better standards of health in Guatemala. In 1955, the number of deaths among children under five constituted a little over one-half (51.2 per cent) of all deaths. In sharp contrast, only 8.4 per cent of all deaths in the United States during 1954 were of children under five years old.[7] The situation in Guatemala seems to be quite typical in Latin America generally. According to Dr. Louis Verhoestraete, 49.1 per cent of all deaths reported in Latin America in 1952 were of children under five, while in the United States and Canada 8.9 per cent of all deaths were of children under five. Only 22 per cent of all deaths in Latin America were of persons 55 years or over, whereas in the United States and Canada it was 70.4 per cent.[8]

According to Table 37, Indians in Guatemala had a life expectancy about eleven years shorter than did Ladinos at birth (38.34 and 49.66 respectively) as well as about nine years shorter at age five (46.84 and 56.04 respectively). The spread between the figures for the two ethnic groups reflects differences in the standard and level of living as well as in the completeness of data.

Demographers consider women to be the tougher of the human species, as life expectancy seems to be longer for them than for males

7. Based on data from *United Nations Demographic Yearbook* (1956), Table 24.
8. Louis Verhoestraete, "Aspectos internacionales de la higiene materno-infantil," *Boletín de la Oficina Sanitaria Panamericana, 40* (1956), Table 1.

in most parts of the world. The generalization certainly holds true for the United States, as can be seen in Table 36. Males in the United States can be expected at birth to have a life expectancy about five and a half years shorter than that of females. The situation in Guatemala is different. In 1949–51, life expectancy at birth for males was .3 of a year longer than that for the females. Analysis by ethnic group shows an even more interesting difference. According to Table 37, life ex-

TABLE 37. *Life expectancy at birth and at five years of age for Indians and Ladinos, 1949–51*

| | | Average future lifetime in years | | |
| | | INDIAN | | LADINO |
Sex		At birth	At five	At birth	At five
TOTAL		38.34	46.84	49.66	56.04
Male		39.60	47.63	49.32	55.98
Female		38.74	46.02	50.00	56.10

Source: Dirección General de Estadística, *Boletín mensual*, No. 54, 1955.

pectancy at birth for Indian males (39.60) was a little higher than that for Indian females (38.74). On the other hand, Ladino females had a higher life expectancy at birth (50.00) than did Ladino males (49.32).

Life expectancy was shown to be somewhat longer in the capital city than elsewhere. In the municipio of Guatemala life expectancy at birth was 46.70, in contrast to 43.64 for the Republic as a whole (Table

TABLE 38. *Life expectancy in Guatemala and in the municipio of Guatemala, 1949–51, by age*

	AVERAGE NUMBER OF YEARS OF LIFE REMAINING AT BEGINNING OF YEAR OF AGE	
Year of age	Republic of Guatemala	Municipio of Guatemala
0	43.64	46.70
1	47.69	51.21
5	50.81	53.33
10	48.08	49.74
15	44.23	45.36
20	40.64	40.28
30	33.61	32.81
40	26.85	25.74
50	20.39	19.24
60	14.42	13.51
70	9.36	8.71
80	5.92	5.04

Source: Dirección General de Estadística, *Boletín mensual*, No. 54, 1955.

38). A glance down each column shows that expectancy was consistently higher in the municipio until the age of 20. From the age of 20 years onward, life expectancy in the Republic was a little higher. The shift at age 20 may be due partly to the high incidence of tuberculosis in congested urban centers. Persons outside of Guatemala City who manage to survive beyond 20 years of age can breathe plenty of fresh air, even if they do not have other advantages conducive to health.

Principal Causes of Death

The principal causes of death in Guatemala reflect the low level of living of the people. The lack of sanitation, inadequate medical facilities, and poor nutrition and housing all contribute to the seriousness of the principal causes (Table 39). Nearly one-fifth of the deaths were

TABLE 39. *Average annual number of deaths from 1950 to 1954, by types of causes*

	Average number of deaths, 1950–54	Per cent
TOTAL	63,741	100.0
Infectious and parasitic diseases	21,922	34.4
Senility and ill-defined conditions	11,836	18.6
Diseases of the respiratory system	10,284	16.1
Diseases of the digestive system	8,972	14.1
Certain diseases of early infancy	3,695	5.8
All others	7,032	11.0

Source: Dirección General de Estadística.

ascribed to "senility, and ill-defined conditions." This category includes deaths where the cause was unknown or undiagnosed. A figure as high as this could only appear in a country where a large proportion of the people never see a physician, even when they are dying.[9] In the United States, the number of deaths coming under the same rubric constituted only 1.4 per cent of the total in 1954.[10]

Chronic illnesses like heart disease and cancer which constitute serious problems in the United States do not appear among the principal causes in Guatemala. The fact that there are relatively few persons

9. According to the Dirección General de Estadística, only 13 per cent of the deaths in 1955 had been certified by doctors.
10. *United Nations Demographic Yearbook* (1956), p. 700.

in the later years as well as the inaccuracy of diagnosis may be partly responsible for the lower figures.

Perhaps the best illustration of the nature of the health problems in Guatemala can be found in the percentage of deaths due to infectious and parasitic diseases. Under proper conditions of sanitation and medical care, most deaths by these diseases could be prevented. In Guatemala, infectious and parasitic diseases were responsible for the greatest bulk of the deaths, about one-third. In the United States in 1954,[11] deaths attributable to these diseases constituted only 2.0 per cent of the total.

Proper sanitation could have prevented deaths by many of the other principal causes shown in Table 39. Some diseases, of course, cannot be entirely prevented, but medical care could help to keep them from having serious consequences.

Having given a brief review of the principal types of causes, we can turn now to an analysis of the more specific causes of death according to regions (Table 40). The figures show the number of deaths per

TABLE 40. *Number of deaths from selected causes in 1950 per 10,000 inhabitants, by regions*

Cause of death	Total	Central	North	East	South	West	North central
Whooping cough	11.5	9.3	5.9	6.7	6.0	17.4	9.3
T.B., all forms	5.5	12.9	3.4	2.9	9.1	3.0	3.7
Dysentery	4.3	1.2	1.1	1.9	6.5	7.0	2.1
Malaria	24.5	3.9	68.1	21.6	43.8	19.4	57.1
Influenza	10.5	4.2	1.7	2.2	2.2	21.2	8.2
Measles	7.8	5.9	2.3	4.2	10.0	11.3	3.0
Helminths	16.7	15.1	5.4	11.9	38.1	15.3	12.4
Bronchitis and pneumonia	22.2	23.5	13.4	19.7	22.5	25.7	12.0
Diarrhea and enteritis	21.9	24.1	26.6	27.6	28.6	17.1	16.8

Source: Dirección General de Estadística.

10,000 inhabitants in 1950. For data on individual departments see Appendix Table 8. Regional differences may be due partly to environmental conditions and to differences in the standard of living. The west, where the ratio of people to land is so high that farm plots are often inadequate for subsistence, had the highest rates in five of the nine causes of death. No region, however, had consistently low rates for all causes; if a region had a low death rate for one cause, it usually had a high rate for at least one other.

11. Ibid., p. 700.

Malaria

According to Table 40 malaria is the chief killer in Guatemala. Except in the central region, it is responsible for a high rate of death almost everywhere and is not confined to the swampy plains of the coast. Certain species of malaria-transmitting mosquitos flourish in the higher altitudes, where they breed in lakes and puddles, as well as in open wells containing water for household use. The seasonal migration of workers from the highlands to and from the plantations in the lowlands also helps spread the disease. A migrant worker who has been bitten by a malaria-transmitting mosquito while in the coastal area may carry the parasites back to the highlands in his bloodstream. Once home, he could be bitten by another mosquito which could transmit the parasites again to someone else. Even when malaria does not result in death, it saps the energy of persons afflicted with it. Thus, the eradication of malaria through strenuous public health measures would help to raise the energy output of the population as well as to lower the death rate.

Bronchitis and pneumonia

Bronchitis and pneumonia together constitute the second leading cause of death in Guatemala. No region has a truly low rate for this cause. The rate for the north central region, 12.0, is the lowest, but it is about four times the rate for the United States.[12] These diseases may be aggravated by the poor housing conditions which prevail, especially in rural areas. Building materials used are not always adequate to keep out the cold, and smoke from the cooking fire irritates the respiratory passages. The marked deficiency of vitamin A in the diet may also lower the resistance of the respiratory tract to bacterial infection.

Diarrhea and enteritis

Diarrhea and enteritis are responsible for almost as many deaths as bronchitis and pneumonia. Diarrhea and enteritis, of course, are general terms which refer to symptoms of loose discharge of the bowels and inflamed intestines. The figures in Table 40 for dysentery are relatively low, but proper diagnoses might have shown that many deaths reported as due to diarrhea or enteritis were really cases of dysentery. The bacteria which produce symptoms of diarrhea and enteritis are spread by the lack of sanitation. Drinking water is frequently polluted, and people rarely boil it before use. Both in the markets and in the home,

12. The rate for the U.S. in 1950 was 2.9, according to the data in the *United Nations Demographic Yearbook* (1953), p. 250.

milk and other foods are commonly left exposed to swarms of flies. The lack of proper facilities for sewage disposal contributes to the spread of dysentery-producing bacteria.

It would appear to be a simple matter to warn people to take precautions about their food, water, and toilet disposal, but the problem is much more complicated than that. The preconceptions which many Guatemalans have regarding causes of disease leave little room for the germ theory, and mere warnings about sanitation would be quite useless. Folk beliefs concerning disease will be taken up in further detail in a subsequent section.

Helminths

Helminths, or intestinal worms, are very common in Guatemala. According to one survey, as many as 84 per cent of the children examined were afflicted with a type which we know as the round worm.[13] This and other varieties of intestinal parasites do not necessarily have fatal consequences, but hookworms can cause anemia and death if a person has enough of them. Hookworms flourish in a warm damp climate; and, according to Table 40, the south has the highest rate for deaths due to helminths. Better sanitation should lower the incidence of intestinal parasites.

Whooping cough, influenza and measles

Whooping cough, influenza, and measles frequently occur in localized epidemics. Thus, data collected over a number of years would be required to determine whether a particular disease was associated with a consistently high rate of death in a given region. However, the highest rates of deaths reported as caused by these three diseases were in the west.

These diseases in themselves do not necessarily cause death. However, they can be followed by fatal complications due to complete absence of medical care and by poor resistance caused by inadequate nutrition.

Regarding whooping cough and measles, the author came upon the following notation in the records of a plantation in Suchitepéquez which he visited in 1945:

In November and December 1934, after the seasonal workers had arrived at the plantation to pick coffee, severe epidemics of measles and whooping cough broke out. Sixty-five children died

13. Francisco Aguirre, "Incidencia de parásitos intestinales en algunas areas rurales de Guatemala," *Revista de la Juventud Médica*, 73 (1952), 34.

on the plantation in a period of a few weeks. Forty of these died from measles, and twenty-five from whooping cough.

Facilities for control of contagious disease have undoubtedly improved since that time, but outbreaks can still be very serious.

Tuberculosis

The highest rate for tuberculosis is in the central region (Table 40). Specifically, it is Guatemala City where tuberculosis constitutes a serious threat to health.[14] The figures may be biased by the fact that actual cases of tuberculosis may be less frequently diagnosed as such outside the capital city. However, we know that in many other countries tuberculosis is a much greater problem in large overcrowded cities than in smaller places. In addition, we can cite earlier data which, although far from ideal, would seem to confirm a higher rate of tuberculosis in Guatemala City than in other parts of the country.[15]

Endemic goiter

Almost any visitor to Guatemala will be impressed by the number of persons who have the enlarged thyroid glands characteristic of goiter. A traveler, as early as 1828, made the following observation:

> In some of the provinces, the inhabitants are dreadfully afflicted with a swelling of the glands of the throat, vulgarly called güegüecho; these sometimes grow to an enormous size and, when accompanied by idiocy or extreme imbecility of mind, which is by no means uncommon, they furnish a most humiliating and painful spectacle. These swellings are generally attributed to some deleterious quality of the water, and are considered by the natives as incurable.[16]

In 1950 the Institute of Nutrition of Central America and Panama (INCAP), with the cooperation of the national health department, began systematic surveys of the incidence of goiter in Guatemala.[17]

14. Appendix Table 8 shows the department of Guatemala to have a rate of 14.0 deaths by tuberculosis per 10,000 inhabitants. Sacatepéquez, the other department in the Central region, has a rate of only 5.0.

15. George Cheever Shattuck, A Medical Survey of the Republic of Guatemala (Washington, D.C., 1938), pp. 84–5.

16. Henry Dunn, Guatimala [sic], or the United Provinces of Central America, in 1827–8; Being Sketches and Memorandums Made During a 12 Month's Residence in That Republic (New York, 1828), p. 256.

17. See J. Antonio Muñoz, Carlos Pérez, and Nevin S. Scrimshaw, "Endemic Goiter in Guatemala," American Journal of Tropical Medicine and Hygiene, 4 (1955), 963–9.

Roughly 40,000 individuals were examined, about 1.4 per cent of the total population. Examinations were made in all 22 departments, but in eight of them only the capitals were visited. School children constituted 70 per cent of the sample, while adults made up 28 per cent, and the pre-school children 2 per cent.

The findings were startling (Table 41). About 40 per cent of the entire sample were shown to have goiter. Only in the sparsely settled

TABLE 41. *Distribution of endemic goiter in sample survey in Guatemala, by region and department*

Region and department	Number examined	Number with goiter	Per cent
REPUBLIC	39,484	15,563	39
Central	13,164	5,497	42
Guatemala	6,948	1,961	28
Sacatepéquez	6,216	3,536	57
North	1,750	278	16
El Petén	659	49	7
Izabal °	1,091	229	21
East	6,112	1,919	31
Chiquimula	1,021	343	34
El Progreso	1,338	411	31
Jalapa °	800	178	22
Jutiapa °	657	242	37
Santa Rosa	1,352	537	40
Zacapa °	944	208	22
South	5,596	1,985	35
Escuintla	3,487	1,186	34
Retalhuleu °	756	293	39
Suchitepéquez °	1,353	506	37
West	10,244	4,534	44
Chimaltenango	2,371	1,422	60
El Quiché	826	366	44
Huehuetenango	2,283	858	38
Quezaltenango °	2,172	666	31
San Marcos °	1,166	636	54
Sololá	834	314	38
Totonicapán	592	272	46
North central	2,618	1,350	52
Alta Verapaz	1,550	657	42
Baja Verapaz	1,068	693	65

Sources: Antonio Muñoz, Carlos Pérez, Nevin S. Scrimshaw, "Distribución geográfica del bocío endémico en Guatemala," *Revista del Colegio Médico de Guatemala,* 6 no. 1 (1955), 40–2; also in "Endemic Goiter in Guatemala," *American Journal of Tropical Medicine and Hygiene,* 4 no. 6 (1955), 964.

° Department in which only the capital was visited.

department of El Petén did less than 10 per cent of the individuals examined have goiter. In eleven of the departments between one-third and one-half of the persons examined had goiter; in four departments, more than 50 per cent.

There was no significant difference in the incidence of goiter between males and females, between Indians and Ladinos, or between residents of departmental capitals or of the outlying villages. However, communities in the higher altitudes seemed to have relatively greater proportions of persons with goiter, which is in line with the tendency elsewhere in the world.

Goiter is generally associated with a deficiency of iodine, and the use of iodized salt is regarded as a preventive measure. The World Health Organization Study Group on Endemic Goiter has recommended a ratio of 1 part of iodine in 100,000 parts of salt. According to tests made by INCAP, the iodine content of salt in Guatemala approximated this ratio quite closely. Yet the high incidence of goiter would seem to show that this was not enough.[18] The experts of INCAP believe that, for some reason or reasons, Guatemalans need a greater amount of iodine than is considered ordinarily adequate, perhaps because of the deficiency of vitamin A in their diet.

Insect bites

As in most tropical countries, a wide variety of insects abound in Guatemala. Some of them are harmful to human beings, others are only annoying. In addition to the malaria mosquito which accounts for the loss of thousands of lives each year, there are other insects, restricted in their habitat but no less dreaded.

In one area along the Pacific piedmont, for example, is the "blinding fly." It plays host to the larvae of a certain worm-like parasite (*filaria*) which, under certain conditions, can blind human beings. When the fly bites the back of the human head, the larvae are deposited there; and when the parasites hatch, they work their way through to part of the brain affecting the eyes and thus cause blindness. For many years, the treatment for this was merely to take a knife as soon as the swollen area was noticed on the back of the head and cut out the egg cyst. In case the swelling was not noticed soon enough or the cyst was not entirely removed, the victim gradually lost his eyesight. In recent years, it has been found that an injection of hexylresorcinol will cause the swelling to disappear and will prevent blindness. Nevertheless, in areas where the blinding effects of the fly bites are observable, there

18. As a result of the INCAP studies, the Guatemalan government passed a law in 1954 requiring the iodization of all salt for human consumption at a level between 1 part of iodine in 10,000 parts of salt and 1 part in 15,000.

is considerable uneasiness, especially among the migratory coffee workers who may not know that a remedy exists, or may not have access to it.

Another insect which causes much inconvenience is known as the nigua. This is a burrowing flea which is reported to infest the ground in certain areas, especially in the vicinity of pig markets. They seem to be particularly attracted to the human foot, and their favorite hideout is to burrow inconspicuously under the toenail. This opportunity is presented by the widespread practice of going barefoot or wearing only sandals. Once securely anchored under the human toenail, they deposit a minute sac full of microscopic eggs. If the eggs are permitted to hatch, a colony of considerable size soon develops. The common remedy is for someone to remove the egg sac with a needle, a rather delicate task since it must be removed without breaking the thin covering. Indian women have become rather skillful in performing this little operation. The housemaid, for example, knew exactly what to do when the author's wife discovered, to her astonishment, a dark, swollen spot under her toe which proved to be niguas. If the sac is not entirely removed or breaks in the process, the eggs hatch and the victim may lose a toe; or in case of serious infection, more disastrous consequences might result.

Unattended wounds

Lack of facilities or knowledge of first aid treatment results in considerable discomfort and at times even the loss of life in isolated areas. The sharp machete is a universal tool of the rural inhabitants, and may cause accidental cuts as well as gashes resulting from skirmishes following overly enthusiastic consumption of alcoholic beverages during the fiesta celebrations. Serious infection of unattended wounds is an ever present danger, especially in the warmer tropical areas.

Malnutrition

As noted in the previous chapter, many of the health and disease problems in Guatemala probably result indirectly from malnutrition in the form of deficiencies in animal protein, vitamin A, riboflavin, and iodine. Such deficiencies are especially common in rural areas, and lower the body's resistance to diseases which might not otherwise prove serious. The incidence of malnutrition is probably greatest among children from one to five years of age and is related to feeding practices that are poorly adapted to the child's needs after weaning.[19]

19. Scrimshaw and others, "Nutritional Problems," *Pediatrics, 16* (1955), 378–97.

MEDICAL BELIEFS AND PRACTICES

The danger of disease and death constantly threatens the lives of many Guatemalans. To allay the anxieties arising from these threats, there has developed in rural Guatemala a body of folklore to explain the causes of disease, and various folk techniques for curing illness. These differ from community to community and from area to area, but there are enough similarities so that we can describe an over-all pattern.

In general, the folk beliefs and practices regarding illness do not differ greatly between Indians and Ladinos. Although sophisticated urban Ladinos resort to modern medical facilities, most Ladinos either cannot afford medical care or do not have access to it. Aside from these factors, however, Ladinos, hardly less than Indians, are conditioned by their cultural history. Even in Europe and North America the theories and techniques of modern medicine are a recent development; in Guatemala they were non-existent when most of the present-day Ladinos became acculturated. The native who became "ladinoized" in the early colonial period did not find the medical beliefs of his Indian background incompatible with those of the Spaniards. For example, the idea then current in Europe that bad air causes illness can be traced to Greek medicine and was comparable to the belief in evil winds among the Maya people. Eventually there developed an integrated blend of elements from both aboriginal and European cultures which persists to this day. Modern medical practices have a long way to go in penetrating the cultural isolation of rural Guatemala.

According to Richard Adams, who has made a first-hand study of the medical beliefs of an Indian village and compared his own data with those of other anthropologists who have worked in Guatemala, the rural inhabitant believes that illnesses are caused by the interaction of a condition within the body and some condition emanating from an external source.[20] It is believed that an internal condition predisposes a person to illness which is brought on when he is exposed to a particular external condition. Without the presence of one condition, the other would not of itself cause illness. The conditions cover a wide range, and not all of them are recognized everywhere. The reader is reminded that the pattern described is only a general one, with exceptions and variations to be found in particular communities.

Internal conditions include such physical states as overexertion, body exposure, infancy, old age, pregnancy, menstruation, menopause,

20. Richard N. Adams, *Un análisis de las creencias y prácticas médicas en un pueblo indígena de Guatemala.* Publicaciones Especiales del Instituto Indigenista Nacional, No. 17 (Guatemala, 1952).

and the improper balance between "hotness" and "coldness." The last mentioned is a concept which appears to be general in Latin America. According to this concept, objects, phenomena, and conditions of various sorts are classified as either "hot" or "cold." Some plants or animals are "hot," e.g., chile and coffee; but some are considered "cold." Often there is no visible relationship between the object described as hot or cold and actual temperature. In some places, chicken meat is considered "hot," but pork is thought to be "cold." A normal person is supposed to have the proper amount of "hotness" in his body, but if he becomes overheated through eating too much "hot" food or through perspiring from hard work, then he becomes susceptible to illness. Certain psychological states such as fear, anger, jealousy, and hysteria are also included among internal conditions predisposing one to sickness. Spiritual conditions are likewise recognized. Lack of sufficient faith in the supernaturals or failure to provide prayers and masses for deceased members of the family can make one prone to illness.

External conditions which interact with internal conditions to cause illness can be natural, magical, or supernatural. Many of the natural ones revolve around the concept of "hotness" and "coldness." The interaction of internal "hotness" and external "coldness"—such as taking in too much chile or hot coffee and then being caught in the rain—is believed to produce a variety of illnesses, such as a common cold, influenza, malaria, stomach-ache, and lung or kidney trouble. Some natural conditions do not necessarily involve the idea of "hot" and "cold." For example, the presence of worms within the body is regarded as fairly normal, and they are thought to lodge in the stomach quietly (an internal condition) until they are disturbed by some rough food (external condition) which stirs them up and makes them rise so that the person vomits or chokes.

Other external factors which cause illness, given the proper internal conditions, can be produced by human or supernatural agencies.[21]

1. *Evil wind* (*aire*). It is believed that a person in a weakened state can become ill if an evil wind invades his body, producing aches or some form of malfunctioning. If an open sore or wound becomes infected and painful, an evil wind, rather than bacteria, is considered responsible. *Aire* may enter the body quite accidentally, or it may emanate from a ritually unclean person, or it may be injected by means of sorcery or black magic by an enemy.

2. *Fright* (*espanto*). Many mental and physical upsets are thought

21. See Charles Wisdom, "The Supernatural World and Curing," in *Heritage of Conquest*, pp. 129–32.

to be caused by sudden fright or shock. Thunderstorms, an unexpected encounter with a snake or a spirit, falling, near-drowning, and similar phenomena may produce fright. Symptoms may include sleeplessness, apathy, loss of appetite, headaches and partial paralysis.

3. *Ritual contamination.* The principal source of ritual contamination is attributed to the evil eye (*ojo*). Some persons are believed to be able to cause illness or harm, often unintentionally, by merely looking at another. Individuals who are considered ritually unclean because of some abnormal condition, such as pregnancy, menstruation, over-exhaustion, hysteria, feeblemindedness, and insanity, are also thought to contaminate others.

4. *Sorcery or black magic.* Certain persons are believed to have power to perform black magic. An enemy may work sorcery on a victim directly, or he may hire a specialist to do so. Sorcery is believed to produce serious illness or death.

5. *Molestation by spirits.* The illness caused by spirits entails various symptoms, including dreams, drowsiness, and general weakness. The spirits may be evil, or they may be angels or the souls of deceased family members who are aggrieved over some failure to perform the appropriate religious ritual.

Occasionally a trained physician or the local pharmacist may be called upon to cure an illness. But more often than not, an ill person resorts to a folk technique, the nature of which depends on what is believed to be the basic cause of illness.

If an individual is reasonably sure of good relations with other persons and with supernatural beings, he may attribute his illness to some natural phenomenon such as becoming chilled after he had been overheated. The cure then may be some herb or other material believed to have a "hot" quality to counteract the abnormal "coldness" of his body. According to Adams, one remedy for lung trouble in Magdalena Milpas Altas consists of a drink containing an herb, boiled either alone or with cinnamon, sugar, and roasted cockroaches broken in two. In the same village, blood from the neck of a freshly killed skunk is also thought to warm the coldness of the body.[22]

When an ill person suspects magical or supernatural causes, he consults a diviner. The latter may question him closely on his movements and on his relations with other persons to determine whether a ritually unclean individual has contaminated him, or an enemy projected black magic against him. The diviner may help him look back over his life to discover some sin or misstep which might have incurred punishment from God. Once it is decided that the illness is attributable

22. Adams, op. cit., pp. 19 ff.

to non-natural causes, then the patient is turned over to the ministrations of a *curandero*, or curer. Sometimes the diviner and curer are combined within the same person. Among the Chorti of eastern Guatemala, a curer can employ such techniques as passing a live turkey or frog or an egg over the patient's body with the idea of attracting the sickness into it and away from the patient. A Chorti curer may also chew tobacco, rue, and other plants, and spray his saliva over the patient. Charms and prayers to the saints may also be used. Herbalists, masseurs, midwives, and "surgeons" are other specialists of rural medicine.[23]

Although there are many instances in which illness is psychosomatic and is undoubtedly helped by the curandero, nevertheless the disorders which stem from bacterial infections, lack of sanitation, and nutritional deficiencies take a heavy toll, as is indicated by the high death rate.

The task of reducing mortality is two-fold: (1) to provide prevention programs, medicine, and personnel; and (2) to introduce these facilities to people whose beliefs of disease causation and cure are fundamentally incompatible with modern medicine.

The problem of personnel will be discussed later, but the fact that even the simplest medicines are almost prohibitive in cost to the rural inhabitant is brought out in Melvin Tumin's study of San Luis Jilotepeque:

> The following should be considered against the background of the fact that the average wage is 10 cents a day: The simplest and most diluted aspirin tablet costs 1 cent. "Very efficient" aspirins cost 5 cents. A quinine injection costs 50 cents. A good cathartic costs between 5 and 25 cents. The services of the average curer retail at 25 cents a visit, plus food and alcoholic beverages for him, plus the cost of whatever patent medicines and herbs he employs in the cure. A visit from the local druggist-dentist-doctor costs 50 cents.[24]

The problem of introducing modern medical facilities in the face of folk beliefs is a delicate one. A doctor who displays nothing but contempt for the traditional practices is likely to fail in his task of raising the health standards. He has to take special pains to explain his techniques in terms that the people can understand. In particular, he would be well advised to work with the traditional curer rather than against him. There have been instances where modern medicine was

23. Wisdom, *The Chorti Indians of Guatemala*, pp. 347 ff.
24. Tumin, *Caste in a Peasant Society*, p. 48.

accepted quite readily, largely because some of the more reliable drugs were placed in the hands of the curandero. Obviously, it is desirable, in the long run, that the rural Guatemalan have some basic understanding of modern medical technology, but the utilization of the existing mechanisms might be justified for the immediate alleviation of the high mortality rates which prevail now.

MEDICAL FACILITIES

Personnel

Both the reluctance of rural inhabitants to accept modern medical practices and the pitifully inadequate supply of doctors contribute to the problem of raising the health standards in Guatemala. In 1950, there were 420 doctors in the whole Republic, or an average of one physician for about 6,600 inhabitants. In 1955, the number of doctors had increased to 469, but the total population had also grown so that the ratio became one doctor for about 6,800 persons.[25] The situation appears to be growing worse rather than improving. The acute shortage can be appreciated even more if one considers that in the United States there were only 760 inhabitants per physician in 1953. In Mexico there were 2,400 persons for each doctor.[26]

Actually the shortage is even graver than the ratio would imply, if one takes into account the distribution of the doctors. In 1950 nearly three-fourths (310) of the doctors were practicing in Guatemala City [27] where only about 10 per cent of the population lived. For every doctor in the capital, there were 917 persons. The ratio for the rest of the country was 22,787 persons per physician.

As can be seen in Table 42 only a few departments had more than a half-dozen doctors either in 1950 or 1954. These were the departments that contained a city, large commercial plantations, or both. Some of the other departments had only one or two physicians. In 1954 Santa Rosa had just one doctor for its estimated population of 126,119.

The concentration of doctors in the capital city is characteristic of most of Latin America. Middle and upper class Latin Americans, doctors included, place a high value upon residence in the metropolis

25. Based on data from the Dirección General de Estadística. A total of 517 physicians is given for 1955: but 48 of these doctors were reported "absent," that is, out of the country.

26. *United Nations Statistical Yearbook* (1956), p. 570.

27. Data from the Dirección General de Estadística. In 1955, there were 341 doctors in Guatemala City.

and regard the hinterland as dull and uninteresting by contrast. A physician can make a comfortable income practicing in the capital city, but the people of the countryside generally cannot pay much, even if they were willing to avail themselves of his services.

TABLE 42. *Number of physicians and number of inhabitants per physician in 1950 and 1954, by region and department*

Region and department	1950			1954		
	No. of physicians	No. of inhabitants	No. of inhabitants per physician	No. of physicians	No. of inhabitants °	No. of inhabitants per physician
REPUBLIC	420	2,790,868	6,645	469	3,202,139	6,828
Central	318	499,037	1,569	352	575,462	1,635
Guatemala	312	438,913	1,407	345	506,581	1,468
Sacatepéquez	6	60,124	10,021	7	68,881	9,840
North	10	70,912	7,091	13	81,644	6,280
El Petén	3	15,880	5,293	4	18,258	4,564
Izabal	7	55,032	7,862	9	63,386	7,043
East	14	554,200	39,586	19	635,950	33,471
Chiquimula	2	112,841	56,420	3	129,594	43,198
El Progreso	2	47,872	23,936	4	54,756	13,689
Jalapa	2	75,190	37,595	2	86,240	43,120
Jutiapa	3	138,925	46,308	5	159,383	31,877
Santa Rosa	1	109,836	109,836	1	126,119	126,119
Zacapa	4	69,536	17,384	4	79,858	19,964
South	37	315,023	8,514	39	361,855	9,278
Escuintla	18	123,759	6,876	20	142,194	7,110
Retalhuleu	5	66,861	13,372	7	75,875	10,839
Suchitepéquez	14	124,403	8,886	12	143,786	11,982
West	36	1,095,571	30,432	40	1,254,143	31,353
Chimaltenango	3	121,480	40,493	3	140,471	46,824
El Quiché	2	174,911	87,455	2	200,851	100,425
Huehuetenango	2	200,101	100,050	3	228,402	76,134
Quezaltenango	16	184,213	11,513	19	210,848	11,097
San Marcos	9	232,591	25,843	8	264,199	33,025
Sololá	2	82,921	41,461	1	95,174	95,174
Totonicapán	2	99,354	49,677	4	114,198	28,549
North central	5	256,125	51,225	6	293,085	48,847
Alta Verapaz	4	189,812	47,453	4	216,788	54,197
Baja Verapaz	1	66,313	66,313	2	76,297	38,148

Source: Dirección General de Estadística.
° Population estimated for end of 1954.

Hospitals

Most of the hospitals in Guatemala are run by the Ministry of Public Health. The Institute of Social Security, to be discussed in the next section, has a few hospital centers and clinics. There are, in addition, a number of private hospitals. The combined total of beds in all these hospitals is low. According to the *United Nations Statistical Yearbook,* there were 6,742 hospital beds in all of Guatemala in 1952. With the population estimated at 2,975,000 that year, there was an average of 441 persons per hospital bed. In contrast, there were 101 inhabitants per hospital bed in the United States in 1953.[28]

The overcrowding of facilities was one of the points raised by Dr. Henry Kolbe in a survey he made in 1948 of the hospitals in Guatemala. Generally, he regarded the administration of the hospitals to be poor and the auxiliary services to be either inadequate or non-existent. He found the hospitals acutely understaffed in regard to doctors, professional nurses, and technicians. The majority of the buildings he thought were antiquated and poorly planned.[29]

Dr. Kolbe's findings were generally confirmed by Leo Suslow when he visited several of the Guatemalan hospitals in 1950. His description of one gives a vivid impression of conditions which existed there at the time.

The National Hospital of Cobán, completed in 1908, is a large cement building which, at the time of the writer's visit, had 120 patients and seventy hospital beds—but the appropriations covered only seventy beds. In the women's ward two girls were sleeping in the same bed—they had the same illness. All the rooms were dirty and poorly equipped. The delivery room served as a central place for getting water (the *pila*), and its equipment appeared unsanitary. The U.S. Army mobile X-Ray was operated by an untrained girl who wore a rubber apron and goggles. The workers in the kitchen were preparing tortillas (little else) and the room was dense with flies. In the isolation ward all contagious ills were interspersed—typhoid, malaria, scarlet fever, etc. Most of the

28. *United Nations Statistical Yearbook* (1954), pp. 519–20. A total of 8,738 hospital beds (including 974 cribs) is cited for 1955–56 in Guatemala by Manuel Antonio Girón, "Consideraciones médico-sociales sobre Guatemala," *Universidad de San Carlos: Publicación Trimestral,* 37 (1956), 51–2. On the basis of the 1950 population, there were 319 persons per hospital bed.

29. Henry W. Kolbe, *Estudio hospitalario de la República de Guatemala: Parte I* (Guatemala, 1949), p. 281.

hospital help were Indians who ranged from twelve to sixteen years of age. Two doctors shared the work with their private practices (the Director, a young surgeon named Dr. Aguilar, received Q200 monthly). Most of the patients were Indians who in the past, the Director said, had been afraid to come to the hospital. Some young nude children ran through the halls; one excreted a large worm on the floor. Only one graduate nurse and five practical nurses were in charge. The pharmacist had no professional training, although the blood bank operator had been trained in the General Hospital [in Guatemala City]. A blood transfusion cost Q3 and it was replaced by a donation from a relative of the patient. There were no retailed regulations governing the administration of the hospital whose budget was Q2,500 per month. A new annex for children was under construction by the Ministry of Public Works.[30]

Just as the capital contains a disproportionate number of physicians, so does it have a good share of the hospital facilities.[31] The largest one, the General Hospital, with a capacity of 1,204 beds, is located in Guatemala City. Another large one, the Roosevelt Hospital, is still under construction with funds from the Guatemalan and United States governments. When completed, it will serve as the principal medical center of the country. The medical school is planning to use it as a university hospital to train personnel.[32]

A Guatemalan working on one of the more progressive commercial plantations has a somewhat better chance of medical attention than do other persons living outside the capital. The United Fruit Company operates two hospitals which are considered superior to most of the other hospitals in Guatemala. One, with 222 beds, is at Quiriguá, Izabal, and the other, at Tiquisate, Escuintla, has 320 beds. The medical care provided by the United Fruit Company is exceptionally good and is not approached by that of other employers. However, some of the larger plantations have an agreement with a doctor in a nearby town, usually the departmental capital, to have him make periodic visits.

30. Leo A. Suslow, *Social Security in Guatemala* (Unpublished PhD. dissertation, University of Connecticut, Storrs, Conn., 1954), pp. 151–2.

31. According to the article by Dr. Girón in *Universidad de San Carlos: Publicación Trimenstral*, 37 (1956), 53, the department of Guatemala had 52 per cent of the hospital beds of the country in 1955–56 (4,535 out of 8,738).

32. At the time of writing, the maternity and pediatrics divisions were completed and in operation. Each of these divisions had a capacity of 150 beds.

Institute of Social Security

The spirit of social reform prevalent among government leaders after the overthrow of the Ubico regime found concrete expression in the establishment of the Guatemalan Institute of Social Security (Instituto Guatemalteco de Seguridad Social) in 1946.[33] Unlike the social security system in the United States which is oriented primarily toward retirement and survivor benefits, the Guatemalan system lays more emphasis on protecting the health of people while they are still part of the labor force. This emphasis would seem to be inevitable in a country where the overwhelming majority of the people cannot ordinarily afford a doctor, and where life expectancy is short.

As originally conceived, the Guatemalan social security system was intended to provide coverage for a wide range of contingencies: industrial accidents and occupational diseases, maternity, general illness, invalidism, orphanhood, widowhood, old age, and burial. Since financial resources were limited, these contingencies could not all be covered from the start. The Institute concentrated first on employment accidents. Later, coverage was extended to accidents in general. Injured persons are paid cash benefits, and wherever possible, efforts are made to rehabilitate them. Some work is done toward the prevention of accidents. In addition, maternity care is available to female employees and to wives of employees who are enrolled in the system.

The social security plan calls for deductions from the wages of workers as well as for contributions from the state and employers. The requirement for payroll deductions excludes the greater proportion of the labor force from participation in the plan. The rural masses who barely extract subsistence from their little plots lie completely outside the scope of the program. Even those persons who work for others cannot all be covered. Where employers are illiterate or hire only a small number of workers, often intermittently, the necessary paper work is not practicable. The system of payroll deductions is best suited to the big urban enterprises and to the large plantations, such as those of the United Fruit Company. Thus, it is more than coincidental that the departments in which the Institute of Social Security operates are those which contain the cities and large plantations. At this writing, maternity care under the social security system can be had only in the department of Guatemala.

For the treatment of workers covered by the system, the Institute

33. Much of the material for this section was taken from Suslow, *Social Security in Guatemala.*

of Social Security operates a number of hospital centers, clinics, first aid posts, and simple medical facilities known as "medicine chests" (*botiquines*). The hospital facilities of the Ministry of Public Health are also available to workers participating in the system.

The Kolbe plan for a hospital system

The Institute of Social Security had not been in existence long before its administrators began to feel that the country should have a completely new hospital system. They believed that the existing hospital facilities were inadequate to meet the needs which were increasing with the expansion of the Institute's activities.

The administrators proposed the adoption of a plan drawn up by a North American hospital consultant, Dr. Henry Kolbe.[34] This plan called for a system containing a central hospital, five regional hospitals, 17 departmental hospitals, and 44 rural hospitals. As envisaged by Dr. Kolbe, every village would ultimately be within reach of some sort of an out-patient clinic or health center. Mobile clinics for isolated communities and various public health activities were also recommended.

For a number of reasons, the plan was never adopted. Although Dr. Kolbe made no estimate of the costs, they probably would have been too high for a country which had also to support on a low per capita income other basic programs of education, communication, and agriculture. There was also rivalry between the Institute of Social Security and the Ministry of Public Health. Moreover, the Institute of Social Security, originally conceived as non-political, did not escape becoming enmeshed in the politics of the Arbenz period. Although bureaucratic rivalries and political embroilments may not work against a similar scheme which might be proposed in the future, the defeat of the Kolbe plan illustrates the need for any ambitious project to be realistic with regard to problems of financing.

In the meantime, the government is doing what it can with the limited resources available. The Ministry of Public Health is replacing badly antiquated hospitals in some areas with new ones, and is improving existing facilities in others. The completion of the Roosevelt Hospital in Guatemala City may result in an increase in the number of doctors trained by the national medical school. The Institute of Social Security plans to continue expanding its services. At the time of writ-

34. Dr. Kolbe, of the hospital consulting firm of Neergard and Craig, New York City, was under contract by the Institute of Social Security to make a survey of Guatemalan hospitals and to make recommendations.

ing, preparations were being made for the coverage of general illnesses under the social security system.

Since the national hospitals and the Institute of Social Security are predominantly urban, the isolated rural areas have to be served by other agencies. For this purpose, the *Unidades Sanitarias* (Health Units) and the *Centros de Salud* (Health Centers) of the Ministry of Public Health are scattered throughout the country. An inadequate budget sets strict limits on what they can do, but they nevertheless serve as the foundation for the gradual extension of health services to rural areas.

The Unidades Sanitarias are concerned particularly with the eradication of malaria and of intestinal parasites. The fight against malnutrition is also being waged through these agencies with the cooperation of such international bodies as INCAP and the United Nations International Children's Emergency Fund (UNICEF). Vaccination programs have also been administered through the Unidades Sanitarias in cooperation with UNICEF and the World Health Organization.

Part 4 SOCIAL INSTITUTIONS

Chapter 12

MARRIAGE AND THE FAMILY

The family in Guatemala follows the same general pattern as that of other Latin American countries. There are some variations, especially in the rural areas, that have come about because of the relative isolation of the communities. This isolation, for instance, has brought about the wide acceptance of common-law marriages.

Briefly, the Guatemalan family may be characterized as the elementary type, consisting of parents and their children; although frequently this is modified to consist of several generations including one or more grandparents and a married son with his family. Occasionally other relatives may also be included. Sometimes married sons in the rural areas live in separate dwellings on the same plot of ground near the parental home. In such cases, they usually retain a close family solidarity with their parents even though living in separate quarters. The family tends to function as a unit in social and economic affairs.

In broad outlines, then, a description of the family in Mexico, Ecuador, or almost any other Latin American country which has a large indigenous population describes the family in Guatemala. The conquistadores left a common imprint on the system wherever they went. The double standard of morality, more common among the upper classes than among the lower, may have been brought from Spain. In any case it was nurtured by the conditions prevalent during the colonial period when, due to the scarcity of European women, Spanish men mated rather freely with Indian women.

As in many isolated rural areas elsewhere in the world, the family is more important in the life of the individual than is any other social institution. In the United States, the school and other agencies participate in preparing the child for adulthood. In rural Guatemala, particularly among the Indian population, the burden of this preparation falls much more heavily on the family. Another basic function of the family, the nourishment of its members, can be performed in a number of ways in different societies. In industrialized societies, a family is usually supported by a single wage-earner; but in the isolated communities of Guatemala, the whole family forms a unit of economic production, more or less self-sufficient.

Although family patterns in the cities and plantations of Guatemala have not been subjected to analysis, they probably differ somewhat from those of the isolated rural communities. Separated from the direct cultivation of the land, the family in the urban centers may be expected to show patterns which vary from those in rural places and also among themselves according to social class. The plantation economy, although rural, involves the family in a network of social relationships quite unlike those in a non-plantation village. As the impact of modern technological change increasingly breaks down the isolation of rural communities, the family patterns even in these places may evolve toward new forms.

MARRIAGE

Marriage in Guatemala may take place in one of three ways: by a civil ceremony which may or may not be followed by a church wedding, by rituals following local traditions, or by setting up a common household without ceremony.

The type of marriage chosen reflects how much significance the national government has in the lives of the people involved. The government recognizes only the civil ceremony. Officially, couples living together as man and wife but who have not gone through a civil ceremony are not married, but are *unido,* or united in common-law alliance. However, the central government is so remote from most Guatemalans that official recognition of marital status actually means very little to them. Many persons view a civil ceremony as merely a legally required preliminary to a church wedding. But priests are scarce, particularly in rural areas, and they charge fees for conducting a ceremony. Thus, many persons do not start their marital life with the blessings of the church; and without a religious ceremony, they see no necessity for a civil one. In isolated areas, a traditional ritual often gives local recognition to the union of a couple. Such rituals have more meaning for the people than recognition by the national government or by the church.[1]

Marital status is given in Table 43 for persons in Guatemala fourteen

1. In 1947, a legislative decree made it possible for a couple living in common-law union to have it legalized by the local authorities. They may do so after three years of living together as man and wife. Indians who have been united through

years of age and over, by ethnic group. The category "married' in this Table includes only those persons who are legally married, i.e., those who were united by civil ceremony. It may be noted that there are

TABLE 43. *Population fourteen years of age and over, by marital status, by ethnic group, and by rural-urban residence, 1950*

| | TOTAL INHABITANTS | | | | | |
| | BOTH ETHNIC GROUPS | | INDIAN | | LADINO | |
Marital status	Number	Per cent	Number	Per cent	Number	Per cent
TOTAL	1,675,146	100.0	890,883	100.0	784,263	100.0
Single	616,754	36.8	280,118	31.4	336,636	42.9
Married	309,506	18.5	126,005	14.1	183,501	23.4
In common-law union	660,421	39.4	436,238	49.0	224,183	28.6
Widowed	84,191	5.0	47,743	5.4	36,448	4.6
Divorced	4,274	0.3	779	0.1	3,495	0.5
	RURAL INHABITANTS					
TOTAL	1,224,211	100.0	768,417	100.0	455,794	100.0
Single	415,463	33.9	234,362	30.5	181,101	39.8
Married	197,928	16.2	96,144	12.5	101,784	22.3
In common-law union	549,229	44.9	397,350	51.7	151,879	33.3
Widowed	60,156	4.9	40,037	5.2	20,119	4.4
Divorced	1,435	0.1	524	0.1	911	0.2
	URBAN INHABITANTS					
TOTAL	450,935	100.0	122,466	100.0	328,469	100.0
Single	201,291	44.6	45,756	37.4	155,535	47.3
Married	111,578	24.8	29,861	24.4	81,717	24.9
In common-law union	111,192	24.7	38,888	31.7	72,304	22.0
Widowed	24,035	5.3	7,706	6.3	16,329	5.0
Divorced	2,839	0.6	255	0.2	2,584	0.8

Source: *Sexto censo de población,* Table 5.

fewer people who are legally married than there are living in common-law union (18.5 per cent and 39.4 per cent, respectively). Among the Indians living together as man and wife, the proportion of persons in

traditional rituals need not wait three years. The number of couples availing themselves of this right is increasing, but the proportion of non-legalized unions is still much greater than that of regularized unions. In 1949, 5.6 per cent of all legally recognized marriages were previous de facto unions; and in 1954, the proportion was 17.9 per cent. Dirección General de Estadística, *Boletín mensual,* 56 (1955), 2–3.

common-law alliance was more than three times that of persons who were legally married. Even among Ladinos, the number living in common-law union was somewhat greater than those who had gone through a civil ceremony. Nearly three-fourths of the rural inhabitants living as man and wife were classified in the common-law category while about one-half of the urban couples were so enumerated.

The extremely small proportion of divorced persons shown in Table 43 (0.3 per cent of all inhabitants fourteen years of age and over) does not necessarily mean that marriages are stable in Guatemala. A divorce is required for the dissolution of a legally recognized marriage only. Since there are relatively few legal marriages, the number of divorces would inevitably be low.[2] The category labeled, "single," probably contains not only individuals who have never been married but also persons who have at one time or another lived in common-law union but are no longer doing so.

Table 44 shows for each region the proportion of persons in com-

TABLE 44. *Per cent of couples living in common-law unions in 1950, by ethnic group and region*

Region	Total	Indians	Ladinos
REPUBLIC	68.1	77.6	55.0
Central	43.1	44.5	42.7
North	72.6	86.4	68.8
East	58.0	65.9	54.3
South	80.8	87.9	74.5
West	77.7	81.9	58.5
North central	72.4	76.9	44.6

Source: *Sexto censo de población.*

mon-law union to the total number living as man and wife in 1950. The prevalence of common-law unions is apparent from the fact that more than two-thirds (68.1 per cent) of all marital unions are of this type. Among the Indians more than three-fourths (77.6 per cent) are living in a common-law relationship, as are 55 per cent of the Ladinos. By regions, the lowest proportions of common-law unions are in the central (43.1 per cent), and the eastern regions (58 per cent). These regions are predominently Ladino and the inhabitants are probably somewhat more accustomed to conforming to the laws of the central government. The highest proportions of common-law unions are found in the south (80.8 per cent), the west (77.6 per cent), and the north,

2. In 1954, the divorce rate in Guatemala was 0.10 per thousand inhabitants. It was 2.35 in the United States. *United Nations Demographic Yearbook* (1956), pp. 729, 731.

(72.6 per cent). It will be recalled that the south has a plantation economy, as does to some extent the north. The inhabitants on the plantations may have some aspects of a rootless proletariat to whom legal marriage does not mean as much, even to Ladinos, as in other more permanently settled areas.

The high rate of common-law unions in the west and to some extent in the north central region, however, may be due in large part to the

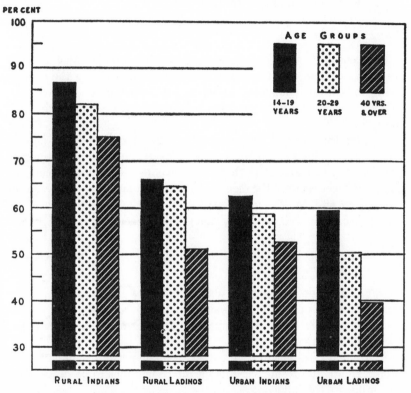

Figure 17. Per cent of all husbands and wives in Guatemala living in common-law unions, by age groups, by ethnic groups, and by rural-urban residence. Data from *Sexto censo de población,* 1950.

predominance of isolated Indian communities. The inhabitants of these areas are more likely to view regulations of the central government as impositions from the outside which have no particular meaning or value to them.

Analysis by age groups of the proportion of persons in common-law union to the total number living as man and wife brings out an interesting pattern. From Figure 17, it can be seen that the percentage of common-law unions decreases with age. Among Indians and Ladinos, both rural and urban, there were proportionately fewer common-law unions among persons 40 years and over than among younger persons. The data suggest that some persons who begin their marital life in common-law unions get legally married when they become older and feel they can afford the costs of both a civil and religious ceremony. It appears from the Table that more Ladinos than Indians do this, since the proportion of common-law unions drops more sharply with age among Ladinos than among Indians.[3]

Age at marriage

The census data on age at marriage are of limited value because they refer only to civil marriages, whereas the majority of the couples living in marital union have either never gone through a civil ceremony, or had lived together for a number of years prior to the civil marriage.

Keeping this in mind, we can point out that the census data on civil marriages, for the years 1948 to 1954, indicate that the most common age for men to marry is in their early twenties, with more than one-third (35.8 per cent) of the men contracting legal marriage between the ages of 20 and 24. Women marry earlier, with 39 per cent of those going through a civil ceremony doing so between the ages of 15 and 19.[4]

Single persons

Data on single persons are also inconclusive, largely because the term refers not only to individuals who have never been married but also to those who have been separated from common-law unions and have not remarried.

In Appendix Table 9 the percentage of single persons is given by age, ethnic group, and residence. Among the conclusions to be drawn from this table are the following:

3. On June 2, 1959, the Guatemalan Congress enacted legislation which in the future may increase considerably the proportion of legal marriages and correspondingly reduce the proportion of common-law relationships. The new legislation enables priests and ministers to obtain authorization to perform legal marriage ceremonies. (Reported in *El Imparcial*, June 3, 1959.)

4. According to ethnographic accounts, Indian girls marry soon after puberty, while Indian boys marry a little later. Wagley states that girls who are 16 or 17 years of age are already past the ideal age of marriage. Op. cit., pp. 36–7. Charles Wagley, *The Social and Religious Life of a Guatemalan Village*, Memoirs of the American Anthropological Association No. 71, 1949.

1. A larger relative number of ladino, as compared to Indian, males are single throughout all age groups in both urban and rural residential areas.
2. Among females, single persons are found in larger proportions among Ladinos than among Indians.
3. There is a large percentage of single Ladinos, both male and female, in the 20 to 24 age groups in comparison with that found among the Indians. This is more pronounced in the urban areas and may have some relation to later marriage as well as to migration to the urban centers in search of employment.
4. The relatively high percentage of single persons 40 years of age and over must be explained in part, at least, by the inclusion in this category of persons who have been separated. This same factor, of course, obtains also but to a lesser degree, in the lower age groups.

The percentage of males 40 years and over who were single in Guatemala (11.6) was higher than that in the United States (8.6 per cent). Among the rural Indians the rate was only 6.8 per cent; but it reached 18.5 per cent among urban Ladinos. Among the females, the relative number of single persons over 40 was 19.3 per cent for the country as a whole as compared with 8.2 per cent in the United States. The per cent of single females over 40 reached as high as 31.4 per cent among Guatemala's urban population. The explanation for these apparent differences is not readily available. Future field research might profitably be directed toward determining exactly how the patterns of interfamily relationships, of courtship, of personality, and family stability, influence the relatively high proportion of unattached persons, especially among the Ladinos.

FERTILITY

Few places have a higher birth rate than Guatemala. Fertility is generally higher in many parts of Latin America than in most other parts of the world, but in recent years Guatemala's birth rate has ranked as the highest in all of the Latin American countries. In 1955, there were 48.8 live births per thousand women in Guatemala. Venezuela had a birth rate of 47.0, Mexico, 46.2; Costa Rica, 40.3; Puerto Rico, 35.0; Chile, 35.0; Peru, 29.5; the United States, 24.6; and Argentina, 23.9.[5]

Comparison with figures for the United States gives a good indication of the high fertility rate in Guatemala. Attention is called to Table

5. *United Nations Demographic Yearbook*, 1956.

45 showing the fertility ratio, or the number of children under five years of age per thousand women between the ages of 15 to 44 inclusive. The over-all fertility ratio for Guatemala was 752; for the United States, it was 473. Throughout the world, fertility is generally lower in urban than in rural areas; and this was the case both in Guatemala and in the United States in 1950, as can be seen in Table 45. However, the fertility ratio for the capital city of Guatemala, the most urban place in that country, was 541, higher than the ratio for all urban places in the United States (422). The ratio for Guatemala City was only a little lower than the over-all ratio for rural non-farm areas in the United States (567). The ratio for rural Guatemala was 808, in comparison to the ratio of 594 for rural farm places in the United

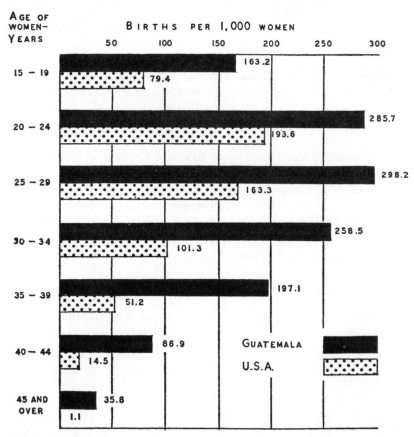

Figure 18. Number of births per 1,000 women in Guatemala and in the United States, by age of the women. Data from the census of population in each country in 1950.

TABLE 45. *Number of children under five years of age per 1,000 women aged 15 to 44 in Guatemala and in the United States, by degree of urban influence*

Country and degree of urban influence	Number of children under 5 years of age	Number of women aged 15–44 inclusive	Number of children per 1,000 women aged 15–44
Guatemala (total)	469,782	624,971	752
Urban	105,021	173,386	606
Guatemala City	42,436	78,485	541
Other urban places	62,585	94,901	660
Rural	364,761	451,585	808
United States (total)	16,163,571	34,205,803	473
Urban	9,772,719	23,142,913	422
Rural	6,390,852	11,062,890	578
Rural nonfarm	3,771,182	6,655,141	567
Rural farm	2,619,670	4,407,749	594

Source: *Sexto censo de población,* and *Seventeenth Census of the United States,* 1950.

States. As might be expected, the fertility ratio was somewhat higher among the Indians (765) than among the Ladinos (736).

Figure 18 contrasts birth rates by age of mother in Guatemala and in the United States in 1950. The rates are given as the number of live births per thousand women in specified age groups. Not only are the rates lower in the United States in all the age groups shown, but the rates of decline with age of the mother are significantly different in the two countries. The number of live births declines much more sharply after age 30 in the United States than in Guatemala. It would appear from Figure 18 that married women in Guatemala continue bearing children about as often as nature permits until menopause.

ILLEGITIMACY

Because of the large number of common-law marriages, an overwhelming majority of the children in Guatemala are technically illegitimate. Until 1943, illegitimacy was officially noted in birth registrations. At that time about 75 per cent of all births were classified as illegitimate, including children of common-law marriages as well as those of unattached mothers; but in keeping with the general spirit of reform after the Revolution of 1944, the distinction is no longer made in the official records. Illegitimacy in this context, however, does not have the social implications that it has in the United States, for instance. Most of these children are living in normal family situations and there is no stigma attached to children of common-law marriages.

There are, of course, many cases of illegitimacy in which the mother is not married, even under common law. This is more likely to be the case in the large urban centers like Guatemala City to which women are drawn to enter domestic service and other occupations; and where there is an imbalance in the sex ratio.[6] In the capital, as in Mexico City and other large cities of Latin America, it is not uncommon for unmarried servant women to have children by fathers with whom they have never lived, but with whom they have simply had a brief affair. Many of these women have migrated to the city from the countryside and hence have no parents or male relatives to shield them from sexual exploitation. The extent to which premarital sexual relations take place varies from one group to another. Traditionally among the upper classes, girls are closely supervised and are permitted to see boy friends only in the presence of some other member of the family. In many rural areas marriage, including common-law unions, is arranged by the parents of the persons involved and is an arrangement that is not to be entered into lightly.

In other areas, however, mating and premarital relations are regarded with apparent unconcern, except that paternity presupposes acceptance of responsibility for economic support.

Wagley describes an illustrative incident in the village of Chimaltenango as follows:

> Few children are born to unmarried mothers in Chimaltenango. Indeed women frequently acquire a husband by becoming pregnant. Two men who had been secretly cohabiting with the same woman quarrelled over her when she became pregnant, although she was a widow with three children and no longer young. Both claimed paternity to the coming child. The quarrel, taken to the *Alcalde* (the village mayor) was ultimately settled in favor of the man who had no wife and could support her. Often a pregnant girl will secure a husband after she has been deserted by her lover. No one counts the months, and the new husband is happy over the fecundity of his wife. Rarely, however, a child is born without a father to claim it. Such children are not looked down upon by the people. When the mother marries, as she is sure to do, the child will take her husband's name, and it may even inherit from the stepfather.[7]

6. In 1950, the sex ratio in Guatemala City was 84.7 males per 100 females among persons fifteen years of age and over.

7. Wagley, *The Social and Religious Life of a Guatemalan Village*, p. 25.

SIZE AND COMPOSITION OF THE HOUSEHOLD

Households are larger in Guatemala than in the United States, averaging in 1950 4.9 persons as compared to 3.4 in the United States. For urban households the average was 4.6 persons in Guatemala, compared to 3.2 persons in the United States. The average for rural households in Guatemala (5.0 persons) was higher than the average for rural farm households in the United States (4.0 persons).

Higher fertility, of course, contributes to the greater size of the household in Guatemala; but the composition of the household is also

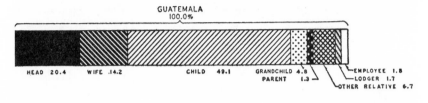

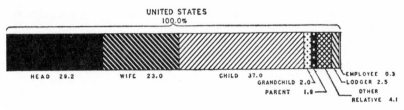

Figure 19. Composition of the household in Guatemala and in the United States, showing per cent of household members consisting of various types of members such as family head, wife, children, etc. Data from the 1950 census of population in each country.

a factor. Newly married Guatemalans sometimes live for a while with their parents, particularly those of the husband. A household may also include miscellaneous other relatives. In addition there may be an *hijo de casa,* a child who is taken into the home as a semi-adopted member.[8]

Figure 19 shows the proportion of persons in the household by relationship to the head in Guatemala and the United States in 1950. As can be seen by comparing the two bars, the proportion of children in the Guatemalan household (49.1 per cent) was considerably higher than in the North American household (37.0 per cent). The proportion of persons outside the primary family but still living within the household—grandchildren, parents, and other relatives, lodgers, and resident

8. The *hijo de casa* will be discussed further in the next section.

employees—was also larger in Guatemala (16.3 per cent) than in the United States (10.8 per cent).

Indian households in Guatemala tend to be larger than those of Ladinos. Excluding lodgers and servants,[9] the average Indian household in 1950 consisted of 5.0 persons, compared to the average ladino one of 4.5 persons. Likewise, rural households generally have more

TABLE 46. *Average size of households by ethnic group and rural-urban residence, by regions, 1950*

| | AVERAGE NUMBER OF PERSONS IN HOUSEHOLDS | | | | |
	Total population	*Indians*	*Ladinos*	*Rural inhabitants*	*Urban inhabitants*
REPUBLIC	4.7	5.0	4.5	4.9	4.3
Central	4.5	4.7	4.4	5.0	4.3
North	3.4	3.7	3.3	3.4	3.3
East	4.8	4.8	4.8	4.8	4.3
South	3.9	4.0	3.9	3.9	3.9
West	5.1	5.2	4.9	5.2	4.7
North central	5.1	5.2	4.6	5.2	4.4

Source: Sexto censo de población. Lodgers and servants were excluded in the calculation of the average size of households.

members than urban ones. The average in rural areas was 4.9 persons and in urban places it was 4.3 persons.

LIFE CYCLE

The life cycle of an individual is patterned by his social and cultural circumstances. The course of a Traditional Indian would differ from that of a Transitional Indian on a coffee plantation. Differences would also be found among the various classes of Ladinos.

Material for a detailed comparison of the life cycle of individuals in all of these categories is unfortunately not available. Thus, the discussion in the following sections relates more to the Traditional Indians than to the Transitional Indians or the Ladinos.[10]

9. In comparing the average size of households of ethnic groups in Guatemala, one must exclude lodgers and servants. This is because the size of the household for each ethnic group was computed by taking the total number of persons in each ethnic group and dividing this by the total number of households in that ethnic group. Thus Indian women who are servants in ladino households were classified as Indian ethnically; and hence their number would be averaged into (increase the size of) the Indian households rather than those of the Ladinos where they were actually living. See *Sexto censo de población,* p. xxiv.

10. Data on the Traditional Indians are to be found in such works as Ruth

Attitude toward having children

According to Guatemalan ideals, a family should be large. In rural Guatemala, children become economic assets at a fairly early age. Moreover, it is only after the birth of the first child that the parents are regarded as fully adult by the community. Barrenness may serve as grounds for terminating a union.

The ideal size is often larger than the actual size. For example, among the Indians of Chichicastenango, the ideal family consists of six sons and six daughters, an ideal which is seldom realized. Ruth Bunzel quotes an informant as disdainfully describing the procession of children of all ages and sizes in his father-in-law's family as "just like a marimba." [11] An Indian with several sons has that many helpers for his work, but he also has to divide his land for inheritance that many more ways. With the increasing population pressures on the land, especially in the western highlands, this often serves as a potential source of conflict within the family. Although we do not have substantiating data, it is likely that the emerging middle classes in the urban centers prefer smaller families than the peasant families of the rural areas.

Despite a tendency to have smaller families than the ideal size, the practice of birth control does not seem to be widespread, particularly among the Indians, although there are some folk beliefs regarding birth control. For instance, the Ladinos of Panajachel believe that lime juice induces sterility in women.[12] The Indians of Santiago Chimaltenango have heard of ladino contraceptives but do not seem to make use of them.[13] However, the Chorti Indians of eastern Guatemala have a variety of remedies to avoid pregnancies.[14]

Bunzel, *Chichicastenango. A Guatemalan Village* (Locust Valley, N.Y., 1952); Gillin, *The Culture of Security;* La Farge, *Santa Eulalia;* Maud Oakes, *The Two Crosses of Todos Santos* (New York, 1951); Benjamin D. Paul and Lois Paul, "The Life Cycle," in *Heritage of Conquest;* Tumin, *Caste in a Peasant Society;* Wagley, *The Social and Religious Life of a Guatemalan Village;* Wisdom, *The Chorti Indians of Guatemala.* The article by the Pauls is a general summary. Information on the Ladinos is to be found in the works of Gillin and Tumin cited above and also in Adams, *Cultural Surveys,* pp. 327 ff.

11. Bunzel, op. cit., pp. 98–9.

12. Sol Tax in a letter comparing Panajachel with Agua Escondida, following Robert Redfield's "Notes on Agua Escondida," in Microfilm Collection of Manuscripts on Middle America Cultural Anthropology, Univ. of Chicago.

13. Wagley, op. cit., p. 20.

14. Wisdom, op. cit., p. 286.

Birth

Beginning with the introduction of the social security program in Guatemala, there has been an increasing tendency for women to patronize the hospital for child delivery. In the rural districts, however, most deliveries take place in the home, with a midwife in attendance. She may have watched the progress of a woman's pregnancy and administered abdominal massages to assure a normal presentation. During the actual labor, the position most commonly taken by the mother is that of kneeling or squatting. Massages, "hot" drinks, and sometimes magic are used to facilitate delivery.

Baptism and compadrazco (Godparenthood)

The idea of baptism and godparenthood came into the New World with Roman Catholicism, but it is more deeply entrenched in Guatemalan life than in Europe. The godparents bring the child to the baptismal font in the church, give an item of clothing or some such gift to the child, and pay the priest's fee. However, the mutual obligations implied in godparenthood extend far beyond the actual ceremony.

Godparents are regarded essentially as auxiliary parents. The child is trained to show deference and respect toward his *padrinos*, as the godparents are called. The godparents and the child's parents refer to each other as co-parents, or *compadres* (and *comadres* in the case of women).[15] Compadres have the right to turn to each other for advice and assistance whenever in need. If the parents should die, the child is often taken into the home of his godparents and reared as an hijo de casa (child of the house).

Parents try to select compadres who will have a genuine interest in the welfare of the child. Generally, the choice falls on a couple for whom they have deep respect. In some areas, the wealth and prestige of the prospective godparents outweigh other considerations. In San Luis Jilotepeque, a high-status ladino couple had over a hundred godchildren.

Indians frequently get Ladinos to be padrinos to their children, but Ladinos rarely reciprocate. Although Indians often seek compadres among their own ethnic group, they sometimes consider it advantageous to be able to turn to an influential ladino compadre for small favors. A Ladino who consents to act as godfather to an Indian child can, in turn, occasionally ask his compadre to do errands or to help out in the fields. If the Indian parents should die, the Ladino would

15. In San Luis Jilotepeque, ladino and Indian compadres do not call each other such, since the term would imply an inadmissible equality.

be expected to rear the orphaned child as an hijo de casa. However, this charitable act would be amply rewarded by the services that the child would render about the house until adulthood.[16] Although an individual may acquire godparents on other occasions (confirmation, marriage, or serious illness), the baptismal godparents are generally regarded as the most important ones.

Infancy

Mothers in rural areas usually nurse their infants for about 15 to 18 months. Ladino women tend to wean their babies earlier than do Indian women who, in some instances, may nurse a child as long as three years if another baby is not born in the meantime. The infant is nursed whenever he cries. If the mother's milk fails, a wet nurse is sought. Unspiced atole is generally the first food given to an infant along with the mother's milk. Other foods are given as teeth appear.

The child receives affection and attention from all members of the household during early infancy. However, the admiration of outsiders is generally not welcome, for fear of contamination by an "evil eye." From the point of view of rural inhabitants an infant's health is guarded by seclusion from outsiders rather than by measures of sanitation.

Among the Indians, toilet training is not forced, and there is no pressure upon the child to develop sphincter control before he is physiologically able and can understand instructions. Full control is not expected until he is two or three years old. Ladinos tend to be somewhat stricter in this respect.

Training

Except among the higher-status urban Ladinos, formal schooling generally plays little part in training a child to take his place in society as an adult. Quite understandably, many Indians and lower-class Ladinos believe that the training their children get in doing the necessary work about the fields or the house is much more valuable than the ability to read and write. From about six or seven years of age, children are gradually given tasks commensurate with their physical and mental development. For example, a young boy may be expected to guard the crops against birds or to bring home small bundles of wood. When he is a little older, he may accompany his father on trading expeditions. A little girl may be given an undersized grinding stone and be taught to make small tortillas; and when she becomes sufficiently skilled, she can begin to use a larger stone. By the time a

16. See Gillin, op. cit., pp. 60 ff. and Tumin, op. cit., pp. 125–40.

child is about twelve or thirteen years old, he or she is considered nearly ready for adult responsibilities.

Attitudes toward disciplining children vary. Scolding and physical punishment may be found in all groups, but Tumin felt that in San Luis Jilotepeque the control of children in Indian families was based on patterns of cooperation among their members while the extremes of permissiveness and authoritariansm were more frequently found in ladino families than in Indian ones.[17]

The attainment of puberty is generally not marked by special ceremonies. However, girls are from thereon watched more closely "for fear something might 'happen' to them." [18] Boys have more freedom, and in some areas have affairs with older women. Adolescent boys in many Indian communities tend to join together in cliques which, among other functions, help to introduce them into courtship practices. A youth learns from his friends how to court girls, and an especially shy boy receives particular encouragement and advice.

Marriage

When the time comes to consider marriage seriously, young Guatemalans may choose their own mates, or their parents may make the selection for them. In the latter event, parents usually take into consideration the wishes of their children. The Indians, especially the traditional ones, have a marked preference for marriage with someone from the same municipio rather than someone from another community. Neither the Indians nor the Ladinos are likely to seek partners across ethnic lines.[19] Within these limitations, a prospective spouse generally can be anyone except a member of the immediate family, a first cousin, a child of one's padrinos, or a person with the same surname. The prohibition against marriages between first cousins is not always strictly enforced.

As indicated in a previous section, few couples undergo a civil marriage, although it is the only union recognized by the government, and is a legal prerequisite to a church wedding. Couples may simply begin living together; but many first marriages are marked by some sort of traditional ceremony which varies from locality to locality. According to Wagley, a father buys a wife for his son in Santiago Chimaltenango,

17. Tumin, op. cit., p. 167.
18. Benjamin D. Paul and Lois Paul, op. cit., p. 187.
19. Between 1948 and 1954, intermarriages constituted no more than 2.2 per cent of all legal unions. The lowest proportion during that period was 1.2 per cent in 1954. Dirección General de Estadística, *Boletín mensual, 56* (1955), 25.

the price depending upon the wealth of the family. After a chiman has divined to see whether the arrangements are propitious, the parents of the boy and girl drink aguardiente until they are quite drunk. The boy then moves into the home of his father-in-law, bringing with him the bride-price, usually in the form of maize or other goods. At the end of fifteen days there is a ceremony with the sacrifice of a turkey and prayers by the chiman. After this ceremony, the couple live with the husband's family.[20]

Wisdom describes the form of wedding ceremony observed by the more ladinoized Indians among the Chorti. It takes place in the village church often without the presence of a priest, and is followed by eight days of feasting and dancing.

> For the ceremony the couple kneel in front of the altar, and the marriage godparents appear in front of them, each holding a lighted yellow candle in the right hand. The godfather, taking a cord in his hand, places the center of its length around the man's neck and hands over the candle to him. The godmother takes the two ends of the cord, twists them once, and places them around the woman's neck, giving the woman her candle. The priest, if present, repeats mass at the church altar. At the conclusion of the mass the priest gives the benediction and places a ring on the woman's finger.[21]

Newly married couples, particularly Indian ones, often live for a few years in the home of the husband's family. Later, they may establish their own households on a nearby site. Often the married son is given a portion of his father's land for his own use. The father eventually makes a final division of the land among his sons, but the anticipation of the inheritance frequently arouses much tension and hostility among the brothers.

In both Indian and ladino households, the husband is regarded as supreme. However, except among some middle- and upper-class Ladinos, wives are by no means meek and submissive. Women have considerable influence in family matters, since without their cooperation much of the work in the fields and in the house would not be done. The time-consuming tasks of grinding corn, carrying water, washing clothes, weaving, and the like are women's work which no man wishes to perform. The Traditional Indian woman has the additional ad-

20. Wagley, op. cit., p. 39.
21. Wisdom, op. cit., p. 300 (footnote).

vantage that her assistance is necessary in the religious rituals her husband performs. In Santiago Chimaltenango, it is believed that the prayers of a man without a wife's backing would always go unanswered.[22]

Middle- and upper-class ladino women tend to be dominated by their husbands more than are Indian or lower-class ladino women. Significantly perhaps, these women are not as essential in the division of labor in the home as are the peasant women, since most of the household tasks are performed by servants. If the husbands choose to maintain mistresses, the wives have little recourse other than to tolerate these affairs. Most husbands are probably faithful, but the double standard of morality nevertheless exists among some members of the middle and upper classes in Guatemala, as elsewhere in Latin America. Moreover, Latin Americans generally seem to place a high value on virility (machismo), and the double standard provides a favorable milieu for extramarital evidence of a man's prowess. As an extreme example, the father of the ladino druggist in San Luis Jilotepeque was reported to have had some 80 children, only three of which were legitimate. He had been a prominent government official, and the druggist was as proud of his father's virility as of his distinction in public affairs.[23]

Regardless of the provocations, a woman of the middle and upper classes generally tries to avoid a divorce, since it is not regarded as respectable in her social circle and is against her religious principles. She tries to maintain the outward appearances of a united family even when her husband is keeping a mistress or two on the side.

Divorce is rare among the lower economic groups, but for reasons different from those among the higher income groups. In the first place, relatively few couples among the lower economic groups are legally married, and divorce is unnecessary for separation from a common-law spouse. Secondly, even those persons who are legally married seldom go to the expense and bother of a divorce. They simply leave and start marital life anew with someone else. In spite of the fact that separation from a spouse is quite easy and, moreover, does not carry the same social stigma as among the higher income groups, it appears that the great majority of the unions are stable and for life. Exceptions are to be found, particularly on the plantations. Richard Adams reported that on one cattle farm in Santa Rosa, the frequent changing of partners seemed to be more the rule than not, and even open polygamy was practiced by some persons.[24]

22. Wagley, op. cit., p. 16.
23. Gillin, op. cit., p. 52.
24. Adams, op. cit., p. 331.

Old age

Not much is known about the status of elderly persons in Guatemala. This may be due to the fact that they do not form a significant proportion of the population. The death rates are so high that relatively few persons reach old age.[25]

Among the Traditional Indians, old age has its disadvantages as well as its compensations. Very few Indians are in a position to accumulate enough property to see them through a comfortable old age. Whatever land a man has, he must sooner or later divide among his married sons. If he puts off the division too long, he may incur the resentment of his children; when he gets around to making it, he runs the risk of becoming completely dependent on one of his sons if illness or senility incapacitates him.

The disadvantages arising from land tenure and division may be offset by the prestige a man accumulates as he grows older and rises in the hierarchy of politico-religious offices of the community. The positive value placed on age in the traditional society, however, diminishes under the impact of social changes which are slowly beginning to take place. The introduction of the political party system, for example, tends to put the leadership of the community in the hands of younger men who can speak and write Spanish and thus to displace older men who have been respected for their traditional wisdom but who, for the most part, are illiterate (see Chapter 15).

Death

Death is a familiar phenomenon in any Guatemalan community. Frequently it does not give the individual an opportunity to sojourn here on earth more than a few days, weeks, or months. Its heaviest toll is taken among infants and small children; but no age group can resist its intrusion. In towns of any size, the daily tolling of the church bells signals the departure of some unfortunate soul who in all probability did not get a chance to live out even half of his "three score years and ten." As indicated in the previous chapter, the average individual in Guatemala can expect to live only 43.6 years; and one out of every ten infants dies before his first birthday.

The rituals surrounding death in Guatemala conform in a general way to those of orthodox Catholicism. However, since deaths occur

25. In 1950, only 4 per cent of the population in Guatemala was 60 years of age or over. In the United States, 12 per cent was 60 years of age or over. See Chapter 3.

so frequently and priests come so rarely to the rural areas, the rituals display local variations and are usually conducted by laymen.

The night before the burial, relatives and friends come to the house of the deceased for a wake. Prayers are said and candles are burned during the night watch. Food and coffee are served to the guests. Among the Indians, some sort of music may be played and aguardiente served. As the night progresses, people often get quite intoxicated on the aguardiente.

A funeral procession accompanies the corpse to the cemetery. If it is an Indian funeral, various articles may be buried with the deceased for use in the other life and aguardiente is often drunk by the mourners to allay grief. Ruth Bunzel reports that at the funerals she has observed in the Indian community of Chichicastenango, there was considerable jocularity and reeling drunkenness among the mourners. She speculates as to whether the great show of merriment might not be due to release of tensions.[26]

26. Bunzel, op. cit., p. 153.

Chapter 13

EDUCATION

During the colonial period, educational programs were almost entirely in the hands of the church. The clergy often combined instruction in the catechism with training in arts and crafts. They also offered instruction in reading and writing along with other rudiments of knowledge to the children of the Spaniards and to sons of other "principal persons" selected to perform roles of leadership in keeping the native population under control. Latin, considered to be the foundation of all education in those days, was taught by Dominican monks even before the middle of the sixteenth century. Plans for a university were discussed by the city council of Guatemala as early as 1581, but the institution was not formally founded until 1679. The Royal and Pontifical University of San Carlos Borromeo, as it was originally called, was patterned somewhat after the previously founded University of Mexico and the University of San Marcos in Lima, Peru. Its first classes were held in 1681.[1]

In the meantime the third printing press in the Americas was introduced into Guatemala in 1660 following those previously established in Mexico and Lima. Thus, Guatemala got an early start in the development of certain aspects of higher education in the New World. Throughout the years, however, educational instruction was confined to a small minority of the population. While training in such specialized subjects as philosophy, astrology, canon law, native languages, and anatomy was provided at the university even before the close of the seventeenth century, comparatively little was accomplished over the years in making education of even the most elementary character available to the common people.

After independence the value and necessity of a more widespread educational system was recognized and the government made some

1. Jones, *Guatemala, Past and Present*, p. 326.

attempt to develop it. Legislation was enacted in 1875 declaring that education must be "popular, obligatory, lay, and free"; [2] but the government was in no position to require all children to attend school because there were not enough school buildings, teachers, equipment, and programs to provide schooling for all. Furthermore, there was little motivation outside of the capital city for parents to send their children to school. Faced with almost insuperable problems, the government began by trying to improve the quality of education in the cities, while the rural masses, speaking their own native languages and living within their isolated cultures, were left largely to themselves, unaffected by the programs instituted by the various governments of the post-independence era.

As the years went by, lack of funds to support rural schools led the government to pass legislation requiring plantation owners to support schools for the children of their employees at their own expense. This legislation is still in effect but such schools have never functioned very efficiently. Usually they have been open for only a few months or weeks during the year and then only with small enrollments. The finquero has tended to comply reluctantly with the law since he has regarded it as a discriminatory measure requiring him to undergo unnecessary expense. Non-compliance was made easier by the fact that neither children nor parents saw any advantages in attending school. The children could make no use of what they were taught and the parents needed what few pennies the children could earn by working on the plantation.

Jones writes that in 1925 only 182 finca schools were functioning. By 1932, he reports that it was a source of considerable pride that there were 367 that were really in operation and not merely open, as formerly, "only during the examination period" or when the inspector came. These schools were usually crude, one-room buildings, poorly furnished and equipped.[3] Nevertheless, without these private finca schools, opportunities for schooling would have been virtually non-existent in many areas.

The curriculum and the methods of teaching in the elementary schools of Guatemala were described as they existed in 1944–45 by William Griffith after a survey of rural education in the Republic at that time.

The course of study followed was hardly more adequate than the buildings and their equipment. It was patterned on the eight-

2. Ibid., p. 331.
3. Ibid., p. 334.

eenth century European model and had reached the ultimate in formalized and sterile intellectualism. Instruction consisted of dictation by the teacher and memorization by the students of large masses of unrelated and irrelevant material on an astounding variety of subjects, few if any of which had any relationship to the life of the student either as a child or as an adult. It was considered an evidence of high academic standards to force difficult subject matter farther and farther down in the curriculum without regard for the ability of the child to grasp the principles which the instruction involved. The proposed reform of the elementary school curriculum after the revolution, for example, included geometry for the first grade. Memorization of subject matter became, therefore, not only an approved practice but a practical necessity to a child who, being unable to understand, could pass the inevitable examination only by a feat of memory.[4]

Thus, despite various attempts to improve the educational program, the schools were in an extremely backward condition at the end of the Ubico dictatorship in 1944. Schools were few in number, buildings and supplies were almost non-existent, teachers' salaries were ridiculously low, and teachers were generally ill-prepared for their work.

ILLITERACY

Guatemala has one of the highest illiteracy rates found in the various countries of the Americas. In 1950, 71.7 per cent of the population seven years of age and older were recorded as illiterate in that they were unable to read and write. This high rate was surpassed at that time in the Americas only by those reported in the Republics of Bolivia, Paraguay and El Salvador.

Illiteracy varied from one region to another, with the highest rates found in the western and north central regions where the greatest proportion of Indians are found. In the north central region 90.4 per cent were illiterate, and in the west 80.7 per cent. The lowest rate was in the central region which contains Guatemala City. In this area 42.1 per cent were so classified. The northern area, though extremely isolated and sparsely populated, is inhabited mostly by Ladinos, who generally have a somewhat lower rate of illiteracy than do the Indians. The southern region had 69.4 per cent illiterate and the east had 76.2 per cent.

4. William Griffith, "A Recent Attempt at Educational Cooperation Between the United States and Guatemala," *Middle American Research Records*, 1 (1949), 175.

The geographical distribution of illiteracy is plotted by municipios on the map in Figure 20. Most of the areas with the highest rates of illiteracy are ranged in a solid block stretching across the nation, dividing the northern region from the central and southern. In most of the municipios in these areas the illiteracy rate was more than 90 per cent. On the other hand, the northern municipios of El Petén and Izabal, as well as municipios in the central, eastern and southern regions, show somewhat lower rates of illiteracy. As has been noted earlier, these areas are more ladinoized than others.

TABLE 47. *Illiteracy in population seven years of age and over, by ethnic group, by rural-urban residence, and by region, 1950, in per cent*

| | Total | RESIDENCE | | ETHNIC GROUP | |
		Rural	Urban	Indian	Ladino
REPUBLIC	71.7	82.4	40.8	90.1	50.5
Central	42.1	72.6	30.6	81.7	31.1
North	55.8	66.7	33.9	87.8	47.8
East	76.2	80.2	50.6	90.6	70.1
South	69.4	75.4	46.5	88.6	54.2
West	80.7	85.1	56.2	89.9	48.0
North central	90.4	93.3	54.9	96.3	58.3

Source: *Sexto censo de población.*

It is logical to expect that in the cities there would be more educational facilities and also greater motivation for parents to send their children to school, which would result in a lower rate of illiteracy than in the more isolated rural communities. This is certainly evident in Guatemala where 82.4 per cent of the rural population was illiterate in 1950 as compared with only 40.8 per cent of the urban. An extreme illustration of the rural-urban contrast in the rate of illiteracy is found in comparing Guatemala City with some of the rural areas. Guatemala City had an illiteracy rate of only 24.7 per cent. At the opposite extreme, the four departments in which the illiteracy rate in rural areas was 90 per cent or more are Totonicapán with 90, Sololá with 92.2, El Quiché with 93.9 and Alta Verapaz with 95 per cent (see Appendix Table 10).

Illiteracy is also closely related to ethnic group composition. Obviously, illiteracy is highest among some of the isolated Indian groups. As noted in Table 47, 90.1 per cent of the Indians in the entire Republic were illiterate in 1950, as compared with 50.5 per cent of the Ladinos. The rate among the Indians was greater than 80 per cent in every region and reached the extreme of 96.3 per cent in the north central region. On the other hand, the rates were generally lower among the

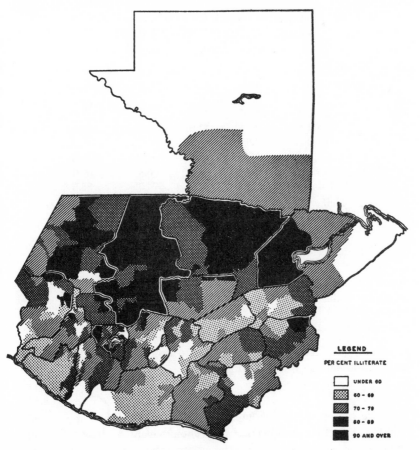

LEGEND

PER CENT ILLITERATE

- [ ] UNDER 60
- 60 – 69
- 70 – 79
- 80 – 89
- 90 AND OVER

Figure 20. Map showing percentage of population seven years of age and older that is illiterate, by municipios. Data from *Sexto censo de población,* 1950.

Ladinos where the range varied from 31.1 per cent in the central region to 70.1 per cent in the east (see also Appendix Table 10).

Finally, it should be pointed out that illiteracy is also associated with age. Among the population ten years of age and older, the illiteracy rate is lowest in the younger age group and increases gradually thereafter. Thus 67.9 per cent are illiterate in the ten to fourteen age group.

This increases slightly to 68.5 in the age group 15–39, and further increases to 75.2 in the age group 40 and over.[5]

This, of course, is a natural expectation where efforts are being made to extend educational facilities and establish new schools that will

TABLE 48. *Illiteracy in population ten years of age and over by age group, rural-urban residence, and by ethnic group, 1950, in per cent*

Residence and ethnic group	Total	AGE GROUPS (YEARS)		
		10–14	15–39	40 and over
Total	70.1	67.9	68.5	75.2
Rural	81.3	77.9	80.3	86.1
Urban	38.7	33.7	35.7	47.8
Indian	89.5	85.1	88.7	94.5
Rural	91.3	86.9	90.8	95.6
Urban	77.9	71.2	74.5	88.5
Ladino	47.9	47.8	45.4	53.7
Rural	64.5	63.4	62.5	70.1
Urban	24.1	19.4	21.5	32.2

Source: *Sexto censo de población.*

reach a higher proportion of the children than was possible previously when the older population was in the school-age group.

FACTORS ACCENTUATING ILLITERACY

Among the factors which combine to accentuate Guatemala's illiteracy problem are the following:

Lack of schools

There simply are not enough schools in Guatemala to accommodate children of school age even if they should want to attend. Adequate educational opportunities for the entire school age population have never been available, and even though at various times new educational programs have been introduced, the facilities are far from adequate to serve the needs. In the rural areas the shortage is especially noticeable. It is not at all uncommon to find that only a one-room school is available to serve an area having several thousand inhabitants.

5. One exception is found among the rural Ladinos where a slightly higher rate of illiteracy (63.4 per cent) is found in the age group 10–14 years than in the succeeding age group 15–39 years where it is 62.5 per cent. The author has no explanation for this.

Therefore, the law requiring compulsory attendance for children of school age is more of an expression of idealism than of expected compliance. Although the number of schools has greatly increased in recent years, it will probably be many years before there will be enough schools to make compulsory attendance practical.

Low school enrollment and poor attendance

Enrollment in the elementary schools of Guatemala increased from a total of 135,150 children in 1944 to 229,267 in 1956. This is an increase of 62.2 per cent in the enrollment. During this same period, however, the estimated number of children of school age, seven to fourteen years, increased from 461,863 in 1944 to 648,254 in 1956, an increase of 40.4 per cent. Thus, much of the gain in enrollment was off-

TABLE 49. *Per cent of population seven to fourteen years of age attending school, by rural-urban residence and by ethnic group, 1950*

Residence	Total	Indian	Ladino
TOTAL	24.4	10.8	40.4
Rural	15.5	9.5	25.0
Urban	55.5	20.6	68.6

Source: Sexto censo de población.

set by the increasing population of school age. Whereas in 1944 there were 70.7 per cent of the population of school age who were not enrolled in schools, by 1956 there still remained 64.6 per cent not enrolled, despite the increase in the total enrollment during this period.[6] Moreover, enrollment data do not even begin to tell the full story since many of those enrolled do not regularly attend. Data were collected through the population census of 1950, showing the number of children actually attending school (Table 49). In that year only 24.4 per cent of the children, age seven to fourteen, were attending school. In the rural areas only 15.5 per cent were attending, while in the urban schools the percentage was 55.5. Thus, it is obvious that fewer rural children attend school than urban. Stated negatively, it may be said that three-fourths of the children of compulsory school age in Guatemala were not attending school in 1950, and that the proportion was

6. Computed from data published by Dirección General de Estadística, in *Boletín mensual*, Nos. 9–10 (1957), 5. Enrollments in urban night schools were not included in these data. Hence, the enrollments appear somewhat smaller than enrollment figures given in Table 51, which also include night schools. In 1944, there were 4,071 enrolled in urban night schools. In 1956, there were 8,851.

44.5 per cent in the urban areas but reached the staggering proportion of 84.5 per cent in the rural districts. As might be expected, the proportion attending school also varied greatly between the two ethnic groups. Only 10.8 per cent of the Indians of school age were attending school as compared with 40.4 per cent of the Ladinos.

Limited progress in school

Most of the children who do enroll in the elementary schools do not progress very far. In 1956 more than one-half of the children enrolled in the elementary schools of Guatemala (51.7 per cent) were no higher than the first grade in school. Only 20.2 per cent were in the second

TABLE 50. *Primary school enrollment by grade and by type of school, 1956* *

Grade in school	ALL PUPILS		IN RURAL SCHOOLS		IN URBAN SCHOOLS	
	Number	Per cent	Number	Per cent	Number	Per cent
TOTAL	228,637	100.0	91,277	100.0	137,360	100.0
Preparatory	14,912	6.5	11,897	13.0	3,015	2.2
First	103,396	45.2	53,835	59.0	49,561	36.1
Second	46,099	20.2	19,317	21.2	26,782	19.5
Third	25,951	11.4	5,318	5.8	20,633	15.0
Fourth	17,706	7.8	658	0.7	17,048	12.4
Fifth	11,938	5.2	199	0.2	11,739	8.6
Sixth	8,635	3.8	53	0.1	8,582	6.2

Source: Ministerio de Educación Pública, Dirección de Estadística Escolar.

* Urban schools are defined by the Ministry of Education as all schools located in the municipal centers; rural schools are those located outside of municipal centers.

grade, and 11.4 per cent in the third. In other words, 83.3 per cent of the enrolled students were in the first three grades in school. In areas where the Indian population is large it is necessary to precede the first grade with a preparatory class designed to teach the children how to speak Spanish. Thus 6.5 per cent of the children enrolled in 1956 were in the preparatory class trying to learn the official language of the nation. In the rural districts 13 per cent were in the preparatory class and 72 per cent were either in the first grade or the preparatory class. Elementary schools in urban areas generally contain six grades while in the rural districts they seldom have more than four, usually only two. Even in the urban schools, 38.3 per cent of the enrolled children had not gone beyond the first grade and 72.8 per cent had not gone beyond the third grade. Thus it appears that even among those children who do enroll, few continue long enough to make schooling important in their lives.

Inadequacy of private rural schools

Many of the rural schools in Guatemala are supported entirely by the owners of plantations. This is due to the Guatemalan law which requires that wherever there is a resident population on a finca containing at least ten families, the finquero must establish and maintain at his own expense a rural school for the children of school age belonging to these families.[7] In 1956, there were 711 of these private rural schools with a total enrollment of 18,860 pupils. This means that 26.6 per cent of the rural schools were maintained by private landowners and these schools accounted for 20.7 per cent of the total rural school enrollment of the nation.

For understandable reasons, the finqueros have not supported these schools with any degree of enthusiasm, but have regarded them as unnecessary expenses which should be borne by the government. Children of school age may help with the work of the finca and one can easily see why it would be to the finquero's interest to permit the children to work on the plantation rather than to send them to school, especially during rush seasons.

The author has visited schools on fincas containing several thousand inhabitants and almost invariably they consisted of one room, with one teacher and an attendance of from ten to thirty pupils. Obviously, several hundred pupils of school age were living on the finca but were not in attendance. Government inspectors visit the finca schools at examination time and give advice to the teacher but rarely do such visits result in improved classroom performance. Occasionally, one finds a finquero who takes pride in his local school and makes it somewhat better than the average. It is generally acknowledged by the Ministry of Education in Guatemala, that the private rural schools maintained by the United Fruit Company are among the best in the nation. Generally speaking, however, for the country as a whole, the finca schools are poor and it is unlikely that they will ever become efficient educational institutions until they are given official public support. Perhaps it should be mentioned that poor quality has not been confined to the plantation schools. Schools maintained by the government have also been inadequate. In recent years, however, the government has given more attention to public education but has continued to neglect the plantation schools.

7. Ministerio de Educación Pública, *Ley orgánica de educación nacional, Decreto número 558,* Art. 99, Guatemala, 1956.

Scattered settlement patterns

It has been pointed out previously (Chapter 2) that many of the inhabitants of rural Guatemala live in scattered settlements strewn over the hills and valleys. We find that 23.6 per cent of the localities outside of the municipal centers consist of isolated settlements where one cannot see one house from another. Such dispersed settlement makes it exceedingly difficult for the people to come together for educational or social purposes. With no transportation facilities, not even riding animals, children have to walk to and from school. It is unlikely that attendance will increase greatly unless and until transportation facilities for school children are available in these areas of scattered settlement.

The problems of Indian education

Many of the educational efforts of the past in Guatemala have been poorly adapted to the situation of the rural Indian living in culturally isolated areas. The Indian probably educates his children to the values, needs, and goals of his culture, and to the means of attaining them as effectively as do his ladino compatriots. Formal education is a new factor which is alien to the cultural tradition of the Indian. Formal is taken to mean the standardized information imparted to the child in subject matter not directly related to everyday life experience. Reading, writing, arithmetic, history, and language are some of the subjects taught to the school child which do not necessarily come within the range of the traditional education imparted by the Indian adult to his child.

Illiteracy has a connotation of backwardness, a connotation which is not welcome in the world of today. It is most commendable that most nations are making concerted efforts to blot it out, because too often illiteracy breeds other less desirable consequences. However, the desire to improve the literacy rates of a nation is only the first step. Building schools and providing teachers is only one side of the equation. There may be schools, teachers, books, and supplies; but unless the children attend, participate, and obtain something of concrete value which can be of use to them in their daily lives, the effort to educate them will probably be wasted and the results a dismal failure.

The social and cultural values of the rural peasant society, bound by traditional ways of doing things, and those of the urban are quite at variance. The motivations to learn in any individual are integrated with the levels of aspiration which the culture has implanted in him and with the means available to attain them. If the goals of the individual are such that formal education is necessary, he will probably be amenable to it. In the ladino society of urban Guatemala, it is necessary to have at least a minimum amount of formal education in order to attain the desired goals.

The average peasant, however, and especially the rural Indian, is confronted with an entirely different complex of needs and rewards. In this isolated culture which may be characterized as agrarian, traditional and conservative, the educational system is governed by local needs and goals. Fully integrated illiterate villagers are the products of their traditional educational system, just as fully integrated individuals in the city are the products of the urban educational system. The content and the method of imparting knowledge in these two systems may be completely different but they are the functional products of their respective cultures and environments.

In rural Guatemala the educational method is usually that of learning by observing one's elders. From the Indian's viewpoint there is no need for formalized schooling. His children receive practical education for the type of life which they are expected to lead by learning through doing. This education is usually fully adequate to the situation and to the future life expectations of the child. Reading and writing do not seem necessary in view of the cultural situation of the rural Indian agriculturalist; but knowledge of the traditional agricultural practices and lore is essential. This is what the rural Indian child receives from the education given to him by his parents and elders—an education aimed at satisfying the needs of an individual growing up in an isolated culture such as his. The individual Indian child probably develops a well-integrated personality, for he has adjusted himself to his cultural environment. He has levels of aspiration which can be attained without going beyond the bounds of his experience or his expected experiences. In other words, his education is integrated with the culture of his own Indian group in such a way that he may attain the goals which his culture sets forth as desirable.

Rural Guatemala is not an airtight compartment, however, into which no alien values can penetrate. It is linked with the outside world; it is interdependent in many ways, and its people are influenced by the non-Indian world outside. The government has seen fit to attempt to incorporate these rural peoples more fully into the national life and culture, and to this end has attempted to introduce schools to educate them.

Yet, in many cases, values which the child is taught in school are not consistent with those he finds prevalent in his home. His parents see little use for the information taught and they may react against sending their child to school. The child fails to see any connection between what he learns at school and the role he is expected to perform in his home or even in his municipio. He may with great difficulty learn to read Spanish, to do simple arithmetic, and to memorize historical facts; but he finds nothing in his social environment that calls for such newly acquired skills (see Plate 19). In the home he finds no books, no magazines, no newspapers, and no writing materials. None of these mysterious facilities are used by his relatives, friends, and neighbors. How then can he hope to use or to retain his newly acquired information? Only if the new set of values can be integrated within the existing cultural framework, can this new information become useful. The endeavor to introduce formal primary education into the peasant societies of Latin America, as elsewhere in the world, is basically the problem of making this adjustment. Wagley points out that regular attendance at school is dependent on the father's attitude toward the school, coupled with the need for the children at home. On the average, girls remain in school longer than boys because boys are needed by their fathers for work in the milpas. "Boys only learn how to be lazy there," he was told by one father. "They do not learn how to plant and harvest corn so they do not tarry long as scholars." There are both economic and moral pressures in the home that prevent attendance at school.[8]

Tumin reinforces the foregoing discussion in his study of the Guatemalan community of San Luis Jilotepeque. As in other rural areas, the children in this community are involved in the economic functions of their families at an early age and

> economic necessity, indifferent attitudes, and inadequate application of the law combine to make formal school systems considerably less significant in the lives of the pueblo residents than might overwise by expected. . . . There seems to be a general tendency . . . to rely on home instruction for adequate inculcation of those values and skills which are requisite to adult survival in the pueblo.[9]

Professor Louis Cooper, who worked with the rural schools of Guatemala in 1949–50, observed that over the years the curriculum generally had not been designed to meet the needs of children at the various developmental levels. Thus, content which might have been quite appropriate at one level was often imposed on another. Many of the teachers were teaching without the least knowledge of child

8. Wagley, *The Social and Religious Life of a Guatemalan Village*, p. 31.
9. Tumin, *Caste in a Peasant Society*, pp. 26–8.

development. The curricula in both rural and urban schools consisted of such things as the memorization of the bones of the body in the lower elementary grades, aspects of algebra in the lower grades, and the memorization of numerous historical and geographical facts. Mathematics seemed to be the memorization of number facts, with little or no attention to functional problem solving. In many schools there were children who knew little or no Spanish and the biggest hurdle to teaching itself was the problem of comprehension of the language of instruction. In many cases the teacher did not have a knowledge of the local Indian language. In such a situation there could be little incentive for the average rural child to attend school.[10]

It seems evident that the school system which operates under such conditions does not impart a training which in any real sense provides a means of facing life in the village. In fact, an individual who effectively absorbed the education imparted could easily become unfit for life in his local municipio. Only when the education imparted in the village is geared to the needs of the villager will it become effective.

What type of education can be offered to integrate the villager and his culture with the national culture? It cannot be merely a watered-down version of the urban curriculum. In many rural areas special emphasis might well be given to educational projects that will show both children and adults alike how to make use of the potential resources of their communities to improve their life. Stress should be placed upon such projects as health and sanitation, gardening, poultry-raising, other small-scale economic activities, and recreation. The school should serve as a center for the efforts to improve all aspects of community life. Not to be forgotten is the problem of continuing education, for to make a man literate is merely the first step in the never-ending process of keeping him literate. The skills learned through childhood exposure to formal schools can be only too easily forgotten if there is no way to utilize and develop them later. The problem of making a person want to learn will be solved only when useful information and knowledge in terms of his culture are available for him to use.

The Rural Functional School Movement

In 1946 Guatemala initiated a program designed to make its rural education functional by training teachers who could adapt the instructional work to the needs of the local communities. For this purpose the first rural normal school was established at one of the national fincas

10. Based on a personal interview.

known as *La Alameda,* situated in a rural area of the department of Chimaltenango in the central highlands about 35 miles from Guatemala City. This project resulted from a cooperative educational agreement signed in 1944 by the Ministry of Education of Guatemala and the Inter-American Educational Foundation, Inc. The program began with a workshop for 65 rural teachers. Emphasis was to be placed on functional education and the development of community leadership in rural school teachers. The first students, carefully chosen from the outlying areas, were adult teachers with families, for the aim was to set up a community at La Alameda, and the children of the teachers were to be enrolled in a demonstration school. In the beginning, the staff at La Alameda was made up of North Americans whose task, among other things, was to train replacements for themselves gradually from students at La Alameda. This was the first of a proposed series of regional normal schools to be carefully distributed about the country in the Indian-inhabited regions of Guatemala, one in each language and culture area. During this period the normal school staff was to develop a full four- to five-year program. This plan of the Institute of Inter-American Affairs in Guatemala was aimed at stimulating the organization of community schools.

Teaching guides were developed. For example, the *Guide of Instruction for Rural Teachers* (Guide No. 1) was prepared.[11] It is described by Cooper as follows:

> Although this guide leaves much to be desired, it is basically sound and is an excellent foundation upon which to start building the curriculum. This guide recommends that the curriculum of the rural schools be centered around the life and needs of the rural people. It would emphasize the teaching of simple agriculture, better health and nutrition, and the improvement of home and family living. Theoretically the entire curriculum would be drawn from the problems of the immediate environment; and the fundamental skills (the three R's) would be developed through the study of these problems. For example, "the school garden" and "how to raise and care for rabbits" might well be basic content units for the elementary grades. Through the study of such units the pupils would learn such things as (a) how to have a better garden; (b) how the vegetables might be used for improving nutrition and general health; and (c) through participation in the units, develop such skills as reading, writing, number work, and

11. Ministerio de Educación Pública, *Guía de instrucción para maestros rurales, 1,* Guatemala, 1948.

concomitant learnings such as sharing responsibility, cooperative planning, and civic responsibility.[12]

In 1949 with the cooperation of specialists from the United States, a program to be known as *Nucleos Escolares Campesinos* was organized. It was patterned after a similar program which had been instituted in Bolivia in 1931. Under this program, the rural schools of a given geographic area are organized in the form of a constellation; with one of the schools designated as the central school and the rest as sectional schools. All are placed under a trained director located at the central school. The director of the nucleo is in effect the supervisor of all the rural schools in the area. The number of schools attached to a nucleo varies from 10 to 30, depending on density of population, accessibility, and other factors. The program in Guatemala included 20 nucleos with an average of about 20 rural schools in each nucleo. The director of each nucleo was to be a graduate of the rural normal school.

It is generally felt that the plan of establishing nucleo schools under the directorship of men trained in adapting the content of education to the needs of the individual in his rural community is sound. Any permanent improvement of the status of education in the nation would also have to incorporate two types of in-service training programs for the nation's teachers. The first would be that of the training of the *maestros empíricos,* rural teachers who have been employed to teach but have received no training for this purpose, and have little besides enthusiasm to qualify them as teachers. Such teachers are desperately in need of help in acquiring additional subject matter, curriculum materials, and information about improved teaching methods. Under the second type of program, graduates of the normal schools would receive supervision and in-service up-grading. While these graduates have been drilled in methods, they have had little experience in actual teaching. The organization of the nucleos escolares was planned with these two basic needs in mind.

Although the program appears to have been soundly conceived, it encountered a great many difficulties in realization. In 1950 the cooperative program ceased to function because the Guatemalan government refused to appropriate its share of the necessary funds. Education in Guatemala, like many other programs, suffers from lack of continuity in personnel and clearly defined objectives. As in many other countries of Latin America, primary and secondary education is organized under the jurisdiction of the Ministry of Education. This means that whenever there is a change in government or even a shift of

12. J. Louis Cooper, unpublished manuscript.

ministers, there is likely to be a shift in policies and procedures as well as a shift in personnel all along the line. With each new minister there is a period of uncertainty and indecision as to just what the new official policy will be, which results in much wasted motion.

In 1956, Congress enacted a new school law defining the programs, policies, and procedures for carrying on education in the schools of Guatemala. Rural education was placed in a new division in the Ministry of Education known as the Division of Rural Social Educational Development. The objectives and purposes of rural education were redefined with emphasis again on functional education related to community and family development. Under the new arrangement, the nation was divided into three broad areas:

(a) An area of intensive work.

(b) An area of extensive work.

(c) An area of preparatory work.

The intensive area includes only those localities where nine of the most successful nucleos escolares have had their greatest development. In this area the work is carried on not only by teachers but also by social workers and by representatives from other government agencies. The activities of all are planned together and coordinated through the nine nucleos escolares. The local school thus serves not only as a place for instructing the children but also as a center for adult education and community development.

The area of extensive work includes a larger section of the country, where the remaining fourteen nucleos escolares are located. Work is carried on largely by the directors of these fourteen nucleos. Efforts are confined to the schools themselves since personnel is unavailable to devote to community problems.

The region designated as a preparatory area includes the vast majority of the rural schools of the nation, where the work is carried on only by the local teachers. Resources in this vast area are grossly inadequate. Teachers have little or no training and are left largely to fend for themselves in conducting their school programs. Lack of teachers, lack of schools, and lack of interest in education all constitute barriers to an adequate program.

In 1956 there were 23 nucleos escolares with a total of 28,324 pupils in all nucleos combined. It was estimated that there were 31,701 children of school age in the same communities who were not being reached by any schools at all. This serves to illustrate the magnitude of the task confronting the school authorities if an elementary education is ever to be provided for all.

CHANGES IN PRIMARY SCHOOLS 1944-56

Although educational facilities are far from adequate in Guatemala, considerable progress has been realized in establishing new schools and increasing school enrollments, especially during the twelve-year period following the overthrow of the dictatorship.

In 1944 the total number of primary schools in the Republic was 2,975, including 102 urban night schools. By 1956 this number had been increased to 3,716, an increase of 24.9 per cent (Table 51). The

TABLE 51. *Percentage change in elementary school enrollment and number of schools, by type of school, 1944-56*

Type of school	1944 Number of schools	1944 Number of pupils	1956 Number of schools	1956 Number of pupils	PERCENTAGE CHANGE 1944-56 Number of schools	PERCENTAGE CHANGE 1944-56 Number of pupils
All Primary Schools	2,975	139,221	3,716	238,118	24.9	17.8
Public	1,798	106,133	2,815	196,510	56.6	85.2
Private	1,177	33,088	901	41,608	−23.4	25.7
Rural	2,044	58,755	2,674	91,277	30.8	55.4
Public	998	35,799	1,963	72,417	96.7	102.3
Private	1,046	22,956	711	18,860	−32.0	−17.8
Urban	931	80,466	1,042	146,841	11.9	82.5
Public	800	70,334	852	124,093	6.5	76.4
day schools	700	66,348	745	115,725	6.4	74.4
night schools	100	3,986	107	8,368	7.0	109.9
Private	131	10,132	190	22,748	45.0	124.5
day schools	129	10,047	183	22,265	41.9	121.6
night schools	2	85	7	483	—	—

Source: Dirección General de Estadística, *Boletín mensual,* Nos. 9–10 (1957), 6–9. These data do not include children enrolled in kindergartens of whom there were 15,286 in 1956. Likewise, persons enrolled in "Industrial centers attached to primary schools" are also excluded of whom there were 3,034 in 1956.

number of rural schools increased 30.8 per cent, while the number of urban schools increased only 11.9 per cent.

The total enrollment in all primary schools of the nation, including night schools, increased 71 per cent during the period 1944 to 1956. In the rural schools the increase was 55.4 per cent while in the urban it was 82.5 per cent.

These data reflect the differences between the recent expansion programs of rural and urban schools. In the rural areas, where the population is scattered over the countryside, there simply have not been enough schools within the reach of all. Since 1944, the major emphasis in these areas has been on the establishment of new schools where they were previously non-existent. This has resulted in greatly augmenting the number of schools and in increasing the total enrollment by 55.4 per cent even though the average number·of pupils per school increased only moderately (13.7 per cent).

In the urban schools, however, the number of schools has increased only moderately since most of these schools were actually in existence prior to 1944, even though they were not well attended. More recently the tendency has been to enlarge the school buildings; or in many cases to replace the small, inadequate and dilapidated buildings by modern, carefully planned, large school buildings. Thus, while in urban areas the number of schools increased only 11.9 per cent during the twelve-year period, the enrollment increased 82.5 per cent, and the average number of pupils per school increased 62.8 per cent. In other words, school expansion in the rural areas has consisted largely of multiplying the number of schools, while in the urban areas it has consisted of enlarging previously existing schools or of replacing these by new and much larger ones.

Attention should perhaps be called again to the decline in the number of private rural schools as well as to the decrease in their enrollment. The number of such schools decreased by 32 per cent from 1944 to 1956, while the number of pupils enrolled in these schools decreased by 17.8 per cent. The explanation for these decreases is not entirely clear. They may be explained partly as an outgrowth of the agrarian reform program of 1952, under which some plantations were taken over by the government and distributed to the workers. The plantation schools then became the responsibility of the government, and were added to the increasing number of publicly supported schools.[13]

ELEMENTARY TEACHERS

The problem of providing trained teachers for the existing elementary schools in Guatemala is a serious one. It is especially critical in the rural areas. The school administrator often has no alternative but to employ anyone who is willing to accept a teaching position. He does

13. This explanation seems plausible because the drastic decrease in the number and enrollment of private rural schools took place after 1950. Thus in 1950 there were 1025 private rural schools while in 1956 there were only 711; and in 1950 the private rural schools had an enrollment of 22,868 while in 1956 this had declined to 18,860.

not pay much attention to the applicant's teaching qualifications since there is practically no choice in the matter. If he can find someone who has had two or three years of primary school education or who can even read and write and is also willing to teach, he is likely to employ that person "sight unseen" in a rural school. Thus, the vast majority of the rural teachers fall into the classification of *empíricos*. An empírico in this sense refers to a teacher who has had little education and no training to become a teacher but who can lay claim to the profession by acquiring a little "experience." In 1955, 84 per cent of all the rural teachers in Guatemala were classified as empíricos. In the private rural schools supported by landlords on the plantations 90.8 per cent of the teachers were empíricos.

TABLE 52. *Teachers in elementary schools by preparation for teaching and by type of school, 1955*

Type of school	NUMBER OF TEACHERS	CERTIFICATED TEACHERS		EMPIRICOS	
		Number	Per cent	Number	Per cent
Rural schools					
Total	3,026	484	16.0	2,542	84.0
Public	2,278	415	18.2	1,863	81.8
Private	748	69	9.2	679	90.8
Urban schools					
Public *	3,935	3,029	77.0	906	23.0

Source: Ministerio de Educación Pública, Dirección de Estadística Escolar.
* No information was collected on this point for private urban schools.

The urban schools are more fortunate in this respect since 77 per cent of their public school teachers hold teaching certificates. It is interesting to note, however, that even in the urban schools 23 per cent are empíricos.

The shortage of competent teachers may be attributed to a number of factors among which the following might be mentioned:

(1) As previously noted, emphasis on widespread public education is a comparatively recent development in Guatemala. Since 1944 schools have been organized more rapidly than have institutions for the preparation of teachers.

(2) The salaries for school teachers are extremely low. As a part of the reform program of the Arévalo government, a salary schedule for school teachers was enacted into law to be known as the *Ley de Escalafón*. This schedule was put into effect and provided for basic salary rates, as follows:

For a primary school teacher holding a teaching degree the beginning salary was $75 per month. A degree presupposes six years of elementary school and five years of normal school training.

Teachers holding the certificate of *maestro rural* (rural teacher), which required somewhat less schooling, might begin at $60 per month.

Empíricos with no degree or certification received a starting salary of $50 per month.

There was no provision for increasing any of these stipends until after the teacher had been in the service for a period of five years, at which time the stipend was supposed to be increased by 20 per cent. Similar increases of 20 per cent were supposed to come at the end of each five-year period for 25 years. Thus after 25 years of service as a teacher the beginning salary would be doubled. By this time, for example, the teacher with a teaching certificate could expect to receive $150 per month and the empírico $100. In 1954, however, Castillo Armas froze teachers' salaries at the basic rates and refused to grant the mandatory increases at the five-year intervals of service rendered. He is reputed to have taken this action because he believed that many of the teachers were communists and it would take time to weed them out. Unfortunately, however, as of 1960 this freeze is still in effect and school teachers feel that it discriminates against them. In 1958 the teachers protested vigorously before Congress, but the latter reacted by insisting that the mandatory periodic increases in salary were unconstitutional.[14] Again in 1960 prolonged and widespread unrest among teachers and students resulted in several unsolved bombings and finally culminated in a teachers' strike. Disorder became so great that President Ydígoras suspended guarantees under the Constitution and declared a "state-of-siege." He insisted that he could not restore the mandatory increases prescribed in the frozen *Ley de Escalafón* because of the economic depression and lack of funds. A settlement was finally reached when the President promised to support beneficial legislation for teachers.

(3) An additional factor making it difficult to get teachers in the rural schools is the tendency for persons with education to shun the isolated rural areas. Since the shortage of teachers is general throughout the Republic, it becomes almost impossible for the rural areas to compete with the urban for teachers. Thus, it would appear that trained teachers will become available for the rural schools only when many more facilities for teacher training are established, when more adequate compensation is offered for the services of the teacher, and when living conditions improve in the rural districts.

14. *El Imparcial,* Nov. 13, 1958.

NATIONAL LITERACY CAMPAIGNS

Guatemala has tried to solve her educational problems in a variety of ways. Since 1944 one of the conspicuous methods has been through the organization and implementation of literacy campaigns.

A national literacy decree was issued on March 8, 1945. This was patterned somewhat after a former Mexican decree which required that "each one teach one." [15] The Guatemalan decree stated that all who know how to read and write are required to teach, without charge, others who cannot. A four-year emergency was declared during which the nation would strive to increase national literacy to 95 per cent. By 1948 five campaigns had been waged by the government. They were far from successful, however, as indicated by illiteracy figures for the Republic as a whole in 1950. Whereas 75 per cent were reported to be illiterate in 1940, the percentage remained at 71.7 per cent in 1950. Thus the objective of attaining 95 per cent literacy in four years was far from realized.

One must continue to ask what the isolated Indian inhabitants would do with literacy if they had it. Until the social economy develops to the extent that books, pamphlets, and newspapers are essential to community life and are generally available, it is unlikely that the literacy campaigns will be successful.

CULTURAL MISSIONS

Another attempt to increase the educational level of the rural population was initiated with the establishment in 1946 of a program to send various units of "cultural missioners" into isolated regions of the country to improve the lot of the peasants. They were also patterned somewhat after the cultural missions of Mexico.[16]

Five missions were sent out into the isolated areas soon after the program was announced. Each mission included a certified teacher, an army official, a student in his last year from the school of medicine and an agricultural expert. Each mission was to work in a given municipio chosen by the President of the Republic in consultation with the Ministers of Education, Defense, Social Welfare, and Agriculture. The missioners were to receive training for one month before going out into the field. Each mission included in its equipment a jeep, a portable electric generator, a movie projector with sound equipment,

15. Whetten, *Rural Mexico*, p. 421.
16. Ibid., Ch. 18.

a phonograph, a loud speaker and microphone, and a portable type-writer.

The missions appeared to be far less successful than in Mexico. They were criticized rather severely at times. It was charged that they did not stay in one place long enough to accomplish much. Some accused them of spreading communistic propaganda and others contended that they did very little or nothing.

Leo Suslow spent considerable time with the Mission No. 2 at Santa Lucía Utatlán in the department of Sololá in 1948. According to Suslow, Mission No. 2 had in addition to the equipment mentioned above the following articles:

> . . . a bingo game, small library, painting sets, drawing pencils, hoes, and rakes; and some equipment for the dispensary, such as hypodermic needles, pills, DDT in dusting cans, and surgical tools for emergency operations of a simple type.[17]

After describing the work of each member of the Mission and its effectiveness, Suslow arrived at the following conclusion:

> Besides insufficient training for their type of work, many other weaknesses in the Mission manifest themselves in practice. The population of the municipio of Santa Lucía Utatlán was estimated to be 6,034 as of December 21, 1946. Of these approximately 10% are Ladinos, of whom almost 80% live in the town center. The job of the Mission is to contact the mass of the population. Not knowing Quiché, the Indian tongue of the municipio, they are forced to approach the Indians through the Ladinos of the region who are not especially interested in aiding the Indians. The missionaries, coming predominantly from the Capital . . . do not have any strong missionary zeal or drive for their work.[18]

In 1954 the mission program in Guatemala was abolished and a new one was instituted in its place. The new one called for sending married couples who had had some experience in teaching out into the isolated communities to live and teach by both precept and example. It proved difficult to find couples with experience and training as well as the willingness to undertake this type of assignment. The program, therefore, floundered and by 1956 had been virtually abandoned.

17. Leo A. Suslow, *Aspects of Social Reforms in Guatemala, 1944–1949* (Hamilton, N.Y., 1949), p. 34.
18. Ibid., p. 38.

THE NATIONAL INDIAN INSTITUTE

In recognition of the tremendous impact of the Indian population on the life of the nation, a National Indian Institute was organized in 1945, as an adjunct to the Ministry of Education. The purpose of the Institute was to study the problems confronting the Indians and to coordinate the information available as a basis for formulating national policy. In an attempt to incorporate the Indians into the life of the nation, studies were launched which were designed to classify and map the various Indian linguistic groups and to study the organization of the Indians in the villages, town, and country areas. Information concerning diet and nutrition based on previous field studies was compiled. Considerable attention was given to alphabets of the Indian languages which could be used in promoting literacy campaigns and various other aspects of national policy. In 1950, the preparation of a book to be written in the Indian languages dealing with "the rights and duties of Guatemalan citizens" and containing the more important provisions of the Constitution of 1945 was initiated.

While the organization of the Institute appears to be a step in the right direction, its work has been greatly handicapped by the lack of sufficient funds to provide adequately trained personnel and the necessary facilities to serve an ethnic group that includes more than half of the total population of the country. Nevertheless, the Institute serves as an important clearinghouse for the government concerning indigenous problems and also serves as an expression of the government's commitment to incorporate the Indian into national life.

POST-ELEMENTARY EDUCATION

This chapter has been concerned chiefly with elementary education, since proportionally few Guatemalans have been fortunate enough to extend their education beyond that level. Indeed, it may quite truthfully be said that post-elementary education is still very much of a luxury for Guatemalans. In 1950, for example, only 2.3 per cent of the population 20 years of age and older had received more than six years of schooling; and only 0.4 per cent had gone beyond the secondary school.[19] Since 1944, however, enrollment in post-elementary schools has been increasing rapidly and for this reason it seems advisable to comment briefly on some of the major types of schools beyond the elementary level.

19. *Sexto censo de población,* Table 24.

Secondary, normal, and vocational schools

Secondary education is available largely in the departmental capitals and mostly in the larger cities. It is divided into two levels of instruction. The secondary level (*nivel secundario*) consists of schools which offer a general pre-vocational course of three years' duration. Schools on the vocational and technical level train students for specialized work by means of a period of study which is of indefinite duration.

In 1944 there were only 28 secondary and normal schools combined, with a total enrollment of 2,763 pupils (Table 53). Of these 1,861 were

TABLE 53. *Number of schools and total enrollments in secondary and normal schools, and vocational and technical schools, by type of school, 1944 and 1956*

| | 1944 | | 1956 | |
Type of school	Number of schools	Number of pupils	Number of schools	Number of pupils
Secondary and normal	28	2,763	84	11,670
Public	13	1,861	28	7,710
Private	15	902	56	3,960
Vocational and technical	35	4,200	62	7,953
Public	10	2,460	20	5,504
Private	25	1,740	42	2,449

Source: Dirección General de Estadística, *Boletín mensual*, Nos. 9–10 (1957), 6–9.

attending public schools and 902 were in private schools. In 1956, the number of schools had increased to 84 and the total enrollment to 11,670. Of the 1956 enrollment, 7,710 were attending public schools and 3,960 were attending private schools.

In 1944 there were 35 vocational and technical schools with a total enrollment of 4,200. By 1956 the number of such schools had increased to 62 and the total enrollment to 7,953 students.

The National School of Agriculture

In 1921, Guatemala established a National School of Agriculture in the department of Chimaltenango. The purpose was to give rural youth training in vocational agriculture. The school was moved in 1944 to Finca Barcenas near the village of Villa Nueva about twelve miles from Guatemala City. At first, the school was under the jurisdiction of the Ministry of Education but later was transferred to the Ministry of

Agriculture. For this reason, it was not included in the data presented above on vocational schools under the jurisdiction of the Ministry of Education. Because of the importance of agriculture in the economy, it seems advisable to draw attention to this particular vocational school. Land for the school originally comprised more than 4,000 acres ranging in elevation from about 4,000 feet to more than 7,500 feet above sea level. The property is almost ideally suited, since it provides a wide range of climatic variations favorable for experimentation with many different crops. Unfortunately, some of the very first land distributed to peasants under the agrarian reform program of the Arbenz government was taken from the property of this school and given to the colonos or peasants who were cultivating it. Therefore, if the enrollment should increase very much, the school might be faced with a shortage of land for instructional and experimental purposes.

At first, the old ranch house of the Finca Barcenas was remodeled and used as the only school building. Later additions were made, one of which includes a modern auditorium. Space now provides for administrative offices, classrooms, laboratories, a small library, a dormitory, dining room, kitchen and storage room. In addition there are barns and pens for livestock.

In 1952 there was an enrollment of 130 boys, most of whom were on scholarships supplied by the National Government. Applicants for admission must have completed at least six years of elementary school work, and be recommended by a responsible person. The requirement of six years of elementary school limits the enrollment quite largely to Ladinos who live in towns large enough to have a six year elementary school.

The period of study is five years and is roughly the equivalent to that of a technical secondary school. Students successfully completing the course of instruction are awarded the title of *perito agrónomo* (agricultural expert). After graduation, students financed by government scholarships are usually expected to work at least one year for the government in some agricultural area. The student mortality rate is quite high, however, with many dropping out after the first year or so. In 1952, there were sixteen teachers, mostly teaching on a part-time basis.

The school attempts to combine class work with practical agriculture. The school day is divided into two parts; mornings are devoted to work in the fields or with the livestock; afternoons are spent in lectures, laboratories, and discussions. After graduation some of the students enter service, while others find employment as consultants or administrators on the coffee plantations and other large farms in the Republic. Some continue their training by enrolling in the College of Agriculture at the University of San Carlos.

The school has an opportunity to perform an important service to the Republic, if it can only maintain freedom from political interference and secure the cooperation of government agencies in providing equipment and adequately prepared teachers.

The University of San Carlos de Guatemala

A college of agriculture was organized as a part of the University of San Carlos de Guatemala in 1950. It constitutes the eighth and most recent school or "faculty" offering college work to be organized as a part of the University. The other faculties are: juridical and social sciences, medical sciences, engineering, chemistry and pharmacy, economics, dentistry, and the humanities.

The name of the University has been changed several times during its history. As noted earlier, it was originally established as the Royal and Pontifical University of San Carlos de Borromeo. In 1875 it was taken over by the government and renamed the National University of Guatemala. This placed it directly under political control where it remained until the end of the Ubico dictatorship in 1944. The revolutionary government through the Constitution of 1945 granted autonomy to the University and changed its name to the University of San Carlos de Guatemala. This autonomy was reaffirmed in the revised Constitution of 1956.

As of 1956, the University had a total enrollment of about 4,000 students. The schools or "faculties" have functioned more or less independently in different locations in the city of Guatemala. A modern campus is now being constructed in a beautiful spot a few miles south of the city where it is expected that most of the schools will be brought together into what is called a *Ciudad Universitaria* (University City).

As in many universities of Latin America, the University arranges most of its classes to accommodate students and faculty members who are employed on a full-time basis in their respective occupations and who attend college or teach on the side. Classes are usually held in the early mornings from 7 to 9 o'clock, and in the evenings from 5 until 9 o'clock, thus leaving the major part of the day free for other occupational activities. Since the University operates on a slender budget, salaries of professors are generally low, with most of them paid on a per course basis. University stipends, therefore, serve largely as supplementary income and members of the faculty depend on their non-university jobs for their principal source of economic support. Such a scheme of university organization has both advantages and disadvantages. On the positive side, it provides a close tie between professional practice and classroom instruction. Doctors, lawyers, and government officials can bring their real life problems into the classroom and vitalize the academic instruction with concrete examples and problems. This should make for stimulating courses. The services of many distinguished professional persons can be made available on a part-time basis that could not possibly be obtained on a full-time basis because the University simply does not have the financial resources with which to employ them. Many of the students who attend on a part-time basis could not attend at all if they could not carry on employment activities to support themselves while attending college.

On the negative side, when the professor must divide his loyalties between his major outside job and the University, it seems likely that the University might suffer from lack of attention, especially when the outside job is responsible for most of the family income. Situations are bound to arise when government and professional work will prevent the professor from appearing at the appointed time to teach his class. Professorial absenteeism is likely to be much greater in a part-time arrangement than in regular full-time university positions. When the professor must rush off to another job the moment his formal class period is over, there is also likely to be less attention given to academic matters outside the classroom in the form of research, advanced study, scholarly writing, and student counseling.

Taking into account the restricted financial support for both students and faculty members, however, it would appear that the University has worked out a reasonably good schedule of operations for the benefit of all. In the author's opinion, the University with its newly confirmed status of autonomy and its freedom to investigate and to disseminate information through its various schools and colleges, offers one of the brightest hopes for Guatemalan education of the future. Properly financed, it should be able to make a tremendous contribution to society in the training of personnel to man the various positions of leadership in government, industry, and the professions. As a center for free investigation and discussion, it should prove invaluable to the nation in the years ahead.

Chapter 14

RELIGION AND THE CHURCH

Religion in present-day Guatemala is a complex of many divergent elements. Although the state does not sponsor any "official" religion, the vast majority of the inhabitants, both Indians and Ladinos, claim to be Roman Catholics. According to the census of 1950, 96.9 per cent of the population are Catholics while only 2.8 per cent are Protestants. Those belonging to other religious groups are negligible. There is a slightly higher proportion of Catholics among Indians than among Ladinos, 98.3 per cent and 95.2 per cent respectively. The relatively few persons expressing preference for non-Catholic Christian religions are largely concentrated in the urban centers, whereas nearly all of the rural inhabitants express a preference for Catholicism. But even in the department of Guatemala, which contains metropolitan Guatemala City, 96.2 per cent of the population claim membership in the Catholic Church.

TABLE 54. *Population by religion and ethnic group, 1950*

	TOTAL		INDIAN		LADINO	
Religion	*Number*	*Per cent*	*Number*	*Per cent*	*Number*	*Per cent*
TOTAL	2,790,868	100.0	1,497,261	100.0	1,293,607	100.0
Catholic	2,703,134	96.9	1,471,595	98.3	1,231,539	95.2
Protestant	78,208	2.8	22,917	1.5	55,291	4.3
Hebrew	829	—	—	—	829	0.1
Others	8,697	0.3	2,749	0.2	5,948	0.4

Source: *Sexto censo de población,* Cuadro no. 34.

INDIAN CATHOLICISM

To say that the vast majority of the population is Roman Catholic, however, implies a uniformity within the nation that does not actually exist. Religion in the rural sectors, and especially in the predominantly Indian areas, is a combination of attenuated Catholic beliefs, coupled with and modified by indigenous beliefs and practices. The two are so completely integrated that they cannot be readily distinguished, nor do the local inhabitants realize that their religion stems from two different sources.

Many factors serve to isolate the official Church from the Indians. Geographical, cultural, economic, and educational isolation all are important, but perhaps even more so are the psychological aspects of the Guatemalan Indian cultures. For more than four hundred years the Indians have practiced their own integrated type of assimilated Christianity, a blend of ancient Mayan practices and the Catholicism presented to them by the early missionaries. Today their religion might be characterized as an "unorthodox orthodoxy," a religious orientation which is perfectly articulated with their way of life, their values and attitudes, and their world view.

There are three general features which characterize religion in Indian Guatemala. First, the religion of the Indian consists of a combination of Christianity and paganism blended together so thoroughly that it is difficult to separate one element from the other. Second, religion displays an extremely local character. Indeed, it may be said that in western and north central Guatemala, there are almost as many variations in religion as there are municipios. Each municipio has its own local adaptations, its own set of supernaturals, prayers, myths, legends, and special formulae for appeasing the gods. Third, religion permeates all aspects of everyday life, so that it cannot be divorced from political, economic, social or personal affairs. Such matters as health practices and the curing and prevention of disease are intimately connected with religious beliefs and practices, as are the ordinary techniques of making a living.

Supernaturals

Each municipio tends to have its own set of supernaturals. The more important ones are the *santos* or saints. In a sense, the inhabitants of rural Guatemala could be called saint worshippers since their major concern is with their relation to the various saints of the particular municipio. The most important of these is the patron saint for whom the local village and municipio were named.[1] One village might be called Santo Tomás after Saint Thomas, who is regarded as the founder, protector, and chief benefactor of that particular village and municipio.

1. Usually the municipio and its municipal center (*cabecera municipal*) bear the same name.

Another might bear the name of San Gregorio in which case Saint Gregory would be the village protector and chief supernatural. In most cases an Indian name is also added to the Spanish name of the particular village in question. Thus, the name of the village and municipio of San Miguel becomes San Miguel *Chicaj;* San Juan becomes San Juan *Ixcoy;* and Santo Tomás becomes Santo Tomás *Chichicastenango.*

Historically, the patron saint probably gained in prestige in direct proportion to the loss in importance of some of the native deities previously worshipped by the Indians. In many cases it seems that the attributes of the pagan idols were merely transferred to the Christian images. Some saints are considered the counterparts of the native Indian deities, who are no longer represented by material images except for stone idols in some localities. The saints, on the other hand, are nearly all represented by images carved of wood and dressed in rich garments. They are said to "live" in the church and each represents a concrete being to whom prayers and supplication may be addressed. Each patron saint is the possessor of a distinct name, personality, reputation, and area of geographical influence. Those of the same name but in a different village are not considered to be the same saint but more like brothers, at least by the less sophisticated worshippers. The patron saint supposedly watches over his group of worshippers and their locality, and may be called upon in times of need to render aid. He receives special attention at an annual fiesta in his honor. The fiesta is attended by most of the inhabitants of the municipio and may be of several days' duration.[2]

Along with the patron saint are found the images of other saints of lesser importance to a particular village, though each may be considered as a specialist in his own right to whom the villager may pray for special favors. One may be especially gifted in providing rain for the parched crops, another may be gifted as a curer for certain diseases. All are considered to be patrons of the local community and different from those found in other localities, even though occasionally possessing the same names.

The care of patron saints and other images is entrusted to the cofradía, a voluntary religious fraternity or sodality. A village may have several cofradías, each responsible for a different saint or shrine or for conducting a fiesta. The cofradía is headed by several mayordomos (headmen) who are chosen by the principales (elders) of the community. The officers change from time to time (usually annually) and the holding of such office is considered an obligation as well as an honor. Young boys become active in the cofradía at about the age of

2. A description of the Fiesta to the patron saint is given later in this chapter.

fifteen in minor positions and often work their way up to become mayordomos of the cofradía or even principales of the village. The cofradía is thus a responsible organization which provides a form of training school in religious and civic responsibility.

There is a general but usually vague belief in God and Christ, who are thought to be all powerful and pre-eminent but are too distant from man to exert influence on him directly. Prayers are, therefore, commonly offered to lesser deities in a hope that they will intercede. Occasionally, God or Christ may be appealed to with the request that he influence the lesser deities to intervene directly in man's behalf.

The vague notions which the Indians may have of Christ, and other biblical characters and events, may be vividly illustrated by the following myth dealing with a combined Genesis-Crucifixion-Resurrection story, as told to Charles Wagley by a resident of the village of Chimaltenango located in the highlands of western Guatemala. This myth is quoted here at some length because it is a beautiful illustration of how biblical characters and episodes are interwoven with local tradition to such an extent that many aspects of the story would not be recognized by Christians. Similar accounts are available in other areas but will vary greatly from one village to another.

Before, the earth was flat and there were no mountains, or *barrancas* (canyons). Father José (Joseph) and Mother María (Mary) Santisima were the first *naturales* (Indians) to live on the earth. The first man was José and he made the earth, and then came María, his wife. José then made men. At the time their burdens were light because there were no hills or *barrancas* to tire them. The world was *puro plano* (perfectly flat). When Father José first made the earth, neither he nor other men could see what they were doing. Then it was always night and people did not know when to sleep and when to work. Then, so he could see men as they went about, Father José made a great machine, the sun and then, later, he made the moon so people would have some light as they slept. He made the moon so it would follow the sun and made it strong part of the time and weak other nights. But then the sun and the moon where not regular; they did not appear at the same time every day. Then, Jesús Cristo, the first son of José and María, was born. While María was pregnant the Devil came to José and told him that he was not the father of the child. He said that María had many lovers. José did not believe the Devil and sent him away. On the first day after Jesús Cristo was born, he sat up and talked, and in four days grew to full size.

He told Father José that his name was Jesús Cristo and told him
that he would not work on this earth for he had houses and land
above. Jesús told his father, "Do not be troubled, Father, for I am
going to make another world and you will be able to help me."
Then, day by day, the mountains began to appear on the earth and
he (Jesús) began to make valleys and *barrancas* for the rivers.
He made the moon weaker (than the sun) so there would be
night and day. He set three times a day for people to eat and told
people when they should sleep. Now a man watches the sun and
eats when it is at regular places (in the sky) and sleeps when the
sun is gone. Jesús made roads over these mountains for the Indians to travel.

The *naturales* were happy but the people of the Devil, when
they saw these mountains appear, were angry and said, "We are
not accustomed to these hills. It is the work of that man José and
his son. It is better that we kill them." Then, they tried to find
Jesús Cristo and they looked for twenty days. During all this time
Jesús fled from them, and the Jews (*Judíos* or "the people of the
Devil") would ask the turkeys, chickens, and all the animals they
met, if Jesús had passed that way. All these animals were gossips,
and told the Jews where to look. Only the mules and horses were
not gossips and would not tell. For this, people do not kill them
now but everyone sacrifices chickens and turkeys today. The cow
was especially at fault and today people kill them to sell for meat.

Jesús ran from the Jews more than forty days and he was very
afraid. One day they were close to him and he found a dead horse.
He jumped far to hide his footsteps and hid in the stomach of the
dead horse. When the Jews came, they could not see him and were
driven away by the odor of the decaying flesh. When they had
gone, Jesús came out of the stomach and went off in the other
direction.

The next day the Jews were about to catch him so he hid in the
branches of a palm tree. At the foot of the tree he made a great
hole in the ground. He walked out of the hole backwards, to show
his foot-prints going in but not out and climbed back into the palm
tree. When the Jews came they rushed into the hole. Jesús hur-
riedly climbed down and filled in the opening, closing many of
them inside.

Then, at the end of forty days, they caught Jesús and tied him
to a tree. Then they made him carry a large cross for many
kilometers to a place where they said he should die. The next day
they crucified him. They nailed him to the cross and gave him a

crown of thorns. He was not dead and he suffered a great deal. After a while a blind man came up and the Jews handed him a knife and told him to kill Jesús. He did not want to, but thrust it into the breast of Jesús. This was a great favor because Jesús was suffering and, for this, blind men may today walk along the road without danger when they cannot see.

Then the Jews placed Jesús' body at the edge of the pueblo. Late that night a burro came along and breathed over the body of Jesús. The breath of the burro made the marks of the nails disappear at once. That same night Jesús went to heaven and has never returned. When the Jews returned next day for the body, they were angry and frightened to find that it had gone. Then they were afraid and went to many people and asked where Jesús Cristo had gone. They were told that he had gone to heaven. Then the Jews hid behind trees and in the brush in fear, but a great storm came and thunder and lightning and with each flash a Jew was killed. Now only those who live beneath the ground where Jesús placed them are alive.[3]

Belief in one or more virgins or female deities is characteristic of the villagers. There are images of Our Lady of Guadalupe, Our Lady of Chinautla, Our Lady of the Rosary, and Our Lady of the Concepción. The virgins usually embody the attributes of mercy, compassion and divine comprehension of the sorrows, tribulations, and frailties of man. It is usually felt that the Virgin is ready and willing to intercede in behalf of man when in trouble. Sometimes, the Virgin may refer to the Virgin Mary who is occasionally thought of as being the Wife of Christ, (*Mujer de Cristo*).[4]

In each village or municipio, in addition to the patron saint there is usually a set of traditional local deities or supernaturals who influence the welfare of the people either directly or indirectly. Some of these are associated with celestial bodies such as the sun, the moon, the stars, and the earth. The sun is often personified as a male deity and in some areas is thought to be the giver of light or the source of all esoteric knowledge. The moon is personified as a female deity or virgin associated with childbirth, with agriculture, and fruition in general. Other native deities are associated with such natural phenomena as mountains, streams, lakes, hills, and valleys. They reside in both the earth and the sky and their activities account for rainfall, rainbows,

3. Wagley, *The Social and Religious Life of a Guatemalan Village*, pp. 51–2. Footnotes omitted.

4. Ibid., p. 54.

lightning flashes, and thunder. Ancient stone or clay artifacts are sometimes believed to contain supernatural powers. Spirits of the dead are thought to exert strong influence over the living. Sometimes they exercise a bedeviling influence. These spirits are honored immediately after death, usually on the anniversary, sometimes for several years afterwards. On the day of the dead (All Souls' Day) they are given food to eat and their graves are decorated. Some supernaturals take the form of apparitions and may be malevolent. These walk at night and may be encountered by single individuals in lonely places. They may make life precarious for the wrongdoer.[5]

Sacred objects and places

Sacred places and objects include: the church, the cross, and the family altar in the home. Sacred places also include hills and mountains, mountain crests, caves, springs, and large bodies of water. These places are sacred because they are inhabited by deities, spirits or apparitions. Dark and secluded places in the forest as well as dangerous spots along the mountain trails are also abodes of apparitions, and are approached with great caution. Other sacred objects include candles, crowns, masks, and incense burners. Certain food plants such as maize, cocoa, and pumpkin seeds may have sacred implications. Turkey blood is used in sacrificial ceremonies and tamales of turkey or chicken meat are eaten on festive occasions. The snake may have symbolic value, being closely associated with rain-making deities and lightning. Intoxicating beverages are widely used as ritual in religious ceremonies, at weddings and funerals, and liquor is ritually sprinkled on objects.[6]

Scattered over the countryside are sacred shelters accessible to the population. In describing these in one rural municipio of Guatemala, Tax says:

> The church in the pueblo is but one of many 'churches.' Scattered throughout the cantones are small shelters, some consisting of a semi-circle of rocks and brush, some more securely sheltered, at which the Indians, especially the *brujos*, (witches) come to perform small rites. Though there is nothing but the shelter—no permanent paraphernalia—the Indians think of them as sacred places. Favorite places for such 'churches' are on the summits of hills—especially on the *cerros* which are small possibly artificial mounds that may have some connection with ancient times. The

5. Wisdom, "The Supernatural World and Curing," in *Heritage of Conquest*, pp. 120 ff.
6. Ibid., pp. 126 ff.

notion that it is best to worship on higher places survives. Figurines and other things like artifacts that are found in the cornfields are considered sacred, are called 'idols' and are worshipped.[7]

Among all the sacred places and objects the church edifice and the cross are perhaps the most important in the lives of the people. The church is important not only in its own right but because it houses the effigy of the village santo and those of other saints. It also contains the church altar and candles; and the cross is conspicuously displayed there. The church is usually located near the center of the village and the market place. When Indians come in from the outlying districts, they usually call at the church and burn incense or pray and worship. Actually, a great deal of the Indian worship such as the burning of incense is carried on outside the church, on the steps or in the yard rather than inside. In addition to the main church building there is frequently what is called a *calvario*. This may be situated on a hill or on high ground on the outskirts of the village. The calvario is a small building, and contains a number of crosses and objects of worship. At Easter time there may be a large procession from the main church to the calvario. The Indians proceed slowly from one station to the other carrying an effigy of Christ on the cross.

The cross is fundamental in rural religious worship. When the Spaniards conquered Guatemala the cross was impressed upon the Indians from the beginning as a fundamental symbol of Christianity. There is also some evidence that it was used even in pre-Columbian days.

La Farge maintains that, among the Indians, the concept of the cross is "definitely un-Christian." Although a particular cross may be considered a "Cross of Christ," others are not associated with the Crucifixion, but are separate entities with their own powers and functions. In short, they form a sort of family, which La Farge divides into the categories of the great cross, guardian village crosses, crosses associated with special places, ancestral or house crosses, and orthodox crosses.[8]

The most important of the crosses, the great cross, is often located in front of the church. This cross ranges in height from 10 to 15 feet up to 70 or 75 feet. It carries somewhat the same relationship to the municipio or village population as does the patron saint, although it ranks below him in importance. This cross sometimes seems to possess some of the attributes of a deity itself. The Indians frequently worship the cross as such and have special prayers directed to it.

In addition to the large cross by the church, however, there may be

7. Tax, *Chichicastenango* (Microfilm), p. 35.
8. La Farge, *Santa Eulalia*, pp. 109–10.

found a wide variety of smaller crosses in various parts of the municipio. One may be located at each road or trail upon entering the village or near the approach to the village. Another may be situated at a strategic point overlooking the village. In general, these crosses serve as protectors, and are also likely to be found at the boundary of the municipio where the trail from one municipio passes into another. There are also crosses associated with special points. Frequently when a trail crosses the top of a high ridge or as it descends into the bottom of a valley there will be found a cross.[9]

Intermediaries between the supernaturals and people

Sometimes the Indian appeals directly to the supernatural being for protection, health, and spiritual guidance. On other occasions, however, he finds it necessary to ask certain specialists to intervene in his behalf. One of these intermediaries, of course, would be the Catholic priest. But the priest rarely resides permanently in the rural areas of Guatemala. He is usually to be found in the larger towns and makes only occasional visits to the smaller isolated villages, sometimes not more than one a year. When he goes to the village he performs such rituals as baptism; but the Indians are not likely to regard him as the only religious leader in the community. It is assumed that in some matters he can exert influence on the supernaturals. If, however, the Indians feel that their interest is outside of his specialty they may appeal to the local practitioners instead. Usually the priest is regarded as a distinguished visitor to the community and is treated with respect. He is not regarded as indispensable, however, and life goes on in uninterrupted fashion whether the priest visits the community or not. The ministrations of the priest are usually confined to the interior of the churches and to a considerable extent are concerned with baptisms. In the more elaborate ceremonies outside of the church the Indian local practitioners take charge.

In most Indian communities contact with the supernatural is made through a mediator known as the chimán (prayermaker, soothsayer). He is considered to be a specialist in the performance of rituals, prayers, and ceremonies, all of which are referred to by the Indians as making costumbre. The chimán is sometimes called by a different name in different villages and even his functions may vary somewhat. In general, however, he is selected from the older persons in the community. He is usually past 45 years of age and sometimes well beyond 60. Old age is respected in the Indian village, for it is supposed to bring experience and wisdom. It is believed that only after acquiring a great

9. Ibid., p. 112.

deal of experience can one hope to master the ritual, wisdom, and religious tradition that has been handed down from the ancestors through the ages.

There may be several chimanes in any particular village. A man or any number of men may be called upon by God to enter into this profession. The chimanes are not organized as a group except that one of their number is designated as the *chimán del pueblo*. In addition to holding a religious office, he has traditionally been regarded as one of the municipal officers and takes part in local government as well as in religious affairs. He serves as a sort of public official-priest. All other chimanes carry on their work in the manner of a doctor in a small country community. Each one develops a clientele of families who call on him to make prayers when they are in trouble or to divine and foretell what the future has in store for them. The chimanes may charge for their services, although the position usually is a part-time job and the incumbent may carry on the regular economic functions of making a living on the side. The function of the chimán in the Guatemalan village of Chimaltenango is quite typical of that in other villages although it would vary in details. It is described by Wagley as follows:

> The ability to look into the future through divination also sets the *chimanes* off from the laity and renders the laity dependent on them in religious affairs. All *chimanes* have a small bundle, given to them by God, which they carry about during all waking hours. It holds a handful of red beans, called *miches*, and a few small rock crystals picked up from the mountain side. Whenever a *chimán* is called by a family to make *costumbre*, he always divines ("questions the beans") in their presence. If he is called to pray for a sick member of the family, he divines to learn the cause (for there are many possible causes) for the illness; then he divines to learn at which shrine he must pray. If he is called to make *costumbre* for the milpa, he will pick out a good day in the calendar and on that day divine to find out at which shrine in the mountains the costumbre should be made. A *chimán* may be called to divine for almost any future event. It is believed that all good things of the future are fixed and that only through the divinations of the *chimán* can a Chimalteco order his life to suit the unchangeable future. A *chimán* was called by Manuel Aguilar to "question the beans" as to whether or not certain girls would make good wives for his son, Pascual. Manuel called a *chimán* for divinations when his wife was pregnant, when his son was sick, when his mule was lost, and when he was cleaning his milpa. All

these divinations were followed, of course, by ritual, but only after the divinations had pointed out the appropriate ritual, the appropriate places for it, and the approximate day for it.[10]

Another method of divination in the village of Chimaltenango is described by Wagley. It is said that this method is a special gift from God and hence is available to comparatively few.

> By this method, the *chimán* asks his question and watches closely the calf of his leg. A twitching of the muscles indicates a positive answer to the question. Pedro Martín seldom practiced this method and, even then, watched only his right calf. Diego Jiménez, however, favored it over the bean technique. Diego of course said that he was unable to control his leg muscles, that "God causes the leg to jump." In these methods of divination, fakery is obviously always a possibility. All testified repeatedly that they had no control over the answer. The answer, they said, is always the word "of God, of the Guardians of the Mountains." [11]

Service as a chiman requires a great deal of sacrifice on the part of the individual. It is his duty to be at the beck and call of those who need his services; and he may be called upon to intercede for others at all hours of the day or night. The reasons for becoming a chiman are varied. In some cases a man will want to become one because his father or his grandfather was one; or he may decide to become one because of a pledge he may have made during a time of illness. A dream may convince him that he should become a chimán; or he may be persuaded by his fellows to do so.

Politico-religious organization

In Indian Guatemala the religious organization has traditionally been closely intertwined with local government. Prior to 1945, the top civil official in each municipio was appointed by the President of the Republic, often upon recommendation of the departmental governor (*Jefe político*). He was almost invariably a Ladino even in cases where nearly all of the inhabitants were Indians. He was called the *intendente*, and was responsible to the President through the departmental governor for his activities.

Subordinate to the official political officer (intendente), however, there has generally existed an informal hierarchy of Indian officials upon whom the intendente relied to maintain order among the Indians

10. Wagley, op. cit., p. 71.
11. Ibid., p. 72.

and to settle local disputes before official action became necessary. At the top of this Indian hierarchy is a small select group of respected older local men known as the *principales del pueblo* (principal men of town). The principal is an honorary position among the Indians and its attainment requires a combination of age, experience, prestige, wealth, and other factors. Once chosen, the principales hold office for life. Upon the death of one member the remaining principales select a successor, so that the group is self-perpetuating. Ranking with them is the chiman del pueblo, or the leader of the chimanes. The principales operate more or less behind the scenes. They have no set of officially prescribed duties to perform but serve more as advisors on general problems of the community, including both religious and secular matters. Below the principales del pueblo, the church offices run almost parallel with the civil offices.

Most appointments to local positions among the Indians, whether of a religious or political nature, must clear through the principales. All offices represent public service to which duty may call a man from time to time as he progresses from boyhood through youth to maturity. Hence, the offices are usually graded in terms of the age which the incumbent is expected to possess in order to discharge his duties satisfactorily. There is no clear dichotomy between civil and church offices, and one may shift from one to the other without realizing it. Only a few, however, aspire to the higher positions since these require considerable wealth and independence. Duties of these higher offices also require a great deal of time, interfering with the regular function of tilling the milpa. Indeed, to seek higher office does not assure its attainment, since the office holders are chosen by the higher officials in the hierarchy on the basis of total suitability for the office and ability to discharge the duties which it carries. The men who attain to the higher posts must be exemplary in their conduct, for only then will their costumbre be good, thus assuring the village of the special favors bestowed by the deities.

Since 1944, however, several developments have taken place that have modified the situation somewhat. In the first place, the Constitution of 1945 established the autonomous municipio in which the officers in the political hierarchy were to be elected by majority vote. Thus, the younger and more vocal members of the municipio, without regard for esoteric and religious considerations, could be elected and given recognition by the government. The types of individuals who might run for elective office would in all probability be different from the ones who would hold office in the traditional hierarchy, and so would, when elected, be outside the old religio-political group. In such a situation, the power and prestige of the older hierarchical group would suffer, causing change within the system of norms and values of the entire society.

Secondly, in recent years certain groups of Catholic priests, particularly the Maryknoll Fathers in Huehuetenango and the Franciscans in Guatemala and Sacatepéquez, have emphasized purification of religious practices to eliminate some of the more obvious non-Christian indigenous customs. This has tended to divide local inhabitants. The conservatives cling to the traditional customs associated with the principales and the cofradías, while the liberals are inclined to break away from these old customs and adhere somewhat more closely to orthodox Catholicism.[12] As will be indicated later in this chapter, the spread of Protestantism in certain areas has also served to undermine the traditional religious customs among the Indians.

To what extent these various developments have reduced the influence of the principales is impossible to say at this writing, but some modification appears to be inevitable. With the return of more conservative government to Guatemala following the overthrow of the Arbenz regime, however, basic changes in religious life are likely to come about more slowly and gradually. Despite the changes mentioned above it seems likely that in the foreseeable future, religion among the Indians will continue to display most of the following characteristics as described by Gillin for the Indians in San Carlos:

> (1) beliefs all function in a Catholic context and explicit recognition of aboriginal pre-Conquest elements is absent; in fact, the average man is now unaware that there ever was a pagan period; (2) priests and other members of the official Church hierarchy function only as administrators of sacraments, but play a very restricted role in the actual religious complex in action; (3) the system is actually administered by a self-perpetuating body of quasireligious officials, called the Principales (Principal Men of the Town), who are not ordained in the official orthodox sense; (4) the outstanding "Catholic" feature of the system is the Cult of Images, which is also supported by the cofradía system; (5) because the orthodox sacraments must be administered by a priest who is very seldom present, they play a relatively small part in the religious life of the ordinary individual; the important cere-

12. See Manning Nash, "Relaciones políticas en Guatemala," *Integración social en Guatemala* (Guatemala, 1956), pp. 139–56. Also see Richard N. Adams, "La ladinización en Guatemala," *Integración social en Guatemala*, pp. 232–4. Also see Chapter 15 on local government.

monies are not the orthodox sacraments, but the fiestas, ceremonies for the images of the saints, a few orthodox religious holidays like All Saints, Christmas, and Easter; and community agricultural ceremonies which are arranged by the Principales.[13]

CATHOLICISM OF THE RURAL LADINO

No attempt will be made to describe the religious culture of the urban Ladino, which is similar to Roman Catholicism found elsewhere in the Western world. The purpose here is merely to point out a few of the major differences and similarities between Indian Catholicism and that of the rural Ladino.

Generally speaking, the religious culture of the Ladino population has both greater uniformity and greater similarity to orthodox Catholicism of the Western world than does the religion of the Indians. However, in those areas which are both culturally and geographically isolated, unique features are prevalent even in the ladino religion, as well as similarities to Indian religious practices.

One of the first noticeable differences is that, whereas among the Indians religion is chiefly the concern of the males, among the Ladinos it is more the concern of the females. Most males do not attend church regularly but confine their participation to special occasions such as Christmas, Easter, or the annual fiesta to the patron saint.

It was noted that among the Indians care of the church and of the images of the saints is entrusted to cofradías or brotherhoods composed of men. Among the Ladinos this responsibility is generally assumed by one or more organizations such as the *hermandad*, composed of women from the higher stratum of the local society who work under the direction of one called the *capitana*.[14] This group exercises considerable influence over affairs connected with the local church.

The Ladinos have no such institution as the principales which dominates religious life among the Indians, nor do they rely so much on witchcraft, magic and exotic medicine. Their religion includes somewhat more instruction in orthodox Catholicism; and there is a greater tendency to separate religious from secular affairs.

Ladinos are more concerned than the Indians about the Catholic rites and ceremonies such as baptism and confirmation. The scarcity of priests in the rural areas, however, and the infrequent visits of a bishop often make it necessary to wait long periods of time for these ceremonies to be performed. Usually confirmation is missed entirely. The

13. Gillin, *The Culture of Security*, pp. 77–8.
14. Adams, *Cultural Surveys*, pp. 355 ff.

rite of marriage can be elaborate or simple, depending upon the economic and social status of the families concerned. Among the poorer classes, marriage is celebrated when and if the financial situation permits it. Since the law requires a civil marriage to be performed before and apart from the religious ceremony it is particularly difficult for the poorer people to celebrate a marriage. Because of widespread poverty and because few priests are available to conduct the religious rites, most couples do not enjoy the benefit of the formal marriage ceremony. They live in common-law unions just as do the majority of the Indians (see Chapter 12).

The religious ceremonies of death provide another important focal point affecting all individuals. There are long established methods of dealing with the ceremonies accompanying it even without the aid of a priest. If the family is financially able and a priest is available, a mass may be said and a *novena* held for the first nine nights after death. If the family has retained the old Spanish cultural heritage they may hold yearly memorial masses on the anniversary of the death. Women are more frequently present at these anniversary masses than are men. In most cases women lead the prayers. There is a significant difference here between the ladino and Indian practices. Among the Indians the man is the principal functionary in the novena, whereas in the ladino groups it is the woman.[15]

As indicated in Chapter 12, the compadre (godparent) relationship, established at the time of baptism, is important in both the ladino and Indian cultures and has important religious connotations. The effectiveness of the relationship varies somewhat from one area to another, but the central concept of the extension of the family by incorporation of the godparental unit is found in all areas. The particular person chosen as godparent depends both upon individual preference and local custom. The godparent may be of the same cultural group as the infant or from the ladino group if the child is Indian. Usually in such a crosscultural situation it is the Indian who has the Ladino for his godparent; rarely, if ever, the reverse.

Fiesta to the patron saint

Like the Indians, the rural Ladinos are also saint worshipers. Of all the supernaturals, the patron saint is probably regarded as the most important. One of the major religious activities of the two cultural groups is the fiesta of the patron saint.[16] This custom seems to be almost universal in rural Guatemala.

15. Ibid., pp. 350–1.
16. This description of the fiesta is drawn largely from Adams, op. cit., pp. 358–60.

The fiesta usually exhibits both a sacred and a secular aspect. Its constituent elements naturally vary in degree depending upon the cultural groups celebrating it. In a community characterized by an integrated politico-religious hierarchy, typical of the predominantly Indian areas, the fiesta has a much more sacred orientation than that found in a characteristically ladino cultural setting where the religious and political hierarchies are separated. In communities where both Ladinos and Indians are found and where the ladino population element is large, the fiesta may be celebrated either by two separate groups or by both groups combined. In the latter case the Indians have responsibility for some elements and the Ladinos for the remaining elements of the fiesta. Since the two groups have different conceptions of Catholicism, their fiesta celebrations vary. The more unorthodox elements of Indian Catholicism are present in the purely Indian fiesta celebration whereas there is greater uniformity and more secularism in the ladino observation.

Among the Ladinos a mass is held on the day of the patron saint and a procession is made up of the images of the saint together with any other saints of the village. In some cases people of the village hold a novena during the nine-day period prior to the fiesta itself. As part of the whole affair, both at the preliminaries and the fiesta itself, elaborate use may be made of fireworks, including *cohetas* (exploding rockets), *bombas* (bombs which are shot into the air and then explode) and firecrackers. Fireworks are also used in the lay part of the fiesta.

The lay aspects of the fiesta are usually either commercial or communal in sponsorship. Such elements as the *sarabanda*, the five-cents-a-dance pavilion; the *chinamas*, temporary stalls set up by the itinerant vendors and local people; the *lotería*, or bingo-like game of gambling run by local persons or outsiders; cockfights; and sometimes a bull fight in which the bull is not killed but only played with to the delight of the audience. Other aspects of the typical fiesta, not commercially oriented, but sponsored by the local people, are horse races, bicycle races, foot races; the *carrera de cintas*, a game of skill in which mounted men on horseback attempt to spear rings tied with ribbons to a rope by riding under them; greased poles, with a prize at the top for the person who can climb to it; sports of all types; and always the *toro de fuego* which is a bull-shaped framework with attached fireworks which are set off as a man, concealed inside, runs about carrying it. Usually each fiesta ground has a *loas*, or stand, from which theatrical performances, usually comic, are staged and dances held. Some dances are free, while others, the *bailes sociales*, are by invitation, which anyone may purchase who possesses the necessary financial capital. Since this is not possible for the average individual, they are actually restricted to the middle and upper classes of the area. Masked dances, performed principally by the Indians, also constitute a very important element of those fiestas in which a relatively large Indian group participates. The Dance of the Moors and the Christians, and the Dance of the Conquest are the two most popular ones, performed by groups of individuals who band together and rent the necessary masks and costumes from certain highland centers. The Masked Dance performance has definite sacred connotations, for costumbre must be done with it in addition to sacrifices and prayers. These elements comprise the typical fiesta as it is known in both Indian and ladino Guatemala.

Pilgrimages

Many good Catholics, whether ladino or Indian, make periodic pilgrimages to the shrines and scenes of miracles in Guatemala or in neighboring Mexico and Honduras. There are at least a dozen pilgrimage centers in this general area, the most important being at Esquipulas, in eastern Guatemala, where the shrine of the "Black Christ" is located, near the junction of the boundaries of Guatemala, Honduras, and El Salvador, and not far from the ruins of the ancient Mayan city of Copán. It seems likely that the spot may have served as a center for important ceremonial functions long before the Conquest. It is now visited by people from other countries in Latin America as well as by people from all regions of Guatemala. According to Adams,[17] the entire period extending from just before Christmas until after Easter is one of almost constant movement of people to and from this shrine.

Other important shrines are those of *Jesús Sepultado* in San Felipe in Antigua and Sonsonate in El Salvador. *El Señor de las Tres Caídas* at Ayutla, *La Virgen de Candelaria* in Chiantla and The Christ of Golgota in Chajul are shrines of regional importance within Guatemala, whereas the first three mentioned are national in importance. The Indian pilgrimage centers appear to be those in Chiantla and Chajul, for they draw upon the northwestern highland population to a large extent. For the ladino population, the two most important shrines are Esquipulas and Sonsonate.

Other religious customs

Another common element in the religious complex of Guatemala is the *rogación*, or prayer for rain. This is the ladino Catholic aspect, but the Indian culture also exhibits the same phenomenon, taken care of by the principales and their ceremonial costumbre. Adams' survey indicated that the custom was followed in approximately 80 per cent of

17. Ibid., p. 362.

the towns. The general procedure is to arrange a procession in which the image of the patron saint is paraded through the village. The procession takes place at mid-day, when the sun is hottest. The saint is shown the arid and dry land, he is made to feel the heat of the hot sun, and is allowed to "perspire a little to feel how much rain is needed." [18] He is then returned to the church. Obviously, this specific type of religious activity is carried out in areas where rainfall is inadequate and less regular than in areas such as the Pacific piedmont, where it is both regular and abundant. The specific ceremonial emphasis varies from locality to locality and, of course, between the two major cultural orientations, ladino and Indian; but all are oriented toward the same objective, to secure divine intervention in order that the needed rains may fall.

The Ladinos commonly celebrate the Christmas season with a *posada,* a ceremonial in which the images of Joseph and Mary are carried for nine evenings from house to house in search of lodging, symbolic of their efforts to find lodging in Bethlehem.[19]

The life of the Ladino is certainly not devoid of religion nor does the ladino culture lack a religious orientation. When contrasted with the Indian, however, he does place less emphasis on religious matters. Among the Ladinos, religion tends to be more compartmentalized and is resorted to largely when a special need is felt for its use. This is particularly true among the males, who, as previously noted, are reported almost everywhere as attending church services only on special occasions.

The religion of the Indian, on the other hand, is regarded as serious business by both men and women. It is much more likely to pervade all aspects of his culture than is the case with the religion of the Ladino. Religion appears to be the cement that binds the Indians into compact rural communities, each differing from the other, yet each making life meaningful to the individual and providing him with a sense of security where other wise he might encounter only insuperable frustration in his attempt to free himself from poverty, disease, and illiteracy.

Catholic Priests

Among both the Indians and the Ladinos lack of priests in the rural areas and lack of leadership from official representatives of the Church have resulted in religious adjustments being worked out at the local level quite independently of the generally accepted regulations and

18. Ibid., p. 361.
19. Ibid., pp. 357–8.

procedures of Roman Catholicism. There are only about 120 Roman Catholic priests [20] in the entire country to serve a total Catholic population, which in 1950 numbered 2,703,134. This adds up to about one priest for every 22,526 people. Despite the increasing population over the years, the number of priests in the country has remained practically constant since 1872, when there were 119.[21] As has been emphasized earlier, the priests are stationed primarily in the larger cities and towns and religious affairs in the rural areas are left largely in the hands of local lay practitioners.

Most priests in Guatemala are foreigners, predominently from Spain. According to Holleran, most of them

> are very poor, and although well-meaning and sincere they are obviously ill-equipped to deal with the problems at hand, the exigencies of the time. They have been brought up in an old world tradition. They are, without exception, courteous and willing to talk all day about the tragedy of the situation, and the plight of the poor people, but seem to be without the semblance of an idea of how to do anything to remedy matters.[22]

Many priests speak only Spanish, although they may be working among parishioners who speak only Indian languages. They confine themselves largely to the routine performance of Church rituals with little or no attempt to provide instruction or guidance, or to improve the social and economic well-being of the people. Reports seem to indicate that the native clergyman is even less well prepared for his work than the foreigner. According to Holleran:

> Often the native clergy is berated because it is ignorant, or dirty, or greedy—because the men live in squalor. The thing goes around in a circle—no matter what it might have been in the distant past, the Guatemalan Church is at present poor; the people are for the most part poor moneywise . . . and the clergyman cannot be, and is not, a more superior product than can be expected from that social and economic environment in which he is is found.[23]

A somewhat different approach is taken by the Catholic missionaries of the Maryknoll Order, located principally in Huehuetenango, the re-

20. Mary Holleran, *Church and State in Guatemala* (New York, Columbia Univ. Press, 1949), p. 235.

21. Ibid., p. 236.

22. Ibid., pp. 236–7.

23. Ibid., p. 238.

mote mountainous department in the northwestern highlands of Guatemala. At present there are about eight missionaries of the order in the nation. Their primary purpose is to impart religious instruction as well as to improve the welfare of the parishioners. To this end they assist in health work, arts and crafts, community recreation, and social service.

HISTORICAL POSITION OF THE CHURCH

One may logically inquire why the Catholic Church in Guatemala has not provided more effective leadership in spiritual affairs, particularly in the rural areas where many aspects of the religious culture and practice cannot even be recognized as Catholic, even though nearly all the inhabitants claim to be Roman Catholics. The explanation is complicated and can only be touched upon here.[24] Perhaps the simplest answer is that after Independence the Church became involved in politics and eventually lost, with subsequent curtailment of its power, its right to hold property, its authority to make unrestricted appointments, and its right to manage its own affairs.

The Roman Catholic Church came into the New World with the Conquest. What put it at the center of the political arena was the question of *patronato real*, or royal patronage—the right or system of rights, granted by the Papacy to the Spanish Crown. Basically, the patronato real involved the right of presentation, that is, the naming of persons to various ecclesiastical positions. In a Catholic country, this privilege carries with it not only prestige but also economic advantages. This right, at first limited in scope and granted only temporarily to individuals, became more far-reaching. By the sixteenth century, it included not only the right of presentation but almost complete control by the King of Spain over the clergy as well as over the erection of religious structures and the administration and collection of tithes.

After the wars of independence, the interpretation of patronato real became of paramount importance. Whether patronage was to be considered as an inherent right of sovereignty, and was thus to be automatically transferred to the new and independent states, or whether it was deemed to be founded on papal concessions which were rescindable and nontransferrable were the questions which would seriously affect the future of the Church in Guatemala. Furthermore, considering the importance of the Church with its large body of adherents, the exercise of the right of patronage would lend prestige and power to the new government. These question, called the laical and canonical inter-

24. For a more complete explanation see Holleran, op. cit.

pretations of patronato real, were the issues in a three-cornered struggle between the Papacy, the Spanish Crown, and the Guatemalan Republic. The colonists, understandably, adhered to the laical position. The Vatican was caught between loyalty to the Spanish monarchy which had done much to further the interests of the Church in the New World and to the many clergy who had participated in the independence movement. For the clergy, the most learned group in the colonies, had become active in the struggle for independence and in the new government, and were sent as diplomats to negotiate with the Vatican. Bowing to the inevitable, the Papacy finally extended recognition to the new government but adhered to the canonical interpretation of patronage.

After Independence, political behavior in Guatemala was channeled through one or the other of two political parties, the Conservative and the Liberal. The Conservatives generally supported measures favorable to the Church. This brought them into conflict with the Liberals, who advocated the curtailment of the power, wealth, and special privileges enjoyed by the clergy. Thus, the Church became aligned with the Conservatives against the Liberals in the minds of the people and was plunged deeply into politics. Its influence waxed and waned with the advent of the particular party in power.

In 1832, and again in 1836, the Liberals put through legislation curtailing the power and special privileges of the Church and the clergy. These measures played a large part in bringing about a popular reaction against the government. Coupled with a cholera epidemic for which the frightened Indians held the government responsible, the anti-Church measures were a major factor in producing an insurrection led by a mestizo, Rafael Carrera, who became a virtual dictator in 1839. Carrera, who assumed the presidency in 1845 and held power for 20 years, restored many of the privileges of the clergy that had previously been taken away, including the right to hold public office. His support of the Church, however, was capricious, depending on whether or not it coincided with his own plans. In return for giving exclusive recognition to the Roman Catholic Church and for other concessions, the President received the right of patronage.

In 1871 the Liberals returned to power and stringent anticlerical reforms were put into effect. Some of the more severe restrictions placed on the Church after the triumph of the Liberals may be summarized as follows:

1. It was deposed as the official state religion with the separation of church and state.

2. The *fuero eclesiástico* (clerical immunity) in both civil and criminal cases was abolished.
3. All Church property was confiscated, including not only the large-landed estates which had been accumulated, but the cathedrals, the other church buildings, and even the cemeteries. The Church was prohibited from holding title to any real estate, or from receiving entailments and bequests. It was permitted merely to use the religious buildings and parochial residences.
4. Education was declared to be lay and free; and all schools were placed under government supervision.
5. The collection of tithes by the Church was prohibited.
6. Civil marriage was made the only legal form, and divorce was made legally possible.
7. Religious orders were suppressed and the Jesuits expelled from the country.
8. Restrictions were placed on the clergy forbidding them to participate in politics in any manner or to express themselves on political issues.
9. Control by the government over the number of clerical appointments was exercised, and sometimes antagonistic members of the clergy were expelled from the country. Thus, the freedom of the Church to manage its own affairs was severely curtailed. Most of these restrictions have remained in force since 1879 or longer.[25] From this time on, the position of the Church has remained relatively static, with occasional concessions to the Church followed by a tightening of restrictions.

With the overthrow of the Arbenz regime in 1954, the anticlericalism of the past century was modified somewhat. When Castillo Armas marched victoriously into Guatemala, he was looking for anticommunists to help strengthen his hand against the lift-wing forces of the previous government. He found in the clergy a most willing ally. Photographs of the President taken with the Archbishop were frequently published in the newspapers, a thing unheard of in the preceding era; and on the first anniversary of the "liberation" Castillo Armas decorated Archbishop Mariano Rossell y Arellano with the Order of Liberation.[26] Article 50 of the new Constitution of 1956 restored to the Church the right to acquire and hold real estate, provided

25. See J. Lloyd Mecham, *Church and State in Latin America* (Chapel Hill, N.C., 1934), pp. 375 ff. Also Holleran, op. cit., pp. 147 ff.
26. John D. Martz, *Central America: The Crisis and the Challenge* (Chapel Hill, N.C., 1959), p. 75.

that it be used for religious, social welfare, or educational purposes. The law was not made retroactive, however, and hence did not authorize restoration of previously confiscated property. Article 51 guarantees religious freedom but still prohibits the clergy from intervening in politics. Thus since 1954 there has been a general relaxation of restrictions against the Church.

PROTESTANTISM

As was indicated in Table 54, there were 78,208 Protestants in the country in 1950. Of these, 55,291 were Ladinos and 22,917 were Indians. Some of the ladino Protestants listed in the census undoubtedly consisted of Americans, English, and German nationals working under the auspices of large foreign-controlled corporations; others had probably acquired landholdings of their own; still others may have been in business for themselves or serving as managers or foremen on the large plantations. Protestant missionaries have also made some headway in Guatemala in recent years. They first entered from the United States in 1882 during the regime of President Justo Rufino Barrios, though they did not penetrate into the highland Indian communities until after 1900.[27] Small Protestant congregations are now to be found in all of the larger towns and cities. The 22,917 Indians listed as Protestants in 1950 probably represent converts by the various Protestant missions that have been operating in the country over a period of years.

The Presbyterians are the largest single group of Protestants in Guatemala. Some time ago they constructed the American Hospital in Guatemala City, which has made a definite contribution to the health facilities in the capital. They have also extended their missionary work into the highland Indian communities. Other Protestant groups operating in the country are the Nazarenes, the Seventh Day Adventists, the Primitive Methodists, the Quakers, and the Mormons. All tend to be designated locally as *evangélicos* (evangelists) and their places of worship are referred to as *capillas evangélicas* (evangelical chapels).[28]

Most of the Protestant missionaries carry on some type of educational work, health education, or social welfare activities, in conjunction with their religious activities. For this reason, Catholics complain that it has been easier in recent years for Protestant missionaries to gain entry into the country than for Catholic priests because the former enter with their families and come as teachers, social workers, or agriculturists.

27. June Nash, "Protestantism in the Highlands of Western Guatemala," unpublished manuscript.
28. Holleran, op. cit., pp. 245 ff.

In some areas Protestant missionaries appear to be received favorably and seem to be making converts both in the cities and among the Indians in the rural districts. In other areas however, they appear to be regarded with suspicion and deep resentment. The latter situation was reported by La Farge in the village of Santa Eulalia.[29]

In 1953–54, June Nash tried to find out why some of the Indians in the village of Cantel, in the department of Quezaltenango, broke away from their traditional religious ties to accept Protestantism. She concluded that in addition to any appeal which Protestantism offered concerning life after death, several of a practical nature related to the improvement of life in this world and in that particular village. One was the appeal of the temperance movement insisted upon by the Protestants. The consumption of alcoholic beverages is high in rural Guatemala and has become a traditional part of fiesta celebrations and religious ceremonial observances. Excessive drinking, especially on festive occasions, is rather common, and some Indians are attracted to Protestantism because of the moral rehabilitation they observe taking place among recently converted neighbors. Others, perhaps, become Protestants to avoid the great expense, in both time and money, involved in the cofradía system.[30]

Other appeals of Protestantism are the literature provided and the opportunities to participate in social and recreational organizations without expense to the participant. The Presbyterian Mission, for instance, holds separate meetings in private homes for societies of men, of women, and of youths. These meetings are frequent and, through a system of rotating offices, provide opportunities for leadership to most of the members.[31]

The arrival of Protestantism sometimes creates a good deal of tension and conflict in the local communities. The Catholic priest often regards the Protestant missionary as an intruder and a parasite who is trying to steal converts from an already established Christian church. The missionary denounces the priest for taking little or no interest in the moral, intellectual, or physical well-being of his parishioners. As Holleran says:

> Between the Catholic and the Evangelical there is a chasm of separation deep and complete. There is no fraternizing between minister and priest, no common cooperational ground. To the padre, the Protestant missionary is an interloper, a usurper, an enemy. To the minister, the priest is only one step removed from

29. La Farge, op. cit., pp. 100 ff.
30. June Nash, op. cit.
31. Ibid.

the witch doctor—he is an agent of ignorance, idolatry and reaction. The minister decries religious monopoly; the priest be-
moans proselytizing which would have his people exchange one
brand of Christianity for another, as if it were an over-the-counter
commodity.[32]

The priests have repeatedly charged that there has been much more
leniency in enforcing the anti-church laws against Protestants than
against Catholics. With the general relaxation of rigid controls over
the Church that has taken place since 1954, however, it is quite possible that such antagonism may gradually subside. At any rate it
would appear that there should be ample room for all who wish to
promote the spiritual, moral, and socio-economic welfare of the inhabitants.

32. Holleran, op. cit., pp. 251–2.

Chapter 15

LOCAL GOVERNMENT

Although the Republic of Guatemala is divided for administrative purposes into 22 provinces known as departments, the government is not federal but is unitary in character. The departments are merely administrative divisions of the national government which has jurisdiction throughout the country except for certain minor functions delegated to the municipios.

The 22 departments into which the Republic is divided are essentially dependencies of the Executive. Each is presided over by a governor appointed by the President and responsible to him. The President may appoint and dismiss governors according to his pleasure. A governor may not remain in one department continuously for more than three years, after which period he is either relieved of his position or shifted to another department. He could presumably return to the original department as governor if appointed again after a lapse of three years. This policy is designed for the purpose of minimizing possible corruption by preventing long periods of tenure, and for training a corps of administrators with experience in different areas of the country and hence familiar with regional as well as national problems.[1]

As a regional officer of the central government, the primary duties of the departmental governor are to transmit rulings and interpretations made by the central government to the officials of the municipios within his department and to see that the local officials comply with them. While his duties are largely administrative and ministerial, he also acts in judicial matters and can apply coercive economic judgments to persons owing money to the government.[2]

As representative of the central government he can act to settle political differences or use his influence to make certain that affairs run smoothly. Clearly the departmental officers are subordinate to the na-

1. Silvert, *A Study in Government*, pp. 69–70.
2. Ibid., pp. 73–4.

tional executive in all areas. They function as administrators of the policy determined in Guatemala City.

Since the departments vary greatly in size, the responsibilities of the governors also vary from one department to another. Gubernatorial responsibility in the department of Guatemala, for example, which in 1950 had 440,000 inhabitants, is considerably greater than that in the department of El Petén which had only 15,900 inhabitants.

MUNICIPIO GOVERNMENT

Each of the 22 departments is divided into municipios, and it is the municipio that has the only form of local self government in the Republic. The municipio is a governmental unit imported by the Spaniards which was designed to facilitate control of the conquered inhabitants at the local level, as well as to insure protection of Indian rights. Village councils were established and local officers were appointed to assist in the settling of disputes and in the maintenance of order. Indians were brought into the councils upon recommendation of the Indian leaders and thus a type of inside control was achieved by using Indians with prestige among their own groups to assist in governing themselves in the interest of the Spanish Crown.

The municipio gradually became the established pattern of local government and has continued to remain so although modifications have been made at various times in the degree of its local autonomy. During the dictatorship of General Ubico, the municipio was essentially a dependency of the central government and had very little local autonomy. Although locally elected municipio councils were retained, the chief presiding officer and legal representative of the municipio was known as the *intendente* who was usually a Ladino appointed by the President of the Republic, often, but not necessarily, upon recommendation of the departmental governor, and responsible to him. After the overthrow of Ubico in 1944, the municipio was declared to have local autonomy with all principal officers to be elected by popular vote of the citizens of the municipio.[3]

STRUCTURE OF THE MUNICIPIO

Physical structure

As previously indicated, each of the 22 departments of the Republic is divided into municipios. Each municipio embraces a specific area of

3. *Constitución de la República de Guatemala* (1950), pp. 116–17. A similar provision was contained in the 1956 revision of the Constitution.

land and includes under its jurisdiction all of the inhabitants living in that area. Municipios differ from each other with respect to the number of inhabitants and the size of their geographical area. In 1950 there

TABLE 55. *Area and population of municipios, by region and department, 1950*

Region and department	Number of municipios	Total area (square miles)	Average no. of square miles per municipio	Total population	Average no. of inhabitants per municipio
REPUBLIC	315	42,042.0	133.5	2,790,868	8,860
Central	33	1,000.3	30.3	499,037	15,122
Guatemala	17	820.8	48.3	438,913	25,818
Sacatepéquez	16	179.5	11.2	60,124	3,758
North	15	17,332.8	1,155.5	70,912	4,727
El Petén	10	13,843.2	1,384.3	15,880	1,588
Izabal	5	3,489.6	697.9	55,032	11,006
East	66	5,878.3	89.1	554,200	8,397
Chiquimula	11	917.4	83.4	112,841	10,258
El Progreso	8	742.1	92.8	47,872	5,984
Jalapa	7	796.5	113.8	75,190	10,741
Jutiapa	17	1,242.8	73.1	138,925	8,172
Santa Rosa	14	1,140.9	81.5	109,836	7,845
Zacapa	9	1,038.6	115.4	69,536	7,726
South	40	3,378.4	84.5	315,023	7,876
Escuintla	12	1,692.7	141.1	123,759	10,313
Retalhuleu	9	716.6	79.6	66,861	7,429
Suchitepéquez	19	969.1	51.0	124,403	6,548
West	139	9,892.3	71.2	1,095,571	7,882
Chimaltenango	16	764.1	47.8	121,480	7,592
El Quiché	16	3,234.7	202.2	174,911	10,932
Huehuetenango	30	2,857.1	95.2	200,101	6,670
Quezaltenango	24	753.3	31.4	184,213	7,675
San Marcos	27	1,463.7	54.2	232,591	8,614
Sololá	19	409.7	21.6	82,921	4,364
Totonicapán	7	409.7	58.5	99,354	14,193
North central	22	4,559.9	207.3	256,125	11,642
Alta Verapaz	14	3,353.7	239.6	189,812	13,558
Baja Verapaz	8	1,206.2	150.8	66,313	8,289

Source: *Sexto censo de población.*

were 315 municipios in the Republic with an average land area of 133.5 square miles per municipio (Table 55). The largest municipios are located in the sparsely settled northern region which, although occupying nearly a third of the entire land area of the Republic, contains only fifteen municipios, with an average area of 1,155.5 square miles per municipio. The small municipios are in the central region and contain on the average only 30.3 square miles per municipio. The region with the second largest land area per municipio is the north central with an average of 207.3 square miles. By individual departments, the smallest municipios are found in Sacatepéquez in the central region which has 16 municipios, averaging only 11.2 square miles per municipio. At the other extreme, the largest municipios are in El Petén whose ten municipios have an average area of 1,384.3 square miles.

In terms of population, the municipios arrange themselves almost in reverse order, with the central region having the largest number of inhabitants per municipio, 15,122 inhabitants. The presence of Guatemala City in this area greatly influences the average number of inhabitants per municipio. At the opposite extreme is the northern region with 4,727 inhabitants per municipio. Broadly speaking, one can say that the large municipios are thinly populated while the small ones are densely inhabited.[4]

Further information concerning the population of the municipios is given in Table 56. Of the 315 municipios, 78 have less than 3,000 inhabitants. These account for 24.7 per cent of all municipios. At the other extreme, 22 municipios have 20,000 and more inhabitants, and 61 have from 10,000, to 20,000. One-third of all municipios (105) have between 5,000 and 10,000 inhabitants.

The exact number of municipios in the Republic may change from time to time. According to present Guatemalan law, the President of the Republic has authority to create new municipios, obliterate existing ones, or combine two or more, when voted by the majority of the inhabitants. Three requisites, however, are necessary for the creation of new municipios. These are: (1) a population of at least 5,000 inhabitants; (2) a land area appropriate to the number of inhabitants; and (3) sufficient resources to meet the necessary expenses of self-government.[5] These restrictions attempt to preclude excessive subdivisions of municipios in the future but they do not apply to those already in existence. It will be noted from Table 56 that 127 municipios, or 40.3 per cent of all municipios now existing in the Republic, actually have less than 5,000 inhabitants and, hence, would not qualify as municipios under the new law.

The municipio usually contains a number of settlements, the most

4. Some idea concerning the density of population by municipios may be obtained from Figure 5 in Chapter 2 which shows the distribution of population.

5. "Ley de municipios," *333 Decretos del congreso de la República*, del 3 de Diciembre de 1944, a Febrero de 1947; Labor Revolucionaria, Boletín No. 7 (Guatemala, 1947), p. 240.

conspicuous of which is the cabecera, or municipal capital, which is somewhat equivalent to the county seat in the United States. It is almost invariably the largest compact village or town in the municipio

TABLE 56. *Municipios by number of inhabitants,*
region, and department, 1950

Region and department	Total number of municipios	TOTAL NUMBER OF INHABITANTS				
		Under 3,000	3,000– 4,999	5,000– 9,999	10,000– 19,999	20,000 and over
REPUBLIC	315	78	49	105	61	22
Central	33	12	6	8	4	3
Guatemala	17	2	3	6	3	3
Sacatepéquez	16	10	3	2	1	0
North	15	9	2	1	2	1
El Petén	10	8	2	0	0	0
Izabal	5	1	0	1	2	1
East	66	11	10	28	13	4
Chiquimula	11	0	3	3	4	1
El Progreso	8	1	3	3	1	0
Jalapa	7	1	1	2	2	1
Jutiapa	17	3	2	9	2	1
Santa Rosa	14	2	1	8	3	0
Zacapa	9	4	0	3	1	1
South	40	13	5	12	7	3
Escuintla	12	1	4	4	1	2
Retalhuleu	9	3	0	4	1	1
Suchitepéquez	19	9	1	4	5	0
West	139	32	19	53	27	8
Chimaltenango	16	4	1	7	3	1
El Quiché	16	2	1	7	4	2
Huehuetenango	30	4	6	15	5	0
Quezaltenango	24	6	7	7	1	3
San Marcos	27	2	4	12	9	0
Sololá	19	13	0	4	2	0
Totonicapán	7	1	0	1	3	2
North central	22	1	7	3	8	3
Alta Verapaz	14	1	4	2	4	3
Baja Verapaz	8	0	3	1	4	0

Source: Sexto censo de población.

and is the place where local government is centralized.[6] In it is found the town hall or courthouse containing the government offices. For the country as a whole, 31 per cent of the population live in the cabeceras

6. The location of all cabeceras, or municipal centers, according to a number of inhabitants was plotted in Figure 6 of Chapter 2.

while 69 per cent live in minor settlements and on farms outside of the cabecera. The variation in the proportion living in the cabecera is quite striking from one area to another. In Alta Verapaz, for example, only 10.4 per cent of the inhabitants live in the cabeceras while in the department of Guatemala the percentage is 74.2. As was noted in Chapter 3, a much higher proportion of the Ladinos live in the cabeceras (46.3 per cent) than is the case with the Indians where only 17.8 per cent live in cabeceras.

Other settlement types, or localities, in the municipios are found outside of the cabeceras and were described in Chapter 2. These consist of the aldeas (villages), the caseríos (hamlets), the plantation communities where resident agricultural workers live with their families, and the small isolated farmsteads. All of these are under the jurisdiction of the cabecera and are subject to local regulations emanating from there.

Formal governmental structure

Municipio government in Guatemala has two fundamental aspects: the formal or legal structure; and the informal structure. The formal structure is duly authorized by law, and thus has official legal status. Municipios with a fairly large proportion of Indian inhabitants are also permitted to participate informally in local government through their own established hierarchies and according to their long existing customs and traditions, apart from any legal authorization or restriction of the law.

The formal or legal structure has its basis in the Constitution of the Republic and in the law enacted by Congress dealing with the municipio. According to law,[7] each municipio is under the jurisdiction of a municipal corporation consisting of an alcalde (mayor) and a municipal council. Members of the council, as well as the alcalde, are elected by popular vote of the citizens of the municipio. Council members are elected annually and serve without compensation. The alcalde may receive compensation provided that the revenues collected by the municipio are sufficient to allow for a salaried mayor; otherwise his services are free. In the latter case, his term of office is for one year; otherwise it is for two years in all municipios except the municipio of Guatemala where the term is for three years. The number of councilmen may vary; and may be increased or decreased by a two-thirds vote of its members.

7. The following discussion is based on the "Ley de municipios," enacted by Congress in 1946. Minor changes in the law are made from time to time.

Service in the offices of alcalde and councilman is obligatory and gratuitous except for stated reasons. Service in responsible posts is regarded as a duty which every man owes to society and one which reflects honor on him and his family. Among the stated reasons for refusing to serve in an elected post are the following: [8]

1. Being more than 70 years of age.
2. Illness and inability to work.
3. Having served in the same or similar capacity within two years previously.
4. Holding another position that would be inconsistent with the one under consideration.

The alcalde presides at the municipio council meetings. He also serves as justice of the peace. It is required by law that council meetings be held at least weekly and as much oftener as warranted by the business to be transacted. Meetings other than those regularly scheduled are called by the alcalde or may be convoked upon the request of two or more councilmen. Ordinarily, sessions of the council are open to the public, although executive sessions may be held when needed.

The municipal corporation has the responsibility of appointing a municipal secretary and a treasurer. Both of these positions are remunerative in character and must be filled by individuals who have the necessary qualifications for the positions and who are not members of the corporation. The secretary must be able to read and write and be able to keep all official records of the municipio. He serves as secretary of the council and is supposed to take complete minutes of each council meeting and present them to the next session for approval, after which they are placed on permanent file for future reference. He prepares the agenda for each meeting and receives and summarizes the various communications from the central government and from the departmental governor. He receives the official daily government paper, *El Diario Official,* and is responsible for transmitting the official decrees of the central government and other pertinent regulations affecting the municipio to the alcalde and the councilmen. He is charged with the duty of writing an annual report of the official activities and accomplishments of the corporation for presentation to its members in January of each year. He is also required to transmit a copy of this report to the President of the Republic through the departmental governor. Although he has no vote in municipio affairs, the secretary is a most important officer. He serves as interpreter of national policy and also

8. Ibid., Art. 30, p. 243.

as a general source of information to the public, since in the more isolated municipios he is one of the few public officials who reads a newspaper or keeps abreast of current events.

The treasurer must have some knowledge of arithmetic, for he is expected to handle official receipts and expenditure of funds for the municipio and keep the inventory of all property. He also keeps the tax records and does the official bookkeeping.

The municipal corporation may appoint such *alcaldes auxiliares* (deputy mayors) as are needed to represent the alcalde in the villages, hamlets and on the larger fincas outside of the cabecera. These auxiliary officers are responsible to the corporation and may be removed at the pleasure of the council. The corporation also appoints the constables needed in the municipio to maintain order. Those in the rural districts outside of the cabecera work under the direction of the local alcalde auxiliar and ordinarily serve without compensation. Local jails are found in most of the larger villages and on the larger fincas. These serve as convenient places to lock up obstreperous persons, as well as those arrested for local infractions of the law and those who are awaiting judgment from higher up. An alcalde auxiliar is usually deputized on each of the larger fincas to enforce order on a temporary basis. It has been alleged that the alcalde auxiliar on the finca has frequently tended to consider himself an employee of the plantation owner and to enforce the latter's will on the plantation community. It is claimed that the local plantation jail has often served to confine labor agitators, workers suspected of planning to escape before finishing their labor contracts, or as a place to punish fugitives caught in the act of trying to escape.

The municipio also maintains a municipal guard consisting of persons appointed by, and responsible to, the alcalde. Members of the guard ordinarily receive compensation for their services. Regulations concerning the guard and its responsibilities are drawn up by the municipal corporation but must have the approval of the governor of the department.

As noted earlier, the municipal corporation has responsibilities to the central government as well as to the local municipio. The alcalde represents the departmental governor in his district and the corporation is required by law to appoint committees to deal with specified problems and programs including local finance, public health and sanitation, public works and ornamentation, education, cultural development, and agriculture. These committees work to improve conditions throughout the municipio and attempt to translate into local action policies established by the central government.

While the municipio is supposedly autonomous and can collect and spend its own funds, it is not entirely free to do so. The taxes it can collect are prescribed by law and are generally limited to items that produce very little revenue, such as a tax on the slaughter of animals, and fines for misdemeanors and minor infractions of the law. Income from taxes on real estate is reserved for the central government.[9]

The amount of annual revenue for 300 municipios as of 1955 is shown in Table 57. Nineteen municipios had a total income that year

TABLE 57. *Municipios (excluding departmental capitals) by annual revenue, 1955*

Amount of income (dollars)	MUNICIPIOS ACCORDING TO ANNUAL REVENUE		CUMULATIVE NUMBER AND PER CENT	
	Number	Per cent	Number	Per cent
TOTAL	300	100.0		
Less than 1,000	19	6.4	19	6.4
1,000–2,999	102	34.0	121	40.4
3,000–4,999	52	17.3	173	57.7
5,000–9,999	75	25.0	248	82.7
10,000–19,999	30	10.0	278	92.7
20,000 and over	22	7.3	300	100.0

Source: *Boletín mensual, 1* (1957), 18.

of less than $1,000; and 121 municipios, or 40.4 per cent, had less than $3,000. The median for all municipios was $4,042. Such meager revenue does not permit much development of community services. Fortunately, such facilities as schools and health services are under the jurisdiction of the central government or they would be even more inadequate than they are. Lack of funds for local services and municipio improvements is a great handicap to the effective functioning of municipio autonomy.

Informal government structure

In municipios where the proportion of Indians is high, there generally exists an informal government structure that is supplementary to the formal and legally constituted government. Until after the Revolution of 1944 it was almost unheard of for an Indian to hold the most

9. The Constitution of 1956 contains an article which states that "The executive shall annually allocate a percentage of the general budget . . . to technically planned projects to satisfy the needs of the municipios. In planning these, preference shall be given to the request of municipal corporations."
Constitución de la República de Guatemala (Feb. 2, 1956), Art. 236.

important official position in local government, no matter how greatly the Indians outnumbered the Ladinos. These positions were nearly always filled by Ladinos through appointment from the central government.

For convenience in administration, however, some of the positions on the municipal council as well as other official positions have usually been reserved for Indians who could be of help in translating the laws and regulations of the municipio to the Indian inhabitants, as well as in obtaining compliance. Furthermore, it has usually proved advantageous to the government to let Indians with local prestige represent it in semi-official positions because such persons would be more likely to win and hold the support of their own people.

Among Ladinos, matters of government are considered secular in nature and separated from religious beliefs and practices. Among the Indians, however, there is no such compartmentalization of religious and political life. They are considered to be aspects of the same thing and are usually so intertwined that they are almost inseparable. (See Chapter 14.)

Nominations for Indian representatives on the municipal council, therefore, always come through the principales. As noted in the previous chapter, these are older men who have served their community throughout their lives and have been elevated gradually through the hierarchy of religious and civil positions to the exalted rank of principal, the highest attainment in the local community, and one which they retain for life. Their functions in San Carlos are described by Gillin as follows:

> These six older men are a sort of supreme court, because they settle disputes between Indians, or try to settle them before they get to the civil magistrate. They are in a sense priests, because they are actually the repositories of the Indians' version of the Christian religion. They have to know the traditional prayers and oraciones in both Spanish and Pokomám and be ready to officiate any time the intervention of God or the saints is desired. They control the Indian representation on the municipal council, or have done so until recently. They control the officers of all the cofradías. Furthermore, they play a role in magical curing. They are, in short, the "head men" in just about everything that goes on in the Indian part of the community.[10]

To reach the high rank of principal, an Indian must have given highly satisfactory service in the hierarchy of other positions along the way.

10. Gillin, *The Culture of Security*, p. 73. The number of principales varies from one municipio to another.

At the age of about 15 to 16, the Indian boy may receive his first appointment to serve in one of the minor positions, probably as church messenger. Most of the appointments are for the duration of one year, after which the individual is entitled to rest for one or more years and then be chosen to serve in some other capacity. One of the more common organizations requiring service is the cofradía. There are usually a number of cofradías (religious cofraternities) in any Indian community, each composed of five to ten adult males who are in charge of a particular saint, including the care and protection of the image and the arranging of fiestas in honor of that saint.

Shifts in the personnel of the religious organizations usually take place annually on the same date that changes are made among the political officers of the municipios. Therefore, the Indian appointees scarcely know which office is civil and which religious.

Since 1944, however, the informal structure of local government has been weakened at the expense of the formal through the attempts by the government to promote democracy and to sponsor widespread programs of social and economic reform. The rise of political parties, the formation of national organizations extending their influence into the rural areas, and the enacting of election laws coupled with the new autonomy of the municipio have all tended to emphasize individual action on the part of the Indians rather than group decisions based on consensus and transmitted through the principales.

During the Arévalo-Arbenz period, political parties sought to strengthen their control by extending their influence into the rural municipios as well as in the urban areas. They sought support among the Indians as well as among the Ladinos. When an Indian joined a political party, he began to derive his political orientation from the party rather than from the principales. As the political parties extended their influence in local areas they tended to ignore the Indian hierarchies and to provide their own slate of candidates for public office. The names of intelligent and ambitious young Indians were sometimes placed in nomination and elected to office without regard to any previous service in the politico-religious Indian organizations and without any endorsement by the principales. Thus the influence and control of the latter was weakened.[11]

It was further weakened by the various national organizations promoted by and directed from Guatemala City. Among these may be mentioned the labor unions organized under the Confederación General de Trabajadores (General Confederation of Workers), and the Confederación Nacional Campesina (National Confederation of Peasants).

11. See Nash, "Relaciones políticas," *Integración social en Guatemala* (1956), pp. 139–56. See also the preceding chapter.

The labor unions made a strong appeal to local workers urging them to demand their rights under the national labor code. Officers of the unions transmitted their complaints to the proper authorities of the central government in an effort to obtain improved working conditions. The Confederación Nacional Campesina was especially influential throughout the country in connection with the land reform program. It sponsored mass demonstrations and membership campaigns designed to enroll all peasants and workers who were not eligible to join labor unions. Local chapters of the national organization were established in practically all municipios; and members were urged to demand their rights to receive land under the terms of the agrarian law.

All of these forces growing out of the revolutionary program had a severe adverse impact upon the informal organization of the traditional Indian communities.[12] Emphasis was shifted to formal organization, as opposed to informal. Indians began to be attracted individually to join local and national organizations, participate in mass demonstrations, vote in elections, and run for local office. In heavily populated Indian municipios, it became possible for an Indian to be elected to the position of alcalde because of the extension of suffrage to male illiterates. Gradually, the Indians were becoming aware of their newly acquired electoral privileges, through which they could by-pass the principales to obtain prestige. Thus, religious activity was gradually becoming separated from the political.

It is still uncertain how permanent these changes will prove to be. With the overthrow of the Arbenz government the land reform program was suspended, the labor unions were greatly curtailed, and the Confederación Nacional Campesina was suppressed. Much will depend on future government policy. If the selection of officers for local municipios continues to be by popular elections; if campaigns for literacy, improved welfare programs, and more effective communication are gradually extended into the isolated districts; and if political parties are permitted to function freely, it may be safely assumed that increased secularization will take place and that the authority and influence of the informal structure of government as reflected in the institution of the principales will gradually decline.

12. Ibid.

Chapter 16

NATIONAL GOVERNMENT

As noted previously, Guatemala's government is highly centralized without the effective regional or state government found in many other Western countries. The national government exercises control throughout the country, delegating only such authority as it chooses to the local municipios. The latter have no representation in the national Congress and hence are in no position to initiate legislation that would enable them to function effectively.

The basis of Guatemalan government rests in the Constitution of the Republic which was drawn up in 1879, and revised recently in 1945 and again in 1956. Despite these revisions, however, and except for social welfare provisions embodied in the Constitution of 1945 and continued in 1956, the general framework has remained the same.

In the Constitution of 1956, Guatemala is declared to have a republican, democratic, and representative type of government, with sovereignty resting in the people and authority exercised by the customary three branches, legislative, executive, and judicial, with none subordinate to the others.[1]

Voting privileges

Guatemala has always had certain restrictions on the right to vote. It was argued in the Constitutional Assembly of 1879 that conditions within the nation made impossible a liberal representative democracy like those of Europe and North America. Certainly the presence of a large group of politically and nationally unsophisticated persons in the nation made very difficult or impossible the functioning of a representative, democratic government.

In recognition of this basic problem, the franchise was not extended to all. A distinction was made between nationals and citizens, with only the latter having voting privileges. Citizens were declared to con-

1. *Constitución de la República de Guatemala* (1956), Art. 2.

sist of (a) those persons over 21 years of age who had a means of subsistence derived from income, business, industry, or a profession; and (b) those over 18 years of age who were in the army. Later, in 1887, the status of citizenship, and hence the right to vote, was restricted to those males over 21 who were able to read and write, or who had an income, business, trade, or profession giving them a means of subsistence, or those over 18 who had graduated from the national schools, or were 18 and were in the army.[2] These qualifications ruled out nearly all of the Indian population and limited the franchise to a very small proportion of the total adult male population.

The Constitution of 1945 extended the suffrage to all males over 18 years of age and those females over 18 who know how to read and write. It was further stipulated that "suffrage is obligatory and secret for those males able to read and write; optional and secret for female citizens; optional and public for all illiterate citizens."[3] The revised Constitution of 1956 retains essentially these same provisions, except that illiterate citizens are not required to vote in public. This, of course, applies only to illiterate males since illiterate females are not technically defined as citizens and hence are not permitted to vote.[4] As indicated in the previous chapter, illiteracy is high in Guatemala (72 per cent in 1950) and increases with age. It was also shown that females are more illiterate than males. Of the males over 18 years of age, 65.5 per cent were illiterate in 1950 as compared with 76.3 per cent of the females. Furthermore, of the Indian males over 18, 85.5 per cent were illiterate as were 96.5 per cent of the females. Since illiterate women are not citizens by definition and hence may not vote, this means that only about 24 females out of every 100 over 18 years of age were granted the right to vote by the Constitution of 1956, and only 3 out of every 100 Indian women.

Congress

Congress is the law-making body of the nation and consists of a Chamber of Deputies elected by the people from the various voting districts (departments) into which the country is divided. Each district elects two deputies except that those districts having more than 100,-000 inhabitants are authorized to elect one additional deputy for each additional 50,000 inhabitants, or fraction thereof, exceeding 25,000.[5] Since there is no senate, Congress is a unicameral body. Deputies are

2. Jones, *Guatemala, Past and Present,* p. 104.
3. *Constitución de la República de Guatemala* (1945), Title II, p. 7.
4. *Constitución de la República de Guatemala* (1956), Art. 16, 17, and 30.
5. Ibid., Art. 133.

elected for a term of four years and are eligible for re-election. Their terms are staggered, with half the deputies elected every two years. If for any reason a deputy's seat becomes vacant before the expiration of his term a substitute is elected within a period of 30 days.

Congress convenes in regular sessions each year on the first day of March. Regular sessions continue over a period of three months, and may be extended for one additional month. Each year before the close of the legislative session, Congress elects a permanent committee of eight deputies to transact business during congressional recess. This committee is presided over by the President of Congress and its members are on call by him or by vote of a majority of the committee members.

The presidency

The executive functions of the national government are exercised by the president of the Republic who operates through his duly authorized cabinet ministers.

The president is elected for a term of six years by an absolute majority of the votes cast, and no president is eligible to succeed himself nor to be re-elected until after two successive terms have expired.

Eligibility to run for president requires that the candidate be a Guatemalan citizen over 35 years of age, in full enjoyment of his citizenship rights, and of secular status. No leader who overthrows the government by armed force or who alters the constitutional arrangement may become president during the period of interruption or the succeeding one; and a provisional president in power at the time of an election or during the preceding year is ineligible for the office of president at that election.

Since there is no elected vice-president, the president each year at the beginning of the regular session of Congress submits a slate of names to Congress of persons he deems worthy to serve as designates to the presidency. Congress, by majority vote of all deputies, elects a first and second designate to succeed to the presidency in case of a vacancy before the end of the incumbent's term of office. The first designate would serve as provisional president pending the election of a new president which must take place within four months of the declared vacancy. In case the first designate should not finish out his allotted time the second designate would take over.

The judiciary

The judicial aspects of government are organized into what Guatemalans call the *Organismo Judicial* (judicial organism). At the apex of the judicial system is the Supreme Court, followed by the Court of Appeals. Then follow the courts of the First Instance of which there were 31 in 1953.[6] Finally, there are the minor courts, or justices of the peace which are found in every municipio.

The judges of the Supreme Court and of the Court of Appeals are all elected by Congress for a term of four years and are eligible for re-appointment. If a justice serves two full terms in succession he then gains tenure until he reaches the age of 70, when he must retire.

Despite any gaining of tenure, however, Supreme Court justices may be removed from office by Congress for commission of a crime, for bad conduct, or for failure to perform their duties.[7] This last reason could lend itself to political interpretation, if the duty as seen by the justice did not coincide with that as conceived by the president or by Congress, especially when laws passed by Congress are being tested for constitutionality. In one instance, referred to in Chapter 8, the majority of the justices of the Supreme Court were suddenly dismissed by the Arbenz government for voting for a temporary injunction against enforcement of the agrarian law.

Constitutional amendment

In Guatemala constitutional amendment has been made simple so that outgrown provisions may be easily discarded. A two-thirds vote of Congress can initiate changes in the fundamental law. After such a vote, Congress must be dissolved, and a general election held for a new constitutional assembly to make the desired reform. After revision of the Constitution, a new Congress is elected. The process of change is so simple in fact that a president in power who has complete control over his political party may change the Constitution almost at will. The role of the Supreme Court as interpreter of the Constitution has therefore been relatively unimportant. It may declare laws unconstitutional but in the past this has had little significance because any powers desired by the government could easily be attained through amendment of the law.

The ease with which presidential terms have been changed when presidents have so desired illustrates the simplicity of the amending process. This is illustrated by Jones in the following quotation:

> The constitution of 1879 established a term of six years without limitation on re-election. The death of Barrios in 1885 removed consideration of his candidacy for a second term. In 1887 his suc-

6. Silvert, *A Study in Government*, pp. 47–9.
7. *Constitución de la República de Guatemala* (1956), Art. 199.

cessor Barillas had an amendment adopted providing a six-year term but prohibiting re-election until at least one constitutional term had intervened. José María Reyna Barrios, wishing a second term, called a constitutional convention which adopted a transitory provision extending his term for four years, to March 15, 1902. He was assassinated and Estrada Cabrera succeeded in 1898. Before his first elective term was finished he called a constitutional convention which re-enacted the six-year term but removed the prohibition on immediate re-election. He was re-elected for terms to end in 1922 but was driven out in 1920. His immediate successor resigned and the next died in office. Lázaro Chacón then became president for the six years beginning March 15, 1927; in that year the presidential period was fixed at "six years without prorogation" and a popularly elected president was made ineligible for a period of twelve years after he had ceased to hold office. Chacón became ill and resigned before re-election became a practical matter, and Ubico was inducted into office in 1931.[8]

Ubico, during the latter part of his term, suddenly announced that there appeared to be widespread clamors among the people for his re-election. He claimed that his only desire was to serve the interests of his people. Therefore, he insisted that a plebiscite be held to determine the people's will. In this plebiscite it was ruled that, contrary to law, women and foreigners should be allowed to vote. After the voting was over it was officially announced that 884,703 votes had been cast in favor of continuing Ubico in office and barely 1,144 opposed him.[9] The legislature did not thereupon change the clause of the Constitution dealing with the presidential term but merely "suspended" it. Thus, it would appear that in the past, strong presidents have not been too much hampered by the limitations of "constitutional" government. Ubico remained in power until he was overthrown in 1944, a period of 13 years. During the period extending from 1839 to 1944 three presidents were in power a total of 61 years. These were Carrera who was president for 26 years, Estrada Cabrera who ruled for 22 years, and Ubico who held office for 13 years.[10] Reaction against renewal of presidential terms became so great at the time of Ubico's overthrow that the new Constitution of 1945 actually legalized rebellion as a means of blocking continuation in office after the presidential term of six years has expired. In Article 2 it is declared that:

8. Jones, *Guatemala, Past and Present,* p. 97.
9. Ibid., p. 97.
10. Silvert, op. cit., p. 2.

The principle of alternate succession in the exercise of the office of President of the Republic is imperative for the national political system, and the people may have recourse to rebellion should anyone venture to violate this principle.[11]

The Constitution did not prohibit re-election altogether but it stated that the "presidential term is of six years and may not be extended; and he who has exercised the presidency may not be re-elected until twelve years after having ceased in the discharge of the post." [12] The Constitution of 1956 also declares that a person serving as president may not hold that office again until two terms have elapsed. It is further declared that any amendment of this ruling cannot become effective until at least twelve years after it has been officially initiated and properly acted upon.[13]

The bill of rights

All of the Guatemalan constitutions beginning with that of 1879 contain a bill of rights protecting the basic freedoms of the individual which is comparable to those found in almost any of the Western democratic constitutions. For example, in the 1956 Constitution it is declared that freedom of speech, of the press, of religion, and of the right to assemble for peaceful purposes are all guaranteed.[14] The sanctity of the home is declared inviolable. It is declared that no one may enter without permission of the owner except by written order from a judge, and even then never before six o'clock in the morning, or after six in the evening. Citizens are given the right to criticize orally or in writing the actions of public officials and government employees without fear of recrimination; and newspapers and radio or television stations may not be closed down, confiscated, or interfered with because of critical remarks or comments. Anyone who is detained for criminal behavior must be informed of the reasons for his detention within 48 hours. He is also to be given the name of his accuser, and the nature of the punishable offense he is alleged to have committed. It is asserted that he shall have access to defense council who can visit him at any time to plan his defense. No one may be convicted of a crime without having been summoned, given a hearing, and judged according to procedures which assure him guarantees necessary for his defense. According to the Constitution, no Guatemalan may be expatriated

11. *Constitución de la República de Guatemala* (1945), Art. 2.
12. Silvert, op. cit., p. 226.
13. *Constitución de la República de Guatemala* (1956), Art. 163.
14. Ibid., Title IV.

nor prohibited from entering the country, nor denied a visa or passport or other documents of identification.

These examples of the safeguards which the Constitution offers for the protection of the rights and prerogatives of the individual citizen appear to be as democratically conceived as those found in any modern constitution.

Law of public order

It should be pointed out, however, that this same Constitution makes provision for abrogating these rights whenever the President feels that a serious disturbance of the peace or public calamity threatens. This is authorized in Article 77 as follows:

> Nevertheless, in case of invasion of the territory, grave disturbance of the peace, of activities against the security of the State, or public calamity, the guarantees . . . shall cease.

In the event that any of the above conditions develop, the President of the Republic with the advice of the Council of Ministers shall issue a decree to this effect invoking what is called the Law of Public Order (*Ley de Orden Público*).[15] The decree shall specify the justification for its promulgation, the particular guarantees to be suspended, the territory to be affected by the suspension, and the length of time it is to prevail. Such decree may not continue in effect for more than 30 days unless renewed by subsequent decree. After a decree is issued, Congress must be called into session within three days, unless already convened, and must be informed of the situation and ratify, modify, or reject the decree.

The Law of Public Order may be invoked in any one of four stages. These are: (a) state of prevention—to invoke which the President need not even confer with his Council of Ministers; (b) state of alarm; (c) state of public calamity; and (d) state of siege and of war. These provisions make it possible for a shrewd executive to build up a case for invoking the law whenever he sees a situation developing that he does not like. For example, he can interpret political opposition as subversion; he can brand criticism of his policies as disloyalty to the nation; and he can always suspect that his former and present opponents are secretly plotting the overthrow of his government. During the Castillo Armas regime it was especially appropriate to charge critics of the government as being "communists," and to invoke the Law of Public Order as a means of stamping out alleged communist activity. This was facilitated by a clause in the 1956 version of the Constitution which

15. Ibid., Art. 77.

despite the emphasis on individual freedom elsewhere, says, "All communistic activity, whether individual or collective, is punishable." [16] Thus, communistic activity is declared to be a crime by the Constitution of the Republic and, since there is no precise definition of communism given, the executive is apparently free to formulate his own definition according to the circumstances of the time and place. This gives the executive a weapon which may be legally used against his enemies in case they appear to display greater leftist or liberal tendencies than he deems wise or expedient.

It is true that in order to maintain in effect the Law of Public Order, the President must have the support of Congress. But a "strong" president almost always has the support of his Congress and it is virtually unthinkable for a Guatemalan Congress to pass a law that the President is known to disapprove, or to refuse to enact legislation that he strongly recommends. This has the effect of authorizing the President to declare an emergency almost at will and to suspend the guarantees under the Constitution whenever they appear to interfere with what he wants to accomplish. This has been commonly accepted procedure not only under dictatorships but also since 1944. It has been estimated, for example, that during the six-year presidency of Arévalo, 1945–51, Guatemala was subjected to the restriction of guarantees for about half of the entire period.[17]

The Problem of Democracy

Democracy as understood in the Anglo-Saxon world would be difficult to achieve on a national level in a country like Guatemala where there are tremendous contrasts in wealth and influence between the few who have and the many who have not; where most people can neither read nor write; where the capital city tends to dominate the entire country; and where most people live in rural communities insulated from the national life by lack of highways, railways, newspapers, or radios.

Under such conditions it is difficult for citizens to make known their wishes on matters affecting the national welfare. The various factors described above set definite limits on the extent to which democracy can operate on a national level; but even within these limits much depends on the attitude, the character, and the aspirations of the chief executive. He has tremendous authority and power in Guatemala, written or unwritten, and has numerous means at his disposal to make his will prevail, foremost among which is control of the army. He may

16. Ibid., Art. 62.
17. Silvert, op. cit., p. 16.

exercise authoritarian control even though this runs contrary to the spirit and letter of the law of the land as written in the Constitution and reaffirmed in legislation enacted by Congress. If he encounters undue opposition and criticism of his policies he can always, as a last resort, invoke the Law of Public Order and declare a state of emergency. In this manner he can subvert the Constitution, unless his policies become so unpopular that the army refuses to support him. He can usually retain support of the leading army officers through special favors such as increased salaries and elaborate expense accounts; and by playing the role of "strong man" which usually has a special appeal to them.

A brief sketch of recent political history will serve to illustrate the degree of authority over the government that can be exercised by the chief executive.

Recent political history

During most of Guatemala's history prior to 1945, her national government was highly centralized, highly personalized, and arbitrary. The prevailing philosophy was one of constraint. Despite the provisions of the Constitution, presidents served as virtual dictators, ruling with varying degrees of benevolence, and managing the affairs of government in their own way without permitting much interference either from the written provisions of the official Constitution or from political opponents. The army and the national police force were relied upon to enforce the decrees and mandates of the chief executive. The inhabitants were kept pretty well under control; there were few political disturbances; peace and order tended to prevail. Prior to 1944, as Silvert says,

> Guatemala has never had a violent social revolution nor even a threat of one; from 1871 to 1944 there was little effective interplay of differing ideologies outside minuscule groups; and Guatemalan presidents have all too often had unusually long tenure in office.[18]

Mass conformity to presidential policy has perhaps been due largely to the president's power to stamp out incipient rebellions before they could get started. Critics and potential political rivals could be quietly banished from the country and their properties confiscated; or in extreme cases, their lives could be snuffed out with little or no explanation of the whys and wherefores. An example of such arbitrary and ruthless suppression of supposed political rivalry by Jorge Ubico in 1934 is

18. Ibid., pp. 1–2.

described by Jorge García-Granados, a former candidate for president, former president of Congress, and former ambassador to the United States, as follows:

> In 1934 he [Ubico] uncovered a conspiracy against him. . . . Seventeen men were seized, given a farcical trial in which they were not even permitted defense attorneys, and sentenced to be shot. Although I [Jorge García-Granados] had no part in this conspiracy, I wrote Ubico a strong letter charging that the trial was a mockery of the law, and urged him to pardon the condemned.
>
> Ubico replied by sending a squad of police to arrest me in my home, take me to the place of execution, and force me to be an eye witness to the shooting of the seventeen. Then I was thrown into prison and held in solitary confinement for months, not even permitted to receive news of my family.
>
> . . . in late 1934 I went into exile to Mexico . . .[19]

Such incidents have been reported as common occurrences under Guatemalan dictatorships. There have been assassinations and torture, not only of political opponents, but also of their families, driving of persons into exile, confiscation of property, executions without trial or with only the most cursory of trials.[20]

And yet there are many in Guatemala who long for a return to the Golden Age of *Ubiquismo* (the policies prevalent under Ubico) where "peace, order, and honest government" prevailed. They long for the alleged harmonious relations between the ethnic groups of former times whereby the Indian was regarded somewhat as a ward of the Ladino with the former obliged to perform those tasks involving the hard, physical labor, and the latter to furnish him with minimum care and protection.[21]

Prior to 1944 there was little or no concern on the part of government to improve the lot of the Indian masses and to incorporate them into the national culture. Generally speaking, they were regarded as inferior persons who could not benefit from education. Illiteracy remained one of the highest in the Americas and widespread poverty was viewed as evidence of the incapacity and indolence of the Indian. Labor unions were virtually nonexistent; collective bargaining was unknown; and forced labor was an official government policy. Government was manipulated in the interests of the large landowners, the foreign cor-

19. Jorge García-Granados, *The Birth of Israel, The Drama as I Saw It* (New York, 1948), quoted in Silvert, op. cit., p. 3.

20. Jones, op. cit., p. 346.

21. Silvert, op. cit., p. 4.

porations, and the small upper class in Guatemala City. The chief executive usually managed to keep himself in power long after the six-year limit prescribed by the Constitution had expired.

The overthrow of General Jorge Ubico in 1944 marked the end of an era. As we have observed, the Constitution of 1945 was democratically inspired and liberal in character, giving the government responsibility for assuring to its inhabitants the enjoyment of liberty, education, economic well-being, and social justice.[22] Political autonomy was granted to the municipio as the local unit of government. A former school teacher, Juan José Arévalo, was persuaded to return to Guatemala from Argentina where he had been living in voluntary exile, and after a short campaign he was elected President of the Republic. Almost immediately his administration initiated widespread social reforms designed to improve the lot of the working man and the welfare of the Indians. New schools were established, campaigns to combat illiteracy were organized, and a social security system was instituted to protect the working population against employment accidents and illnesses. An elaborate labor law was enacted, in accordance with the provisions of the Constitution of 1945, giving labor the right to organize, to bargain collectively, to strike, and to receive severance pay when discharged without just cause.[23] Freedom of speech and of the press was encouraged and political parties were permitted to organize and to function. Arévalo described the predominating ideology behind his program as that of "spiritual socialism."

In carrying out these reforms a great deal of opposition was encountered, especially from conservative groups. Arévalo ran into difficulties in trying to finance his government, and plots were continuously being "discovered" to overthrow his regime, with the result that, as previously noted, he repeatedly invoked the Law of Public Order. He served out his six-year term, however, and in 1951 withdrew quietly in favor of his elected successor, Jacobo Arbenz Guzmán.

Arbenz was a military man who had played an important role in bringing about the revolution of 1944. He had served as a member of the three-man governing *junta* along with another military man, Colonel Francisco Javier Arana, and a civilian by the name of Jorge Toriello, pending the election of the new President, Arévalo. During the latter's regime Arbenz had served in the cabinet as Minister of War while Arana served as Chief of Staff of the Armed Forces. Arana was very popular, especially among the moderate and conservative

22. *Constitución de la República de Guatemala* (1945), Art. 1.

23. Ministerio de Economía y Trabajo, *Código de trabajo*, (Decreto no. 330 del congreso, Guatemala, 1950), Revised by Presidential Decree No. 570, 1956.

groups; he also had a following among the supporters of the revolution who were growing disillusioned with the Arévalo program.[24] Arana announced his candidacy for the presidency in 1948. This evidently was not pleasing to the government, which shortly afterwards endorsed the rival candidacy of Arbenz. Partly because Arana was regarded as the more conservative of the two, and partly to counter-balance the influence of one military man with that of another, the government chose Arbenz. But on July 18, 1948, the country was shocked to learn that Arana had been killed under circumstances which took on all the aspects of deliberate assassination. The details are described by Silvert as follows:

> There are many accounts of what occurred on that fateful July 18, still mourned by many groups in Guatemala, and still a nervous day for the government. What is certain is that Arana was lured to the town of Amatitlán, near the capital, on the pretext that an arms cache had been discovered. He was allegedly lulled into a feeling of security by the presence of Arbenz's personal chauffeur, now a Deputy in Congress. As his weapons carrier passed over the narrow crest of the aptly named *Puente de Dolores* (Bridge of Sorrows) on the edge of Amatitlán, he was caught in enfilading fire and killed.[25]

The death of Arana had such an impact on his followers that huge crowds gathered in front of the National Palace and observed a *minuto* (minute) of silence in protest of the assassination. This demonstration was repeated annually in downtown areas of Guatemala City while Arbenz was president.

With Arana out of the way and with strong government support, Arbenz won the election with little difficulty. He attempted to speed up some of the social reforms initiated by the Arévalo government and to carry out others as well. His government was strongly pro-labor, and he was determined to liquidate the latifundios. As noted in Chapter 8, his administration enacted the agrarian reform law, over bitter opposition, and full speed was ordered in putting it into effect. Protests over the constitutionality of the law were quickly answered

24. Silvert, op. cit., pp. 9 ff. Many are convinced that the infiltration of communists into the Guatemalan government actually began during the Arévalo administration. According to Martz, "During his presidency the Communists burrowed into the vitals of Guatemalan life. He was aware of their presence and made only half-hearted efforts to uproot them." Martz, *Central America: The Crisis and the Challenge*, p. 30.

25. Silvert, op. cit., p. 12.

by dismissal of several Supreme Court justices who had voted for an injunction against taking private property until the law could be more thoroughly studied. It became immediately evident that the government would push through its program despite any protests or technicalities that might arise with reference to the constitutionality of the law.

Evidence of communist influences became increasingly apparent both in domestic and foreign relations. Trips behind the Iron Curtain were made by labor leaders and others who appeared to be exerting considerable influence on national affairs. The government-controlled newspaper repeatedly contained headlines denouncing the leaders of the Western democracies as war mongers and praising the peaceful policies of the Soviet Union and of Communist China. As discontent developed in Guatemala, the Arbenz government tried through bitter denunciations to shift national resentment against the United States,[26] using the United Fruit Company as a prize example of U.S. colonialism.

During the latter part of his administration it seemed apparent that along with carrying out of some badly needed reforms, Arbenz was also permitting the utilization of the illiterate masses and laboring groups as a tool for political purposes. A constant barrage of propaganda denounced the large landholders and urged the landless to demand land. The emotions of the workers and peasants were fanned into a flame that became difficult to control; and, in many cases, they seized properties unlawfully. Open conflicts developed between finqueros and workers; and the economy seemed to be rapidly falling apart.

In the meantime, international tension was building up, partly because of the constant government propaganda against the United States; partly because of the protests of American-controlled corporations in Guatemala who considered their enterprises to be disastrously threatened; and partly because of protests by the United States growing out of fear that International Communism was getting control of the Guatemalan government and thus successfully establishing a "beachhead" in the Americas.

Guatemalan exiles in the neighboring Republic of Honduras managed to get foreign support [27] to help finance an invasion from that

26. Martz, op. cit., p. 47. For a thorough analysis of communism in Guatemala during this period, see Roland M. Schneider, *Communism in Guatemala: 1944–1954* (Frederick A. Praeger, New York, 1959).

27. According to Martz, the invading forces "were armed almost entirely by the United States. This has been denied repeatedly by United States officials. Yet there can be no serious doubt of United States intervention." Ibid., p. 60. It is beyond the scope of this work to discuss in detail the problem of international relations involved here. This would require a book by itself.

country under the leadership of Colonel Carlos Castillo Armas, a former classmate of Arbenz who had assisted in bringing about the revolution of 1944. He had become a strong follower of Arana and when the latter was assassinated, presumably by persons connected with the government,[28] Castillo Armas participated in minor uprisings of protest. For these, he was taken into custody with others and supposedly executed by a firing squad. Although abandoned as dead on the firing field, he survived the bullet wounds of the executioners, was revived, and thrown into the penitentiary. He managed to dig an underground tunnel through which he escaped and took refuge in the Colombian Embassy. Later he fled in exile to Honduras where he began making plans for an invasion. He was joined by other disappointed followers of Arana and gradually received support from conservative groups and from persons disillusioned by the Arbenz regime.

Evidently, dissatisfaction with the Arbenz government in Guatemala had spread to the army, which offered only token resistance to the small invading force of Castillo Armas. Perhaps it should be observed here that despite whatever assistance Castillo Armas may have received from the outside, his invading force was so small and so poorly equipped that he could not possibly have overthrown the Arbenz government without substantial help from within.

Although not many persons lost their lives in the actual fighting, it appears that a considerable number were killed by the Arbenz supporters on the way out; and by the liberation army or its supporters on the way in. Bodies found after the Arbenz capitulation indicated that prior to execution severe torture methods had been applied by the national police of the outgoing government to some of the victims suspected of collaboration with the invaders.[29]

Castillo Armas and his "Army of Liberation" entered Guatemala City in July 1954. Arbenz and his associates had taken refuge in the foreign embassies and later fled to foreign countries. Hundreds of *Arbencistas* were rounded up and thrown into temporary prisons pending investigation of their alleged communist activities; and a goodly number were executed in retaliation for alleged crimes committed under the Arbenz regime. Most of the executions apparently took place in the small towns and villages outside of Guatemala City in what were labeled "spontaneous uprisings of the people against the communists." Ironically, all of the known communist leaders affiliated in any way with the Arbenz regime escaped, either by fleeing the country directly or by taking refuge in the foreign embassies and later going into exile. It was only

28. Silvert, op. cit., p. 12.
29. Martz, op. cit., pp. 56-7.

some of the petty officials and alleged collaborators who were caught and liquidated. Many of these were persons with leftist leanings who had risen to minor posts in the labor unions. It is said that 17 labor leaders were taken out and shot in the vicinity of Tiquisate alone. John Gillin reported that in the village of San Luis Jilotepeque nine persons were rounded up by the invading army and executed. While killings were reported in various other parts of the country it would be difficult to estimate the total number with any degree of accuracy. They were certainly few in number in comparison with the executions that took place in Cuba under Fidel Castro in 1959.

When Castillo Armas took over the government he quite understandably regarded with suspicion anyone who had participated actively in the Arbenz government. The pendulum, therefore, swung from extreme leftism to authoritarianism of the rightist variety. He surrounded himself with advisers from the more conservative groups including former officials of the Ubico regime, the large landowning groups, and the clergy. He suspended the agrarian law [30] and the Constitution of the Republic and called for a constitutional convention to rewrite the Constitution.[31] A plebescite was held to determine whether the voters were willing for him to serve as President for a regular six-year term of office; and, there being no opposition candidates, he was overwhelmingly approved.

Convinced that labor unions and political parties had played leading roles in spreading communism in the nation, he severely restricted the activities of both. He allowed no political opposition; and the activities of labor unions were greatly curtailed. Union leaders had to receive government clearance. Friendly relations were re-established with the United States and arrangements were made for extensive financial assistance under foreign aid programs. Most of the lands distributed under the agrarian program of Arbenz were returned to the former owners. Settlements were reached with the large corporations that had been harassed by the Arbenz regime and a new petroleum law was enacted granting liberal concessions to foreign corporations for exploration for oil in the vast department of El Petén. A much more favorable environment for foreign investment was established. Emphasis was placed on highway construction, for which 39 per cent of the total national budget was spent in 1956. Serious efforts were also made to improve business conditions generally; and a colonization program was organized to bring new land into agricultural production.

30. The agrarian law was later revised and supplemented by a colonization program. See Chapter 8.
31. The revised Constitution was officially adopted on Feb. 2, 1956.

While Castillo Armas evidently tried to follow a middle-of-the-road course between liberalism and conservatism, he was not always successful. Some Guatemalans would classify his regime as extremely conservative, or even reactionary. They point out, for example, that freedom of speech and of the press were much more restricted under Castillo Armas than under either Arévalo or Arbenz. Even under Arbenz, although a few foreign correspondents were sent out of the country, local opposition newspapers continued to denounce his regime until the very end with little fear of suppression. The government of Castillo Armas, on the other hand, maintained tight control over the press and did not hesitate to suppress editions of newspapers and to send out of the country writers who were unduly critical of his policies. It was claimed that any criticism of the regime or any incipient political opposition was dealt with swiftly. Such action was comparatively easy to justify under the guise of combatting communism because, as we have noted, the new Constitution specifically declares that "communism is punishable." Castillo Armas appointed a secret National Defense Committee to root out communists and Arbencistas. Members of this committee were authorized to search homes, make arrests without warrants, and throw people into jail.[32] To the dismay of many, Castillo Armas also appointed to the position of Chief of the National Police the same individual who had served in this capacity under the dictatorship of General Jorge Ubico, and who was remembered for his ruthless methods of suppressing opposition. This was evidence enough to some people that the government was reverting to a dictatorship. Justification was claimed by the government on the grounds that strong methods had to be used to stamp out communism.

The regime of Castillo Armas ended suddenly with his assassination by one of his own palace guards in July 1957. The first designate by Congress to the presidency, Luis Arturo González López, was automatically declared provisional president upon the death of Castillo Armas. General elections were held in October 1957, and the government-sponsored candidate for president, Miguel Ortiz Passarelli, who had resigned as Chief Justice of the Supreme Court to run for president, was officially declared the winner. His leading opponent, however, General Miguel Ydígoras Fuentes, a right-wing candidate who had previously been defeated by Arbenz, charged that the elections had been rigged by stuffing the ballot boxes and falsifying the results. His followers held large demonstrations in front of the National Palace.

32. Martz, op. cit., p. 72.

Riots broke out in Guatemala City, a national emergency was declared, and a military junta took over the government, deposing the provisional President on the grounds that he could not maintain order. It was later declared that widespread irregularities actually had occurred in the election proceedings.

The elections were nullified and the junta asked Congress to declare the second designate provisional President of the Republic and to call for new elections. Guillermo Flores Avendano thus became provisional President in October 1957, and new elections were held in January 1958. President Flores had repeatedly assured the electorate that the government would not sponsor any candidate this time; that the polling booths throughout the nation would be well policed; that the army would be used to maintain order if necessary; and that the people could choose their candidate freely and fairly.

Evidently, President Flores fulfilled his promise, and for the first time in Guatemalan history a national election took place without official government endorsement of any presidential candidate and without any attempted coercion at the polls. It was reported that the votes were divided among the four candidates for President as follows: General Miguel Ydígoras Fuentes, who was a candidate of the Party of National Redemption and sponsored by the more conservative groups, received 190,972 votes; Colonel José Luis Cruz Salazar, avowed middle-of-the-road candidate sponsored by the National Democratic Party of the late Castillo Armas, received 138,488 votes; and Mario Méndez Montenegro, candidate of the Guatemalan Revolutionary Party which included the more liberal groups, received 132,824 votes. A fourth candidate by the name of Colonel Enrique Ardón Fernández from the Liberal Party of National Action received only 5,834 votes.

One need not point out that such an even distribution of votes among the three leading candidates is unprecedented in Guatemala or in almost any other country of Latin America. It is especially significant that candidates representing contrasting political views could even campaign freely without inciting political violence. Usually, through official endorsement, the incumbent President has been able to choose his successor and announce the official results through a cooperative Congress; and, as noted previously, the successor all too frequently has turned out to be the incumbent himself, despite the provisions of the Constitution which prohibit re-election.

Guatemalan law requires that, to be elected, a presidential candidate must receive a majority of the total votes cast—not merely a plurality. Otherwise Congress must choose the President by naming one of the two leading candidates. In this instance, after considerable hesitation, Congress finally chose the man receiving the largest number of votes, General Miguel Ydígoras Fuentes.

Signs of uneasiness were widespread as President Ydígoras took over the reigns of government on March 2, 1958. Some felt certain that his administration would swing back toward a dictatorship similar to that of General Ubico. They pointed to the prominent role played by Ydígoras in the former dictatorship, and identified numerous other *Ubiquistas* who were unusually active in support of his election, and noted that he had the support of most of the large landholders.

As of November 1960, the term of office of General Ydígoras is less than half expired. It appears that his government is highly conservative, although he is continuing some of the previous reforms and is evidently trying to promote industrialization and to encourage greater agricultural diversity. Unfortunately, he has been confronted thus far with a severe economic depression due to the decline of the price of coffee on the world market. He has been criticized for failure to launch programs of socio-economic reform or to execute vigorously those reforms already endorsed. Social unrest has been evident intermittently in various parts of the country. A rebellion broke out in November 1960 centered in the small city of Puerto Barrios on the Caribbean coast. This resulted in the suspension of guarantees under the Constitution and the declaration of a state of siege. The rebellion, which was stamped out within a short time by the army, was alleged by the Guatemalan government to have been inspired by Fidel Castro of Cuba in an attempt to export his revolution (*Fidelismo*) to Guatemala with the connivance of the supporters of former President Jacobo Arbenz, who was reported by the newspapers to be in Havana making speeches against the Guatemalan government at that time. Excitement ran so high that Guatemala in conjunction with Nicaragua called on the United States for protection. President Eisenhower promptly dispatched an aircraft carrier and four destroyers to patrol their coasts as a precautionary measure against possible invasion. Whether or not Castro had anything to do with instigating the rebellion in Guatemala, certainly unrest and discontentment with the status quo offer a fertile seed bed for political agitation to any leader who displays sufficient talent to unite the discontented elements into an organized, resistant force.

Perhaps the foregoing brief review of the highlights in the recent political history of Guatemala will serve to emphasize the importance of the human equation in bringing about democratic government. Neither beautifully constructed constitutions nor enlightened and humane legislation can be of much avail unless they are administered in accordance with both the spirit and the letter of the law. During the brief period described above there was a swing all the way from reactionary, personalized government to extreme leftism and almost back again. Ubico tended to ignore the Constitution except insofar as it served his particular purpose. Arévalo took the social welfare aspects of the revised Constitution of 1945 very seriously and introduced fundamental socio-economic reforms. Arbenz became an extremist and tried to remake society too fast. Castillo Armas became so preoccupied with stamping out communism and constructing highways that he had little time to devote to encouraging democratic procedures. Ydígoras began his presidency by trying to stabilize government at a conservative level.

Thus, the attempts to establish democratic government and to inaugurate important social reform programs, which were undertaken enthusiastically after the downfall of the dictatorship in 1944, have encountered tremendous difficulties along the way. Despite the fluctuations, however, it appears that at least a few permanent gains have been achieved which the people will probably not relinquish willingly.[33]

Lack of trained personnel

Some of Guatemala's difficulties stem from the problem of recruiting adequately trained personnel to man the various posts in government. This problem is apparent almost everywhere, from the positions of mayor and councilman in the rural municipios to the highest positions in the national government in Guatemala City. As we have noted previously, only a very small percentage of the inhabitants have had schooling beyond the six years of the elementary school and only an infinitesimal proportion have had a college education.

During the era of the dictatorships prior to 1945 there were comparatively few government positions to fill. Only a small bureaucracy was necessary since all decisions of any importance were made by the chief executive. With the attempt to establish democratic government after 1944, however, the need for trained personnel greatly increased, especially with the establishment of government agencies and services such as social security, public health services, expanded educational opportunities, economic development programs, land reform legislation, and supervisory functions growing out of the enactment of elaborate labor legislation.

The fall of the dictatorships left Guatemala without trained human

33. Some of these will be discussed in the final chapter.

resources adequate to discharge the many responsibilities that the government was called upon to perform. Some of the failures and inefficiencies of government programs can probably be attributed, at least in part, to this lack.

The Castillo Armas regime was doubly handicapped by problems of personnel. Not only were trained people scarce but the stigma of communism was pinned on persons who had cooperated with the Arbenz government. Some of the communistic labels were undoubtedly justified, but others were not. Many patriotic Guatemalans holding responsible positions in the Arbenz government were doing so because they wanted to serve their country and help improve the welfare of the population. They had no thought of promoting the interests of either local or international communism. The fact that they were associated with the Arbenz regime, however, placed them under a cloud of suspicion and many of them were, therefore, unwanted and unused by the succeeding government. After the fall of the Arbenz government it was also relatively easy to pin the tag of "communist" on anyone who ventured to express liberal ideas or to criticize the policies of the government in power. Some of these persons, though competent, were ostracized, with the result that Guatemala's scarce human resources were depleted still further by restrictions imposed by political considerations.

Political integrity

Lack of opportunities for employment in business, industry, and elsewhere cause many to look for jobs in the government service. Political influence thus becomes important, not only as a means of getting a job for oneself, but also for friends and relatives. Unfortunately, it happens many times that a man's political connections turn out to be much more important than his education, training, or experience for the job. Some regard appointment to high public office as their chance to make their financial stake. This gives rise to various types of graft or bribery such as the following: (1) The payment "under the counter" of a small, or large, sum of money to a public official by one who wants to get his business with the government transacted efficiently without lengthy delays. (2) Refusal by government officials to legalize documents requiring their stamp of approval until they have received some sort of "consideration" for their efforts.[34] (3) Failure to account for all of the funds channeled through the hands of government officials,

34. These two forms of bribery are referred to in Guatemala as the *mordida* ("bite"). The term in Guatemala is generally used in a somewhat more restricted fashion than in Mexico. See Whetten, *Rural Mexico,* pp. 545–6.

such as those received through the operation of the national fincas or other official government enterprises. (4) "Deals" whereby government officials are granted shares of "interest," in, or "kick-backs" from, business concerns in return for special considerations in allotting government contracts, making government purchases, or in manipulating fees, taxes, or concessions in the interests of the particular enterprise.

Guatemalans have been aware of the existence of graft and bribery for a long time. The Constitution of 1945 contains a clause designed to preclude the acquiring of unexplained wealth by high governmental officials while in office. It states that all high officials and all persons who manage or administer funds of the state or of the municipios,

> shall deposit a declaration of all their goods and debts so that, upon completion of their duties or even during their course, any person may, without incurring responsibility, press demands for a comparison of goods and properties.[35]

This provision is also contained in the Constitution of 1956 where it is said that any person is free to check the financial accumulations of any public official to determine whether or not he is acquiring, or has acquired, undue financial gain while in public office. This article of the Constitution is frequently referred to as the "law of honesty" (*ley de probidad*).[36]

Nevertheless, despite these precautionary measures written into the Constitution of the Republic, Guatemalans can point with embarrassment to numerous ex-government officials who entered office with practically nothing, and came out of office as wealthy owners of coffee fincas or other expensive real estate worth many thousands of dollars which could not possibly be accounted for through their modest salaries.

An editorial in one of Guatemala's leading newspapers serves to illustrate the point of view of many Guatemalans with reference to honesty in government.

> For about a quarter of a century our constitutions have contained a beautiful paragraph referring to honesty (*probidad*) in government. Even the creators of this so-called law of honesty did not consider themselves obliged to comply with it completely and the law has remained ineffective either because officials have failed to declare their property and debts as the law requires, or else because no one dares to make accusations or denounce any-

---

35. *Constitución de la República de Guatemala* (1945), Title III, Art. 24.
36. *Constitución de la República de Guatemala* (1956), Art. 121.

one for non-compliance because of the difficulties in the way and the risks which one might run in doing so in our environment. The shady business transactions and the ingenious deals seldom leave any material traces and the eventual witnesses turn out to be either accomplices or parties interested in maintaining the greatest reserve.

The same may be said with reference to the bribe known as the *mordida,* a practice of immemorial standing also, but which not long ago achieved the distinction of becoming a veritable institution in our country. Neither those who give nor those who receive the *mordida* think that they are doing anything wrong. It is merely considered as a gratuity in order to obtain from a government employee prompt attention in expediting one's business. It is really a kind of open sesame regarding which everyone involved remains happy; but whose consequences are paid for by the one who does not pay the bribe since he has to content himself with getting his business transacted at turtle speed instead of at the accelerated tempo available to others. . . .

One curious phenomenon is frequently present. Persons who in private life, whether in business or the professions, would be incapable of trying to profit through shady deals or bad practices and who would not think of taking a cent that did not belong to them, do not appear to have any scruples at all about participating in any ingenious deal that is proposed to them while in public office, many times without doing anything very bad but merely by closing their eyes or by recommending a proposition favorably to a third party. It seems unbelievable that such flexibility of conscience could exist; but it is based on the assumption that the state never loses; and that its resources in addition to being inexhaustible do not belong to anyone in particular. Perhaps only when a complete team of persons arrive in public office who have such Spartan honor that they are absolutely incorruptible; only then can we believe that complete administrative honesty in government has ceased to be an Utopia in Guatemala. In the meantime, vigilance and control should be intensified and sanctions imposed, as educational devices.[37]

Many Guatemalans have expressed the opinion to the author that the national fincas have served as tremendous sources of graft for high government officials. It is pointed out that, through the sale of coffee,

37. "The Policy We Need: Effective Honesty in Government," *El Imparcial,* Feb. 8, 1958. Translated by the author.

these fincas bring in hundreds of thousands of dollars every year, and it is suspected that some of the managers have made deals with their supervisors whereby some transactions go unrecorded on the official records and the proceeds are quietly distributed among "appropriate" individuals.

It is impossible to make any valid estimate of the amount of graft involved in all government transactions; and it might very well be that some claims have been exaggerated. The author is of the opinion, for example, that although the mordida certainly exists in Guatemala, it is not so widespread or so institutionalized as in Mexico. Nevertheless, a country like Guatemala that is struggling to free its inhabitants from poverty and illiteracy and to provide them with minimum health and welfare services, can ill afford to tolerate any graft or bribery at all among her public officials. Not only do these divert much-needed public funds into the pockets of private individuals, but what is worse, they weaken the moral fabric of the nation and undermine the confidence of the people in their own government.

The foregoing discussion serves to emphasize the many factors in Guatemala which converge to make the development of democratic government on a national scale exceedingly difficult. In previous chapters we have noted the prevalence of geographical isolation, high rates of illiteracy, language barriers, widespread poverty, and tremendous contrasts between the few who have wealth and the many who live near the subsistence level. All these factors tend to prevent effective communication and understanding among the diverse population elements and hence serve as obstacles to the development of national ideals and aspirations which appear to be basic ingredients of democratic government.

Part 5 *THE OUTLOOK*

Chapter 17

THE OUTLOOK

Guatemala, like many other economically underdeveloped countries of the world, is faced with the problem of trying to overcome poverty, illiteracy, and disease. Her people are seeking the basic personal freedoms of which they have been deprived throughout a succession of dictatorships. It is a long, rough road ahead; and their aspirations will probably be accompanied by many frustrations and disappointments along the way.

Viewed from the standpoint of a modern democracy, one of Guatemala's crucial problems appears to be the lack of social integration at the national level. She is not a homogeneous, closely integrated society with common traditions, ideals, and aspirations. On the contrary, many factors accentuate diversity and contrast rather than integration among her people.

Lack of communication is one of the chief barriers to social integration. This is manifest in a number of ways, most noticeably in the geographical isolation of the inhabitants in different parts of the country. Attention has been called to the mountainous nature of the areas in which most of the inhabitants dwell, and to the lack of roads and transportation facilities that might encourage travel among the various regional and local communities. Three-fourths of the inhabitants live in small, rural communities, many of which are virtually unconnected with the larger towns and cities. It has been pointed out that those areas having more or less level terrain are virtually uninhabited and almost completely lacking in roads and facilities for transportation. In rural areas much of the settlement pattern tends to accentuate isolation, with farm families on their small plots of land scattered over the hills instead of grouped into villages as in central Mexico and elsewhere. This scattered pattern of settlement without transportation facilities makes it difficult for people to come together for programs of community development, and multiplies obstacles to the organization of educational institutions, health services, and participation in local government.

The high rate of illiteracy creates another serious barrier to social and cultural integration. With more than 70 per cent of the population unable to read and write, it is almost impossible to overcome geographical isolation through communication by means of the printed word. Newspapers, magazines, and books are conspicuously absent outside of the major cities, and could not be read by the general population even if they were available. Information concerning national affairs must be passed along by word of mouth, a slow and ineffective process indeed where scattered settlement and rugged topography impedes contact with the outside world.

A further obstacle to social integration is the ethnic division which splits the inhabitants into two different cultural worlds. As previously noted, more than half of the people are classified as Indian in that they maintain local customs, attitudes, and dress which set them apart from the Ladinos. Not only do the Indians constitute more than half of the total inhabitants but they themselves are divided into numerous, small, isolated societies. In the highland communities each municipio is characterized by its own religious beliefs and practices, its distinctive dress and, in many instances, even its own language. Obviously, the language problem seriously interferes with the development of literacy and education. In most communities the first year or two of schooling must be devoted to learning Spanish, the official language of the country; and children in the rural areas seldom attend school for more than two years.

The Indian is not particularly interested in what goes on beyond the boundaries of his local municipio, even though he may be aware of the existence of larger towns and cities. He characteristically looks inward to the elders in his local community for his models of aspiration. Unfortunately the elders tend to know only what their forefathers knew. They are shut off from the streams of knowledge and information about modern techniques of living that have become available to other peoples having more highly developed avenues of communication. Standards of housing, of diet, and of health education are those that have prevailed in the local communities for many generations.

The Indian's religion, his customs, and his traditions all emphasize the importance of his relations with the supernatural world. His religion is a combination of Christianity and paganism adapted to the local situation so neatly that it is difficult to separate one element from another. The supernatural is seen in the wooden images of the local saints as well as in the mountains and streams, and in numerous traditionally sacred places. While nominally Roman Catholic, the Indian's religious life goes on, for the most part, without benefit of priest or catechism; and local practitioners administer their own local brand of religious ceremonies in their own way. He adjusts his behavior to conform to the standards of acceptance deemed important by his ancestors many generations ago.

Although the Indian is highly integrated into his local community, he is effectively insulated from events taking place beyond the borders of his municipio, except as these impinge on his economic situation or find expression in government regulations enforced by local representatives of the central government.

The Ladino, on the other hand, tends to be more aware of life in Guatemala City and is influenced to a greater extent by urban standards. This is probably because, speaking Spanish, he hears more about what is going on outside of his local community even if he is unable to read. While it is true that many rural Ladinos are almost as isolated as the Indians, nevertheless, participation in national affairs is almost entirely confined to Ladinos. Indians are regarded as culturally and socially inferior by most Ladinos; and cultural barriers between the two groups constitute an important obstacle to social integration.

With more than half of the total population consisting of Indians, it is difficult to see how national integration can be developed without widespread programs to incorporate the Indian into the national life. This will mean breaking down the geographical, cultural, and economic barriers that now isolate him in small, tradition-bound communities. Part of the solution may come by erasing the language barriers through a more widespread use of Spanish, promoted through long-neglected rural educational programs. Improved transportation facilities and expanded economic opportunities would further tend to attract the Indian into the national stream of socio-economic life.

As mentioned in Chapter 4, it is fortunate that the social barriers separating Indians from Ladinos in Guatemala are not focused to a great extent on differences in race or color. Enough race mixture has gone on during past generations to obliterate marginal distinctions in racial features; and skin color tends to fade gradually from the brown of the direct descendant of the pre-Columbian Indian to the lighter color of those Ladinos with a heavy proportion of European ancestry. A dividing line on the basis of color between Indian and Ladino would be impossible to draw with any degree of accuracy. Ethnic distinctions define one as an Indian if he lives like one, clinging to antiquated customs, in what is regarded by Ladinos as a lower socio-economic position.

The process of ladinoization, or acculturation, has been going on slowly for generations, but numerous barriers have prevented it from developing fast enough to obliterate distinctions between Indian and ladino society. Many Indians are at an intermediate stage of acculturation between Traditional Indians (those described in the preceding paragraphs) and Ladinos. These intermediate peoples have been referred to in this study as Transitional Indians since they stand between two cultures, not belonging entirely either to one or the other. They have begun but have not completed the process of acculturation. A number of problems have been identified in connection with transitional status. Ladinoization will inevitably be speeded up if and when communication systems become more highly developed, educational programs become widespread, and economic opportunities become more abundant.

Some lament the progressive ladinoization of the Indian which will ultimately eliminate his colorful dress and the distinctive features of his tradition-bound isolated communities; but this would seem to be inevitable if the Indian is to share in the social, educational, and economic progress of the nation, or to participate intelligently in a national democracy.

As indicated in Chapter 5, poverty is one of Guatemala's chief problems. Her economy is agricultural, and yet many of her excellent agricultural resources remain essentially undeveloped. Large areas of potentially valuable farm lands lie virtually unused; and those under cultivation are very unequally distributed between large-scale holdings and tiny subsistence plots. There is little between these two extremes that would resemble the family farm as generally known in the United States.

Most plantation agriculture is devoted to the growing of coffee, Guatemala's principal export. Coffee is so important to the economy of the nation that minor fluctuations in the price of this commodity exert a profound impact on business conditions. For this reason, it might be wise to encourage greater agricultural diversification so that the country would not be so dependent on the price of one single crop.

Plantation farming in Guatemala, in most cases, makes use of an abundant supply of cheap hand labor working without benefit of modern tools and equipment. It minimizes reinvestment of capital in the farm and the utilization of modern techniques that might greatly increase productivity per acre or per man.

Most Guatemalan farmers, however, are concentrated in the high-lands where good farm land is scarce. They farm small plots of land devoted to subsistence crops, principally corn, and the income is gen-erally insufficient to support a family. The farmer must seek outside employment as a migratory worker on the plantations, or supplement his income in some other way.

Health problems are so serious that Guatemala has one of the high-est death rates in the world. Over the years physicians, hospitals, and other health facilities have tended to be concentrated principally in Guatemala City, while the vast majority of the inhabitants have had to depend largely on remedies prescribed by local, untrained practition-ers. Malnutrition is widespread, especially among children in the rural areas, and a high proportion of infants fail to survive the first year of life. The average person born in Guatemala in 1950 could expect to live only 43.6 years as compared with 68 years for a person born in the United States at the same time.

A further obstacle to social and economic development in Guatemala might be phrased as the traditional commitment of government to the maintenance of the *status quo*. Rulers have governed largely in the interests of the few and have tended to ignore the plight of the Indians and the aspirations of the vast majority of the common people. Gov-ernments generally have failed to accept the responsibility for promot-ing the welfare of the masses, and their primary concern has usually been to maintain "law and order" by whatever means appeared most conducive to achieving the desired results. If this required banish-ment, imprisonment, execution, or assassination, these could all be justified in terms of the necessity to preserve order and to retain con-trol. For this reason the government has remained highly centralized and no effective regional government has been allowed to develop. Laws and decrees are issued from Guatemala City; but the population of the hinterland, with the exception of large landowners, is generally powerless to influence legislation for its own welfare.

Despite the many obstacles to social and economic development in Guatemala, however, the outlook is not hopeless. Looking back care-fully over the recent past, one may detect signs of progress. Among the important gains since 1944 has been an increase in the amount of individual freedom enjoyed by the average person. Even though this has suffered serious limitations at various times in recent years, re-strictions have not been as severe as they were under the dictatorships. One need only recall that prior to 1944 forced labor was widely prac-ticed under the guise of the vagrancy laws which made it possible for government agents to round up Indians and assign them to work on the plantations or highways whenever there appeared to be a shortage of cheap farm hands or of road workers. Furthermore, each person had to carry an identification card (*cédula de vecindad*) so that his residence and identification could be checked at all times, and his mobility from one place to another might be restricted whenever it was deemed advisable.

Although farm wages have remained low and the economic conditions of most of the rural workers have improved little, if any, nevertheless, there is tremendous relief for them in being able to choose when, where, and how long they will work. It seems unlikely that forced labor will again be tolerated in Guatemala.

Freedom of speech and of the press, although still curtailed at times during declared national emergencies, has been much more prevalent since 1944 than previously. Under the former dictatorships, banishment into exile was a weapon that was commonly used against anyone who criticized the state of affairs in the nation, or who was suspected of creating a threat to the unlimited authority of the chief executive. Any paper carrying an uncomplimentary article or an editorial that was displeasing to the ruling power could be instantly suppressed, and severe reprisals inflicted against the critics.

Since 1944 there has been an attempt to stimulate local self-government through autonomy of the municipio, permitting the population of the municipio to elect its own local officials, including the mayor. It is assumed that in this way local communities will gradually develop self-government. One of the most serious obstacles preventing the realization of true self-government on the local level, however, is the lack of a sound financial structure to support community development. The important sources of revenue are pre-empted by the national government, leaving little with which to finance local improvements. In spite of the many restrictions and problems connected with local autonomy, it appears to be an important step in the right direction and is obviously an improvement over the policy existing prior to 1945 when all mayors of municipios were appointed by the President of the Republic and were responsible to him.

It seems unlikely, however, that Guatemala will develop into a national democracy of the Anglo-Saxon variety within the near future. To do this would presuppose a literate population, a common language, and communication facilities that would acquaint the people with their rights, duties, and responsibilities under the law. It would require a level of living high enough to permit the average citizen to devote a little of his time to the consideration of local, regional, and national problems, instead of having to devote himself entirely to the immediate task of trying to make a living. These things cannot be attained overnight or even during one generation; but many Guatemalans are willing and eager to work for them.

Since 1945 there have been serious attempts to incorporate the Indians into the national life. The revolutionary government of Arévalo was oriented toward improving the lot of the masses generally, and to assimilating the Indians into the socioeconomic life of the nation. Campaigns against illiteracy were organized; new schools were constructed; organization of political parties was encouraged; labor laws were enacted authorizing the formation of labor unions and collective bargaining; forced labor was abolished; a social security system was set up to protect workers from accidents and certain types of illnesses; and a national institute was established to give special attention to the problems of the Indians.

Arbenz continued to emphasize some of the Arévalo reforms. He also initiated a vast program of land reform. Unfortunately, however, during the administration of Arbenz, the programs were allowed to fall increasingly under the influence of extremists interested in using the government programs as political weapons for achieving objectives of International Communism. The widespread resentment that was aroused finally resulted in the overthrow of the government by Castillo Armas and his "Liberation Army," and Castillo Armas returned to highly conservative policies. Concentrating on stamping out communism and constructing highways, he tolerated no opposition, political or otherwise. Although he retained some of the reforms instituted by the previous governments, he suspended the agrarian program and, with the assistance of United States technicians, replaced it, on a small scale, with a program of colonization and land settlement. He also instituted a much needed agricultural extension service.

The Ydígoras government is also conservative in nature, but the few reforms that were supported by the Castillo Armas government have been continued. Programs to promote industrialization are being planned. Many Guatemalans, however, feel that the government is concerned largely with maintenance of the *status quo* and that its reform programs are inadequate to meet the essential needs of the people. Unrest is abroad in the land and the future is uncertain. In an effort to maintain order, reversion to conditions that existed during the Ubico dictatorship is certainly within the realm of possibility, although a dictatorship of the extreme right would encounter resistance from a number of groups in Guatemala that are now beginning to exercise a significant influence. Some of these groups are the following:

1. *University students and teachers.* The university is now an au-

tonomous institution where teachers and students are relatively free to discuss problems of their country. Many of the professors have studied abroad in Mexico, France, the United States, and elsewhere. They are familiar with programs of social welfare and with democratic procedures in other countries, some of which they would like to introduce into Guatemala. The students take some of the teachings of their professors seriously and believe that through protests and demonstrations they can influence their government in the direction of liberal policies. In their student newspaper they do not hesitate to denounce those government policies which they deem detrimental to the progress of the nation. They engage in student strikes and mass demonstrations; they march down the streets of Guatemala City to the National Palace and shout their objections to decisions they do not like. As in many other Latin American countries, student discontent furnishes a favorable environment for communist agitation.

2. *Returning exiles.* Guatemala has many returning exiles who were banished for political reasons during one regime or another. Familiar with life in other countries, they are often resentful at any signs of dictatorial policies· in Guatemala. Some have felt the impact of the dictator's heel and want no more of it either from the right or from the left. Others return to pursue the very political activity for which they were previously banished.

3. *The rise of a middle class.* While anything resembling a middle class in Guatemala is still insignificant in numbers, this small group is beginning to exert some influence on national affairs. It is eager to do away with poverty, expand educational opportunities, and promote democracy.

4. *Disappointed agrarians.* There are many *campesinos* who received land under the agrarian law of 1952 only to have it taken away from them again after the fall of the Arbenz government. They might be receptive to any revolutionary scheme that promises to restore to them the land of which they were the proud possessors for such a short time.

5. *Frustrated labor leaders.* The activities of organized labor have been severely restricted since 1954, and potential labor leaders are anxiously maneuvering to bring about a situation upon which they might capitalize to restore labor to its former influential position.

6. *Communist sympathizers.* Finally, there are communists and sympathizers with the former Arbenz government who are still working under cover and eagerly awaiting every opportunity to take advantage of popular discontent. Uprisings have occurred with disconcerting frequency in various parts of the country, and some have been

of considerable magnitude. It seems likely that a government of the extremely reactionary type would have the effect of providing a fertile field for the reception of communist propaganda and might even facilitate the return of a communist-controlled government. Obviously, either dictatorial extreme, whether of the right or the left, would be detrimental to the orderly development of Guatemala. Therefore, it is to be hoped that present and future governments will pursue a middle course in which basic social reforms will be soundly conceived and carried out carefully and consistently, so that the fundamental needs of the people might be gradually satisfied and revolution averted.

In her efforts to develop into a modern democratic nation, Guatemala will need the encouragement, sympathetic understanding, and cooperation of those sister republics of the Western Hemisphere that have already been fortunate enough to achieve a considerable degree of industrialization. Programs of technical cooperation, for example, can be especially valuable in transferring to Guatemalans some of the more efficient techniques of agricultural and industrial production that have recently been developed elsewhere. Cooperation of this type could be carried out under the auspicies of the various agencies sponsored by the United Nations, such as the Food and Agriculture Organization, the World Health Organization, the United Nations Children's Fund, and the World Bank; or it could be achieved through bilateral agreements between individual countries. Perhaps both types of collaboration should be encouraged.

Much of Guatemala's social and economic development, however, will depend on the competence and integrity of her own present and future government officials and the degree of their orientation toward the improvement of the lot of the common man. Will they display the initiative and the courage to formulate and carry out basic social reforms to improve the health, education and economic well-being of the general population? Will they enforce the democratic provisions of the Constitution so that freedom and justice under the law will be available to all on an equal basis? Will they carry out programs of land reform and resettlement on the large areas of unused land in the Republic? The future of the Republic of Guatemala will probably depend to a large extent on the manner in which these questions are answered.

APPENDIX TABLES

APPENDIX TABLE 1. *Land in Guatemala by types of use, 1950* *

Types of use	Acres (thousands)	Per cent of total
TOTAL	9,052.4	100.0
Croplands	2,302.1	25.4
Fallow lands	907.0	10.0
Lands in natural pasture	1,417.9	15.7
Lands planted to coffee and fruit trees	368.3	4.1
Wooded areas	3,253.6	35.9
Unusable lands	803.5	8.9

* *Source: Investment in Central America,* (U. S. Department of Commerce, Washington, D.C., 1956), p. 149.

APPENDIX TABLE 2. *Number of municipios, ciudades, villas, pueblos, aldeas and caseríos, by region and department*

Region and department	Municipios	Ciudades	Villas	Pueblos	Aldeas	Caseríos
REPUBLIC	322	28	29	265	2,483	4,441
Central	33	3	3	27	164	114
Guatemala	17	2	3	12	142	109
Sacatepéquez	16	1	0	15	22	5
North	15	2	0	13	90	249
El Petén	10	1	0	9	29	71
Izabal	5	1	0	4	61	178
East	66	6	8	52	990	1,342
Chiquimula	11	1	3	7	235	354
El Progreso	8	1	0	7	106	124
Jalapa	7	1	1	5	125	164
Jutiapa	17	1	1	15	219	375
Santa Rosa	14	1	2	11	120	181
Zacapa	9	1	1	7	185	144
South	41	3	5	33	116	40
Escuintla	12	1	1	10	37	26
Retalhuleu	9	1	1	7	36	2
Suchitepéquez	20	1	3	16	43	12
West	145	11	11	123	882	2,012
Chimaltenango	16	2	4	10	91	201
El Quiché	18	1	2	15	78	416
Huehuetenango	31	1	1	29	306	687
Quezaltenango	24	2	2	20	92	79
San Marcos	29	3	1	25	207	532
Sololá	19	1	0	18	49	76
Totonicapán	8	1	1	6	59	21
North central	22	3	2	17	241	684
Alta Verapaz	14	1	1	12	157	440
Baja Verapaz	8	2	1	5	84	244

Source: Dirección General de Estadística, *Departamentos, municipios, ciudades, villas, pueblos, aldeas y caseríos de la Republica de Guatemala,* 1953.

TABLE 3   363

APPENDLX TABLE 3. *Rural-urban distribution of Indians and Ladinos, by region and department, 1950*

Region and department	Total number	INDIANS Per cent rural	Per cent urban	Total number	LADINOS Per cent rural	Per cent urban
REPUBLIC	1,497,261	87.3	12.7	1,293,607	60.9	39.1
Central	110,508	51.7	48.3	388,529	22.1	77.9
Guatemala	79,514	58.1	41.9	359,399	20.6	79.4
Sacatepéquez	30,994	35.3	64.7	29,130	40.3	59.7
North	13,897	87.1	12.9	57,015	62.9	37.1
El Petén	4,431	98.9	1.1	11,449	86.5	13.5
Izabal	9,466	81.6	18.4	45,566	57.0	43.0
East	163,231	91.4	8.6	390,969	84.9	15.1
Chiquimula	69,843	95.3	4.7	42,998	80.5	19.5
El Progreso	4,482	87.8	12.2	43,390	83.0	17.0
Jalapa	38,004	87.0	13.0	37,186	73.0	27.0
Jutiapa	27,249	98.1	1.9	111,676	88.1	11.9
Santa Rosa	10,294	60.7	39.3	99,542	90.5	9.5
Zacapa	13,359	94.9	5.1	56,177	81.3	18.7
South	138,608	87.5	12.5	176,415	73.9	26.1
Escuintla	19,660	82.3	17.7	104,099	78.0	22.0
Retalhuleu	34,696	84.4	15.6	32,165	71.0	29.0
Suchitepéquez	84,252	90.1	9.9	40,151	65.5	34.5
West	854,933	89.0	11.0	240,638	71.6	28.4
Chimaltenango	94,243	71.6	28.4	27,237	51.3	48.7
El Quiché	147,094	92.5	7.5	27,817	80.4	19.6
Huehuetenango	146,628	96.6	3.4	53,473	85.0	15.0
Quezaltenango	124,473	85.7	14.3	59,740	56.5	43.5
San Marcos	168,540	97.0	3.0	64,051	85.1	14.9
Sololá	77,817	81.2	18.8	5,104	38.3	61.7
Totonicapán	96,138	85.5	14.5	3,216	8.8	91.2
North central	216,084	95.4	4.6	40,041	78.2	21.8
Alta Verapaz	177,308	95.6	4.4	12,504	56.6	43.4
Baja Verapaz	38,776	94.3	5.7	27,537	88.0	12.0

Source: Sexto censo de población.

Appendix Table 4. *Population distribution by age and sex, 1950*

Age groups	TOTAL POPULATION		MALE		FEMALE	
	Number	Per cent	Number	Per cent	Number	Per cent
TOTAL	2,790,868	100.0	1,410,775	100.0	1,380,093	100.0
Under 5	469,782	16.8	239,511	17.0	230,271	16.7
5–9	380,877	13.6	195,380	13.8	185,497	13.5
10–14	328,958	11.8	172,596	12.2	156,362	11.3
15–19	306,613	11.0	150,294	10.6	156,319	11.3
20–24	276,725	9.9	135,014	9.6	141,711	10.3
25–29	219,432	7.9	109,588	7.8	109,844	8.0
30–34	163,207	5.9	84,738	6.0	78,469	5.7
35–39	156,195	5.6	78,442	5.6	77,753	5.6
40–44	117,918	4.2	57,043	4.0	60,875	4.4
45–49	104,631	3.8	53,262	3.8	51,369	3.7
50–54	84,924	3.0	41,767	3.0	43,157	3.1
55–59	58,531	2.1	30,955	2.2	27,576	2.0
60–64	54,220	1.9	27,825	2.0	26,395	1.9
65–69	27,206	1.0	14,607	1.0	12,599	0.9
70–74	17,065	0.6	8,158	0.6	8,907	0.7
75–79	10,459	0.4	5,254	0.4	5,205	0.4
80–84	8,230	0.3	3,521	0.2	4,709	0.3
85 and over	5,895	0.2	2,820	0.2	3,075	0.2

Source: *Sexto censo de población.*

TABLE 5   365

Appendix Table 5. *Population of Guatemala City
by age and sex, 1950*

| Age | TOTAL | | MALE | | FEMALE | |
---	Number	Per cent	Number	Per cent	Number	Per cent
TOTAL	294,344	100.0	139,604	100.0	154,740	100.0
Under 5	42,436	14.4	21,384	15.3	21,052	13.6
5–9	31,940	10.9	16,220	11.6	15,720	10.2
10–14	28,572	9.7	14,234	10.2	14,338	9.3
15–19	32,513	11.0	14,723	10.6	17,790	11.5
20–24	34,412	11.7	16,367	11.7	18,045	11.7
25–29	26,596	9.0	12,615	9.0	13,981	9.0
30–34	20,088	6.8	9,648	6.9	10,440	6.7
35–39	19,641	6.7	9,037	6.5	10,604	6.9
40–44	14,331	4.9	6,706	4.8	7,625	4.9
45–49	12,644	4.3	5,595	4.0	7,049	4.6
50–54	9,916	3.4	4,521	3.3	5,395	3.5
55–59	6,963	2.4	3,019	2.2	3,944	2.5
60–64	5,585	1.9	2,224	1.6	3,361	2.2
65–69	3,675	1.2	1,449	1.0	2,226	1.4
70–74	2,302	0.8	892	0.6	1,410	0.9
75–79	1,476	0.5	533	0.4	943	0.6
80–84	728	0.2	280	0.2	448	0.3
85 and over	526	0.2	157	0.1	369	0.2

Source: Sexto censo de pablación.

APPENDIX TABLE 6. *Distribution of plows,*
by region and department, 1950

Region and department	Total no. of farms	Farms with plows Number	Per cent	Total no. of plows	Number wooden	Number metal	Per cent wooden
REPUBLIC	348,687	25,376	7.3	37,284	32,284	5,464	85.5
Central	27,394	842	3.1	1,061	212	849	20.0
Guatemala	18,352	619	3.4	784	112	672	14.3
Sacatepéquez	9,042	223	2.5	277	100	177	36.1
North	7,607	127	1.7	122	96	26	78.7
El Petén	2,206	46	2.1	6	0	6	0.0
Izabal	5,401	81	1.5	116	96	20	82.8
East	78,715	9,345	11.9	13,600	11,902	1,698	87.5
Chiquimula	16,428	1,210	7.4	1,678	1,300	378	77.5
El Progreso	5,619	564	10.0	849	774	75	91.2
Jalapa	12,091	1,063	8.8	1,504	1,394	110	92.7
Jutiapa	22,982	4,139	18.0	5,680	5,144	536	90.6
Santa Rosa	15,346	724	4.7	800	257	543	32.1
Zacapa	6,249	1,645	26.3	3,089	3,033	56	98.2
South	32,340	705	2.2	1,392	154	1,238	11.1
Escuintla	10,662	301	2.8	1,007	90	917	8.9
Retalhuleu	8,943	137	1.5	132	31	101	23.5
Suchitepéquez	12,735	267	2.1	253	33	220	13.0
West	162,289	12,973	8.0	19,848	18,372	1,476	92.6
Chimaltenango	18,059	436	2.4	569	68	501	12.0
El Quiché	26,469	1,657	6.3	2,804	2,723	81	97.1
Huehuetenango	32,027	7,127	22.3	11,426	11,063	363	96.8
Quezaltenango	20,292	490	2.4	534	237	297	44.4
San Marcos	34,261	3,158	9.2	4,438	4,271	167	96.2
Sololá	13,561	87	0.6	43	4	39	9.3
Totonicapán	17,620	18	0.1	34	6	28	17.6
North central	40,342	1,384	3.4	1,725	1,548	177	89.7
Alta Verapaz	28,571	143	0.5	68	32	36	47.1
Baja Verapaz	11,771	1,241	10.5	1,657	1,516	141	91.5

Source: *Censo agropecuario,* 3 (1950), *Población agrícola y otros aspectos,* 76.

TABLE 7   367

APPENDIX TABLE 7. *Number of holdings and average size (in acres) by ethnic group, region and department, 1950*

Region and department	ALL OPERATORS		INDIANS		LADINOS	
	Number	Average number of acres	Number	Average number of acres	Number	Average number of acres
REPUBLIC	348,687	26.3	224,840	7.6	123,847	60.4
Central	27,394	19.2	12,973	6.6	14,421	30.4
Guatemala	18,352	23.9	7,132	6.9	11,220	34.4
Sacatepéquez	9,042	9.9	5,841	6.1	3,201	16.6
North	7,607	71.3	1,851	8.3	5,756	91.5
El Petén	2,206	16.8	708	10.7	1,498	23.7
Izabal	5,401	93.4	1,143	6.7	4,258	116.8
East	78,715	27.7	25,527	8.3	53,188	36.8
Chiquimula	16,428	13.3	10,492	6.6	5,936	25.3
El Progreso	5,619	38.6	536	6.1 '	5,083	42.0
Jalapa	12,091	23.9	6,997	10.2	5,094	42.4
Jutiapa	22,982	22.3	4,788	8.1	18,194	26.0
Santa Rosa	15,346	42.4	1,410	8.7	13,936	45.7
Zacapa	6,249	46.4	1,304	14.7	4,945	54.7
South	32,340	58.6	16,399	4.7	15,941	114.2
Escuintla	10,662	105.4	1,898	3.8	8,764	127.3
Retalhuleu	8,943	37.4	5,111	4.7	3,832	80.8
Suchitepéquez	12,735	34.6	9,390	4.8	3,345	117.8
West	162,289	15.1	133,922	7.4	28,367	51.6
Chimaltenango	18,059	17.1	14,611	8.3	3,448	54.7
El Quiché	26,469	18.9	22,751	10.2	3,718	72.0
Huehuetenango	32,027	18.5	24,762	8.7	7,265	52.1
Quezaltenango	20,292	16.8	15,487	4.7	4,805	55.5
San Marcos	34,261	16.4	25,986	9.0	8,275	39.4
Sololá	13,561	7.1	12,970	5.0	591	56.2
Totonicapán	17,620	2.8	17,355	2.8	265	5.0
North central	40,342	39.8	34,168	9.9	6,174	205.5
Alta Verapaz	28,571	42.7	27,066	9.9	1,505	635.3
Baja Verapaz	11,771	32.7	7,102	10.2	4,669	67.1

Source: Censo agropecuario, 3 (1950), *Población agrícola y otros aspectos,* Table 27, 118.

APPENDIX TABLE 8. *Number of deaths from selected causes in 1950 per 10,000 inhabitants, by region and department*

Region and department	Whooping cough	T.B.– all forms	Dysentery	Malaria	Influenza	Measles	Helminths	Bronchitis and pneumonia	Diarrhea and enteritis
REPUBLIC	11.5	5.5	4.3	24.5	10.5	7.8	16.7	22.2	21 9
Central	9.3	12.9	1.2	3.9	4.2	5.9	15.1	23.5	24.1
Guatemala	7.5	14.0	0.9	4.0	3.8	5.0	11.3	21.2	24.2
Sacatepéquez	22.0	5.0	3.5	2.5	7.5	12.3	43.4	40.4	22.8
North	5.9	3.4	1.1	68.1	1.7	2.3	5.4	13.4	26.6
El Petén	12.6	3.8	1.9	72.4	2.5	—	2.5	9.5	32.1
Izabal	4.0	3.3	0.9	66.9	1.5	2.9	6.2	14.5	25.1
East	6.7	2.9	1.9	21.6	2.2	4.2	11.9	19.7	27.6
Chiquimula	7.5	1.0	4.3	51.0	2.2	7.0	2.7	11.2	17.4
El Progreso	7.1	1.0	1.9	30.1	2.5	5.0	5.9	20.3	36.8
Jalapa	12.6	2.3	0.9	12.4	3.1	2.4	10.2	29.7	26.1
Jutiapa	6.8	1.7	0.4	5.6	2.6	2.0	16.6	20.9	26.1
Santa Rosa	2.4	4.5	1.0	7.6	2.2	4.3	25.9	25.3	31.1
Zacapa	5.3	7.8	3.2	31.9	0.3	4.9	1.6	10.9	36.7
South	6.0	9.1	6.5	43.8	2.2	10.0	38.1	22.5	28.6
Escuintla	5.9	11.5	3.2	28.6	1.4	11.9	48.9	27.5	33.0
Retalhuleu	5.5	6.3	5.8	63.0	4.9	2.2	27.5	12.3	20.3
Suchitepéquez	6.4	8.3	10.2	48.6	1.5	12.2	33.3	23.0	28.7
West	17.4	3.0	7.0	19.4	21.2	11.3	15.3	25.7	17.1
Chimaltenango	11.3	1.7	4.0	7.7	7.2	9.3	18.6	46.3	20.0
El Quiché	4.1	0.6	4.3	22.6	29.6	33.9	7.8	15.1	10.7
Huehuetenango	13.9	1.7	7.0	18.5	35.9	6.0	8.1	14.9	9.9
Quezaltenango	7.2	6.5	6.6	20.2	6.4	6.6	23.6	19.7	26.4
San Marcos	42.4	1.9	11.1	29.5	16.7	5.2	20.2	15.3	16.6
Sololá	8.7	2.0	10.1	14.7	23.3	11.1	3.7	69.7	18.2
Totonicapán	23.2	8.5	4.1	9.3	30.3	8.0	21.4	39.7	22.0
North central	9.3	3.7	2.1	57.1	8.2	3.0	12.4	12.0	16.8
Alta Verapaz	10.5	4.2	2.4	44.2	8.4	0.4	12.3	10.8	18.4
Baja Verapaz	5.6	2.6	1.1	94.1	7.7	10.6	12.5	15.2	12.1

Source: Dirección General de Estadística.

TABLE 9   369

APPENDIX TABLE 9. *Percentage of single persons fourteen years of age and over, by age groups, sex, ethnic group, and rural-urban residence, 1950*

	MALES								
	TOTAL			RURAL			URBAN		
Age groups	Total	Indian	Ladino	Total	Indian	Ladino	Total	Indian	Ladino
14	99.4	99.1	99.7	99.3	99.1	99.7	99.7	99.5	99.8
15–19	92.5	88.7	97.3	91.2	87.9	96.9	96.6	93.6	97.9
20–24	57.5	46.5	70.0	52.9	44.7	66.5	70.3	57.8	75.1
25–29	30.0	22.3	38.7	26.4	21.3	34.9	40.6	29.6	44.6
30–34	19.2	13.6	25.5	16.7	12.8	23.1	26.6	19.4	29.1
35–39	14.7	10.0	19.7	12.6	9.3	17.5	20.7	14.5	22.9
40 and over	11.6	7.4	16.3	9.9	6.8	14.9	16.3	10.8	18.5
	FEMALES								
14	96.0	93.9	98.3	95.0	93.2	97.8	98.9	98.4	99.1
15–19	68.3	60.3	77.8	63.0	58.0	72.1	83.1	76.0	85.3
20–24	32.5	24.7	41.4	26.6	22.9	32.9	47.9	35.8	52.3
25–29	20.5	15.2	26.6	16.2	14.0	20.2	31.8	23.1	34.8
30–34	17.5	13.2	22.2	13.9	12.1	17.0	26.4	20.0	28.6
35–39	16.1	11.1	21.0	12.1	10.0	15.2	25.4	17.5	28.0
40 and over	19.3	13.9	25.3	15.5	13.0	19.8	28.0	18.5	31.4

Source: Sexto censo de población, Table 5.

APPENDIX TABLE 10. *Illiteracy in population seven years of age and over by ethnic group, by rural-urban residence, and by region and department, 1950, in per cent*

Region and department	Total	RESIDENCE		ETHNIC GROUP	
		Rural	Urban	Indian	Ladino
REPUBLIC	71.7	82.4	40.8	90.1	50.5
Central	42.1	72.6	30.6	81.7	31.1
Guatemala	40.2	75.5	27.6	84.9	30.5
Sacatepéquez	56.7	57.5	56.2	73.2	39.4
North	55.8	66.7	33.9	87.8	47.8
El Petén	49.2	53.5	13.2	91.9	32.2
Izabal	57.7	72.3	35.5	85.9	51.7
East	76.2	80.2	50.6	90.6	70.1
Chiquimula	82.6	87.3	44.5	94.2	64.2
El Progreso	68.8	72.4	51.3	88.7	66.8
Jalapa	76.9	82.2	56.7	87.6	66.0
Jutiapa	76.7	79.9	48.7	85.6	74.5
Santa Rosa	73.8	76.3	56.6	86.6	72.4
Zacapa	72.5	78.2	43.8	93.7	67.5
South	69.4	75.4	46.5	88.6	54.2
Escuintla	63.8	69.0	44.7	88.3	58.8
Retalhuleu	71.0	77.4	49.5	88.1	52.6
Suchitepéquez	74.3	80.5	46.7	88.9	43.3
West	80.7	85.1	56.2	89.9	48.0
Chimaltenango	78.6	83.4	69.1	87.7	47.2
El Quiché	91.6	93.9	70.5	97.3	61.7
Huehuetenango	85.9	88.6	48.9	94.7	61.8
Quezaltenango	67.7	77.6	38.0	82.7	36.8
San Marcos	74.5	77.2	35.8	85.4	45.6
Sololá	88.6	92.2	75.4	93.1	21.9
Totonicapán	85.7	90.0	65.4	88.1	16.6
North central	90.4	93.3	54.9	96.3	58.3
Alta Verapaz	92.1	95.0	54.8	96.7	27.6
Baja Verapaz	85.5	88.3	55.1	94.7	72.4

Source: Sexto censo de población.

BIBLIOGRAPHY

BIBLIOGRAPHY

ADAMS, Richard N. *Un Análisis de las creencias y prácticas médicas en un pueblo indígena de Guatemala.* Publicaciones Especiales del Instituto Indigenista Nacional, Guatemala, 1952.

—————. *Cultural Surveys of Panama-Nicaragua-Guatemala-El Salvador-Honduras.* Pan American Sanitary Bureau, Regional Office of the World Health Organization, Washington, D.C., 1957.

—————. "La ladinización en Guatemala," *Integración social en Guatemala,* Seminario de Integración Social Guatemalteca, Publicación No. 3, 1956.

————— (ed.). *Political Changes in Guatemalan Indian Communities: A Symposium.* Middle American Research Institute, Tulane University, New Orleans, 1957.

—————. "Social Change in Guatemala and U.S. Policy" in *Social Change in Latin America Today,* Council on Foreign Relations. Harper & Brothers, New York, 1960.

ADLER, John H., Eugene R. Schlesinger, and Ernest C. Olsen. *Public Finance and Economic Development in Guatemala.* Stanford University Press, Stanford, Calif., 1952.

AGUIRRE, Francisco. "Incidencia de parásitos intestinales en algunas áreas rurales de Guatemala," *Revista de la Juventud Médica,* No. 73 (June–December 1952).

ALEXANDER, Robert J. *Communism in Latin America.* Rutgers University Press, New Brunswick, 1957.

ARBENZ, Jacobo. *Discursos.* Guatemala, 1951.

ARÉVALO, Juan José. *Discursos en la Presidencia, 1945–47.* Tipografía Nacional, Guatemala, 1947.

ARIAS B., Jorge. "Aspectos demográficos de la población indígena de Guatemala," *Boletín estadístico,* Dirección General de Estadística, Guatemala, 1959, Nos. 1–2, pp. 18–38.

—————. "Estudio sobre las condiciones de vida de 776 familias en 10 ciudades, 1952–53," *Boletín mensual de la Dirección General de Estadística,* Nos. 3–4 (March–April 1957).

373

——. *Estudio sobre las condiciones de vida de 179 familias en la ciudad de Guatemala*, Publicaciones de la Dirección General de Estadística, Guatemala, 1948.

ARRIOLA, Jorge Luis (ed.). *Integración social en Guatemala*, Seminario de Integración Social Guatemalteca, Publicación No. 3, Guatemala, 1956.

ARROYAVE, Guillermo. *Estudios sobre el mejoramiento de la tortilla de maíz en Centro América*. A mimeographed publication of the Instituto de Nutrición de Centro América y Panamá, Guatemala (April 1955).

ATWOOD, Rollin S. "The Intercommunity Trade of the Indians of the Utatlán Basin in Guatemala," *Annals of the Association of American Geographers*, 25 (1), 1935.

BANCROFT, Hubert Howe. *History of Central America*. 3 vols. The History Company, San Francisco, 1883–90.

BAUER PAÍZ, Alfonso. *Cómo opera el capital Yanqui en Centroamérica (El caso de Guatemala)*. Editora Ibero-Mexicana, México, 1956.

BEHRENDT, Richard F. "The Uprooted: A Guatemala Sketch," *New Mexico Quarterly Review*, 19 (Spring 1949).

BILLIG, Otto, John Gillin, and William Davidson. "Aspects of Personality and Culture in a Guatemalan Community: Ethnological and Rorschach Approaches," *Journal of Personality*, 16, 1947–48.

BOGARDUS, Emory S. "A Social History of Guatemala," *Sociology and Social Research*, 38 (5), 1954.

BRITNELL, George E. "Economía nacional y economía internacional," *Integración social en Guatemala*, Seminario de Integración Social Guatemalteca, Publicación No. 3, 1956.

——. "Problems of Economic and Social Change in Guatemala," *Canadian Journal of Economics and Political Science*, 17, No. 4, 1951.

BUNZEL, Ruth. "The Role of Alcoholism in Two Central American Communities," *Psychiatry*, 3 (3), 1940.

——. *Chichicastenango, A Guatemalan Village*. American Ethnological Society Publications, Locust Valley, New York, 1952.

BURBANK, Addison. *Guatemala Profile*. Coward-McCann, New York, 1939.

BUSH, Archer C. *Organized Labor in Guatemala 1944–1949*. Colgate University, Hamilton, New York, 1950.

CAPLOW, Theodore. "The Social Ecology of Guatemala City," *Social Forces*, 28 (2) 1949.

CIRO BRITO, José. "La Pelagra y la extinción de la civilización Maya,"

Universidad de San Carlos Publicación Trimestral, 11, (April-May-June 1948).

COE, William R. "Tikal 1959," *Expedition,* Bulletin of the University Museum of the University of Pennsylvania, *1,* No. 4, 1959.

CORREA, Gustavo. *El Espíritu del mal en Guatemala.* Middle American Research Institute, Tulane University, Publication 19, New Orleans, 1955.

DEL VALLE MATHEU, Jorge. *Sociología Guatemalteca.* Editorial Universitaria, Guatemala, 1950.

Diario de Centro America.

DIESELDORF, Erwin P. *Las Plantas medicinales del departmento de Alta Verapaz.* Anales de la Sociedad de Geografía de Guatemala, Guatemala, 1939.

DOLL, Eugene. *The Stewardship of the Saint in Mexico and Guatemala.* M.A. Thesis, University of Chicago, 1950.

DUNN, Henry. *Guatimala [sic] or the United Provinces of Central America, in 1827–8; Being Sketches and Memorandums Made During a 12 Month's Residence in that Republic.* G. and C. Carvill, New York, 1828.

DUTTON, Bertha P. "All Saints' Day Ceremonies in Todos Santos, Guatemala," *El Palacio, 46,* Santa Fé, New Mexico, 1939.

EBAUGH, Cameron D. *Education in Guatemala.* Federal Security Agency–Office of Education, Bulletin No. 7, Washington, D.C., 1949.

El Guatemalteco: Diario oficial de Guatemala.

El Imparcial.

El Triángulo de Escuintla. Primer Congreso regional de economía, Junio de 1945. Guatemala, 1946.

EWALD, Robert H. *Bibliografía comentada sobre Antropología Social, 1900–1955.* Seminario de Integración Social Guatemalteca, Guatemala, 1956.

———. *San Antonio Sacatepéquez: Culture Change in a Guatemalan Community.* University of Michigan, Ph.D. Thesis, University Microfilms, Ann Arbor, Michigan, 1954.

FLORES, Marina and Emma Reh. "Estudios de hábitos dietéticos en poblaciones de Guatemala: I. Magdalena Milpas Altas; II. Santo Domingo Xenocoj; III. San Antonio Aguas Calientes y su aldea, San Andrés Ceballos; IV. Santa María Cauqué," *Suplemento* No. 2, *Boletín de la Oficina Sanitaria Panamericana, Publicaciones Científicas del Instituto de Nutrición de Centro América y Panamá* (November 1955).

GALLENKAMP, Charles. *Maya: The Riddle and Discovery of a Lost Civilization.* McKay, New York, 1959.

GARCÍA GRANADOS, Jorge. *The Birth of Israel, The Drama as I Saw It.* Alfred A. Knopf, New York, 1948.

GEIGER, Theodore. *Communism versus Progress in Guatemala.* Planning Pamphlet No. 85, National Planning Association, Washington, D.C., 1953.

GILLIN, John. "Cultura emergente," *Integración social en Guatemala,* Seminario de Integración Social Guatemalteca, Publicación No. 3, 1956.

——. "Ethos and Cultural Aspects of Personality" in *Heritage of Conquest,* by Sol Tax and members of the Viking Fund Seminar on Middle American Ethnology. The Free Press, Glencoe, Ill., 1952.

——. "Houses, Food and the Contact of Cultures in a Guatemalan Town," *Acta Americana, 1,* 1943.

——. "Magical Fright," *Psychiatry, 11,* 1948.

——. "Parallel Cultures and Inhibitions to Acculturation in a Guatemalan Community," *Social Forces, 24,* Chapel Hill, 1945.

——. " 'Race' Relations without Conflict: A Guatemalan Town," *American Journal of Sociology, 53,* 1948.

——. *The Culture of Security in San Carlos: A Study of a Guatemalan Community of Indians and Ladinos.* Middle American Research Institute, Tulane University, Publication No. 16, New Orleans, 1951.

GIRARD, Rafael. *Los Chortis ante el problema Maya: Historia de las culturas indígenas de América, desde su origen hasta hoy.* Collección Precolombiana, Antigua Librería Robredo, 5 vols. México, 1949.

GIRÓN CERNA, Carlos. "El Indigenismo y el Indio," *Américan Indígena, 1* (1), 1941.

GIRÓN, Manuel Antonio. "Consideraciones médico-sociales sobre Guatemala," *Universidad de San Carlos: Publicación Trimestral,* No. 37 (April-June 1956).

GOUBAUD CARRERA, Antonio. "Del Conocimiento del Indio Guatemalteco" *Revista de Guatemala,* Año I, No. 1, 1945.

——. *Distribución de las lenguas indígenas actuales de Guatemala.* Boletín del Instituto Indigenista Nacional, Guatemala, 1946.

——. "Some Aspects of the Character Structure of the Guatemala Indians," *América Indígena, 8* (2), 1948.

——. "Indian Adjustments to Modern National Culture," *Acculturation in the Americas,* ed. Sol Tax. Proceedings and Selected Papers of the XXIX International Congress of Americanists, University of Chicago Press, Chicago, 1952.

GRIFFITH, William. "A Recent Attempt at Educational Cooperation Between the United States and Guatemala," *Middle American Research Records, 1*, No. 12, May 15, Tulane University, New Orleans, 1949.

Guatemala. *Constitución de la República de Guatemala,* decretada por la Asemblea Constituyente en 11 de Marzo de 1945, Guatemala, 1950.

————. *Constitución de la República de Guatemala,* decretada por la Asemblea Constituyente en 2 de Febrero de 1956, Guatemala, 1956.

————. *Estatuto agrario,* Decreto número 559. Guatemala, 1956.

————. "Ley de municipios." *333 Decretos del congreso de la República,* del 3 de Diciembre de 1944, a Febrero de 1947; Labor Revolucionaria, Boletín Número 7, Guatemala, 1947.

————. *Ley de reforma agraria,* Decreto número 900. Guatemala, 1952.

Guatemala, Dirección General de Asuntos Agrarios. *Tierra en Propiedad,* Guatemala, 1956.

————. *Boletín No. 2,* 1958.

Guatemala, Dirección General de Estadística. *Anuario de Comercio Exterior,* 1954.

————. *Boletín mensual.* Selected issues from August 1950 to October 1957.

————. *Censo agropecuario, 1950.* Vols. *1, 2, 3.*

————. *Censo cafetalero 1950,* Boletín. Nos. 44–45, (August-October 1953).

————. *Censo de la vivienda urbana, 1,* 1949.

————. *Departamentos, municipios, ciudades, villas, pueblos, aldeas y caseríos de la República de Guatemala.* Guatemala, 1953.

————. *Guatemala en cifras,* 1955 and 1957.

————. *Mensaje quincenal de estadística.* No. 122 (April 15, 1956).

————. *Quinto censo general de población,* Levantado el 7 de Abril de 1940, Guatemala, 1942.

————. *Sexto censo de población.* Abril 18 de 1950.

Guatemala, Instituto Guatemalteco de Seguridad Social. *Ley orgánica del instituto guatemalteco de seguridad social,* Guatemala, 1956, 1957.

Guatemala, Instituto Indigenista Nacional. *Alfabeto para los cuatro idiomas indígenas mayoritarios de Guatemala: Quiché, Cakchiquel, Mam y Kekchí,* Guatemala, 1950.

————. *Organización de municipalidades indígenas.* Boletín del Instituto Indigenista Nacional 2 (1), 1946.

————. *La Población de habla indígena en Guatemala.* Boletín del Instituto Indigenista Nacional 1 (4), 1946.

————. *Mercados regionales guatemaltecos.* Boletín del Instituto Indigenista Nacional 2 (3–4), 1947.

————. Publicaciones especiales. Eight mimeographed monographs of rural communities in Guatemala, 1948 and 1949.

Guatemala, Ministerio de Agricultura. *SCIDA, Informe anual 1956.* Guatemala, 1957.

————. *SCIDA, Informe anual 1958.* Guatemala, 1959.

Guatemala, Ministerio de Economía y Trabajo. *Código de trabajo.* Guatemala, 1950. Revised by Presidential Decree No. 570, 1956.

Guatemala, Ministerio de Educación Pública. *Guía de instrucción para maestros rurales, I. El Maestro rural en la comunidad.* Guatemala, 1948.

————. *Ley orgánica de educación nacional,* Decreto número 558, Guatemala, 1956.

Guatemala, Oficina Central del Café. *Informe cafetalero de Guatemala,* 1946. Guatemala, 1949.

GUINEA, Gerardo. *Evolución agraria en Guatemala.* Impreso en La Nueva Editorial, Guatemala, 1958.

HANKE, Lewis. *Bartolomé de las Casas.* The Hague, 1954.

HAY, C. L. (ed.). *The Maya and their Neighbors.* Appleton-Century, New York, 1940.

HIGBEE, E. C. "The Agricultural Regions of Guatemala," *The Geographical Review,* 37, No. 2 (April 1947).

Hispano Americano. 3 de Febrero de 1958, México.

HOLDRIDGE, L. R., et al. *The Forests of Guatemala.* Turrialba, Costa Rica, 1950.

HOLLERAN, Mary. *Church and State in Guatemala.* Columbia University Press, New York, 1949.

HOPPENOT, Hélène. *Guatemala.* Editions Clairefontaine, Lausanne, Switzerland, 1955.

HOYT, Elizabeth E. "El Trabajador indígena en las fincas cafetaleras de Guatemala," *Ciencias Sociales,* 6 (35), Pan American Union, Washington, 1955.

————. "Indian Laborers on Guatemalan Coffee Fincas," *Inter-American Economic Affairs,* 9 (Summer 1955).

HUXLEY, Aldous. "Religious Practices in Central America," *Geographic Magazine 1* (5), 1935.

Instituto de Nutrición de Centro América y Panamá (INCAP). *Boletín de la Oficina Sanitaria Panamericana,* Suplemento No. 1, 1953; and Suplemento No. 2, 1955.

International Bank for Reconstruction and Development. *The Economic Development of Guatemala*, Report of a Mission, Washington D.C., 1951.

JAMES, Preston E. *Latin America.* (Revised Edition.) The Odyssey Press, New York, 1950.

JIMÉNEZ, Adalberto. *La Otra Mitad del Pueblo.* Ministerio de Educación, Guatemala, 1947.

JONES, Chester Lloyd. *Guatemala, Past and Present.* University of Minnesota Press, Minneapolis, 1940.

KELSEY, Vera and Lilly de Jongh Osborne. *Four Keys to Guatemala.* Funk and Wagnalls, New York, 1943.

KING, Arden R. "Changing Cultural Goals and Patterns in Guatemala," *American Anthropologist, 54,* 1952.

KIRK, William. "Social Change among the Highland Indians of Guatemala," *Sociology and Social Research, 23,* 1939.

KOENIG, Nathan. *The Agricultural Development Program in Guatemala —An Appraisal and Recommendations.* Guatemala, 1956.

KOLBE, Henry W. *Estudio hospitalario de la República de Guatemala: Parte I.* Instituto Guatemalteco de Seguridad Social, Guatemala, 1948.

LA FARGE, Oliver. "Adaptations of Christianity among the Jacalteco Indians of Guatemala," *Thought* (December 1927).

———. "Maya Ethnology: The Sequence of Cultures" in *The Maya and their Neighbors,* ed. C. L. Hay, Appleton-Century, New York, 1940.

———. *Santa Eulalia: The Religion of a Chuchumatán Indian Town.* University of Chicago Press, Chicago, 1947.

——— and Douglas Byers. *The Year Bearer's People.* Middle American Research Series, Tulane University, Publication 3, New Orleans, 1931.

LANNING, John Tate. *The Eighteenth-Century Enlightenment in the University of San Carlos de Guatemala.* Cornell University Press, Ithaca, New York, 1956.

LASTRES, Juan. *La Curación por las fuerzas del espíritu en la medicina aborigen.* Universidad de San Carlos, No. 3, Guatemala, 1946.

LeBEAU, Francis. "Agricultura de Guatemala," *Integración social en Guatemala,* Seminario de Integración Social Guatemalteca, Publicación No. 3, 1956.

LEMOS, Pedro José. *Guatemala Art Crafts*. Davis Press Co., Worcester, Massachusetts, 1941.

Life. October 13, 1958.

LINCOLN, J. Steward. "The Maya Calendar of the Ixil of Guatemala." Carnegie Institution, Publication 528, Washington, D.C., 1942.

MANGELSDORF, Paul C. "Corn Origins Clarified," *Science News Letter* (March 6, 1954).

———. "Hybrid Corn," *Scientific American* (August 1951).

——— and Robert G. Reeves. "The Origin of Corn," *Botanical Museum Leaflets*, Harvard University, *18*, Nos. 7, 8, 9, 10, 1959.

MARTZ, John D. *Central America: The Crisis and the Challenge*. The University of North Carolina Press, Chapel Hill, 1959.

———. *Communist Infiltration of Guatemala*. New York, 1956.

MASON, J. Alden. "The Native Languages of Middle America" in *The Maya and their Neighbors*, ed. C. L. Hay, Appleton-Century, New York, 1940.

MAY, Stacy and Galo Plaza. *The United Fruit Company in Latin America*. National Planning Association, Washington, D.C., 1958.

McBRIDE, George McCutchen and Merle A. "Highland Guatemala and its Maya Communities," *Geographical Review, 32* (2), New York, 1942.

McBRYDE, Felix Webster. *Cultural and Historical Geography of Southwest Guatemala*. Smithsonian Institution, Institute of Social Anthropology, Publication No. 4, Washington, D.C., 1945.

———. *Sololá: A Guatemalan Town and Cakchiquel Market-Center*. Department of Middle American Research, Tulane University, New Orleans, 1933.

McDOUGAL, Elsie. "Easter Ceremonies at San Antonio Palopó, Guatemala," *Notes on Middle American Archaeology and Ethnology*. 3 (81), Carnegie Institution, Washington, D.C., 1947.

———. "Observations on Altar Sites in the Quiché Region, Guatemala," *Notes on Middle American Archaeology and Ethnology, 3* (62), Carnegie Institution, Washington, D.C., 1946.

McQUOWN, Norman A. "The Indigenous Languages of Latin America," *American Anthropologist, 57,* 1955.

MECHAM, J. Lloyd. *Church and State in Latin America*. University of North Carolina Press, Chapel Hill, 1934.

MELHUS, Irving E. "A Preliminary Study of the Diseases of Corn and Some Related Hosts in Guatemala," *Iowa State College Journal of Science, 27*, No. 4, (July 1953).

———, Franciso Aguirre, and Nevin S. Scrimshaw. "Observations on the Nutritive Value of Teosinte," *Science, 117,* No. 3028 (January 9, 1953).

MÉNDEZ, Rosendo P. *Leyes vigentes de agricultura.* Publicaciones de la Secretaría de Gobernación y Justicia, Guatemala (November 1937).

————. *Leyes vigentes de gobernación y justicia.* Publicaciones de la Secretaría de Gobernación y Justicia, Guatemala (February 1937).

————. *Leyes vigentes de educación pública.* Publicaciones de la Secretaría de Gobernación y Justicia, Guatemala (June 1941).

Microfilm Collection of Manuscripts on Middle American Cultural Anthropology. University of Chicago Library, Chicago. (Contains field notes by most of the anthropologists who have worked in Guatemala.)

MILLA, José. *Historia de La América Central.* 2 vols. Guatemala, 1879.

MOLINA, M. F. "Study of a Psychopathic Personality in Guatemala," *Psychiatry, 10,* 1947.

MORGADANES, Dolores. "Similarity between the Mixco (Guatemala) and the Yalalag (Oaxaca, Mexico) Costumes," *American Anthropologist, 42* (1), 1940.

MORLEY, Sylvanus G. *The Ancient Maya.* Stanford University Press, Stanford, Calif., 1946. Revised edition by George W. Brainerd and Sylvanus G. Morley, 1956.

MOSK, Sanford A. "Indigenous Economy in Latin America," *Inter-American Economic Affairs, 8,* No. 3 (Winter 1954).

MUÑOZ, J. Antonio, Carlos Pérez, and Nevin S. Scrimshaw. "Endemic Goiter in Guatemala," *American Journal of Tropical Medicine and Hygiene, 4,* No. 6 (November 1955).

————. "Distribución geográfica del bocío endémico en Guatemala," *Revista del Colegio Médico de Guatemala, 6,* No. 1 (March 1955).

MUNSELL, Hazel E., et al., "Composition of Food Plants of Central America: II, III, VIII. Guatemala," *Food Research, 15,* 1950.

NASH, June, "Protestantism in the Western Highlands of Guatemala," unpublished manuscript.

NASH, Manning. *Machine Age Maya: The Industrialization of a Guatemalan Community.* The Free Press, Glencoe, Illinois, 1958.

————. "Relaciones Políticas en Guatemala," *Integración Social en Guatemala,* Seminario de Integración Guatemalteca, Guatemala, 1956.

————. "The Reaction of a Civil-Religious Hierarchy to a Factory in Guatemala," *Human Organization, 13* (4), 1955.

————. "The Multiple Society in Economic Development: Mexico and

Guatemala," *American Anthropologist*, 59, No. 5 (October 1957).

NEVINS, Albert J. *The Meaning of Maryknoll*. McMullen Books, New York, 1954.

NEWBOLD, Stokes. "Receptivity to Communist-Fomented Agitation in Rural Guatemala," *Economic Development and Cultural Change*, 5, No. 3, 1957, pp. 338–61.

New York Times. April 7, July 16, August 13, 1957 and February 5, 1958.

NORIEGA MORALES, Manuel. "El Indio como factor económico de Guatemala," *Anales de la Sociedad de Geografía e Historia de Guatemala, 18* (2), Guatemala, 1942.

NOVAL, Joaquín. "Algunas modalidades del trabajo indígena de Guatemala," *Publicaciones del Instituto de Antropología e Historia, 4,* (1) Guatemala, 1952.

OAKES, Maud. *Beyond the Windy Place. Life in the Guatemalan Highlands*. Farrar, Straus and Young, New York, 1951.

———. *The Two Crosses of Todos Santos: Survivals of Mayan Religious Rituals*. Bollingen Series XXVII, Pantheon Books, New York, 1951.

O'NEALE, Lila M. *Textiles of Highland Guatemala*. Carnegie Institution, Publication 567, Washington, D.C., 1945.

OSBORNE, Lilly de Jongh. *Guatemala Textiles*. Middle American Research Series, Tulane University, Publication 6, New Orleans, 1946.

———. "Guatemala: on Indian Foods," *Boletín Indigenista, 4* (1), México, 1944.

———. "Influencias de la época colonial sobre la indumentaria indígena de Guatemala," *Anales de la Sociedad de Geografía e Historia de Guatemala, 18* (4), Guatemala, 1944.

PACHECO HERRARTE, Mariano. *Agriculture in Guatemala*. Pan American Union, Washington, D.C., 1944.

PARSONS, Elsie Clews. *Mitla: Town of the Souls*. University of Chicago Press, Chicago, 1936.

PAUL, Benjamin D. "Life in a Guatemala Indian Village," *Patterns for Modern Living, Division 3, Cultural Patterns*. The Delphian Society, Chicago, 1950.

——— and Lois Paul. "The Life Cycle," in *Heritage of Conquest* by Sol Tax and members of the Viking Fund Seminar on Middle American Ethnology. The Free Press, Glencoe, Illinois, 1952.

RECINOS, Adrian. *Popol Vuh: The Sacred Book of the Ancient Quiché Maya*. English version by Delia Goetz and Sylvanus G. Morley, University of Oklahoma Press, Norman, Oklahoma, 1950.

REDFIELD, Robert. "Culture Contact Without Conflict," *American Anthropologist, 41* (3), 1939.

———. "Culture and Education in the Midwestern Highlands of Guatemala," *The American Journal of Sociology, 48* (6), 1943.

———. "Primitive Merchants of Guatemala," *Quarterly Journal of Inter-American Relations 1* (4), 1939.

REH, Emma with the collaboration of Aurora Castellanos and Yolanda Bravo de Rueda. "Estudio de la dieta y de las condiciones de vida existentes entre los trabajadores de una plantación azucarera de Guatemala," *Boletín de la Oficina Sanitaria Panamericana, 37* (1954).

REYNOLDS, Dorothy. "Guatemalan Market Day," *Yale Review, 21* (4), 1942.

RICKETSON, Oliver G. "Municipal Organization of an Indian Township in Guatemala," *Geographical Review, 29,* 1939.

ROBERTS, Robert E. T. "A Comparison of Ethnic Relations in Two Guatemalan Communities," *Acta Americana, 6,* 1948.

SAENZ DE SANTA MARÍA, Carmelo. *Diccionario Cakchiquel-Español.* Tipografía Nacional, Guatemala, 1940.

SAMAYOA CHINCHILLA, Carlos. *Madre Milpa.* Tipografía Nacional, Guatemala, 1934.

SAPPER, Karl. *Die Soziale Stellung der Indianer in der Alta Verapaz.* Petermanns Mitteilungen, Heft 4, 1890.

———. *Das Nördliche Mittel Amerika.* Braunschweig, 1897.

———. "Die Feldbäuliche Anpassung der Indianer Guatemalan an die Geographischen Bedingungen ihrer Wohnorte." *Proceedings of the XXVth International Congress of Americanists, 1,* Buenos Aires, 1934.

SCHNEIDER, Ronald M. *Communism in Guatemala: 1944–1954.* The Foreign Policy Research Institute Series No. 7, University of Pennsylvania. Frederick A. Praeger, New York, 1959.

SCHULTZE JENA, Leonhard. "La Vida y las creencias de los Indios Quichés de Guatemala," *Anales de la Sociedad de Geografía e Historia de Guatemala, 20,* Guatemala, 1945.

———. *Leben, Glaube, und Sprache der Quiché von Guatemala.* Indiana I. Gustav Fischer, Jena, 1933.

SCRIMSHAW, Nevin S., Moisés Behar, Carlos Pérez, and Fernando Viteri. "Nutritional Problems of Children in Central America and Panama," *Pediatrics, 16,* No. 3 (September 1955).

SHATTUCK, George Cheever. *A Medical Survey of the Republic of Guatemala.* Carnegie Institution, Washington, D.C.. 1938.

SHAW, Richard L. "The Flour of San Vicente: Central America Fights Malnutrition," *Americas, 12,* 1960.

SHOOK, Edwin M., William R. Coe, Vivian Broman and Linton Satterthwaite. *Tikal Reports Numbers 1–4.* Museum Monographs, University of Pennsylvania, Philadelphia, 1958.

SIEGEL, Morris. "Religion in Western Guatemala: A Product of Acculturation," *American Anthropologist, 43,* 1941.

——. "Resistance to Culture Change in Western Guatemala," *Sociology and Social Research, 25,* 1941.

——. "Problems of Education in Indian Guatemala," *Journal of Experimental Education, 9* (4), Madison, Wisconsin, 1941.

——. "Culture Change in San Miguel Acatán, Guatemala," *Phylon,* 1954.

SILVERT, K. H. *A Study in Government: Guatemala.* Middle American Research Institute, Tulane University, Publication No. 21, New Orleans, 1954.

——. "Nacionalismo," *Integración social en Guatemala,* Seminario de Integración Social Guatemalteca, Publicación No. 3, 1956.

SIMMONS, Charles. *Geografía de los suelos de Guatemala.* Folleto misceláneo No. 5. Secretaría de Agricultura y Ganadería Oficina de Estudios Especiales, México, 1955.

SIMPSON, Lesley Byrd. *The Encomienda of New Spain.* University of California Press, Berkeley, Cal., 1938.

SKINNER-KLÉE, Jorge. *Recopilación de legislación indigenista de Guatemala.* Ediciones especiales del Instituto Indigenista Interamericano, México, 1954.

SLOWING H., Otto. *Estudio sociológico sobre la vivienda rural guatemalteca.* Guatemala, 1955.

SOLOW, Anatole. *Housing in Guatemala.* Mimeographed, Pan American Union, Washington, D.C., 1950.

SQUIBB, Robert L. "Native Feedstuffs developed by Guatemalan Research," *Foreign Agriculture, 14,* No. 2, 1950.

—— et al. "Ramie—A High Protein Forage Crop for Tropical Areas," *Journal of British Grassland Society, 9,* 1954.

STADELMAN, Raymond. "Maize Cultivation in Northwestern Guatemala," *Contributions to American Anthropology and History, 6* (33), Carnegie Institution, Washington, D.C., 1940.

Statistical Abstract of the United States, 1955, 1956.

STEPHENS, John L. *Incidents of Travel in Central America, Chiapas and Yucatán,* edited with an introduction and notes by Richard L. Predmore, 2 vols. Rutgers University Press, New Brunswick, 1949.

STOLL, Otto. *Etnografía de la República de Guatemala.* Guatemala, 1938. (Translated from the German by Antonio Goubaud Carrera.)

STUART, L. C. "El Ambiente del hombre en Guatemala," *Integración Social en Guatemala,* Seminario de Integración Social Guatemalteca, Publicación 3, 1956.

SUSLOW, Leo A. *Aspects of Social Reforms in Guatemala, 1944–1949.* Mimeographed, Colgate University, Hamilton, New York, 1949.

———. *Social Security in Guatemala.* Ph.D. dissertation, University of Connecticut, Storrs, Connecticut, 1954, University Microfilms, Ann Arbor, Michigan.

TAX, Sol. "Changing Consumption in Indian Guatemala," *Economic Development and Cultural Change,* 5, No. 2, 1957, pp. 147–58.

———. "Culture and Civilization in Guatemalan Societies," *Scientific Monthly, 48* (5), 1939.

———. "Ethnic Relations in Guatemala," *América Indígena,* 2, México, 1942.

———. "La Economía regional de las Indígenas de Guatemala," *Boletín del Instituto Indigenista Nacional,* 2 (3–4), Guatemala, 1947.

———. *Penny Capitalism: A Guatemalan Indian Economy.* Smithsonian Institution, Institute of Social Anthropology, Publication No. 16, Washington, D.C., 1953.

———. "Relaciones económicas," *Integración social en Guatemala,* Seminario de Integración Social Guatemalteca, 1956.

———. "The Municipios of the Midwestern Highlands of Guatemala," *American Anthropologist,* 39, No. 3 (July 1937).

———. "World View and Social Relations in Guatemala," *American Anthropologist, 43,* 1941.

TAYLOR, Douglas McRae. *The Black Carib of British Honduras.* Viking Fund Publications in Anthropology, No. 17, New York, 1951.

——— and others. *Heritage of Conquest.* The Free Press, Glencoe, Illinois, 1952.

TERMER, Franz. "Ethnographische Studien Unter den Indianen Guatemalas," *Zeitschrift für Ethnologie, 61,* Berlin, 1929.

———. *Etnología y Etnografía de Guatemala.* Seminario de Integración Social Guatemalteco, 1957. (Translated from the German by Ernesto Schaeffer and Alicia Mendoza H.)

THOMPSON, Donald E. *Maya Paganism and Christianity: A History of the Fusion of Two Religions.* Middle American Research Institute, Tulane University, Publication 19, New Orleans, 1954.

THOMPSON, J. Eric S. *The Rise and Fall of Maya Civilization.* University of Oklahoma Press, Norman, Oklahoma, 1954.

TORIELLO, Guillermo. *La Batalla de Guatemala.* Ediciones Cuadernos Americanos, 39, México, 1955.

TUMIN, Melvin M. *Caste in a Peasant Society: A Case Study in the Dynamics of Caste.* Princeton University Press, Princeton, 1952.

————. "Culture, Genuine and Spurious: A Re-evaluation," *American Sociological Review,* 10 (2), 1945.

————. "Reciprocity and Stability of Caste in Guatemala," *American Sociological Review,* 14 (1), 1949.

————. "Relaciones de castas y clases," *Integración Social en Guatemala,* Seminario de Integración Social Guatemalteca, Publicación No. 3, 1956.

United Nations Demographic Yearbook, 1953, 1955, 1956, 1957.

United Nations. Department of Economic Affairs. Statistical Office. *National and Per Capita Incomes of Seventy Countries in 1949 Expressed in United States Dollars.* Statistical Papers, Series E. No. 1, New York, October 1950.

United Nations. Statistical Office. *Per Capita National Product of Fifty-five Countries, 1952–1954.* Statistical Papers, Series E. No. 4, New York, 1957.

United Nations. *The Population of Central America (Including Mexico), 1950–1980.* ST/SOA/Series A, Population Studies, No. 16, 1954.

United Nations Statistical Yearbook, 1954, 1955.

United States Department of Commerce. *Investment in Central America.* Washington, D.C., 1956.

United States Department of Health, Education and Welfare. National Office of Vital Statistics. *Vital Statistics—Special Reports: United States Life Tables 1949–51,* 41, No. 1.

United States Department of State Publication No. 6465. *A History of Communist Penetration: Guatemala.* Washington, D.C. (April 1957).

Universidad de San Carlos de Guatemala. *Ley orgánica y estatutos.* Guatemala, 1947.

VALLADARES, León A. *El Hombre y el maíz.* Guatemala, 1957.

VERHOESTRAETE, Louis, "Aspectos internacionales de la higiene materno-infantil," *Boletín de la Oficina Sanitaria Panamericana,* 40, No. 3 (March 1956).

WAGLEY, Charles. *Economics of a Guatemalan Village.* Memoirs of the American Anthropological Association, No. 58, 1941.

————. *The Social and Religious Life of a Guatemalan Village.* Memoirs of the American Anthropological Association, No. 71, 1949.

WAUCHOPE, Robert. *Modern Maya Houses: A Study of Their Archaeological Significance.* Carnegie Institution, Publication 502, Washington, D.C., 1938.

WHETTEN, Nathan L. "Land Reform in a Modern World," *Rural Sociology, 19* (December 1954).

———. "Patrones de población," *Integración social en Guatemala,* Seminario de Integración Social Guatemalteca, Publicación No. 3, 1956.

———. *Rural Mexico.* University of Chicago Press, Chicago, 1948.

——— and Robert G. Burnight. "Internal Migration in Mexico," *Rural Sociology, 21,* No. 2 (June 1956).

WISDOM, Charles. *The Chorti Indians of Guatemala.* University of Chicago Press, Chicago, 1940.

———. "The Supernatural World and Curing," in *Heritage of Conquest,* by Sol Tax and members of the Viking Fund Seminar on Middle American Ethnology. The Free Press, Glencoe, Illinois, 1952.

INDEX